Caribbean Green

Caribbean Green

*To Don Rogers:
Best wishes to one of the
best 508th M.P.s.
Regards,
Jim (CJ) Westwick*

CJ Westwick

Copyright © 2003 by CJ Westwick.
Cover illustration by Jimmie W. Hanes III.
Cover assembly and prepress by Steven James LaMont Co.

Library of Congress Number:	2002096146
ISBN : Hardcover	1-4010-8397-8
Softcover	1-4010-8396-X

All rights reserved. No part of this book may be reproduced or transmitted in any form or by any means, electronic or mechanical, including photocopying, recording, or by any information storage and retrieval system, without permission in writing from the copyright owner.

The events and characters in this book are fictitious. Certain real locations and public figures are mentioned, but all other characters and events described in the book are totally imaginary.

This book was printed in the United States of America.

To order additional copies of this book, contact:
Xlibris Corporation
1-888-795-4274
www.Xlibris.com
Orders@Xlibris.com
16668

TO MY DEAR WIFE SANDY, WHOSE UNEQUALED
ASSISTANCE AND LIMITLESS CONFIDENCE HAS
BROUGHT THIS WORK TO THE PRINTED PAGE.

Chapter One

At times Bernie Lustfield even amazed himself. *Eleven big ones,* he thought. A broad smile enveloped his round, fleshy face. *An' Dom's certain to get more than double that in the States. Musta near shit when I faxed him total carats, high quality and first-rate price.*

As Bernie relaxed on the oversized pool lounger, he gazed toward the heavens. The sky was so brightly lit over the shimmering Caribbean he glanced around to see the moon. *No moon,* he noted. *Sky's so clear I could read by starlight.*

Bernie loved Anguilla. He especially loved it here at Rendezvous Bay's "Casablanca" resort. *Twelve hundred bucks a day,* he reflected. *And worth every cent.*

The small sixteen-square mile island commonwealth of Great Britain was his idea of what the Garden of Eden must have been like. *No crime. No poverty. No unemployment. No welfare lines or food stamps.* He loved the talcum-powder white sandy beaches and smiling, happy islanders. Even Anguilla's main industry, tourism, was held to acceptable moderation. The island government limited the number of hotels and resorts. It also confined the length of the main runway of Wallblack Airport to small jets and turboprop planes. By imposing strict regulations, American, Canadian, South American and European visitors were kept to a respectable, read "controllable," number. *Good thinkin',*

Bernie thought. *Maybe I'll immigrate here and be a beach-bum the rest of my days.*

Bernie was good at his business. Many people said he had the magical gift of gab needed by an outstanding buyer of precious gemstones. He'd gone to a less-pretentious shop in Philipsburg this time. Sure, Colombian Emeralds International, Caribbean Gems and Gemsland Jewellers were well-known for their high-quality emeralds. Still, their markups were higher because of the fancier stores, and he wanted the absolute best deals available.

Fortunately, on his second evening on St. Martin, at a café in Grand Case, he overheard four tipsy Canadian computer salesmen from Quebec City. They bragged about the superb emeralds they'd bought for their wives and girlfriends. The shop was the Bombay, just off Front Street along a narrow, nameless lane. The proprietor and his family were the only salespeople, and they were East Indians. Bernie trusted the Indian shopkeepers in Philipsburg for their honesty.

St. Maarten is reputed to be the principal emerald center of the Caribbean. Philipsburg, the capital of the Netherlands Antilles side of the island, was noted for its tax-free, duty-free shops. Unfortunately, it was also known as the destination for many smuggled items of great value and high demand. The South American coasts of Colombia and Venezuela were only 600 miles and 500 miles away, respectively, across the Caribbean from St. Martin/St. Maarten, and Colombia produced the finest emeralds in the world.

A few store owners on the Dutch side of the island were suspected of being less than honest about selling jewelry and gemstones. Some tourists returned home to Peoria or Poughkeepsie to discover their eighteen carat gold bracelets left an embarrassing green ring around their wrists. Many "Grade-A quality Colombian emeralds" were produced in New York City's emerald laboratories.

Again, Bernie smiled when he thought of *his* purchases. The eighteen emeralds were top of the line, truly magnificent specimens. Dark green—so green they cast a bluish tint. "Mint quality," Bernie mumbled in half-darkness beside the large pool. *Carat for carat*, he reminded himself, *more precious than blue-white diamonds.*

A sudden, high-pitched screech from one of the small finches called Sugar Birds startled Bernie. The tiny bird fled into the night sky, unaware it wasn't a bat, screeching loudly every few seconds. It headed north for the inner safety of the island.

"Little shit scared the crap outta me," Bernie declared, and laughed.

Suddenly he stopped smiling. *What th'hell startled the little bastard?* He stared back at the main hotel, a hundred feet beyond the large, splendid swimming pool. Bernie's smile returned. About halfway between the rear hotel entrance and where he sat, a tuxedoed waiter approached the corpulent American, carrying a large silver serving tray. *About time*, Bernie thought. *Startin' to get a bit dry.* His last Bloody Mary had been drained ten minutes earlier.

"Good evenin', Mistah Lustfield. Are you 'bout ready for anotha drink?" The black waiter was not the same one who'd served him a half-hour before.

"You betcha," Bernie smiled. "Where's Buford?" Buford Buchanan was always Bernie's waiter in the lavish dining room. Buford had brought him his drinks tonight while he lounged beyond the pool on the pink, cream and light blue-fired tiles.

The tall black man smiled. "E'en ole Buford gotta rest sometime, Mistah Lustfield." The waiter glanced at his watch. "Time's little past 'leven, suh. I jist come on an' Oliver assign me to you. Name's Benjamin, suh."

"If Oliver sent you, you're all right. Another Bloody Mary, Ben. An' leave out the leafy old stalk of celery, hear?"

"Bloody Mary, suh. No celery. Only be a minute." Benjamin turned and briskly retreated toward the dining area that overlooked the pool and the placid Caribbean.

Bernie turned his gaze back to the sea. About five miles due south of the main pier on the south west end of Anguilla lies Ferry Pier at Marigot, St. Martin. Marigot is the capital city of the

French West Indies' side of the island. The evening spring trade winds had quieted and the warmth from the heavy pool side tiles blended with the not-unpleasant briny sea odor just twenty feet away. The balmy evening turned Bernie's thoughts to the opulent resort. *Casablanca*, he reflected. *Place actually looks like the Taj Mahal*, he squinted back at the resort's unique outbuildings. *Egypt? India? Nope, Morocco. French Morocco, that's where Rick's Bar was in the movie. Bogart, of course, was Rick.* Bernie tried to remember the other actors and actresses in "Casablanca." *Yeah, Ingrid Bergman was Ilsa. Then there were Paul Henreid, Claude Rains, Peter Lorre, even Sydney Greenstreet.* He pondered the cast. *Shit, with real pros like that, who needs the current crop of no-talent kids?*

Twelve hundred a night, he pondered again about the pricey resort's rate. *Probably Bogie's weekly salary during the filming of "Casablanca."* Bernie smiled at the idea. This afternoon's single buy would find him banking some $300,000 before taxes from Dominick DePalma with his three percent of the anticipated profits. *Jist 'cause I'm the world's all-time greatest gemstone buyer.* His smile widened.

"Shit," Bernie grumbled, "where the hell's Ben? Fer these rates they could hire five native boys to take care of me." The portly buyer wasn't used to being neglected. When you have a reputation for buying collections of precious gems costing ten million to twenty million dollars a pop, people catered to your every whim.

Bernie picked up the portable telephone from the table next to his lounger and began to dial the hotel dining room. It was as if he'd sent a signal to Benjamin, for the lanky man immediately appeared at the far end of the tile pool deck. He carried the shiny silver serving tray at shoulder height, bearing its single, heavy crystalline goblet.

Why'd I start gettin' uptight? Bernie asked himself as he flicked off the talk switch on the phone. *What's Sol's kid always sayin'? 'Chill out, Unca Bernard.'? Asshole kid, but probably right about me bein' too tense.* "Gotta chill out," he remarked aloud.

"Beg pardon, Mistah Lustfield?" Benjamin asked as he reached Bernie's lounger. "You like to order something else, suh?"

"No. No, Ben. Talkin' t'myself, I guess." He grinned.

Benjamin smiled in return, but properly only half-nodded at the wealthy guest's joke. "One Bloody Mary. No celery." He set the reddish-hued cocktail next to two empty tumblers, a billfold and the portable telephone. "Will that be all, suh?"

"Jist perfect, Ben. Have one on me," Bernie said. He pulled a twenty-dollar bill from his billfold and placed it on the tray.

Benjamin smiled, nodded to Bernie and said, "Many thanks, Mistah Lustfield." He turned and strode off toward the resort buildings.

Twelve hundred dollars a day at the Casablanca included all meals and all the drinks a guest could possibly belt down. Bernie knew the worth of a good tip every once in a while, however. *Ya catch more flies with honey than with pee*, he always figured.

Sixty feet away, Benjamin picked the twenty off the tray and stared at it. He smiled again, wadded the bank note tightly and flicked it into the pool.

Bernie salivated as he anticipated the tangy drink. Holding it to his lips he inhaled its bouquet. *Smells better than Buford's,* he grinned. *A kind of sweet nutty aroma, pecans maybe, or almonds.* He held the glass up and said, "Here's to the great Bernard Lustfield and his stack of precious Caribbean green." Bernie almost finished the large Bloody Mary with one gigantic swallow. He set the nearly empty glass on his thigh and sighed with satisfaction. The pungent combination of vodka, tomato juice, spices and hot sauce slowly inflamed his mouth, then his throat and finally Bernie's stomach. His eyes teared from the fiery drink.

"Kee-rist," Bernie reckoned, "sucker's got the kick of an Ar-Kansas mule." He shook his now-swimming head and slapped the glass hard onto the table. The whack against the steel-topped stand sounded like a gunshot to his ears.

"Better call it a night," he suddenly decided, feeling a nauseous quake in the pit of his belly. He tried to stand, but fell back, missing the lounger as he reeled to his left. He landed on all fours, panting as a shooting pain raced throughout his chest. "Doc-tor," he shouted in his brain, while the actual sound was a whimper more like, "tah-choor." The nausea he experienced frightened him more than the hundred knife blades in his chest. With strength no one would have expected, he forced his legs to lift him to his feet. "Run—is—only—hope," Bernie decided. *I'll stay alive if I keep movin'.* However, the large man's resolve lasted but one step. He tumbled in a heap, half on the pool tiles and half on the sand twenty feet from the beautiful, shimmering Caribbean. *Musta been some real bad food*, he presumed, as his bowels erupted and he vomited with a deathly wail. The convulsions continued for several minutes, even after Bernie Lustfield quickly fell into a coma and stopped breathing.

Almost instantly, a silent, swift figure appeared by the body. He reached into the inner pocket of Bernie's swim trunks and removed the safe key for Suite 212. He stuffed it into his right front pocket, then turned to the thick pigskin leather billfold. With white gloved fingers, the man pulled out the plastic card-key to Lustfield's suite and pocketed it as well.

In a matter of minutes, he entered the resort hotel's propped-open rear door and loped up the back staircase to the second floor. Entrance to 212 was quick and effortless, as was opening the safe in the master bedroom closet. The killer pulled out the locked leather case, neatly slit around the latch with a cardboard box cutter, and checked the contents. The emeralds shone like small green flames. It was completed.

The man Bernie knew only as Benjamin was nearly halfway across the bay between St. Martin and Anguilla fifteen minutes after the emerald buyer died. The powerful speedboat would soon be moored at the same place where Benjamin stole it. The silver serving tray and weighted-down tuxedo now wobbled on the bottom of the sea, not even visible through the glistening, clear water. Benjamin occasionally eyed the small leather case containing eleven million dollars' worth of extraordinary emeralds.

Don e'en t'ink 'bout coppin' them, Benjamin, he thought, smiling in the dark night. *Wi' de monies I get from Mistah Mercedes-Mon, I be hoppy for de res' a me life.* Benjamin hummed a little calypso tune that went along with the words to his thoughts. He loved the lights of Marigot from the sea, especially on a beautiful night like this.

Chapter Two

Two hundred fifty thousand dollars. Bret Lamplighter repeated the amount again in his head as he glanced out the small crackled window of the tourist-packed 727. *Two hundred fifty thousand and all expenses paid.* That was the figure the Board of Directors had authorized Henry Gruener and George Princeton of Multistate Insurance to pay him to recover more than 2,000 carats worth of emeralds.

Multistate never spent their money frivolously. In fact, they had the reputation for being frugal. According to George, the theft was their biggest loss in over forty years, and they were going to be out eleven million dollars if the gems were not recovered. The owners of Ultragem, R. Conrad Douglas and his wife, held a double indemnity policy on the emeralds. Multistate would be forced to pay out twice the premium because their courier died—murdered. Bret didn't have to find the killers, all he had to do was locate the gems and Multistate would bring in the authorities. His job would be done.

There was only one problem, two actually. First, George and Henry wanted the emeralds within two weeks. Bret thought about this with little enthusiasm. The crime was more than two weeks old already, with little hope of the Anguilla and St. Martin police departments finding a quick solution.

The second problem: he had to return to St. Martin. There would be memories to confront. *Why'd I agree to go back?* he wondered. *Too many memories. Too many ghosts and too much pain.* There had been five killed: Harriet, three Netherlands Antilles police officers, two French West Indies *narcs*, plus a total of seven badly wounded personnel. That didn't even count the two American tourists or the police informants. The body count had been nine, and he would have to face it all again. *Have to forget Harriet, have to forget Robert and all the others.* How could he?

* * *

Two years before he'd been covertly assigned to French St. Martin to train a handpicked group of locals in the DEA's methods of drug enforcement. The team had been training for nearly twelve weeks. Then a police snitch tipped off his handler in Marigot about a large drug shipment. It was due to arrive in two days—by sea, probably in a powerful cigarette-style speedboat.

After three months of intensive physical training and instruction, the nine recruits had become superbly fit. Each man and woman was skilled in unarmed defense, small arms use, judo, remote-area survival techniques and the discipline of forced marches under an eighty-pound pack that included M-16 rifles.

Sous-inspecteur Jacques Beauville was the equivalent of chief of police of St. Martin. Beauville had delegated the attack to Lamplighter, but the Frenchman would be certain his superiors in Paris were aware that *he* had coordinated the entire operation.

On the evening of the 23rd of April, the boat was supposed to land on the northern beach of Oyster Bay. It was less than one kilometer from the invisible border with the Netherlands Antilles' Sint Maarten. There was a full moon that night, perfect for an early morning drug run.

Even with the brilliance of the Smuggler's Moon, Bret and his anti-narcotics team had found it hard to distinguish each other from trees, shrubbery and shadows. There had been little breeze, and the occasional gust that flitted across the dune grass was noiseless and modest.

At one-fifteen in the morning a radio warning from the southernmost beach lookout reported two tourists. They were settled in for the evening on a blanket with a twelve-pak and another bag with food. Two strangers on the beach could easily spook the smugglers, maybe even scrub the drop. Similarly, the concealed pickup team would either eliminate the couple or hightail it back to Marigot or Philipsburg. Neither option had been workable to Bret.

He radioed for Harriet Chanson to grab a blue carryall and meet him on the beach, fast. Rapidly, Bret had stripped down to his boxer shorts, snatched a bottle of Volvic spring water, a two-way radio and his .38 caliber Colt Cobra. It was a struggle through the beach sand to where he'd seen the young black woman advancing at a trot. Harriet's light-hued skin had shone in the starlight as she'd kicked up powdery sand in her haste.

Bret had grabbed the blue bag, stuffed in the radio and revolver—and zipped it shut. Harriet had carried the bottled water. Quickly he'd explained the situation that they had two love birds on the beach. The plan was to appear drunk and obnoxious to drive the couple away.

The plan worked until the older couple angrily disappeared from sight. Then a loud crack had hurled Harriet backward with a fatal round to her chest. In rapid succession, her head, neck and stomach had ripped open by high-powered slugs. In an instant Bret had hugged the sand. Stunned, he'd stared in horror at Harriet's torn body, knowing she was already dead and beyond his help.

He'd snatched his pistol and radio from the bag and called his team to give them his location. Heavy gunfire continued, but the snap of slugs fell no lower than a foot above his head. A slight rise, where the sand had met the scrub brush, prevented the shooters from picking him off.

Over the radio, the rattled under-inspector had spoken in French, "Hawk Two, *je suis* Nighthawk. *Comment*, uh, how many enemy? Team is on way, Lamplighter."

It had pissed him off. Beauville had used his surname over

the base radio. Bret had known the attackers probably had radios as well.

"*Les touristes*. Was it them, Hawk Two?"

He'd screamed into the radio, "Christ man, no. It's a goddam army."

The attackers had laid down a furious barrage from positions stretched out more than one hundred yards along the deep bushes above the sandy beach. Muzzle flashes had lighted the entire area in eerie yellow-white strobe flashes.

"Cap'n, dees be Robert. We almos' on toppa de *narcos*. We give them own med'cine in ten, twenny secon'. You hol' on, mon!"

"Hawk Commo, *arrêt, arrêt*," Beauville had yelled into the base radio at Robert. "I will be there to lead the assault." No sooner had Jacques Beauville hollered 'stop' in French than eight M-16A1 assault rifles doubled the disorder of the once quiet morning.

The sound of automatic rifle slugs had cracked over Bret's head with renewed fervor. However, they came from the west rather than the northwest, and were more irregular and were directed higher. The drug enforcement team had sprayed M-16 fire wherever they had spotted gun barrel flashes from the attackers. Beyond the shooting, he'd heard the screams and shouts from the opposing groups.

The gunfire had increased from the region of St. Martin's rookie drug enforcement team. Feeling more exposed than ever, Bret had begun to scuttle along the beach like a noiseless crab.

"Headquarters," he'd almost missed hearing from the radio that had swung loosely in his hand, " . . . radio Philipsburg for reinforcements."

Bret had stopped in his tracks, plopped down in the cool sand and slapped the radio speaker to his ear. *That wasn't right. They were supposed to call Marigot for reinforcements.* A cold sweat had covered his body in an instant and bad vibes had surrounded him. The brief transmission had sounded like Verhouten from the Philipsburg police.

"Nighthawk base," Bret had shouted. "Who called for

P'burg?" Only silence had come from the two-way radio for a few seconds.
Then, "N-nighthawk people," a flustered Dutch-accented voice had mumbled. "Are, are you Marigot officers?"
"*Mon Dieu*," under-inspector Beauville had sputtered. "Is that Verhouten?"
"*Mein Gott*," had come the response. "Jacques, you are the other force?"
Bret's heart had frozen. It was as he had feared. The two friendly police agencies on the island had been intent on mowing each other down.
"Hawk team, *arrêtez-vous de tirer*—halt shooting!" Beauville had screeched into his radio. "We shoot at the Netherlands Antilles police."
The fusillade had slowed, then ceased altogether. Bret now remembered the exact sound of the attackers' weapons. They were 5.56mm M-16A1's, the same American-manufactured rifles his own force carried—and was the assigned weapon for *both* island special assault teams. At that moment he'd wished he were anywhere else but on the beautiful, isolated beach in St. Martin.
His wish quickly came to pass. Bureaucrats in Paris promptly notified the Pentagon that Lamplighter's covert anti-narcotics training on a French *territoire* was politically unacceptable. Four days later, at Justice Department headquarters in Washington, D.C., he was discharged from the DEA.

* * *

His financial troubles had forced him to accept Multistate's offer. The two hundred, fifty thousand dollars was more money than he could turn down. It would cure his economic distress and let him carefully choose his cases from now on.
As Bret peered out the plane's window, he noted wispy white clouds far below, set against a deep blue backdrop of water. Even at 33,000 feet he could see a ship and fishing boats leaving trails of white in their wakes.

The Atlantic Ocean at this point south of the U.S. mainland and east of Central and South America was customarily lumped into one word, Caribbean. The thousands of islands were known as the Leeward *and* Windward Islands, the Greater *and* Lesser Antilles, *and* the West Indies. Depending on the cartographers, all the names were correct—or *none* of the names were correct.

An abrupt atmospheric disturbance shook the aircraft and the sign to fasten seat belts blinked on. Bret's ghosts faded and he glanced down, his eyes focused on the open file folder resting on his lap.

A photocopy of the Anguilla Colonial police report displayed a classic cover-up. All references to the murdered emerald buyer, Bernie Lustfield, referred to the American *accident* victim. A separate report prepared by Anguilla's top forensic pathologist, a funeral director by trade, described a bizarre cause of death. What first seemed like a fatal seizure or stroke turned out to be terminal voodoo.

Lustfield's last Bloody Mary had been laced with synthesized raw root of the *Manihot angustiloba* plant. Native to North and South America, including the Caribbean, some species of *Manihot* contain amygdalin, a soluble cyanogenetic glycoside. In layman terms, *Manihot* is the source of cyanide poison, a very lethal, almond-scented preparation. "Of late," according to the pathology report, "this substance has been associated with many West Indies quasi-religious cult activities."

Bret found himself more interested in another autopsy report provided by George Princeton. The corpse of one Benjamin Claypool had been discovered in Philipsburg's Great Salt Pond two days after Bernie Lustfield was robbed and murdered. The autopsy report carefully detailed something the police report totally omitted, the empty leather gemstone case had been tightly bound around Claypool's genitalia. It had been tied so securely his genitals remained attached to his body only by several small strips of scrotal tissue.

The *cause* of Benjamin Claypool's death was also interesting. The St. Martin native's throat had been cut from ear to ear. His death exactly matched those of the two partying American tourists at Oyster Pond beach when they were found dead after the fiasco. It was almost two years ago, but Bret clearly recalled the genital mutilation of both the male and female victims. All three murders were too grotesquely-similar to disregard as coincidence. *Why pointless disfigurement of all three victims after they'd been killed?*

Gotta be a confederation, an organization with some form of hierarchy and established structure, Bret mulled over in his mind. *Maybe they arranged that massacre last time I was there. Didn't seem like a loosely-planned scheme. Most small groups of penny-ante thieves and pickpockets would have almost no access to multimillion dollar emerald purchases.* Bret knew gemstone buys like Lustfield's were usually carried out in secret negotiations. The only people privy to such deals were the buyer, the seller and, occasionally, the middleman.

Break time, Bret decided. The tiny front toilet's IN USE light shone, and two people waited impatiently near it. "Step to the rear of the bus," he muttered as he unbuckled the seat belt and edged his six-foot, 190-pound frame into the narrow aisle.

Not an empty seat on the plane, he thought as he made his way toward the rear. *Shit!* he nearly spoke aloud. *Know them.* Bret tried to act normal as possible. He'd flown with those two people before. *Where? Last time in St. Martin?* He drew closer. The man looked up.

"Hi there," he greeted Bret. "Been a long time, friend."

"Hi, how are ya?" Bret went along, trying to place the man.

"Yeah, must be two years at least." It must have been during his farewell flight from the island.

"Sounds about right. How 'bout it, Ellen? Last time we saw Burt here was at Princess Juliana Airport during that wild monsoon, right?"

He didn't correct the man about his name. *That's right, I remember that storm before the plane took off.*

The attractive woman glanced at Bret and nodded. "Surely do, Claude honey. We ran the bar clean outta beer and rum that night."

Ellen's right on that count, Bret recalled. Every passenger was stoned by the time the airliner's crew got permission to take off.

"Business again, Burt?" Claude asked.

"Yeah, same old thing." *Wonder what I told them I did?* He hesitated only a moment. "Say friends, I better get to the rear toilet before things get outta hand." Smiling, he started to walk away.

"You betcha, Burt. Stayin' at the same place? Give you a call, okay?"

Bret nodded. "Right, Claude. You folks keep in touch." After extending a slight wave, he continued toward the tiny restroom.

Glad I'm not stayin' at La Residence this time, he thought. *Gonna keep my distance from those two. Too much of a coincidence meetin' them here.*

La Residence was a small hotel in the center of Marigot on Rue de General DeGaulle. The lodging was quiet and pleasant. It had been just right for his role as DEA advisor. There were no beaches or pools to keep his mind off the training of his nine recruits. Now, however, his client would have arranged for him to stay at a posh resort on beautiful Nettle Bay. The necessary reservations would be with his contact at the airport.

On the way back from the cupboard-sized toilet he hailed a stewardess serving food and drinks from a cart. "Excuse me, miss. Wonder if you could help me."

"And *how* may I help?" she countered.

"The two passengers in 'B' and 'C', about row twenty, are they regulars?"

"We're not allowed to give out that information, sir." The flight attendant looked down the aisle at the passengers Bret spoke about.

"Too bad. Met them before, and was wondering if you've ever noticed them on other trips."

The attendant smiled and adjusted a group of soda cans. "No harm, I guess. Yes, they're in import-export from what I've overheard."

"So they fly back and forth from the Mainland to St. Martin quite a bit?"

"Pretty often. Maybe once, twice a month." She opened cans and dropped ice into plastic glasses.

"Wouldn't know what they import and export?" Bret smiled. The flight attendant straightened, gazed at Bret and ran fingers through her hair. "Not certain about their exports *from* St. Martin." Her smile revealed even, white teeth.

"Makes me think you know about the *imports*, though," he said, grinning.

"Yes," she said and arched an eyebrow, "but you'll have to buy me one of their products if I tell you."

"Can't promise that," Bret replied. "What if it's something like Rolex watches?"

"That'd be a drop in the bucket," the flight attendant said, softly laughing. "They import luxury cars, mostly Mercedes."

He had just returned to his seat when Bret felt the airliner bank sharply. It wasn't a gentle ten-mile swivel like most landing approaches he'd experienced. Nervously, he glanced through the semi-transparent port six inches from his face. Water. Wavy sea water. Close. Lapping at the landing gear—well, not quite. But it looked very near.

Pilot must've flown jet fighters during the Gulf War or Kosovo. It was a strafing run. Bret sighted the intended targets on a public beach. Sailboats' masts snapped . . . well, again not quite. *Near miss.* They were close. Bret could almost count the freckles on the bathers' bare chests. Whooosh . . . the plane streaked down the landing strip of Princess Juliana Airport, having touched down scant centimeters beyond the white sand of Maho Bay Beach.

His head jerked forward as plane flaps adjusted, brakes were applied and the jet engines' thrust was reversed. The Captain worked to halt the airliner before it came to a stop in Airport Parking Lot Number Two. It was a typical 'Welcome to Sint Maarten/*Bienvenue à* St. Martin' landing. White-faced passengers nervously glanced around to see if friends or spouses noticed their near-hysteria.

After several minutes, the doors were opened. Warm, tropical air stole through the passenger compartment. Another safe landing in Paradise. The airplane stood about 100 yards from the terminal. All 150 passengers unsteadily filed out the door and clambered down the portable ramp. It was a pretty day on St. Martin, super-bright sun and a temperature of about 82 degrees.

The short walk across the tarmac was totally opposite of his last walk across this stretch of concrete. His seven remaining drug enforcement "trainees" had seen him off that morning. They'd spoken little, still showing the shock of their recent ordeal. Now, walking through the warm, humid air, it seemed as if only yesterday he'd shaken the hands of the survivors. But that was in the past, this was now.

Where's my contact? Bret wondered. He scanned the several dozen men and women who watched the new arrivals from large windows in the terminal building. He entered an ARRIVALS gate and waited in line to clear customs. Once finished with the brief questions, Bret stood in the terminal—waiting for someone to approach him. After fifteen minutes he began to walk around the airport gift shops. They sold everything from Guavaberry liqueurs to fake Movado watches. As he casually studied T-shirts in a little souvenir shop, he felt a hand on his elbow. He spun around to confront a very short, Hispanic-appearing man in a beige-colored suit. Even his tie was beige.

"Jou are Lamplighter," he stated.

". . . and you are?"

"Meester Johnson. I am here as representative of Multistate Insurance."

"You're on Multistate's payroll?"

"Correc'. Thees week, jes."

"Other weeks?"

"I serve many masters." Johnson began walking. Bret stayed by his side. "I have many paychecks."

"George Princeton said you'd give me some papers and equipment."

"Iss hokay. I have what jou were promised by Meester Princeton."

"Multistate trusts you? Even when you 'serve many masters'?"

"I am on the side of the law."

I hope George knows what he's doing. "How can I contact you if I need more information or help?"

"All information jou need is in here." He handed Bret a twelve-by nine-inch manila envelope. He paused and glanced around. "Jou are too visible on thees small island. There are those who remember what happens when jou were last here. Jou have enemies on St. Martin, Meester Lam'lighter."

Johnson continued walking. Bret followed the small man. In several minutes, they stopped near the security and x-ray devices. Departing passengers put luggage on a conveyor belt that scanned their possessions for illegal weapons. Passengers walked through several metal detection portals.

"People involved in the bloodbath two years' ago?" Bret asked.

"Involved? Jes." Johnson glanced toward the walkthrough metal detectors. "Mostly because jou are in search of certain emeralds." He spoke to Bret without looking at him. His lips barely moved as he talked, muffling some words.

"Know who leaked the assignment?" Bret also discreetly observed departing passengers walk through the tunnel-like detectors.

"Many know of it . . . both theft and murder." Johnson turned toward Bret, and asked, "Do jou see breeches in security over there." He shifted his eyes toward the three native women at the metal detectors.

"Been watchin', Johnson," the investigator nodded slowly. "Lots of alarms ringing. No checks of passengers to find the cause. Musta forgot September 11, 2001."

Johnson nodded. "*Si, verdad*, Lam'lighter. And *why* no checks of passengers?"

"Missed it at first. But the large woman doesn't permit cameras and film canisters to be handed around the detectors." He added, "She almost seems to delight in people's complaints that the electromagnetic field in the detectors will ruin the film."

"And then . . . ?" Johnson waited so he could be sure Bret caught his meaning.

"Then . . . nothin'," Bret answered. "The screeners laugh at the passengers' complaints and figure the detector alarm only caught the camera or film canister metal."

"Right, Lam'lighter," Johnson grinned, "and the upset passenger walks to his plane with discolored film in camera or boxes. And . . . ?"

". . . and any *other* metallic objects they carried with them," Bret realized.

Chapter Three

Claude Tomasso placed his second call from one of his office telephones, the phone with the scrambler attached.

Ellen hadn't come with Claude to their Island Luxury Imports car showrooms and offices. She'd continued on in the white Mercedes limousine toward their magnificent home in the lush volcanic foothills above Marigot. She was going to hurry home, grab some leisure clothing and drive directly to their yacht anchored in Marigot Harbor.

"Rupert Morgan," Tomasso said to the person who answered the phone.

"Ay', Mistah T'masso, suh,' the elderly woman hurriedly spoke. She'd recognized the voice as one would recognize the voice of one's closest relative . . . or of one whose voice was far too menacing *not* to recognize.

"Dees be Rupert, suh," a man breathlessly answered. He'd run from a shed where he'd been caulking a rickety sailboat. "Hope de trip was a good one, Mistah T'masso."

"Profitable, Rupe. But challenging on the return flight."

Morgan was not always certain what Mister Tomasso meant when he spoke. The Man often used English beyond his educational level . . . that of a first-grade dropout. Just by hearing Tomasso's tone, he knew there was a problem. "Needs he'p, Mistah T'masso? You a'ways got Rupe to do a job."

"Know I can always depend on you Rupe." There was a pause

while Claude Tomasso sipped a very dry martini. "Remember the American drug agent we, er, helped leave the island a couple years ago?"

"Yessuh. Man name of Lam'light. Sure do 'member that fella, Mistah T'masso."

"Bastard's back, Rupe." Another slurping sound as the martini lost volume. "We do *not* want him here, understand?"

The enormous black man smiled. Rupert seldom smiled since the incident four years before with sulfuric acid. The scars and pustules still hurt horribly with any facial expression. However, this was one of the rare times Rupert permitted himself the insufferable pain. A cocaine lab processor had tossed a beaker of acid into his face in a coke-high fit of rage. Rupert would have only broken his knee caps and elbows for skimming off coke if he'd taken his punishment like a man. Instead, his death took five days after he'd dashed the acid into the enforcer's face. Rupert had tied Diego spread-eagled atop a table in the Colombian coke house. Each hour for five consecutive days, the St. Martin native poured one tablespoon of sulfuric acid on another portion of the shrieking man's naked body. After three days, the four other coke cookers left, repulsed by the sight and stench of their dying *compadre*. To this day, no one else even considered ripping off a single grain of cocaine destined for St. Martin. A lot of people still recalled 'Rupert's Formula.'

"He still be a narc, Mistah T'masso?"

"No, Rupe. But he's a private investigator snoopin' around about the emeralds, according to Danny. Just talked to him in Chicago at the Dirksen Federal Building."

"T'ink *Señor* Vargas be unhoppy wi' de Lam'light mon here. Emeralds be ver' important to C'lombia boss."

"That's right, Rupe. The *Patrón* would be most discouraged if he were to lose those emeralds. We want Lamplighter dead."

Rupert shivered with anticipation. Of all the shoo-flies in the Caribbean who'd gladly waste the American, Tomasso wanted *him. A man gotta have a fine rep'tation so he be called on first t'inking*. Rupe definitely *enjoyed* that reputation.

"Where we find th' narc, Mistah T'masso?" Rupert could only picture Bret Lamplighter as the DEA officer involved in the Oyster Pond episode.

"Just found out he's booked at the Amsterdam House in P'burg. Put two bricks of Semtex in his room. Get the exact room number from Prescott."

A brick of Semtex weighed one kilogram, two and one-fifth pounds. The Czech-made *plastique* consisted of near-pure nitroglycerine. In its solid state it was incredibly stable, until an electric impulse activated the easily-inserted detonator.

Morgan had never used two full bricks of plastic explosive to eliminate someone. He'd vaporized the two occupants of a Rolls Royce Silver Shadow five years before in Port-au-Prince with a half-brick of the yellowish-colored explosive. The make of the vehicle, thus the probable identity of its occupants, was finally determined by a Haitian police officer who found a distinctive "RR" hubcap a block from the blast scene.

"Det'nate from Front Street, suh?" Rupert was already planning the assault.

"You'll be down at The Pier, Rupe." Tomasso knew this would hurt the black man's pride, but he needed as clean a job as possible. "My wife and I'll be on my yacht. You make sure the limos and SL650 are parked together across from the Plaza. Get on it right now."

"Timer det'nate, Mistah T'masso?"

"No. Prescott sets it off with a hand-held detonator from outside Lamplighter's door. Understood?"

Morgan knew Tomasso had been unhappy with Prescott. The older man had failed to report at least three instances where outside law enforcement officers visited the hotel. He was a loose cannon in Tomasso's airtight vessel.

"Un'stan, suh." Rupert ventured another painful grin. The distrusted front desk manager would disappear a split second after he pressed the red button on the remote control detonator.

Chapter Four

Johnson slit open the flap of Bret's manila envelope with an ominous-looking switchblade. "My Haitian Army Knife," he'd called it. The Multistate rep reached into the envelope and removed a reservation confirmation voucher for the Amsterdam House, on Front Street near Wilhelminastraat in downtown Philipsburg. When he handed it to Bret, the American noticed that someone at Multistate had made an open-ended reservation for him in a room at the hotel. Johnson gave Bret his business card, presented a mock salute, turned on his heels and left the busy terminal.

The "meeting" had ended. Bret grabbed his carryall bag and pushed his way toward the taxi stand. "Taxi Stand" was a polite phrase, he knew from experience. Hawkers held signs telling their clients' taxi company names and cab numbers. Each man shouted a different ride rate, and prospects then haggled for even lower prices.

The prime concern with St. Martin's cabs was that most of them were large American or Japanese SUVs, comfortable, but eight-seaters. Almost no island driver would pass up a fare. Some cabbies stopped and attempted to solicit pedestrians to take their taxi, much like jitneys in New York, Chicago, San Juan and Manila. Thus, a ride that may normally take ten minutes could run to a half-hour or more.

Before Bret exited the terminal, he studied a large map of the Philipsburg area that included Princess Juliana Airport. *About four miles to his hotel,* he concluded. Another map on the opposite side of the entrance automatic doors showed the airport in relation to Marigot. It was about the same distance from the airport following the highway paralleling Simpson Bay. *Should be staying near Marigot,* he thought. *Know some police and attorneys there.*

First things first, he decided. *Go to the hotel and get my bearings.* He walked through the doors and strode directly to the nearest taxi . . . a Toyota van. Bret had violated all airport taxi etiquette by avoiding both "hawkers" and "starters" and slid the rear door open, stepping inside. Before either cabby, starter or hawker could protest, he pulled a ten-dollar bill from his pocket and set it next to the driver.

"That 'Alexander Hamilton' has a twin brother for you soon as we get to the Amsterdam House in P'burg."

"A'ways did like them two Hamilton boys," the cabby said. He pulled out of the bewildering jam of taxis, buses and motor scooters, then headed for the airport terminal's main entrance/exit turnoff.

"Good afternoon, sir. Would you care to register for a room?" The desk clerk at Philipsburg's old-but-immaculate Amsterdam House looked to be in his early fifties. He wore a grey suit and tie in the air-conditioned lobby. The comfortable quiet contrasted with the mass of tourists and automobile traffic only inches away outside on the tiny brick sidewalks and narrow one-way lane of Front Street.

"Afternoon," Bret said. "My company booked me with you yesterday. Here's my reservation confirmation." He handed the desk clerk his triplicate sheets of paper.

"Very well, Mr. Lamplighter," the clerk pleasantly said as he studied the document. He set a sign-in sheet in front of the American. "Please fill this out. Also, may I see your passport, sir?"

Bret placed his passport on the counter for the desk man to

see. The clerk looked at the credentials, wrote the serial number at the top of the sign-in sheet and picked up a rubber stamp. He inked it and whacked it directly over Bret's passport number and casually slid the passport back across the counter.

"Will you be with us for a long stay?" the clerk asked.

"I hope not. Want to finish my business as quickly as possible." *This isn't where I want to stay*, Bret finally decided. He'd been mulling this over ever since Johnson gave him the hotel reservations at the airport. Now he'd decided. *Most of my contacts are gonna be in Marigot. Why'd George book me into a hotel on the Dutch side?* George knew he worked for the French authorities when he was here before. *That's where I'll have the best chance getting answers.*

Fifteen minutes after Bret entered his room, he sat on the bed and placed a station-to-station call to Multistate Insurance in Chicago. It was about one-thirty p.m. in St. Martin . . . which meant it was eleven-thirty a.m. Chicago time.

After speaking with the Claims Adjustment Department's receptionist, George Princeton answered. "Bret, *cómo está usted?*"

"Don't speak Spanish here, George . . . or French, either."

"No? Where the hell *are* you?"

"I *wanted* to be in the French West Indies, but somebody booked me into a hotel in the Netherlands Antilles."

"Ida's not too good with geography, Bret. Look, tell me where you wanta stay and I'll personally make the reservations for you."

"Just checked out some spots closer to Marigot." Bret stared at one of several brochures he'd picked up at the airport. "Phoned a place already and they have one last opening. Sounds just right."

"Okay, old friend. Gimme the details."

"Called Sunshine Pointe Resort. It's at Pointe des Pierres a Chaux on Nettle Bay, west of Marigot."

"Don't need all that crap. Just give me the phone number."

"George, you *do* need some information when you call. Phone number's (590) 87.91.20. The opening is for villa number twelve. Got that?"

"You said '*villa*'?"

"Sure did, my friend. Henry okayed all reasonable expenses."

About five dollars' worth of silence followed Bret's comment.

"I gotta bury *that* charge in some other assignment. Okay, I'll book you at Marigot's Sunshine Pointe and cancel the Amsterdam in Philipsburg."

"You're a gem . . . a real, um, blue-green emerald in a sea of zircons."

"*Auf Wiedersehen*, Bret."

"Don't speak German here, either. 'Bye, George."

Bret slammed down the receiver. Looking at his watch, he noted he'd been on St. Martin more than an hour. He grabbed the ever-present carryall and a securely-wrapped package that had awaited him in the room. When Bret first picked it up from the bed, he read a brief note that said, "Lamplighter. Wear this in good health. Johnson." *Odd character, but seems to know his way around.*

The private investigator locked the door behind him after tossing the key on an end table. He entered the closest of two elevators. As the sliding door nearly fully closed, he just managed to see the desk clerk who'd waited on him earlier. Now in shirt sleeves, the man appeared to be heading toward Bret's vacated room.

A young woman was now tending the desk, obviously the older man's replacement. She sifted through a pile of mail and only briefly looked in his direction. Bret pushed through the heavy wrought-iron front entrance and stood on the sidewalk in tourist-packed Front Street. Three cabs waited outside the hotel entrance. Fortunately, one was an automobile . . . a full-size Ford Fairlane. *Don't wanta waste any more time ridin' with a half-dozen other fares.* Hurriedly, he walked to the taxi and pulled open its right rear door.

Tons of debris preceded a blinding flash of intense flame directly above him. In peripheral he could see the falling rain of bricks, mortar, glass, wood and metal shooting out from a huge hole in the side of the Amsterdam House. The wreckage spread for hundreds of feet over and beyond Front Street. A prolonged, deafening rumble followed the deadly shower of thousands of pounds of rubble, a scant instant later.

Bret dove to the rear floor of the cab as the plunging debris rained down on the busy mid-afternoon street. He had no doubt the tumultuous blast had just destroyed his second floor room with the view of Front Street. *His* room was now scattering its ceiling, floor, walls and furniture on pedestrians and vehicles. *Is the desk clerk part of the falling dust?* he oddly wondered.

A quarter-ton section of wall suddenly replaced the taxi's windshield. Before he could move, the driver was crushed beyond recognition. The Ford's roof crumpled almost to the rear seat underpinning. Bret managed to twist and wrench his small carryall from beneath the roof frame. The small package from Johnson had fallen to the floor and was untouched except for several scuff marks.

Gagging on roiling dust, he tried to kick open the door. He found the left rear door handle, and twisted it down, but it remained fast. "Open, you lousy sucker," he ordered. He felt some outward movement as he pushed, though he felt as if his arm was exploding. The door moved more with a nerve-grating "scrunch." He pushed harder. The door slowly moved outward far enough for him to squeeze through. Mortar, bricks and more dust fell from atop the door jamb to the now-filthy street.

Bret dragged himself through the narrow opening and tumbled to the littered pavement. He shook his head and checked himself for injuries. No wounds, but he was covered in dirt and grime. His trousers had several small rips and tears at knees and cuffs. His shirt was missing buttons and the pocket was hanging by a few threads.

Dust filled the air. Other vehicles around him were crushed. A horn sounded endlessly. Three bodies lay on the street, bleeding and unmoving. Others screamed with pain at their horrible injuries. Reaching back in the car, he grabbed his dirty, crumpled carry-on bag of belongings from the rear seat and retrieved Johnson's airport terminal 'Welcome Home' gift.

"Sonuvabitch was meant for me," he muttered. He knew it as he peered up at the gaping hole in the side of the hotel. *A couple pounds of C-4 or Semtex,* he realized. *Only plastique flashes without a raging fire afterward.* The four rooms above, below and to the sides of Bret's brief second floor lodging were also blown over half of Front Street. "Bastards took no chances," he grumbled aloud, unheard amid the screaming, groaning victims lying and staggering around him, most still in shock.

"Here be 'nother one," a uniformed young man yelled behind him as he ran up to Bret. "Look dazed, but 'live."

"I'm okay," Bret assured the man. "Go help the worse hurt."

"Ver' well, suh. Sorry 'bout all this," he said, indicating their surroundings. It was as if the Philipsburg civil servant somehow felt responsible for the carnage and destruction.

Sirens could be heard nearing the scene of the disaster. Only two or three minutes had elapsed since the explosion, but he had to get away, fast. *Murdering bastards could still be around to admire their handiwork.*

Unsteadily, Bret dragged himself to his feet. Bag in one hand and grubby package in the other, he briskly walked past hundreds of shouting and terrified tourists, shopkeepers, and curious bystanders. At the first cross-street, he turned south . . . toward The Square adjoining Philipsburg's Pier on Great Bay. Outside the Bay's entrance between Fort Amsterdam and Point Blanche lay the Caribbean.

There were always taxis in The Square, he remembered. It would be best to get a cab and check into Sunshine Pointe, fast. The side street was barely as wide as its single, narrow sidewalk. Two ambulances and a police van skimmed past Bret as he flattened his back against the bricks of a souvenir shop. They hurriedly raced toward the scene of the Front Street explosion. As begrimed as he looked, he appeared no worse than dozens of other men, women and children fleeing the carnage. Many people were cut and bleeding, but clearly those who were walking didn't need immediate medical attention.

As he reached The Square, many people fleeing the bomb

scene stood around the central plaza. Some still were in shock, while others milled around trying to find a means of transportation to their home or hotel. Fierce screaming and fighting centered on several taxis and city buses, and near a few tour buses and private vans. The Square was crowded in "normal" times, so with the fear generated by the horrific blast, confusion and apprehension were prevalent.

Bret scanned the length and breadth of The Square for a free taxi. Several cabs arrived and dropped off passengers. Waiting police instantly commandeered these to load cut and bleeding casualties. For no apparent reason, he suddenly wondered, *What happened to the hotel manager? Why was he headed for my room?*

As he continued his search for an empty cab, Bret's eyes focused on a curious sight. Three Mercedes Benzes were parked in a row directly in front of the now-empty fire station on the north edge of the plaza. Two of the vehicles were white limousines, and their drivers stood next to the cars . . . occasionally laughing and joking with each other. The third Mercedes was a new, bright red SL650. *What'd that stewardess say?* Bret thought back to the 727. *Claude and Ellen imported Mercedes.* Glancing toward the limos and personal luxury car, he wondered how they could park with impunity directly in front of the municipal fire station. *Average firefighter doesn't drive a Mercedes.*

He wasn't thinking clearly, yet. He needed to get to the resort and shower. Too much happening too fast. Before him was one of the many small tour buses that appeared to roam everywhere on the island. The driver was nervously herding his passengers inside. He obviously didn't want police putting casualties in his bus. A side trip to the hospital would waste time, and with him, time in his vehicle was his only source of income.

Bret saw a sign inside the windshield. It depicted an orange fruit superimposed against an outline map of St. Martin . . . Guava Tours, Ltd. He raced to the bus and wedged in front of the weaving line. Most of the tourists were talking about the explosion on Front Street, so nobody complained about his cutting in line. Several people who'd been near the Amsterdam House when the bomb exploded were covered with gray dust, a few others had torn clothing, but nobody appeared to be hurt.

"Got ticket stub, mon?" the bus driver asked. "Don't 'member you from b'fore."

Bret had anticipated this problem. He placed a twenty-dollar bill in the man's outstretched hand and said, "Musta lost the stub in all the confusion. This should get me to Sunshine Pointe, don'tcha think?"

The driver leisurely looked into his hand and said, "Now I place de face, mon. Welcome back."

Sunshine Pointe Resort was the fourth stop on the driver's agenda, following the west coast road from Philipsburg. Bret and two couples got off at Sunshine Pointe. The couples walked toward their accommodations while Bret went directly to the main desk in the lobby. A very tan young woman with long, brown hair and large hazel eyes gave him a professional smile, but also seemed to question his threadbare appearance.

"Name's Lamplighter," Bret informed her. He looked down at his shirt and slacks. "I was walking along the wrong street in Philipsburg when the whole side of a building blew off."

"Oh, we are so sorry, *Monsieur* Lamplighter. I hear that news on the radio one or two hours ago." She was suddenly very concerned for this pleasant looking man. "We have you for the *reservé* in Villa *numero* twelve."

"Wonderful," Bret smiled politely. "I'm glad George got through to you."

"My name is Yvonne, *m'sieur*. If you are in need of a taxi, tours, restaurant *reservés* . . . ask for me. I will be of service in every way." Yvonne's light green blouse was unbuttoned to the waist since she wore a bright print halter top beneath it. The remainder of her outfit consisted of short, beige culottes and sandals.

"*Merci*, Yvonne," Bret replied. He hesitated briefly, then added, "I'd like to ask a very big favor of you."

The young woman smiled as if this sort of thing happened often. "It *may* be my pleasure," she answered in French-accented English.

"It's nothing improper . . . maybe awkward, however."
"I can answer only after you make the question."
"*Big* favor," Bret said again. "There are people in St. Martin who want to know I'm here . . . but I don't *want* them to know. Does that make sense?"
"You want to use the *faux* name, Monsieur Lamplighter?"
Her outwardness and obvious understanding took Bret aback.
"Yeah. Yes, Yvonne. Umm, did *you* take the reservation from my friend in Chicago?"
"*Oui, il était je, Monsieur.*"
"Good, er, *bon,*" Bret responded, smiling. "No one else on your staff could know me by my real name?"
"*Non,*" she said, shaking her head. "I make copies for files and French government tax records, but they are locked away. No one else has the file cabinet keys."
Bret knew how easy breaking into an average file cabinet was. He understood how disastrous a paper trail could be . . . receipts, ticket stubs, credit card invoices. A practically endless list.
"Perhaps you'll book me as my friend who made the phone call to you."
"George Princeton? I will do that. His name appears on some records I have filled out here."
"Thanks for your help, Yvonne. Please keep this arrangement to yourself."
She nodded and handed him two keys. "This *clef*, um, key is for your villa doors. This other key is for the room safe found within the bedroom closet."
"*Merci, mademoiselle,*" Bret thanked the young desk clerk.
"You are welcome, sir," she said, and briskly shook his hand.

Chapter Five

After a quick shower, Bret had tried to reach Johnson at the telephone number on his business card. Maybe the little man had information that could help him find the people who wanted him dead. Johnson was gone, so Bret left a message on his answering machine. He had tried to contact several other people he knew two years before, but none were available. He had left messages with family members, but not with the people he really needed to speak with.

Time is already running out, he'd thought. *And I only arrived here a couple of hours ago.* He had sat on the edge of his bed, ears still ringing from the powerful bomb blast at the hotel. His ripped and filthy shirt lay in the bathroom waste basket. He'd begun to read more of the Anguilla medical examiner's report with weary, bloodshot eyes, but the words no longer had made sense. *Damn. Need to calm down just a bit,* he'd thought. Bret then slipped into swim trunks and sat on the sofa. He'd tried to pay attention to the news on CNN, but began to nod off. The day had been long and exhausting, both emotionally and physically.

Maybe a quick dip will bring me back to reality. He grabbed several towels, left his villa and walked twenty feet to the large fresh water pool. It was only available to the occupants and guests of the twelve villas spaced around it in a staggered semicircle. Five or six other male and female guests reclined or sat on loungers. No one wore clothing above the abdomen, common sunbathing attire in the French West Indies. He settled into a shady lounge chair on the pool tiling. A light northwesterly breeze off the Caribbean drifted over Bret, and he immediately fell asleep.

Bright sun awoke Bret, stinging his eyes. A young woman lay on her back in the lounger next to him. A trim, unclothed and very tanned body glistened with suntan lotion. She had closely-cropped, wavy auburn hair, and no makeup. Her oval face was turned slightly toward Bret.

The slender woman wore very dark sunglasses. *Maybe in late twenties, early thirties*, he tried to judge. Narrow hips, athletic build, about average height, 5' 6" or so.

Pain, Bret discerned. His body ached and he instantly realized he was sunburned. *Time?* He groped around next to him in and around the towels. His watch, when he finally retrieved it, showed 6:20. He'd been asleep more than two hours. He glanced to his right again, and wondered how long she'd been there.

Bret's forehead and nose stung. "Damn sunburn," Bret said and sat up.

"You are American?" The woman rose onto her left elbow. "Your face and arms are sunburned."

"I know," he said.

The sunglasses hid her eyes, but he saw her smile. "I have some aloe vera lotion." She grabbed a bottle of aloe from beneath a towel and passed it to him.

"Thanks," Bret said. Although the woman spoke perfect American English, she did so with a slight French accent.

She swung her legs off the lounger, leaned forward and thrust out her right hand. "Name's Abby Duchamps."

Bret shook her outstretched hand. "Hello, Abby. You go to college in the States? You've got all the right American expressions."

"Wellesley," she nodded. "Spoiled French brat." She paused a moment, then leaned back on the lounger.

"How long have you been on St. Martin? You're darker than some natives."

Abby cocked her head to one side. "Why do you want to know?"

"Like I said, you can't get tanned *that* dark overnight. Live here?"

"No, I grew up in Grenoble . . . and I don't live here." She hesitated. "I'm starting my fourth week of holiday . . . just sun, sea and sand."

"Good paying job? A full month at an expensive resort."

"No. Government civil servant. About the lowest paying job in France."

"Work in Paris?"

"Marseille."

"Kinda seedy place as I recall."

"Definitely not the *Riviera*, that's true."

"What government agency do you work for?" Bret was fascinated that a young woman who earned low wages could afford a $600 a day resort villa for a full month.

"*Pourquoi?*"

"Just curious, I suppose. A graduate of an expensive, prestigious American college. Working as a civil servant."

"What's your name? I told you mine."

"That's a major change of subject." Bret mulled over her question for several seconds. "George," he answered. "George Princeton. Chicago. Insurance, also low-paying." He wished he could see her eyes through the dark sunglasses. A person's eyes reflected a lot. He'd like to assess her reactions to his answers.

Abby straightened up, moving her arms to her sides. "I'm ready for a dip, um, George. You coming?"

"No, gonna put on your aloe lotion. Nose must resemble a stop light." *Had she hesitated when saying 'George'? Better call Bertrand about her.*

Bertrand Hough was U.S. Assistant Consul General at Fort-de-France, Martinique. The consulate handled U.S. affairs on the French Caribbean *departmentes* of Martinique and Guadeloupe, and the *territoire* of St. Martin, French West Indies. He came to know Bertrand during his temporary duty assignments on St. Martin and Guadeloupe. Hough had been his only contact between DEA headquarters in Washington. It was Hough who personally delivered his farewell airline ticket to him that last day in Marigot. *Wonder if he's still at the consulate?* Almost two years had passed.

Abby slipped off the lounger, picked up a bath towel from the chaise, and stood in front of Bret. Her bare breasts were low-slung and quite full and haughty on her slender, shapely frame.

Bret slowly shook his head. "That's the smallest bikini bottom I've ever seen," he said as he peered at the tiny triangle of blue cloth barely covering her lower abdomen.

"Next best thing to *au naturel*," she chuckled. Abby turned and walked to the edge of the pool. Her deeply-tanned back and bare, undulating *derrière* matched the brown tan of her stomach, legs and gently swaying breasts.

Bret dabbed huge globs of aloe onto his ruddy face, shoulders and chest. He watched as Abby expertly shallow-dove into the clear pool water.

He glanced at his watch as he enjoyed the cool, soothing effect of the aloe. *Shit, six-thirty. Three hours ago someone nearly killed me. Have to start scouring the island for answers to lots of questions.*

He definitely needed this small amount of rest to get his brain and body functioning again. He couldn't shake the queasy feel of fear and apprehension in his stomach. *The only Mercedes' I've seen in St. Martin this time around . . . and all three were illegally parked two blocks from my intended funeral.* He attempted to link his data. *The only two people I saw on my previous trip to St. Martin are the only two I met on this trip, and they import Mercedes. I need to get the last name and address of Claude and Ellen.*

Abby waved as she splashed in the pool. *Seems pleasant for a Wellesley woman.* He'd dated a Smith grad for six years. Came very close to wedding bells. Discovered her one afternoon totally naked in the back seat of her father's Bentley . . . in *flagrante delicto* with another completely unclothed young lady. Bret, Adele and her friend agreed that marriage was not a good idea. Adele's father phoned him several times after that, but Bret never mentioned the reason they'd ended their engagement. Adele's mother dropped in at DEA headquarters once. That time, he *did* give the reason for the sudden broken engagement. None of the family contacted him after that. One year later, the *Washington Star* announced Adele's high-society nuptials to a Georgetown attorney. The accompanying glossy showed that her spouse was male.

"George, that was wonderful." Abby approached Bret's lounge chair, wet feet splatting on the pool tile. There was a scant instant when Bret nearly looked around to identify Abby's 'George'.

"Looked like great fun." Bret watched Abby dab the towel on slicked-down hair.

"Very pleasant," she nodded. "Interior."

"Fascinating comment," Bret said, also nodding. "Decorating problem in your villa?"

Abby sat on the edge of her lounger, elbows perched on her thighs. "Interior Ministry. That's where I work."

"I see. I wasn't really pressing you for an answer, Ms. Duchamps." He hesitated several seconds. "What kind of work at the Ministry of the Interior?"

"Statistics. Research and Development. Some typing, some filing. Busy work."

"That's it?" Bret was doubtful. Her background and lifestyle didn't call to mind the menial chores of a clerk-typist.

"It's an honest living," she replied. Abby began to apply suntan lotion to her still-wet skin.

Bret stared into impossibly-light blue eyes, so pale they shown nearly ice-blue. He involuntarily shuddered at the intense depth of those orbs.

Abby turned around so her bare buttocks were perched on the near horizontal support of the lounger, and placed her feet against the far chair support. "Put some lotion on my back . . . thickly, would you, please? I would hate to burn near the final days of my holiday."

Bret took the lotion from her and splattered a big daub on Abby's upper back.

"*Ummm*, good hands." She sounded drowsy.

"You're buffed," Bret noted. "Robust muscle tone . . . you seem strong, athletic."

"Thank you. I follow a strict regimen of strenuous exercises and aerobics. Also, I *am* a marvelous athlete."

"Glad you agree with my appraisal," Bret smiled. "Okay," he gave her a slap on the butt, "grease job and oil change finished . . . you're good for another 10,000 miles."

"*Merci*, you are a most competent 'body mechanic'."

Bret busied himself wiping excess lotion on one of his towels, trying to ignore Abby as she turned over and lay on her stomach.

"Excuse me, *monsieur* Lamp-, Princeton." Yvonne from the front desk noticed Abby as she walked up to Bret's lounge chair.

"Hello, Yvonne," Bret greeted her. He glanced toward Abby, but she showed no evidence of having heard anything out of the ordinary.

"I phoned your room to give you this message." She handed Bret a slip of pink paper. "It was not until now that I received my replacement at the lobby desk."

"Been out here a coupla hours," Bret explained. He read the note. "This is the time," he pointed with a finger, "when they called?" The note had "1730 *heures*" printed on it.

"Yes, it was the first of three calls from this person to you," she smiled. "He was most insistent."

The caller was 'M. Henri Bouchard'. Although nearly two years had elapsed, Bret immediately recognized the caller's phone number . . . 87.50.06 was Marigot, St. Martin police headquarters. *Dammit*, he said to himself, *didn't waste any time— even after I changed locations.*

"Many thanks, Yvonne. I appreciate your bringing this to me."

"We do all we can for our guests," she said. Yvonne briefly glanced down at the prone figure on the lounge chair next to Bret. "I am on dinner break, *m'sieur*. I must leave now. *Au revoir*."

"G'night. Thanks again." He watched the young woman walk away. *Nice girl*, he thought. *Glad she's on my side.*

Bret grabbed his towels and hurried toward his villa. He unlocked the rear door and slid the double-thick glass portal aside. He'd left the air conditioner on, so cool air soothed his face and body.

Should call the gendarmerie, he thought. Bret went to the phone and dialed the number Yvonne had printed on the message slip.

A woman's voice answered, "Marigot police."

"Monsieur Bouchard," Lamplighter said.

"The *sous-inspecteur* he leave for th' day," she responded. "Is there someone else who may be helpin' you?"

"No, Bouchard tried to contact me earlier." His watch showed it was nearly seven P.M. "I'll call him tomorrow."

"Your name, suh?"

Bret hesitated, then, shrugging, said, "Lamplighter, Bret Lamplighter."

"Ah, *oui, m'sieur* Lamplighter. Indeed, *sous-inspecteur* Bouchard do want to talk to you. Monsieur Bouchard be here 0700 *heures* tomorrow. Phone him then."

"Very well, miss. Goodbye."

"*Au revoir, m'sieur.*" Dead line. Dial tone.

"Damn," Bret yelled into the inanimate phone. He hung up and leaned back on the sofa. "I'm here five hours and already the *gendarmes* want to talk to me."

Johnson's package sat on the glass-topped coffee table in front of the sofa. Bret started to reach for it, then shook his head. *Shower first.* He stripped and traipsed into the bathroom.

A half-hour later, he lay on top of his bed sheets, clean and soothed with his own aloe vera. His eyes were closed when the telephone chirp-chirped. *Who else knows I'm here?*

Bret answered, "Princeton." *Johnson getting back to me?*

"Monsieur Lamplighter, here is Yvonne from the lobby desk."

"Yes, Yvonne?"

"I want to speak information for you."

"What information?" Bret felt wary again. *Should never drop my guard.*

"The woman on the swim pool *lit* adjoining yours."

"Woman? Yeah, Abby Duchamps. What about her?"

"Does she tell you where she is employed, *m'sieur?*"

"Yes, she works for the government in Marseille. She's been here on vacation nearly four weeks."

"Monsieur, she is not being truthful. She has been in St. Martin for *deux jours*! I see her passport when she arrives yesterday *matin*, um, morning."

"Impossible. Nobody can get a suntan like hers in two days, Yvonne."

"This I do not know, *m'sieur*. She gives the name of her employer for our *territoire* tax records."

"Yes, she told me. Works for the French Interior Ministry."

"*Oui, monsieur*, but she registers at Sunshine Pointe forty minutes before you *arrivé* here. Did she also tell you she works for the *Sûreté Nationale Français* . . . the government secret police?"

Chapter Six

Bret awoke at 5:30 A.M. to the clanging of his portable alarm clock. He quickly showered and shaved, then dressed in fresh, though wrinkled, slacks and a short-sleeved cotton shirt. He planned to phone Bertrand Hough in Martinique. At least he'd phone the consulate in hopes Hough was still there.

"Damn, Johnson's box," Bret said. He had not yet opened the shoebox-size package after he'd carried it through two countries . . . one with a sixteen square mile area, the other measuring some twenty-one square miles.

He sat on the sofa, picked up the package and stared at it. He gently shook it. *Perfect size for a bomb, especially plastique.* "Should trust Johnson," he spoke aloud. *"Don't* trust him."

Carefully, he removed the light brown wrapping paper. It literally *was* a shoe box . . . Keds sneakers, size 7B. He took a razor-sharp pen knife and very carefully cut a rectangular hole in one end. *No plastique. No detonator. No fuse.* He noticed several dozen sheets of paper in two or three file folders, also a cloth-wrapped object on top of the folders. Wadded-up newspaper filled open spaces to keep everything from bouncing around. Bret pulled the lid off the box and picked up the cloth-wrapped object. A Sint Maarten souvenir T-shirt shrouded a matte-gray automatic pistol. Bret hefted it as it lay in his hand. The long barrel stuck beyond his palm by nearly seven inches. The professional hit man's pistol: a High Standard Dura-Matic-101.

The High Standard is a .22 caliber automatic, so accurate it's often used in shooting matches. It breaks down in six seconds for cleaning, and uses powerful .22 caliber Quik-Shok Long Rifle ammunition for killing . . . ten deadly fragmentation slugs to a clip.

He smiled to himself. Today's action movies and novels emphasize muscle hand guns . . . Glocks, Ingram Mac-10's, .44 and .357 Magnums, H & K 9mm P7M8, and many more. In the real world, nevertheless, *accurate* and *efficient* weapons kept a man alive. Johnson had provided the ultimate survival weapon . . . a mob-endorsed High Standard. *This is the 'extra equipment' George mentioned*, he realized. *Guess he knew what was goin' down in the islands.*

Included were two 50-round boxes of .22 Quik-Shok Long Rifle ammunition and two loaded clips from the box. He slipped a clip into the hand grip and set the weapon and ammo aside.

On the top folder, the word ANGUILLA was written on the outside with a red felt marker. He began to read the first file. It was an addendum from the forensic pathologist in The Valley, dated twelve days after the death of Bernard S. Lustfield at Casablanca Resort. A laboratory in San Juan had analyzed minute particles of matter taken from Lustfield's trouser cuffs and pockets. Lustfield didn't smoke, but there had been traces of cigarette tobacco, with South American origins. There were minuscule emerald particles with soil and shale from Boyacá province . . . not at all surprising. Of greatest interest to technicians at the Puerto Rican lab, however, was an abundance of coffee grounds. Again, detailed tests showed their origin to be South American—specifically Choco province in western Colombia. *Colombia seems to be the source for damn near everything sticking to old Bernie's clothing*, Bret reflected.

A blue, penned-in asterisk followed the remarks by the Anguillan coroner: "Addendum to addenda," the footnote related in longhand. "To BLL [Bret's initials] from GRP [Princeton's initials] through Johnson: Lustfield's wife and personal physician swear that deceased had a potentially life-threatening allergic reaction to several common chemical substances. Highest on the allergy list was caffeine in *every* form . . . coffee, colas, pain killers, analgesics, *ad infinitum*. Deceased would experience epileptic-like convulsions after ingesting or breathing the smallest amounts of caffeine (and at least eight other basic drugs, including *nicotine*)."

Damn, Bret thought, *why would someone who's deathly allergic to caffeine and nicotine have coffee grounds and tobacco in his clothing?* Less than twenty-four hours into the case and the private investigator was already up to his ass in alligators. *All this nonsense and now I gotta phone Bertrand in Martinique.* He'd read the other files Johnson provided before the day was out.

Bret checked a phone book for the area code of Martinique. The number was the same: (596) 63-13-03. The number he'd dialed rang.

Connection. "Hello."

"Bertrand Hough, please."

"Speaking. How are you, Bret?"

"Great, old buddy. You don't sound surprised to hear from a ghost."

"Expected it. Your name appeared in our computer data bank yesterday. Welcome home."

"Home is where the heart is, Bertrand. Heart's not in St. Martin this time around."

"Bastards screwed you royally. No way they shoulda axed you from DEA."

"Couldn't agree with you more. Justice needed a scapegoat to placate Paris."

"True. At least they drummed out Beauville, too."

"No shit! Hadn't heard."

"Yeah. Day after you survived Hurricane Leona and flew back north."

"Transferred . . . or booted clean out?"

"Gave him a choice: a bust down to *gendarme* in St. Martin or full pension back home in Loire-Atlantique."

"Obviously, Jacques took his pension and *la belle Français*."

"Bet your ass. Now he's tellin' the citizens of Nantes how he singlehandedly took on the Colombian *narcos* . . . and won."
"Believe it!" Bret exclaimed. He paused momentarily. "Bertrand, on the subject of French police, does your computer list members of the *Sûreté Nationale*?"
"*Sûreté*? Damn, man. How do the French feds fit into your latest travels?"
"Wish I knew. Wasn't here four hours before my hotel blew up and a female *Sûreté* agent contacted me. Think she knows . . ."
"Stop! Halt!" Bertrand interrupted. "The Philipsburg disaster was *your* room!?"
"I was gonna mention that fray my next sentence." Despite his brush with death, Bret suppressed a slight smile.
Silence on the satellite hookup. "Christ almighty," his friend cursed. "Do you have a scrambler?"
"No, why should I carry around . . . ?"
"Okay, okay," Bertrand interrupted again. "I'm comin' to St. Martin. We gotta talk. Say no more. I'll phone you from Grand Case Airport around two P.M. We must speak in private. Understand?"
"Yeah. And information on the girl?"
"From the *Sûreté*? Got her name?"
"Duchamps. Abby Duchamps . . . from Marseille."
"Maybe she's from Marseille, maybe not. Stay away from her, Bret. Bye."
"Won't go near her. Bye, Bertrand."
Bret placed the phone in its cradle. *Sounded like a dozen AWACs monitored our conversation.*
Bret realized he'd have to phone Marigot's under-inspector and check in. The inspector was upset about his arrival, from the phone calls he'd made the previous day. When he dialed police headquarters, a woman answered who sounded like the one he'd spoken with the previous evening. "Do you work twenty-four hours a day?"
"Mistah Lamplighter?"
"Yes."

"Please remain on th' phone for *sous-inspecteur* Bouchard."

Bret was put on hold. He thought it was strange the French police had gotten to him before the Dutch. The bomb was on Netherlands Antilles soil.

"*Bon jour Monsieur* Lamplighter."

"*Bon jour Inspector* Bouchard. The resort desk clerk left a message that you wanted to speak with me."

"True, we know you were registered in a room at the Amsterdam House yesterday. We also know you vacated the room a short time before it blew up."

"Correct, inspector. I have no idea who set the bomb."

Bouchard managed a chuckle. "Monsieur," he continued, "a faulty gas line valve at the hotel caused the tragic explosion. You were lucky you escaped with your life."

"That the story you gave the press, inspector?"

"It is the sad fact, Lamplighter. Four innocent people died because of the accident at Amsterdam House."

The desk clerk, Bret wondered. "Did a hotel employee die in the, um, accident?"

"Yes, the day manager. Why do you ask?"

"When I got in the elevator, I noticed him walking toward my room. The explosion happened no more than thirty seconds after that."

"*C'intéresse, Monsieur.* I must now invite you to make a statement for us regarding that information."

That's an order . . . not an invitation. "Your place or Philipsburg? The incident was *not* in French St. Martin."

"*Monsieur* Lamplighter, we work closely with the Netherlands Antilles authorities. St. Martin is a small island, so the two countries cooperate as one. With mutual teamwork we solve our mutual problems."

"When do you want my statement?"

"Immediately," the *sous-inspecteur* replied. "We have questions to ask you, also."

"Editorial 'we', inspector?"

"I am not certain . . ."

"Sorry. Does your use of the word 'we' mean only you, or you and others?"

"The Philipsburg police chief has questions, as well."

"Unm hunh. Marigot police station?"

"*Oui, monsieur. Au revoir.*"

Bret set the receiver on its cradle. It immediately chirp-chirped like one of the pesky little island sugar birds. He lifted the receiver and said, "Hello. This is Princeton."

"No, you're not!" George Princeton bellowed into Bret's ear.

"Right, George. Bret here." George sounded upset.

"Cut the shit. It's still dark here in Chicago," Princeton shouted. "What happened at the Amsterdam House, fer crissake?"

"How'd you hear about that? This is a no-news, third world country."

"Mrs. Douglas saw one of those bleached blond newsreaders on CNN mention it. She phoned Henry to see if her investigator was one of the dead."

"Then Henry called you," Bret completed the progress.

"Yeah . . . and I went through hell getting hold of someone at State in D.C."

"Okay. Then the State Department filled you in."

"Some cock-and-bull nonsense about a faulty gas main valve at the hotel."

"That's the police coverup story for the news media."

"All right, what's *your* story?"

"*Plastique*, probably. Definitely an explosive device. I missed being part of the rubble on Front Street by thirty seconds."

"Shit, Bret. You hafta be damn careful out there."

"Reconsiderin' the assignment, George. Now I know why a quarter-million sounded okay with Multistate. My life's worth a lot more'n that."

"Bret old buddy. Henry, both Mr. and Mrs. Douglas, *everybody*'s counting on you. One bad little . . ."

"George, save it for some insurance investigator intern. I've got the French *Sûreté* checking on me, and some mob's gotta . . ."

"Hold on a second," Princeton interrupted. "What's that about the *Sûreté*?"

"Yep. Met her at the resort pool. Said she was a tourist, but a desk clerk identified her through her passport. Came in the day before I arrived. Has a villa not far from mine. Says she's from Marseille."

"Any way to check her out?"

"Already on it. Consular friend in Martinique's lookin' through computer files for any confirmation of her background."

"You've gone to a heluva lot of trouble to be considerin' reneging on the assignment. Just bullshittin', hunh buddy?"

Bret knew Princeton's question would come up. He actually *had* considered backing out. Then he thought of his finances. He owed thousands of dollars in past due bills, his lease and other commitments. This one job for Multistate would pay off all his debts and leave him with money in the bank. Even after taxes. "Yeah, bullshittin' you, George. Your insurance company's got me by the *huevos*."

"Okay, Bret . . . glad to hear you're with us 'til the end. Oh," George remembered another question. "you get our rep's equipment, all right?"

"Sure did. Think the metallic item's necessary?"

"You just got done tellin' me several good reasons for that metallic equipment. Stay healthy."

"Thanks. I better get hiking for beautiful downtown Marigot. Have an appearance with the island's top law enforcement people."

"Really? The little gas leak in Philipsburg?"

"Yep."

"Any chance it *could* be a gas leak?"

"Nope. Before any town or city on St. Martin had electricity, their only fuel and light sources were imported kerosene, coal and oil. That supplemented wood and dried kelp they already had here."

"No gas at all?"

"Some bottled propane, now. St. Martin *never did* have gas mains . . . for businesses or homes."

"You sound awfully sure about that."

Bret took a deep breath. He replied, "My last stint in St. Martin, George. I managed to become friendly with several natives. They told me a lot of island history." He still recalled conversations with Harriet that lasted 'til the wee hours of the morning.

* * *

"We do not need to read you your rights, M'sieur Lamplighter," *sous-inspecteur* Bouchard reminded Bret. "We observe the Napoleonic Code here, not the United States Constitution nonsense that gives criminals more rights than the innocent."

"Whatever works for you, inspector," Bret retorted. He knew American Constitutional law was often slow to convict the guilty. However, Bret admired a system that assumed a person was innocent until proven guilty beyond any doubt.

"Why are you in St. Martin, Mr. Lamplighter?" Horst DeGroot was Philipsburg Chief of Police. He'd replaced Andres Verhouten immediately after the bloody battle between French and Netherlands Antilles forces nearly two years before. He and Under-Inspector Bouchard sat opposite Bret across a small, littered desk in a small, littered conference room in Marigot police headquarters. A stenotypist sat in a neutral corner.

The room air conditioner in its single window cranked out more noise than cool air. With the two stern police officials and the stenotypist watching his every movement, Bret felt like a live lobster in a seafood café water tank . . . ready to be consumed.

"I'm investigating a murder for an insurance company, Chief," Bret explained.

"Mr. Lamplighter," it was Bouchard's turn, "we are not happy that you are on the island of St. Martin."

"Inspector," Bret said, "I feel the same way. When I finish my business . . ."

"Your business," Bouchard broke in, "does not interest us. Your presence does. This is a peaceful country."

"*Two* peaceful countries," DeGroot amended. "One hour after you arrive, my city experiences the deaths of four innocent citizens."

"It was 'an unfortunate accident caused by leaking gas'..."

"I'm certain you know the cause of the explosion," DeGroot continued. "If you hadn't appeared on our peaceful shores, the bomb would not have been set."

"That's your theory, Chief."

"Mr. Lamplighter, you were present on Sint Maarten during the last, and only *other*, massacre we have experienced, no?"

Bret smiled and said, "At least since the original Dutch and French explorers exterminated every Arawak and Carib Indian who lived here three centuries ago."

The room became silent for several moments. The slaughter of the native Arawaks and Caribs, and the subsequent slave breeding of captured black Africans, were not comfortable topics for French and Dutch permanent residents.

Bouchard and DeGroot ignored Bret's comment. "Do you still work with the American government, Mr. Lamplighter?"

"No, Inspector. We went our separate ways after the incident the Chief spoke about."

"Most unfortunate, er, foul-up for all concerned," Bouchard said.

"It was awful that so many good people died because of a communications problem," DeGroot added.

"Mr. Lamplighter, partially due to your, er, the Oyster Pond Bay massacre, Philipsburg and Marigot routinely inform each other of *any* operation that could possibly pose a hazard to the other country."

"Guess it was constructive in *that* sense."

"Mmm, *oui*. Perhaps," Bouchard nodded.

By now the heat in the room had definitely overwhelmed the air conditioning. Bret felt sweat trickle down his side from his arm pits. *Sunburn sure doesn't help matters*, he realized.

"Are you *performing* work for the American government?" DeGroot asked.

"No, I'm investigating an emerald theft for an insurance company. No connection with *any* government."

"The CIA have freelancers for some of their assignments," Bouchard said.

"Wouldn't know, inspector," Bret replied.

"The emerald theft you speak of occurred in Sint Maarten?" DeGroot asked.

"Anguilla."

"Then why are you in St. Martin?" Bouchard asked.

"They were purchased in Sint Maarten . . . Philipsburg."

"Gems International? The Gold Mine? Ballerina Jewelers?"

"None of the large shops. A small store off Front Street. Called Bombay."

"I know the place. Did the gem theft have any connection with the Amsterdam House explosion?"

"Maybe, indirectly. I'm stumped about it. Somebody wants me taken out, but it *could* be in retaliation for the Oyster Pond Bay massacre."

"Only our police officers, and your drug enforcement people, were killed. Do you suspect police officers of the bombing?"

"Maybe their friends, possibly relatives. *Could* be the police." Bret noticed DeGroot and Bouchard exchange quick glances. *Know something?*

"Saw an odd thing on my way home from a hotel bombing," Bret continued. "Three Mercedes Benzes were parked right in front of that fire station across from your Pier, Chief."

Another pair of police executive glances. Bouchard's was an angry glance.

"In Chicago, Chief, that kind of protection usually means money under the table for a district police captain."

Bouchard stared at DeGroot. DeGroot checked the condition of the room air conditioner. The stenotypist examined the condition of her fingernails.

"Did you get the registration numbers of the vehicles, Lamplighter?" the Philipsburg police chief asked.

"No, but in the thirty-six square miles of St. Martin, I bet you'll have no trouble identifying two white Mercedes limos and one red SL650."

No comment. Instead, Bouchard reached into a green box and pulled paper from it. "What do you know about this person?" He handed Bret a photo of himself and Abby beside their resort pool.

Bret studied the photograph. "Young lady I met at Sunshine Pointe resort yesterday. She's French."

"Her name, Mr. Lamplighter?" Bouchard probed without so much as a smile.

"Duchamps, Inspector. Abby Duchamps from Marseille."

"Did she tell you where she works?" DeGroot asked.

"Interior Ministry." Bret figured he wasn't lying by failing to mention the specific department she worked for. *Besides, hafta see Bertrand before I'm certain who she is and how she fits in.*

"Did Mademoiselle, umm, Duchamps initiate the meeting between you two?"

"She was lying on a lounger. *I* initiated the meeting by asking her for some aloe vera lotion."

"I see. And how much longer do you intend to remain on St. Martin?"

"Only as long as it takes to complete my investigation, Chief."

"Yes, *monsieur* Lamplighter? The Chief and I are open-minded, but we do note you brought *two disasters* to peaceful St. Martin on *two visits*."

"That's *hardly* being open-minded. In no way did I cause either incident."

"Lamplighter," Chief DeGroot spoke, "*sous-inspecteur* Bouchard and I discussed your visit before you came here this morning. We want you to complete your business by the 23rd of the month . . . six days from today."

"S-six days?" Bret was dumfounded. "Chief, I need at least twice that time to finish my investigation."

"You are not a law enforcement officer. We don't mind tourists or legitimate businessmen. You belong in *neither* category."

Inwardly, Bret fumed. In a way, though, he understood the

predicament of the two chiefs. Their bosses in France and the Netherlands would already have questioned Lamplighter's presence on the island. They may already have mainland investigators on the way to St. Martin. Abby was DST *Sûreté*, but she was here before the Amsterdam House bombing. *She was here during the damn thing, too,* Bret realized. *Would the DST have reason to eliminate me?* Bret hoped not. "You don't understand."

"We understand. As we already told you, we are a peaceful island. We know what you are investigating . . . and it could cause ill will with many of our citizens. Complete your work by next Thursday."

Shit. Virtually impossible. "Inspector," Bret looked at Bouchard, "did the French *Sûreté* become involved with the Oyster Pond Bay, um, episode two years ago?"

Bouchard leaned back in his chair and stared at Bret. "St. Martin can handle its own concerns, monsieur."

"I'm certain of that, inspector." He waited a couple of seconds. "*Did* the *Sûreté Nationale* undertake an investigation here?"

Chief DeGroot turned his gaze toward Bouchard.

"Mr. Lamplighter," Bouchard finally replied, "the DST branch of the *Sûreté—Direction de la Sécurité du Territoire*—has the responsibility of investigating criminal offenses or provocations of French citizens on overseas French soil."

"Then your Bureau of Territorial Security sent a team of investigators to St. Martin, Inspector?"

"Two investigators . . . *not* a team." Under-Inspector Bouchard was not very enthusiastic about Bret's questions.

"The DST ousted Beauville from St. Martin, then."

More silence. Finally, "That was their decision . . . just as the DEA decided to 'oust' *you* from St. Martin."

Bret ignored Bouchard's comment. "Do you expect more *Sûreté* here, now that four people died in yesterday's terrorist bombing?"

"It is quite likely," Bouchard acknowledged.

"The explosion took place on Netherlands Antilles soil."

"Certainly," Bouchard raised his voice slightly, "but two of the victims were French Nationals. It is *also* most likely the Netherlands Antilles authorities from Curaçao will visit us." Bouchard couldn't hide a smile directed at Chief DeGroot.

"Is that all, Inspector, Chief? Seems I have much work and little time to do it in."

"*Oui, monsieur* Lamplighter." Bouchard stood. "If you discover anything important regarding the Anguilla murder, contact us immediately."

Fat chance, Bret thought as he stood up. "Anything you wish, Inspector." He walked toward the door, then stopped and turned. "If you or the chief find anything regarding Lustfield's murder, please contact me."

"We will help as much as possible," Bouchard answered. The two police officials nodded to each other, then Bouchard said, "*au revoir.*"

Bret left the hot, stuffy room one step behind the police stenotypist.

As Bret reached the front door of the police station, the stenotypist approached him. "Mistah Lamplighter. M'name is Loretta Chanson. Harriet was my fav'rite cousin."

"Very sorry, Loretta. Harriet was a favorite friend of mine, too. She was an outstanding *narc* and a wonderful human being."

"I know that, suh. She talk of you of'en when fam'lies come t'gether. She *très* fond a you, Mistah Lam'lighter. You lose fine friend, true 'nuf said."

Shit, Bret thought to himself, *two years is too short a time to forget some things.* "One of a kind that woman, Loretta."

"You ask de question 'bout *Sur'té*, suh. I know answer."

"About Abby Duchamps?"

"No, suh. You ask when DST team *arrivé* on St. Martin island."

"You mean a team's already plannin' to come here?"

"Ay', m'sieur. Three *Sûr'té* 'ficial *arrivé* Princess Juliana six 'clock dees night."

Chapter Seven

The gentle sound of lapping waves nearly mesmerized Bret as he sat in the villa's spacious living room. It was just past Noon and between phone calls he'd tossed together a sandwich from a loaf of French bread and some sliced lunch meat. A local grocery store two blocks away was always full of tourists buying small deli items. Most favored were bottles of beer and mineral water to take back to hotel rooms and suites.

He glanced down at the seemingly bottomless pile of copied reports, memos and files given to him by Johnson. The phone rang. *Only person knows I'm here is George.*

"Hello." Bret wasn't about to give *any* name over the phone again.

"*Allô*, George. This is Abby Duchamps . . . from the swimming pool."

Not too surprising, Bret thought. *Seems I'm the one she's checkin' up on.* "Hi, Abby. Comment-allez-vous?"

"Very well, thank you," she answered. Slight pause. "I was surprised yesterday when you left without saying goodbye."

"Needed rest and another dose of aloe vera. You looked happy just gettin' sun."

"Yes, I suppose that's my one vice, George."

"All that tan during *this* holiday, right?"

A slight pause. "This holiday, yes."

"All on the island of St. Martin, in other words?"

Now the pause was a full two or three seconds. "What are you getting at?"

"No one tans as brown as you are in two days. No way."

A third long pause. "Perhaps we should meet for a talk. What do you say?"

"My place in a half-hour?"

"See you in a half-hour." Abby now sounded solemn.

"On my back patio, *s'il vous plaît.*" The number of people on the mile-long private beach was usually small, seldom more than ten or twelve sunbathers and strollers. Even so, Bret figured the woman wouldn't try a broad-daylight assassination attempt.

"Thirty minutes."

As Bret replaced the receiver, the phone immediately chirped back to life. "Now what?" Bret yelled into the mouthpiece.

"Seenk jou want to talk to me, Lam'lighter," Johnson responded. "Jou leave message on my recorder."

"Johnson? Sorry, thought you were someone I just spoke with. Got your supplies. Many thanks. The information is perfect . . . very helpful."

"Jou just want to thank me. Jou could do it into my recorder." Johnson seemed angry he'd gotten through to the American.

"Okay, Johnson, I've got some more questions. You got five or ten minutes' time for me?"

"What else jou are wanting to know?"

"Mercedes Benz dealer and his wife. They may be involved in more than selling cars. Three of his vehicles were parked two blocks away when my room went into orbit. Looks like Philipsburg's police chief knows something about it."

"Clever of jou, Lam'lighter. Claude Tomasso ees well-connect with the Medellín family . . . although he keep the low, um, profile."

"Would he have put a contract out on me, Johnson? After all, emeralds might be another luxury item Tomasso's in to."

"Possibly jou are correct, *amigo.* Claude's partner, Rupert Morgan, is doing mos' wet work for him."

"This is an open phone line, Johnson." Bret began to worry about his contact.

"We speak only of things *mucho* known, Lam'lighter. Jou and French 'thorities are threats to emerald smugglers; from this come jour enemies."

"Does the cartel use boats to smuggle in emeralds?"

There was a longer than usual pause. Finally Johnson said, "Sometimes, but jou mus' think of coffee and tobacco." Now he was choosing his words more carefully.

"You mentioned in your notes that those items were found in Lustfield's clothing, plus traces of emeralds."

"*Si*, I do. Ask jourself why they come together." The telephone went dead.

Fifteen minutes later, Bret sat on his patio. He watched two older couples noisily play a card game twenty feet from the lively waters of the bay. Sunbathing parents closely watched several unclothed children as they thrashed about in the balmy sea. According to a large thermometer on the patio wall, the temperature in the shade was a very warm eighty-six degrees Fahrenheit.

"Just another day in Paradise," Abby Duchamps remarked. She stepped from the sandy beach to Bret's tiled patio and slowly pulled the wooden gate door closed. She wore a diminutive, light blue halter and white hiphugger shorts. He watched as she brushed off-white sand from snow-white canvas deck shoes. Sunglasses hid her ice-blue eyes. Abby carried a clutch, but it was nothing more than billfold-sized suede.

Satisfied that her shoes were immaculate, she took a seat in one of the three unoccupied white metal chairs around a large white metal table. "It took you no time at all to 'finger me', as Americans so coarsely put it."

". . . along with a little help from my friends."

"We are using some tired, old clichés," Abby noted. "Maybe it's time we got down to business."

"French *Sûreté Nationale* . . . DST branch," Bret said. "Kinda like our domestic FBI with a dash of CIA thrown in." Bret looked at Abby's cleavage and skin-tight shorts. *Weapon's hardly possible*, he thought. "Mind if I look at your wallet?"

"Yes, I do . . . but suit yourself." Abby flipped the small billfold to within an inch of his hands on the table top. "No insects, George."

Bret examined the suede pursette. He even ran his fingers over the soft material itself. It passed the close review. "*Merci*, Abby," he said as he slid the wallet back to the young woman's side of the table.

Abby smiled. "Bret Lamplighter, age 40. Failed ex-DEA agent. Presently investigating a murder committed on a British colony. However, Mr. Lamplighter makes his investigation from *French* soil."

Bret flipped open one of several file folders on the table. He pulled the top document out. "Police report," he pointed. "St. Martin, repeat *French* St. Martin, police report," he indicated again. "*Pourquoi?* Because the man presumed to be Lustfield's murderer is in the Marigot morgue. Killed by, St. Martin police believe, person or persons unknown from St. Martin, *French* West Indies."

"May I see the report?" Frowning, Abby Duchamps reached for the document.

"Sure," Bret handed it to her. "I admit I'm surprised the *Sûreté Nationale* doesn't have these files already. The murder happened two weeks ago."

"*Merde*," Abby swore under her breath as she scanned the report. "DST should have been notified immediately. Or at least the Ministry of the Interior."

"I think St. Martin's covering something up. I've already dug up facts the police kept under tight wraps."

Abby looked over at Bret, then back at the sheet of paper. "*Sous-inspecteur* Bouchard has an impeccable record."

"Better men than Bouchard . . ."

"I know," she interrupted. "I've read or heard of them all. But Bouchard was handpicked from more than thirty superior candidates."

"As I recall, ex-*sous-inspecteur* Beauville came here highly recommended, too."

"So? I didn't know him." Abby took a scrap of paper from the billfold and wrote some notes with a tiny pencil she pulled from the suede folds. "Where did you get this police report?"

"Sorry. Privileged information." Bret took the document and put it back into its file folder.

Abby looked as if she wanted to demand an answer, but her severe countenance softened. "I *could* have the local police insist on an answer from you, Mr. Lamplighter."

"That's not the way old swimming pool buddies act, is it?" Bret said. "Besides, I don't think the inspector's happy having the *Sûreté* on his turf."

The sound of children screaming and squealing intruded on the conversation. Bret and Abby turned to look toward the shoreline some fifty feet away. A rather large cruiser motored dangerously close to the beach. Several parents joined in with the youngsters in shouting and waving away the craft. Three men aboard the cruiser also waved. It was as if they thought the children were good-naturedly welcoming them.

"Idiots shouldn't be anywhere near that close to shore," Bret criticized. "Props could carve up those kids." He stood up.

Sun's glinting off something they're holdin', Bret noticed. The short distance of sixty or seventy feet from boat to patio abruptly revealed the reason the cruiser pulled up to the beach. "Dammit, they've got weapons! Aimin' them this way."

Almost as a single entity, Bret and Abby grabbed the heavy metal table. They quickly spun it on its side and dropped behind the improvised shield. Loud automatic rifle gunfire rang out as the table edge clanged against the hard tiled patio. The heavy glass doors directly behind the couple shattered as powerful slugs rained a tattoo against them. A staccato din of drumming clangs hit the table that was the only shelter for Bret and Abby. They knew the table wouldn't take much more heavy fire. Already, several slugs pierced the steel top where others hit before.

"Boat's movin' closer," Bret shouted. The sunbathers on the

private beach had vanished completely in the ten or fifteen seconds since the shooting began. Towels, clothes, blankets, toys, playing card were all lying where the resort's vacationers had left them. An abandoned portable radio played a noisy Reggae tune to nearly the same beat as the automatic weapons.

"Shooters jumping off the cruiser," Abby yelled. "We must retreat through your back door." Briefly, they noticed that one man was white, the other black . . . and both wore ski masks over their heads. Frantically, they dragged the heavy shielding table to the left rear portion of the patio. When they reached the doorway, they dashed inside the living room crouched low.

"My weapon is in my villa," the young woman screamed to her companion. "Perhaps we can get there in time." She didn't sound too certain of their chances.

"The bedroom," Bret bellowed as they snaked through the villa. "Our only hope."

Abby stared at him as one regards a madman. Nevertheless, she followed closely behind the "crazy" American. They raced into the bedroom where Bret slammed the flimsy wood-louvered door shut. Abby rapidly locked the door and slipped behind a heavy wooden dresser. Bret sprinted into the large clothes closet, safe key already clutched between his fingers.

"They're in the villa," Abby whispered across to Bret in the sudden stillness.

The private detective rapidly opened the heavy safe and pulled the High-Standard automatic from within. A rapid movement jerked the .22's slide back, arming the weapon. He edged along the wall to within two feet of the closed door, pistol at the ready.

Suddenly the entire top half of the door crumbled and the black shooter thrust an M-16 and his two arms through the fragile wood. Bret was ready for this explosive thrust and aimed the .22 caliber semiautomatic point blank at the man's neck. Three rounds spit out so rapidly it was as if one long discharge erupted. The man silently dropped as if his feet had been kicked out from under him.

"*Merde!*" cursed the man directly behind him. His partner was killed in an instant and he wasn't ready to die himself. Noisily he raced back through the hallway and living room. Bret eased himself out of the bedroom and saw the man leap over the low railing along the front of the patio. Abby stayed behind to make certain the other assassin would do no more harm. He had no pulse.

Bret ran to the broken-glass-covered patio entranceway and fired two more shots at the fleeing man. He watched as the man skipped a beat after the second shot and slow noticeably in the impeding sand. Still, he was now at the cruiser and being helped on by the man who'd been left aboard.

Abby breathlessly ran up. "I think you just saved our lives." She took a deep breath. "That one's dead," she cocked her head back toward the shattered bedroom door.

"Think I winged the other guy." Bret pointed at the rapidly accelerating cruiser as it headed close along the eastern shore toward the city of Marigot.

"You're very competent with that mafia gun of yours." She looked at the deadly .22 magnum. "Unfortunately, you've committed a major crime in St. Martin, *mon ami*. Foreign nationals can receive a harsh sentence for possessing an unregistered firearm on this *territoire* . . . not to mention killing someone with one."

"Hey, lady. Don't give me 'illegal possession' threats." Bret was becoming testy. "I notice you're still breathing."

"Sorry. Guess I'm far too 'professional' at times," Abby admitted. "Truly, I'm totally indebted to you," she said. "We're on the same side"

"I've wondered on occasions."

Abby smiled. "Now I'll protect your sunburned ass. Give me that thing," she nodded toward the weapon.

Bret handed her the pistol butt first after clicking on the safety.

"Still warm," she noticed. "Get me a towel." Abby closely examined the .22 caliber automatic.

Bret turned, stepped over the dead hit man and grabbed a bath towel from a rack in the bathroom. He returned several seconds later and gave Abby the clean towel. "This should do . . ."

"Untraceable, it seems," she said of the automatic. "Serial numbers routed out and treated with acid. Your average disposable assassination tool."

Abby carefully buffed every portion of the High Standard until she was certain any trace of finger or palm prints was deleted. She then grasped the slide and poked the red-tipped button next to the trigger guard. The half-empty clip slipped into her other hand. She then emptied the remaining rounds and wiped each clean. Next, she wiped clean the clip itself. Finished cleaning, she reversed the entire process, making certain her own prints were clearly in evidence.

"I wiped the inside parts clean when I broke it down," Bret mentioned. "Oh . . . something else. I've got extra rounds and another clip in my safe."

"Well," Abby feigned disgust, "I just don't know *what* to do with you, Bret."

The private investigator smiled as he pulled out the clip and boxes of ammunition from the safe. "Think maybe you should take these to your place."

Abby grinned. Bret was doing his best to be cooperative and refrain from issuing orders. Placing the semiautomatic weapon on the coffee table, she reached out her hand. "Give them to me. I'll run to my villa right now. The police will be here any minute." Barely five minutes had passed since the attack began on the beach, though it seemed like a century ago.

"Look Abby, I want . . . thanks. I mean, really, you don't have to . . ."

"You're welcome," she yelled as she ran toward the front door. "Pool buddies, remember?" Bret heard the door slam behind her.

Damn, putting her own ass on the line, he said to himself. *Could be kicked outta the Sûreté if the truth became known.*

Thirty seconds later the door slammed again. Abby puffed back into the room. She now wore a lightweight, dark brown windbreaker despite the upper-eighty-degree warmth. Across the back of the jacket—stenciled in large, yellow letters—was **DST**.

They discussed their line of defense when the police arrived, predicting questions they would pose and their answers. Before they could lay down any clear-cut plan, the doors at either end of the villa burst open without warning. At least a dozen heavily armed police officers pointed assault rifles, shotguns and pistols at the two remaining living occupants. Apparently, the St. Martin police were trying to catch the pair of gunslingers in the act. Not a minute had gone by since Abby rushed back into Bret's suite of rooms.

Bret leaned over toward Abby. "Did they see . . . ?"

"No," she whispered. "No one was out there when I returned." She then loudly shouted, "*Sûreté Nationale Français . . . Direction de la Sécurité du Territoire. Je suis agente Duchamps.*"

About a dozen assorted armed weapons slowly lowered their muzzles toward the floor . . . much like wilted wildflowers. *Sous-inspecteur* Bouchard holstered his French-manufactured MAS 1950 automatic.

"*Bon jour, mademoiselle,*" he managed to say after regaining his composure. "Perhaps you will explain this affair. We received reports of a raiding party from the sea." The police official spoke in English for the benefit of his native officers and the lone American. "Shipley and DuBois, secure the entrances; everyone else outside."

All but the two named police officers filed out of the villa. The last two were stationed at each door. Bouchard sat in an easy chair while Bret and Abby attempted to relax on the sofa.

"As a fellow law enforcement officer, *mademoiselle,*" Bouchard began, "you understand this session is merely a discussion of the incident you and mister Lamplighter recently experienced."

"Of course, *sous-inspecteur,*" Abby smiled. "We understand the facts are necessary for your official report."

Bouchard slowly nodded his head, barely glancing at the young woman. He tape recorded all his questions and the answers given by the French *Sûreté* agent and the American. Bouchard didn't skip a beat, even when evidence technicians arrived to 'sweep' the scene of the killing. The questioning went without incident . . . up to a point.

"*Maintenant, agente* Duchamps," the under-inspector continued, "I am curious about the .22 caliber semiautomatic pistol. It is not French government issue. In *no* country is it standard police or government issue." He glanced at Bret.

"I believe you're right, Inspector," Bret nodded. "Usually .38's. Or 9mm's like your French MAS 1950, as I recall."

"*Sous-inspecteur*," Abby stood and peered down at Bouchard. "DST has no restrictions on the number of weapons, their make or their caliber, an agent may carry."

The under-inspector's temples tightened perceptibly. The tendons of his neck stood out farther than usual. "*Mademoiselle, je vous regarde . . .*" Bouchard's words halted as he realized he might say too much to the DST agent in their native tongue.

In English, Abby said, "Please continue, *monsieur* Bouchard. I missed your last remark." In the French law enforcement pecking order, Abby Duchamps wielded a good dozen giant pecks above the *territoire* police under-inspector. She sat back down.

"I withdraw the previous statement," Bouchard said, biting his tongue. He considered the direction of his questions for a moment, then continued:

"*Peut être* a social visit with Mr. Lamplighter would have been more appropriate without a DST jacket and a weapon."

"Perhaps, but we know about the hotel bombing in Philipsburg, *n'est-ce pas?*"

Everything became clear to Bouchard. "Then you were protecting *m'sieur* Lamplighter?"

She nodded. " . . . and myself, of course."

"Of course," Bouchard again nodded. "Is not the MAS a more, er, reasonable weapon to carry in a jacket pocket?"

"Reasonable, *sous-inspecteur*? The High Standard and the MAS are *both* reasonable firearms . . . practical, as well."

"Length, *mademoiselle*," Bouchard blurted out. "The MAS is barely 190 millimeters long. The American assassination pistol is twice that length."

"That's a truism," Bret said, feeling a need to contribute some input.

Bouchard and Abby stared at Lamplighter. Abby grinned while Bouchard's face went totally blank.

"Inspector," Bret continued, "Miss Duchamps had the High Standard stuck in the waistband of her shorts . . . not a jacket pocket. Her pockets were full of I.D. and other documents we were examining."

An evidence technician sidled up to his boss, interrupting the conversation. He bent over and whispered into Bouchard's ear.

"*Merde! C'est impossible!*" the under-inspector roared, leaping to his feet. The technician quickly followed Bouchard to the outstretched form of the dead gunman. A .22 caliber magnum slug had passed through the bottom of the ski mask. Consequently, the mask had not been removed until the other two slugs were marked and photographed. When the mask was finally removed, a remarkable discovery was made.

"It's Barnstable," Bouchard mumbled with a pained expression. The three police technicians looked at the corpse. Then they studied the M-16 assault rifle lying on several sheets of white paper. A couple dozen shell casings and three empty M-16 clips lay next to the weapon. Bouchard shouted an order and the officer standing at the front entrance hurriedly joined the group standing above the body. Questions, asides, exclamations and accusations seemed to accelerate through the group of police officers.

Abby and Bret walked to the bickering gathering. "One of your police officers, Inspector?" Bret asked.

"Why do you think . . . ?" Bouchard began, then shrugged and asked, "How did you come to know this?"

"It's certainly not magic, *sous-inspecteur*," Abby interrupted. "Your own reaction, your instant recognition of the man . . ."

" . . . and this morning," Bret broke in, "at our meeting. You and DeGroot seemed to realize the possibility of police involvement in the Amsterdam House bombing."

"*C'est vrai*," Bouchard agreed. "Chief DeGroot and I thought such a situation could be possible."

"*Un moment*," *agente* Abby Duchamps remarked. She was unhappy at the way she was being kept out of the entire investigation. Her remarks were aimed at *sous-inspecteur* Bouchard and his men. The pitch, timbre and speed of her French left no doubt to Bret that the *Sûreté* agent was kicking St. Martin police ass.

It was at this moment when the reason for her lightweight windbreaker suddenly became evident. As if to clarify a particular statement, Bret saw *mademoiselle* Duchamps pull a wad of identification—including a badge—from a jacket pocket. Next, she produced another handful of official looking documents from the other outer jacket pocket. A sheet of flimsy paper was thrust upon Bouchard. His teeth were tightly clenched as he took the paper.

"*Mademoiselle* has further questions?" Bouchard asked.

"Yes. Don't you believe that after two years, one of the '*wrong*' police officers tries to murder Mr. Lamplighter?"

Everyone knew what she meant. No French St. Martin police had died in the Oyster Pond Bay tragedy. Only police officers from the Netherlands Antilles were killed.

"Relatives of Lamplighter's drug enforcement team?" she undertook a guess. Abby knew all the details of the fouled-up drug raid.

"We investigated for eight weeks after I arrived here," Bouchard answered. "Relatives, friends, acquaintances, anyone remotely associated with one of the victims."

"You drew a complete blank?" Bret asked.

"Nearly everyone felt the *real* blame lay with, with *monsieur* Beauville," the under-inspector related.

"Interesting," Bret contemplated. "I didn't agree with his methods of preparation for the raid. But the actual assault was highly professional. The drug enforcement team operated straight from the book. Everyone acted with great competence."

"All boards of inquiry cleared you and the police . . . on both sides," Abby said. "There was no doubt in the final review that it was a carefully directed plan to generate a double ambush."

"Someone excelled at their homework," Bret nodded.

"We're talking professional mobsters, not local St. Martin gangs."

"The reason for the *Sûreté*'s DST?" Bret wondered.

Abby didn't answer the obvious. The phone suddenly rang. Bret had turned its volume up full blast while he was on the patio, so everyone was startled. He darted to the device and answered. Bret thought he knew who it would be. "Hello."

"*Monsieur* Lamplighter, here is Yvonne at the front desk. I have the *téléfon* for you from a man at Grand Case Airport. Are you available to connect?"

"Did he identify himself, Yvonne?"

"*Oui*, a *monsieur* Hough, U.S. consulate *de* Martinique."

"Thanks, please put him through."

One lonely click, this time. "Bret, you got the desk clerk screening your calls?"

"She's okay." Bret didn't care to identify the caller with a roomful of police listening.

"You got company?" Bertrand had heard some conversation in the background.

"Seven."

"Seven people? Let me guess . . . the *gendarmes*."

"Go to the head of the class, *mon ami*."

"Whew. More trouble?"

"Affirmative. More about that, later. What about the data you were checking?"

"*Côte d'Azur* for three weeks prior to Marigot. Marseille pulled her off a legit month-long vacation to check your bonafides."

"I see. Any more?" Bret wondered why the *Sûreté* was so eager to check him out, but he couldn't ask Hough right now.

"On Duchamps? Yeah, age thirty-one. Originally from Grenoble. Father's a big-time lawyer in the old hometown... very wealthy. She graduated *Magna cum laude* from Wellesley ten years ago. Major... political science. Master's from Harvard one year later in political science. Very bright girl.'

"How long at... you know?"

"Breathing down your neck, hunh, buddy?" Was that a snicker, Bret heard? "Okay, went directly from Boston to *Sûreté Nationale* training center in Le Mans. Six months later assigned to Marseille. Still there... highly regarded."

"Thanks. Feel a lot better, now."

"Me too. Thought you were assassin fodder 'til I learned the truth." Bertrand was silent for a moment, then said, "We've gotta meet, *amigo*. Other things to relate that shouldn't be mentioned over Ma Bell's lines."

"Gotcha. You name it."

"Damn, this is great. You're usually ranting and raving up a storm, old buddy. Never had such a pleasant conversation with you."

"Please continue, *mon ami*." Bret watched as Abby continued to speak with the St. Martin police investigators. Right then, two ambulance attendants came through the rear doorway, nudging a gurney over the broken glass and metal.

"Sounds like a wild party at your place. I can hardly hear you." Another short silence. "Meet me the last place you and I had dinner. Remember?"

Bret remembered. It had been his last meal in St. Martin after the massacre. The ex-DEA agent would always remember. "You're on, friend. Eight o'clock, okay?"

"Right, Bret. With bells on." The line went dead.

Chapter Eight

Grand Case lies about four miles from Marigot as the Sugar Bird flies. Bertrand Hough and Bret had spent the final evening after the dreadful Oyster Pond Massacre at Alabama restaurant in Grand Case. Tonight they discussed more recent incidents.

"Yeah," Bret looked at a high resolution fax sheet, "that's Abby Duchamps. A little younger. Hair's a trifle longer."

"Okay. It's her most recent I.D. shot." Bertrand took the fax back. "Photo's three years old. Attractive young lady."

"Beautiful woman. Intelligent."

"Records show she was tops in her undergraduate class. Also, one of the top ten at Harvard in her graduating class."

"Odd that I suspected her of the Amsterdam House bombing. Guess it was her chance appearance on St. Martin. Still don't know how she ended up at the same resort as me. She was here *first*—by forty minutes—and mine was a last minute change . . . thank God."

"Best decision you'll make in your lifetime. As for her being here, it's not *too* surprising. Always stays first class. Your place is considered number one or two on everybody's St. Martin resort rating list."

"I lucked out with her being so close. Abby pulled me out of a tough spot when I shot that cop during the failed hit."

"Surprising, really." Hough looked back at her fax photo. "Always follows the letter of the law. Never even bends the rules, according to her DST associates." Bertrand placed the photo back into his attaché case. "That's one reason they called her away from a vacation on the Riviera and sent her to check on you."

"Knows my illegal gun saved her. Guess taking the heat was her payback."

"Probably right. On the subject of the dead cop, Bret . . . did Bouchard say if anyone ever suspected the man would turn rogue?"

"Didn't have a clue. Six years as a police officer. Average personnel ratings down the line . . . investigations, reports, arrests, effectiveness. Even average number of sick days taken a year." Bret cut into his tender, succulent pork chop. "One two-day suspension for sleeping on duty, graveyard shift."

"Bouchard's checkin' further, now? Mob connections, smuggling rings, drug running, any possible underworld dealings?"

"Absolutely, my friend. Only not Bouchard. Three *Sûreté* investigators are hassling Marigot's Internal Affairs office. Internal Affairs are breathing down the necks of anyone *gendarme* Barnstable had connections with . . . police and civilians."

"More *Sûreté*, so quickly?" Bertrand asked. He'd only known about Abby.

"Yep, just flew in. They were on their way here *before* the incident at Sunshine Pointe."

"Is the girl part of their investigative team?"

"No, she's prohibited because of her involvement in the beach assault. Abby's working on the emerald buyer's murder. That could help me a heluva lot"

"Bret," Hough slowly shook his head, "seems wherever you show up on St. Martin, the statistical averages for local mayhem do a flip-flop."

"Thanks for your confidence, Bertrand." Bret speared another juicy chunk of grilled pork, mixed it in delicate wine sauce gravy and thrust it into his mouth.

The consular officer grinned at him. "Haven't lost your appetite, buddy."

"No. Forgot how great the food is on the island's *côte Français*."

Hough nodded agreement, smothered a gigantic shrimp in a delightful Caribbean tartar sauce. Between bites he said, "Somebody's making a statement, Bret."

"Good shrimp?"

"You know what I'm talking about." Bertrand tossed the shrimp tail aside. "First the Amsterdam House. Less than twenty-four hours later, *your* house!"

"Heluva coincidence . . ."

Hough ignored him. "State contacted me right after I arrived at Grand Case Airport."

Bret sighed and said, "Bertrand, you didn't come from Martinique just to invite me to dinner and talk about the *Sûreté Nationale* investigation."

Hough stared at him. "Time was when the central Caribbean was far removed from crime and corruption."

"What's your point?"

Hough absentmindedly tapped his dessert spoon against the empty dish. "State's Bureau of Intelligence and Research concludes that eighty percent of felony crime in the Caribbean has direct links to organized crime. Equally divided between U.S., Mexican and Colombian operations."

"Reading between the lines, I think you're saying some country's mobsters are tryin' to silence me."

"We believe so."

"Gotta be Colombia."

"How'd you know?" Bertrand asked with a puzzled expression.

"The blend of emeralds and coffee. Big Colombian products."

"I understand why you mention emeralds. Where do you come up with coffee?"

"Bernie Lustfield's clothing. Lab reports showed an excessive amount of emerald dust, coffee grounds and tobacco residue in his pockets, pants cuffs, jacket lining."

"Strange. Why all that loose waste in someone's clothes? Even a heavy coffee drinker doesn't get grounds on him."

Bret related all the reports of Lustfield's allergies. He told Bertrand the strange, almost ritualistic cause of his death on Anguilla, and explained that the coffee was a variety grown only in Choco state.

"Choco?" Bertrand asked with interest. "You got any idea what *else* comes from the highlands of Choco?"

"Guess you're gonna say the coca plant and its derivatives."

"You're correct about the coca. Just now, though, I was going to say *tobacco* . . . and the world's highest quality *emeralds*."

"Ole Bernie was carrying most of Choco state around in his clothing,"

"Hardly," Bertrand smiled. "Choco's emeralds *are* fine quality. In fact, when you include those of Muzo in Boyacá state, they comprise ninety percent of the world's total emerald production."

"Incredible. Place must be Colombia's most prosperous state."

Bertrand shook his head. "One of the poorest. Little cultivatable land. Mountains, hills, rain forests, mud slides. All agricultural and natural resources, read emeralds, are exploited by the drug cartels. The *paisas* reap chaff, *narcos* reap wheat."

"Colombia's cocaine cartels also control the emerald, coffee and tobacco trade?"

Hough nodded. "They limit the coffee harvest to keep prices high. Even so, Colombia's *still* the world's second largest coffee-producing nation."

"Do they limit emerald export, as well?" Bret was becoming interested in Colombia's particular interpretation of Keynesian economics.

"Same principle as their coffee. Emeralds from Muzo state are *incredibly* high-quality. They're literally ground into dust whenever they exceed five kilos in weight. The dust is used as a fine dye for expensive designer lines of clothing."

"Nobody sells eleven pound emeralds, Bertrand. That's hundreds of carats."

"Hundreds, buddy?" Hough chuckled. "A five-kilo emerald would weigh about *25,000* carats! A carat is the equivalent of 200 milligrams . . . about one-fifth gram." He waited to let the enormity of such a gemstone sink in. "You see, those are what marketable emeralds are cut *from*. Then they're sold to expert jewelers for faceting. The largest emerald ever faceted for sale is a 632-carat whopper from Muzo . . . discovered in 1905. And *that's* where your Bernie Lustfields of the world come in."

"Damn, they get deals from the middlemen, no matter how the middlemen managed to get the emeralds. Lots of smuggling."

"Incalculable, actually. It's major crime. Also, *très* dangerous for the emerald-mining smugglers and their families. If the Syndicate catches them, they sure as hell wish the National Police caught them instead."

"*Narco* penalty for ripping off what they consider their own property is death?"

"Hopefully, quick death for the smugglers," Bertrand nodded grimly. "The common penalty is genital amputation. They shove his genitalia down the culprit's throat 'til he suffocates. Then they cut the victim's throat open. Symbolic blood spilling."

"M'gawd," Bret blanched, "you're describing five killings here in St. Martin. One way or another they've been part of my personal experiences on this island." One by one he described the deaths of the American tourists during the Oyster Pond bay debacle and the death of the two police informants. Finally Bret related the elimination of the probable killer of Bernard Lustfield.

"Genital mutilation and amputation prove nothing, of course," Bertrand Hough admitted. "The circumstances, nevertheless, make me suspicious that at least one Colombian crime cartel has a branch right here in St. Martin."

"I think the local lawmen know this, Bertrand." Bret leaned forward. "You're a font of knowledge . . . anyone know who the Godfather of the Caribbean cartel is?"

"Not 'Godfather', although it's the same idea. Czar, king, literally *patron*. State's BIR and CIA came up with two probable cartel *patrons* for this part of the Caribbean."

"You mean they somehow overlap?"

"No, it's the old separate-but-equal rule. The rivals despise each other." Hough consulted some notes. "For St. Martin, State believes it's the Cali cartel, Gonzalo and Miguel Rodriguez Gacha, for coke, heroin, cannabis and control of the telephone system. Emeralds, coffee and apparently tobacco, as you suggest, come under the authority of Medellín's Enrique Vargas Mantilla."

"Looks like I'm buckin' shadows. Can't fight what I can't touch."

"Don't think your insurance company really wants you taking on the Medellín cartel. They want the emeralds, and I doubt Enrique Vargas has 'em."

"Figure they're still on St. Martin?"

"That's your job to find out, buddy. I'd guess yes, but no way of telling."

"Yeah, if a buyer had been arranged before the theft, those emeralds could be in the Virgin Islands, P.R., maybe Cuba."

"Right, and if the heist was done on spec, they could still be negotiating a price."

"That's two totally opposite 'ifs', Bertrand." Bret's police-ordered deadline looked more ludicrous. He glanced around the attractive French garden setting. "Think I'll be back in Chicago sooner than originally planned."

"Hope you get lucky," Bertrand said. The consular officer caught the eye of the waiter. Hough's Air Martinique return flight to Fort-de-France was scheduled to depart the French side's Grand Case Airport at one A.M., an hour from now.

Antonio Locksley deposited two quarters, dialed the four-digit Dutch code plus five business phone digits on Alabama's old rotary-style pay phone. He watched the two Americans say good night to the tall, blond hostess. Tony's was a perfect vantage point, next to the rarely-used coat room.

"Police Hotline. Please leave your message at the tone." A beep sounded.

"Tony Alabama," the waiter said. "Twelve-ten A.M. Mart go to G.C. airport... Blue Toyota. Chi to Mar'got... red Subaru M-80." He hung up.

Like most "confidential" messages phoned to the special

police number, the sender's telephone digits were automatically "stamped" to the message. A skinny man with long corn row hair ringlets recorded the message on an expensive Nagra reel-to-reel tape machine. He expertly "burst" transmitted the data to two separate mobile locations within fifteen seconds. The 'stalk' directive was initiated.

Bertrand Hough thought about Bret. *Bastard's got two crazy deadlines. Multistate gave him one ultimatum and the two St. Martin police departments gave him another.* Hough knew *sous-inspecteur* Bouchard would escort Lamplighter to a stateside-bound flight in five days. *Hope Bret gets partial payment for his trouble.*

One of St. Martin's countless 'HUMP' signs suddenly appeared out of the darkness in the Toyota's headlights. Hough jammed on the brakes. *Damn these forty k speed bumps*, he thought. The car immediately behind Bertrand squealed its tires and swerved as its driver braked to avoid rear-ending the car he followed. Very cautious now, Hough kept his speed down for the remaining short distance to Grand Case airport.

Off-duty Marigot police officers hired by DST branch of the *Sûreté* followed the rental cars driven by Lamplighter and Hough. A confidential Marseille directive was in the hands of the last three temporary duty officers assigned to St. Martin. The memo ordered the officers to "monitor" all activities of officer Abby Duchamps.

"Shotgun" microphones at the Alabama had picked up every word spoken by the consular officer and the private investigator. Video cameras recorded the entire scenario. If the Americans were concealing any important information, the *Sûreté Nationale Français* would know.

The DST was to keep close tabs on everyone involved in the two recent deaths. The Anguilla murder, and subsequent death of the suspected assassin, had definite ties to the French *territoire* of St. Martin. The attack by sea at the Sunshine Pointe resort beach, with the death of one attacker, was even more important to the DST. Agent Duchamps was well-regarded in Marseille. Jacques Chirac was a close friend of Antoine Duchamps, Abby's influential father. The attempt on her life was viewed as a personal affront to the *Sûreté Nationale*. The killing of the attacker was certainly justifiable, regardless if Duchamps or the American fired the weapon. For now, DST sanctioned their account, however questionable.

Bret pulled off the highway into the entrance driveway of Sunshine Pointe. The black Suzuki drove on. It had followed him from the Alabama restaurant, never allowing more than a fifty-foot distance between the two cars. He parked at the lobby entrance and stepped out. *Local cops. No one else would tail me that close.*

Bret entered the lobby where a young man ran the desk on this graveyard shift.

"Hi," Bret acted jauntier than he felt. "Do you know if my villa's habitable? My name's George Princeton, number twelve."

"Ah, Mr. Princeton. Yvonne asked me to tell you the broken glass door and windows were boarded up. You don't have a rear entrance/exit, but you may certainly stay if you wish."

"Probably no choice, hunh?"

"No, *monsieur*. There are no villas available for three days." The desk clerk reached into a drawer beneath the computer console. "Yvonne wanted me to give you this note." He pulled a sealed envelope from the drawer and set it on the counter. 'Mr. George Princeton. Villa 12' was printed on it.

Bret thanked the young man and returned to the car door. The lobby area was well-lighted, so he ripped open the envelope as he stood next to his car. On a sheet of light blue paper was written, "Mr. Lamplighter. At *vingt-et-un cent heures*, the wood mechanic shows to me two electrics. He finds these one *dans* the kitchen & one *sous la table à café*. I hide them *maintenant, sous votre lit*. Keep safely. Your friend, Yvonne."

"Two 'electrics'?" Bret asked his car. "In the kitchen and under the coffee table?" *What does she mean?*

He unlocked the front door, switched on the hall light and warily walked inside. The smashed wooden door had been replaced. *They keep spare doors for terrorist attacks?* The floor and walls were washed and sanitized. The scene of the shooting smelled of disinfectant, but it was neat and clean. Double-thick plywood covered the entire fifteen foot wide north living room wall. All shattered glass and metal had been swept from the tile floor.

Satisfied the once-trashed villa was habitable, he went to the large bed, kneeled and peered beneath it. There sat the Ked shoebox he'd tossed into the waste basket many hours before. He slid it out, then sat on the floor with his back against the king-size mattress.

He removed the contents. *'Electrics', all right*, Bret mumbled, and held up two tiny radio transmitters. The bugs were so minuscule they could both be hidden under a nickel if placed side-by-side. An infinitesimal on/off switch could only be activated with a pin or needle point. A nearly-invisible quarter-inch filament antenna was capable of relaying hundreds of hours of sound a distance of more than 3,000 feet.

Carpenter found two of 'em near where he was working, Bret realized. *Place must be infested with little black bugs. Who the hell planted them? DST? Bouchard?*

"Assholes!" Bret shouted. "You're all assholes." He hoped a human being heard him rather than a recording device.

Carrying the shoebox in hand, he searched for bugs. In thirty minutes he collected seven tiny radio transmitters. Bret set them in the box with the two found by the maintenance man. *Gotta be others*, he knew. *Just checked obvious spots. Damn*, he suddenly wondered, *did they wire Abby's room, too?*

He picked up the phone receiver, then quickly hung up. *First place they'd tap. Better warn her before she says something incriminating.* Bret wrote a short note and grabbed a microtransmitter from his collection. He left the villa, locked the door and walked to Abby's residence. A light shown through the door slats, so he lightly rapped on the wooden frame.

"*Oui?*" Abby's voice asked softly after several moments.

"George . . . um, Bret," he answered.

A wooden louver edged up. Bret stared at a small rectangular mirror attached to a metal rod. He saw the reflection of an ice-blue eye. The mirror turned back and forth. When she was certain Bret was alone, Abby said, "One moment." The sound of two locks clicking open reached the American's ears.

The door opened. Abby sported bikini bottoms and a cropped tank top . . . as well as a nasty-looking Walther P-38. The 9mm automatic was in her right hand, the mirror device in her left. She smiled and Bret felt younger.

The American immediately held up his note for Abby to read, while he held an index finger to his lips.

Her smile disappeared, and her eyes flicked about the bedroom. He shut and locked the door behind him. He tossed the tiny transmitter onto her king size bed . . . a black fly speck atop a mint green bedspread sea.

He checked the clock-radio on her night stand. A small voice/sound transmitter stuck to the bottom. It was attached at the same location as the one he'd found in his room. On the note paper he wrote, "They follow same script for each place they bug."

Abby nodded. She took the paper and pencil and wrote, "Who's *they*?"

The DST officer held the note as Bret wrote, "Think either your people or Bouchard's. Can't tell."

The *Sûreté* agent nodded again. They went through the villa, onto the patio and continued toward the gentle surf lapping at the beach, until they stood inches from the water. She still carried the pistol in her right hand.

"Let's sit. Not even a directional mike will pick us up down here."

"Whether you know it or not," Bret squirmed to find a more comfortable spot on the sand, "three more *Sûreté* folks are nosing around the island."

"Shit, that's what you meant by 'my people' planting bugs." Abby gazed up at the quarter-moon. "Wish I were still on the beach at the *côte d'azure*. Never had to worry about my own company until I came to the Caribbean."

"You're no teenager, Abby, so simply act your thirty-one years. We're here to iron out our problems. You were lucky today . . . you might live to see age thirty-two."

"How do you know my age?"

"*Are* you thirty-one? Lucky guess." Bret felt foolish getting caught in a silly lie.

"Lucky, my ass," Abby grinned at him. "What else do you know about me?"

Bret told Abby about his visit with the assistant U.S. consul general. He related everything Hough revealed. Finally he told her about his "tail" from Grand Case to Sunshine Pointe.

Abby occasionally asked Bret to fill in relevant points. Meanwhile, she absent-mindedly slipped the clip in and out of the P-38.

"Where'd you get the Walther? You're issued the French MAS 1950."

"Never hurts to have extra firepower." She paused. "Besides, Bouchard took the MAS away from me. Said he would keep it and your High Standard forty-eight hours after the fatal shooting of our attacker."

Abby's agitation became apparent. She'd assumed the blame for Barnstable's death, although Bret Lamplighter was the shooter. Logically, *sous-inspecteur* Bouchard suspected the American, so he'd ragged on the DST officer.

"Sonuvabitch," Bret grumbled. "I'm really sorry that happened."

"No problem, *mon ami*." Abby smacked the clip into the Walther another time. "Tit for tat! I told him DST needed you here as long as you wanted . . . to finish your investigation, and help me with mine."

"He bought it?" Bret beamed at Abby.

"Turned crimson, but couldn't do a thing about it. After all, I'm here to assure the security of the *territoire* . . . by any means." She casually twirled the Walther by its trigger guard after picking it up from between her crossed legs.

"Those safeties don't always work, Abby," Bret advised as he stared at the pistol.

"Safety's not on," she smiled. Abby Duchamps stopped whirling the weapon.

The nearly-motionless water shimmered with the moon—and star-light. Further to the east of Nettle Bay the lights of Marigot were brightly mirrored in the sea. Two large cruise ships were anchored in the harbor of the French West Indies' capital. Hundreds of glowing lights were strung between their masts and down the sides of the vessels. The bay was alive with gleaming reflections.

Abby felt the presence of Bret without actually looking at him. She envied him his life of transient adventures. *Does he see it as adventurous?* she wondered. She recalled how calm he appeared as he placed three slugs in their attacker's throat, and wondered how many people he had killed. She'd witnessed a professional at work. *The killing was necessary, but not pretty.* Abby Duchamps had never before seen a person killed. In her near-decade of service at the *Sûreté*, she'd never fired a weapon in anger. The good-looking American, on the other hand, was as cool as an automaton in the face of death, while she had been sick and scared.

Bret glanced at her gun and said, "Tomorrow I'm gonna check out the little store where Bernie Lustfield bought his emeralds. It's possible Colombia's Medellín cartel supplied these particular emeralds to the Bombay shop."

"Possibly professionals," she agreed. "Why the Medellín cartel?"

"State Department sources and the U.S. consulate in Martinique have conclusive proof that they're the principal suppliers to this part of the Caribbean."

"I'll go with you if you want, *monsieur le investigateur privé*."

"Good. A tourist couple might seem more convincing. Call you at seven. We'll be on the front stoop of Bombay when they open at eight o'clock."

"And if we can prove the Colombian cartel supplied the stolen emeralds?"

"I'll go to Colombia . . . to the source. Find the supplier or smuggler. They must surely keep some kind of records or transactions of St. Martin's major buyers. Then it's back here to locate the exact whereabouts of the emeralds."

"It could be dangerous . . ."

"That's what I was hired for, Abby. Find the emeralds and get 'em back to their owners, Ultragem, Inc. My employer doesn't want to shell out eleven million bucks." It was the first time Bret had mentioned the actual dollar value of the Caribbean Green.

"*Merde!*" Abby exclaimed, "No wonder your insurance company wants those emeralds returned." Satisfied, she knew *he* wanted to locate his emeralds, and *DST* needs the names of St. Martin's local smugglers and distributors.

Chapter Nine

Tourists, taxis, hustlers, clamor . . . Philipsburg's Front Street was the same as ever. Wood scaffolding covered the outer wall of the Amsterdam House. An army of acrobatic workers scampered over the structure, tearing out fractured bricks, loose mortar and ruptured metal framework.

"My room was right where the guy in blue shorts and red shirt is standing," Bret said as he nodded toward the hotel.

"Nearly the center of the crater," Abby judged. She cocked her head to one side and said, "Powerful explosive. Nitro or plastique."

"My guess, too. Don't know if Sint Maarten has a police bomb squad to make a thorough examination."

"Doubtful," Abby shook her head, "and any overt investigation would discredit their gas leak story."

Dressed in typical tourist attire, both wore blue denim cutoffs, but the description ended there. Bret had chopped the legs off his blue jeans at the point where his knees had finally split the material. Abby's cutoffs were newly purchased designer denim shorts. She wore a snug, sleeveless T-shirt, white with small crimson letters across the upper right front that read "Grenoble." On the back, a logo of the five linked Olympic rings was surrounded with the words, "Grenoble, France. 1968 Winter Olympic Games." Bret's tan T-shirt hung loosely on his rugged frame and advertised Red Stripe Lager.

Foot and vehicular traffic detoured the extensive scaffolding by using the narrow cobblestone street and the opposite-side walkway. Pedestrians passing the construction rarely perceived the amount of damage to the Amsterdam House.

"Philipsburg's finest," Bret remarked.

Abby looked at him, then followed his gaze across the street. "You know them?"

Neither man wore a uniform, but Bret recognized Chief DeGroot immediately. He believed he'd seen the other man at the police station. They were the only men in sight dressed in slacks and jackets on this warm Sint Maarten morning.

The chief and his companion glanced at the exterior damage to the vintage hotel briefly. DeGroot said something, then motioned to the other man. They disappeared through the doorless entranceway.

"Chief DeGroot and friend," he explained. He thought for a moment. "Your directive to Bouchard won't carry any weight in Sint Maarten. DST has no authority on the Netherlands Antilles side."

"I realize that. We should tie up all loose ends here before your time's up."

Bret nodded but wasn't convinced. *Oyster Pond massacre on the Dutch side. Bomb at Amsterdam House . . . Dutch side. Three illegally-parked Mercedes . . . Dutch. Two dead snitches and the dead probable killer of Lustfield . . . Dutch.* "We better check out Bombay."

They hurried east on Front Street. It still wasn't eight A.M., yet both knew the local store openings were conducted with drill team-like precision.

Abby put her arm around Bret's waist. "We better look like proper vacationers, mon ami. Don't want the Bombay staff to become suspicious of us."

Bret said, "Good idea," and relaxed his arm over her shoulder. "We'll be lookin' for a nice but not-too-expensive emerald ring."

They continued to walk along Front Street much as hundreds of other tourist couples were doing . . . window-shopping and people-watching. "This the street?" Bret stopped and looked down a lane not wide enough for any vehicle except bicycles, scooters and motorcycles.

Abby pulled some notes and a brochure from her tiny clutch purse, as they halted at the corner of two converging thoroughfares. "Camera shop across the street?"

Bret peered kitty-corner and said, "Boston Baked Cameras." He stared harder. "Can't believe that name."

Abby chuckled. "Right alley, apparently. Come on, we're supposed to be engaged or very fond of each other." She handed Bret the brochure.

Steel shutters were slowly rolled upward from across the front facade of Bombay Gems, Ltd. by an East Indian or Pakistani. His gray-black complexion and Caucasian features were a sharp contrast against his white, short-sleeved cotton shirt and trousers.

The security shutters covered both the front entrance and the window facing into the narrow, long shop. Bombay was no more than fifteen feet wide, but the store's length was close to fifty feet. Show cases the entire store length stood on each side of the long, narrow center aisle.

A dozen prospective customers stood along the confined sidewalk in front of the store. Most looked like prosperous tourists, while two or three appeared to be professional gem buyers.

"Who's the bimbette with the bodacious ta-tas?" Abby whispered.

Bret had no doubt who she meant. A busty, dark blond woman wore a flame-red dress cut very low on top, very high at the bottom.

"Possibly a buyer," Bret speculated. She was one of a half-dozen women on or near Front Street wearing high heels. Her tan looked more like a tanning salon job and she held a large briefcase in each hand. A purse with long straps was draped over her left shoulder.

When the East Indian swung open the front door, the woman in the red dress pushed in ahead of everyone else. As she entered, the proprietor greeted her with a half-bow as if she were a long-lost sister.

"Think you're right about her being a heavy player," Abby said. "The owner nearly kissed her feet."

The tall, curvaceous woman and several other people walked directly to the rear of the shop area stocked with first-class, big ticket items. The man who'd opened the shop hurried to the rear, ahead of the customers. An older lady and two young women appeared from a door at the back. All three dispersed to strategic locations behind the showcases and immediately spoke to customers. They appeared to be members of the same family.

Bombay specialized in rare gemstones, primarily exquisite blue-green emeralds. Showcases nearer the front door held a mishmash of real and fake watches on the line of Rolex, Piaget and Movado. Also, there were inexpensive necklaces, bracelets and rings. Only nearer the rear of the store were the collector-quality gemstones displayed. At least six large signs arrayed throughout the shop proclaimed, "NO LAB-CREATED GEMSTONES SOLD AT BOMBAY. OUR PROMISE."

"I've seen large banks with less security," Bret whispered to Abby. At least a dozen surveillance cameras swung slowly back and forth. "Inventory must be millions of dollars on any given day."

Abby threw back her head and giggled, as if her companion had said something clever and humorous. "Let's go nearer the rear of the shop."

Abby took Bret's hand and led the way along the aisle. Everyone who'd been waiting for the store opening was now examining either gems or jewelry. The young salesgirls appeared about twenty-one and twenty-three years old, probably university graduates and quite attractive. They wore pastel short-sleeved blouses that accented their dark complexions, long black hair and light brown eyes. Both were friendly, slender and very knowledgeable about gemstones and other merchandise in the store.

"*That* is a totally gorgeous emerald, sweetheart," Abby exclaimed, pointing to a dark green gem nearly as large as an ice cube. The stone was unmounted, rectangular and cut with no more than twelve or fourteen facets.

"It's superb," Bret agreed, "but probably beyond our budget, princess."

The younger of the two daughters walked over to the showcase where Abby and Bret stared at the emerald. "Only if your budget exceeds one hundred thousand dollars U.S., sir." She reached into a skirt pocket and retrieved a ring of keys. Selecting one, the young woman unlocked the heavy, sliding panel in the showcase. "It's exquisite, miss," she spoke directly to Abby, "and virtually flawless."

The pretty woman brought the emerald out on its crinkled white satin bed. She gently set it on the top of the showcase and smiled up at Bret.

"Remarkable," Abby marveled. "It doesn't seem to need facets to catch the light like diamonds do. It almost has an inner fire of its own, deep inside." She peered into the large gem. "It's radiating light and energy," Abby exclaimed.

"Many people say that," the salesgirl agreed. "Much of the luster lies in their composition. Emeralds are a variety of beryl . . . a silicate. The more chromium found within an emerald, the deeper the green, greatly increasing its value."

"I'll leave you with your knowledgeable emerald friend, Abby. I'm gonna wander farther toward the rear of the shop." Bret smiled and slowly ambled along the aisle. The man who'd opened the shop spoke to the three potential emerald-buyers from behind his counter. Everyone gazed at the counter-top as the merchant quietly spoke to them. Bret craned his neck to see what they all gazed at. It didn't surprise him to see an emerald as large as a rectangular 9-volt battery resting on a thick white cushion atop the counter.

" . . . straight from Number Six site at Muzo. The three-phase inclusions are quite visible with this hundred-power loupe, Beverly." The proprietor glanced at the woman.

The woman took the small device, put it to her right eye and leaned forward. The far edge of the magnifying loupe was no more that a centimeter from the large, octagonal emerald. The other two buyers carefully inspected the magnificent emerald.

"There's a cluster," she slowly intoned. "Gas bubble's perfect." She paused. "No doubt about the saline suspension." Another short hesitation. "Ah yes, a perfect salt crystal," she sighed with seemingly carnal satisfaction. She handed the loupe to a short, balding man on her right, who quickly began to examine the gemstone.

The proprietor spoke again, but in reverently hushed tones. "There are only eight three-phase inclusion cavities in this specimen, Walter. All align perfectly."

"Yes, I see," Walter breathed quietly. "Definitely Muzo or Chivor, Colombia."

"Most certainly Muzo, Walter," the proprietor amended. "When it arrived here last month, much of its dark shale was still attached."

"Calcite?" Beverly asked Bombay's proprietor.

"Heavily embedded in calcite crystals, yes indeed," he assured her.

The prospective buyers fascinated Bret. They definitely weren't novices at their trade, but then this was not a profession for amateurs. Millions of dollars could hang in the balance at the slightest miscalculation.

"Here's my offer, Ravi," the man named Walter said. He handed the man behind the counter his business card. Ravi backed away from the group and studied the back of the card. He nodded, showing neither pleasure nor annoyance, placing Walter's card in his transparent cotton shirt pocket . . . bid side in.

"And mine, my friend," the man farthest away spoke. He palmed his business card and placed it directly into Ravi's outstretched hand. "Just gift wrap the bauble and I'll be on my way." He spoke with a decidedly British accent.

The proprietor smiled and peered at the bid as a poker player craftily peeks at a newly-dealt card. "Many thanks, Mr. Calvert." Ravi smiled at the tall man. This card, too, went into the shirt pocket.

Bret was now only six or seven feet from the woman named

Beverly. He saw her take an expensive pen from her purse. The purse, now perched on the counter, hid the card from the two men at her right. Bret saw her write 800K on the back of her business card. *Damn,* he thought, *this isn't a trade for the timid.*

Beverly picked up her card and handed it to Ravi so only he could see her offer. As Bret glanced at the information on the front of the business card, his heart skipped a beat. It read: Beverly L. Maitland, Caribbean Sales Manager, ULTRAGEM, INC. *Bernie Lustfield's old company*, Bret silently reflected. Ravi put the card in the same pocket with the other two.

"How much does that emerald weigh?" Bret impulsively asked, pointing to the gemstone on the counter.

All four people in the group looked surprised at Bret's question, and at his presence in their corner of the shop. The woman from Ultragem looked Bret up and down.

"You wanta buy it?" Beverly finally managed a smile. The three men in her group smiled at her retort.

"Not a major league stone like that," Bret grinned. "Just curious."

The man who Ravi called Mr. Calvert seemed to relax at Bret's good humor. "What would you guess, Ravi," he winked at the East Indian, "about a quarter-pound?"

Ravi pulled a small calculator from behind the counter, set it next to the emerald and tapped on several keys. "This beautiful specimen weighs slightly more than two ounces," he looked up at Bret. "However, I do not sell my gems as one sells sliced ham at the corner delicatessen." His small audience laughed at Ravi's analogy.

Bret pretended humiliation at his original question, placing both elbows on the counter-top. "Sorry, folks," he feigned a sober *faux pas*, "guess I'm outta my element." He raised up, turned and slowly began to walk away.

"Wait, Mr., uh . . . ?" Beverly Maitland turned toward Bret.

Bret stopped and turned. "Princeton," he said. "George Princeton."

"Look, George," she continued, "maybe we were a little

rude." She glanced at the three men. They slowly nodded their heads.

At the front of the narrow shop, Abby Duchamps smiled to herself. The young saleswoman continued to show Abby some less-pretentious emeralds on display.

"It's just that we weigh emeralds in *carats*, Princeton," Calvert spoke again.

"The specimen you see here, George," Beverly said, "is 220 carats of velvety green Colombian supreme."

"Gorgeous," Bret observed, walking over to the matchless emerald. "Looks heavier than, you said two ounces, sir?" he asked Ravi.

"It is as I say," Ravi nodded. "One English pound is equal to twenty-two hundred, eighty-eight carats, thus one ounce equals 143 carats."

"Weight is similar to hardness," the British-accented Calvert intervened. "So, at 7.5 on the Mohes and Knoop hardness scale, emeralds are not particularly heavy or hard."

"What he's saying," Walter broke in, not wanting his expertise to be overlooked, "is that an emerald like that," nodding toward the gemstone on the counter, "the size of a match packet, weighs two ounces. A diamond of that same volume, having an M & K hardness of ten, would weigh about four ounces."

". . . and a mass of graphite that size," Beverly interrupted, "with a hardness of only one, would weigh no more than a half-ounce."

"Of course we are speaking of great rarity," Ravi said, "when we talk of five-ounce diamonds. The largest diamond *ever* found weighed slightly more than six-tenths of a kilogram . . . about twenty-one of your ounces."

"3,106 carats, from the Premier Mines, South Africa, 1905," Beverly added.

" . . . which did not last long," Calvert breathlessly appended, "since it was cut into one hundred, five smaller stones. Most famous diamond of this collection was the Star of Africa, having a total weight of 530 carats."

"Damn," Bret remarked, "so, at 2,280 carats a pound, that's on the line of four ounces, or a quarter-pound diamond."

"Mr. Princeton," Ravi managed a smile, "you still use your delicatessen weighing standard for precious gems."

Got what I came for, Bret thought. He said, "Thanks, folks," and with a slight nod, walked away. The buyers, proprietor and several other customers continued to discuss gemstones in a gradually heated conversation. No one noticed when Bret left the gathering.

As he walked up to Abby, Bret smiled broadly and asked, "You find that little trinket you was aching fer, princess?" He clamped a hand on one of Abby's shoulders.

"Not really, sweetheart," Abby grinned at him. "Their line runs somewhat higher than the two hundred dollars we planned to spend."

"Not surprised, dear heart. Those emeralds at the rear of th' store were downright outta sight . . . beauties, but more expensive'n yer daddy's new John Deere tractor."

Abby blinked at Bret's comparison. She suppressed laughter by clamping a hand over her mouth. Speaking between her fingers, she managed to say, "Sweetheart, I do believe I'm coming down with a fit o'sneezin'. Must be a bit dusty in here. We best go."

Outside the Bombay, they walked beyond the large shop windows. Abby placed the palms of her hands against the warm brick building, her forehead pressed against the back of her hands and giggled. "Princess? John Deere tractor? Oh, *mon Dieu*, Bret. Where'd you come up with those, those . . . um, *bon mots*?"

"I'm gratified you saw some humor there, Abby," mock-serious Bret stood back and watched the young woman. "As for me, it was a way to get out of the place without causing suspicion."

"Okay, okay. Sorry." Abby turned around and wiped tears from her eyes. "Only, it was, er, rather funny . . ."

"Yeah, sure," Bret nodded. "Now let's get serious, all right?" He gently took her elbow and walked further down the alley.

"You said you had all the information you needed?"

"Bombay's better emeralds come from Muzo in Colombia,"

Bret replied. "Apparently, Muzo's emeralds are found in dark shale."

"You learned a lot in a short time. What's with the lady in red?"

"Very interesting. Name's Beverly Maitland. Represents Ultragem, Incorporated out of Boston."

"I've heard of that company before, I believe."

"Bernie Lustfield's stompin' grounds before he was neutralized in Anguilla."

"Didn't take Ultragem long to stop mourning Lustfield and send in the reserves."

"Definitely knows the gemstone business," Bret said. "Quoted all kinds of facts and data on emeralds and diamonds. Knew precisely what to look for in a huge emerald's three-phase inclusions."

Abby smiled at Bret. "Three-phase *what*?"

"Appears to be a tiny imperfection in an emerald that literally proves it's the real thing. Every natural emerald has several of them deep down inside. Looked to me like it established a higher value on the gem."

"Sounds strange . . . the more imperfections, the rarer the stone."

"It's reliable. If an emerald has *no* imperfections, it's lab-created." Bret pulled Abby to a halt outside a high wood-slat fence paralleling the lane. "This should be the rear of Bombay Gems." He glanced around. "Nothing to climb up on."

"Give me a boost and I'll scope out the other side," Abby suggested.

"Um, I'm lookin' for a way to get over it. I want to pick through Ravi's trash." He still scanned the narrow, deserted street.

"Think you'll find a few errant emeralds?" Abby smiled.

"Hardly," the American investigator mumbled. "I'm bettin' we'll find lots of empty coffee cans or cigarette cartons, though."

"Bombay's a gem shop, not a grocery store."

"Lots of indications point to Bombay Gems, Ltd. as one of the collection points for smuggled Colombian emeralds," Bret said.

"You think they're smuggled in coffee or tobacco containers?"

"Makes sense. Bernie's clothing was full of bits and pieces of coffee, tobacco—and emerald granules."

"Not normal for him since he was allergic to caffeine and nicotine."

"Yeah, but he'd certainly risk an allergic reaction to dig out some extraordinary emeralds he particularly prized." Bret moved to the fence and peered between the edge of the wood fence and the heavy, bolted gate.

"Very clean back yard," he murmured. "Big green dumpster up near the back door." Bret paused. "No windows looking out from the store."

"Really?" Abby asked. "Okay, help me over the fence and I'll tackle the trash."

Bret backed away from the gate. "Don't like you taking that risk. The stolen emeralds are my responsibility."

"Bret," Abby said, giving him a stern look, "their eventual recovery is between you and your insurance company. Any smuggling onto the French *territoire* of St. Martin, however, is my responsibility."

"Even Dutch Sint Maarten?"

"Yes," Abby responded as if she'd anticipated the question. "Major crimes such as murder, grand larceny and felony illegal commerce of merchandise, *smuggling,* are given reciprocal status on this island. Lesser crimes remain under the jurisdiction of the individual colonial law enforcement authorities."

"Goddam, officer Duchamps," Bret pretended surprise, "you sound like a paragraph straight out of the *Sûreté Nationale*'s training manual."

"Forgive me. Occasionally cops recall rookie training."

"Still don't like you goin' in there. You'll be trapped in that compound if someone knows you're going through the dumpster."

"I have a much better chance of getting in and getting out with you boosting me. I'm in excellent condition, but holding up two hundred pounds on this side and pulling two hundred pounds out from the other side is ridiculous."

"One-ninety," Bret corrected. "You're what, about one-twenty?"

"I've *never* been one hundred twenty pounds. I weigh exactly fifty-two kilograms . . . perfect for my height." Abby smiled, but seemed annoyed at Bret's guess.

"All right," he agreed, "about one-fifteen. You're right, it might be hard for you to lift me outta there."

Bret leaned a shoulder against the wooden fence and intertwined his fingers. Abby kicked off her sandals and slipped her right foot into Bret's cupped hands. Bret lifted her, and Abby pulled herself up and over the fence, dropping out of sight.

"It's not too bad here," Abby whispered through the small opening between fence and gate. "Don't see any surveillance cameras. No watch dogs or booby traps."

Any surveillance equipment or booby traps would be well-hidden, Bret thought. He didn't say it, knowing Abby understood the fact. *The building itself must be tightly secured.*

"Okay," Bret whispered through the opening. "Just one sample if you find anything in the dumpster. That's all we need."

"On my way. Be here when I return."

"Right. Be careful. I'll be waitin'."

All Bret could hear from the far side of the fence was a slight rustling. *Probably sand covering the ground at the rear of the store.*

Leaning against the fence, he noticed a native woman dressed in a white uniform park her bicycle about fifty feet away. She pulled the detachable rear wheel from the bike and padlocked the remainder to a telephone pole using a link of chain. The woman looked in Bret's direction momentarily, then entered a shop's front door carrying her bike wheel. Since he could see no business sign from where he stood, Bret checked the location against his brochure's local street map. *Small restaurant*, he noted from the Philipsburg city diagram. *I could use the bike. Gotta get Abby back over the fence as quickly as possible.*

His thoughts kept returning to the short conversation with the Bombay's proprietor and his buyers. *Something Ravi did as* he explained the weight of emeralds. *Something odd about it.* "Dammit," Bret quietly exclaimed. "Can't put my finger on it."

"Who are you talking to?" Abby's whisper came from behind Bret's ear.

"Myself," Bret retorted, slightly startled. "Find anything?"

"You bet. I'm tossing something over the fence for you."

"Great," Bret said. He folded the brochure and put it in a back pocket. "Toss it over . . . not too far. No one in sight."

"Here it comes. It's not heavy."

Bret stood away from the fence. Suddenly, a brown object cleared the fence and dropped in front of him. He grabbed the small coffee bag and set it against the fence.

"Good work. Now I have to . . ."

"Hold it," Abby interrupted. "I'm tossing you something else. Here it comes."

Before he could protest, something else cleared the fence. He leaped toward a white and red carton and grabbed it before it hit the bricks paving the small street. *Told her one sample*, he said to himself.

"Get it?" Abby asked from behind the barricade.

"Yeah, yeah," Bret muttered. "Gotta get you out now." He glanced at the second package from Bombay's dumpster. It was a ten-pak Marlboro cigarette carton, apparently still filled with packs of cigarettes. He set the carton next to the coffee bag and raced to the padlocked bicycle carcass.

Bret looked up and down the tiny street, but saw no one. Fortunately, the bike was chained to the pole by nothing more than two spokes of the rear wheel. "Sorry, lady," he whispered as he yanked the bicycle away from its wooden anchor. The two spokes popped away from the rim and the bike was free. Pushing it somewhat like a wheelbarrow, the investigator swiftly ran back to the hinges of the gate at the fence.

"You there, Abby?" Bret quietly called, face pressed against the dark wood.

"Where were you?" the DST officer asked, some tension evident in her voice.

"Got something to climb up on," he answered. "Just a second." Bret shoved the bicycle against the fence and climbed up on the wobbly seat. He could barely get both feet to stay on the shaky piece of smooth vinyl. His eyes were at the same level as the top of the eight-foot-high fence.

They both heard the metallic scraping noise at the rear of the Bombay building. It came from inside the back door.

"Someone's unlocking the rear entrance," Abby whispered, her eyes wide.

Immediately, Bret boosted himself up until his stomach rested on the top of the fence. The T-shirt gave scant protection against his skin, but there was no time to cushion himself. He reached down with both arms and grabbed Abby's outstretched hands. He grasped her wrists firmly and dragged her up, until she grasped the top of the fence. Then he dropped down and jumped back out of the way.

Once she clutched the top of the fence, Abby pulled herself to the top, and swung her legs over. She then let herself drop several feet to the pavement. Bret helped her to a less-abrupt landing on bare feet. They crouched with backs against the fence, as Abby crossed both arms over her chest and carefully smothered the sound of her heavy breathing.

"Oh, yes. I thought I heard noise out here, Mr. Pundamaj. But all looks to be fine," a clipped English remark reached Bret and Abby's ears.

"Very well, Clarke," the voice of Ravi replied. "Check the dumpster," he said.

The sound of shoes on wooden steps. The squawk of rusted metal on metal. A hesitation. "All trash here and ready to be picked up, Mr. Pundamaj. Special garbage truck will be here in two hours, sir." Another squawking sound ended with a loud clang. Seconds later, shoes on wooden steps and then the slam of a heavy door. Again the unmistakable bolting and locking sounds of the rear door.

"*Merde*, as you'd say, Abby," Bret whispered.

Abby let out her breath. "Used quite correctly," she said, nodding.

"How come *you* didn't make noise with the dumpster?"

"Because I'm careful. Just opened it slowly and no more than five or six inches. It was filled with coffee bags and cigarette cartons."

Bret nodded. "You did great, Abby. We'll have to analyze the contents, but that's almost certainly the way they smuggle in their emeralds." He looked at the young woman. "You all right? You look upset, Abby."

"I'm okay, but don't think my boobs will ever be the same after you hauled me up against that fence." She glanced down at her smudged and dirty T-shirt.

"Lucky your shirt didn't rip or you may have had some major wounds to patch up." Bret said, "We'd better get away from here. I'd hate to have Ravi's friends find us with his dumpster 'trash'."

"Where'd you get the unicycle?" Abby asked as she attempted to brush dust and grime off her T-shirt.

"Borrowed it from a waitress at the restaurant next door." Bret grabbed the crippled bicycle and half-filled coffee bag, while Abby pulled on her sandals. Quickly, they retreated down the alley.

At the telephone pole, Bret slipped the chain around the broken bike spokes and adjusted them to look undamaged to passersby. He stuck two wadded-up ten-dollar bills into a chain link hidden from plain view. "That should pay for a repair," he noted. He grabbed the coffee bag again and they set out for Sunshine Pointe.

Chapter Ten

Claude Tomasso listened as Rupert Morgan fussed with the tape recorder. *Can't count the hours I've spent with Rupe on that equipment*, Tomasso thought. *At least he managed to hook up the scrambler right this time.*

From his vantage point on the sidewalk on Front Street, Rupert Morgan looked like any Sint Maarten native listening to his Walkman. He'd been so far from the American and the Frenchwoman that neither noticed him over a hundred yards from them in the tiny street behind Bombay Gems. The parabolic eavesdropping unit itself looked like an antenna on the small "radio." The conversations Morgan picked up were recorded on a tiny tape machine hidden beneath his floppy shirt.

"Got it workin' yet, Rupe?" Tomasso was impatient, but was well aware that his enforcer might mistakenly erase the tape if pressured.

"T'ink he comin' 'long now, Mistah T'masso," Morgan answered unsurely. Rupert was still pissed-off that his Semtex failed to kill the man at the Amsterdam House.

"Just take your time, Rupe. No hurry." *What were those sonsabitches doing at Bombay?* Claude Tomasso wondered.

"Got it goin', Mistah T'masso, suh," Rupert's muffled voice sounded over the scrambled phone. "Switchin' on."

Tomasso listened to idle chitchat between the two foreign annoyances. *It provided incredible clarity from nearly a hundred yards away*, he judged the equipment Morgan had used. *Just clutchin' at straws?* Then the luxury car dealer's throat went dry . . .

" . . . *you'll be trapped in that compound if someone knows you're going through the dumpster*," Tomasso heard.

"Goddam bastards," he shouted. "They're onto us." Claude leaned back in the huge leather lounge chair, both knuckles holding up his chin. More inane talk between the two proved nothing. *Maybe they didn't find anything in the trash, he told himself. Oh oh, sounds like Ravi.* Tomasso sat up.

" . . . *Check the dumpster.*"

"The idiot dothead's laughing." Claude jumped up from his chair, screeching to the walls of the empty office. "He should have the fuckin' trash removed by this time!"

Then Tomasso heard the clincher. " . . . *have to analyze the contents, but that's almost certainly the way they smuggle in their emeralds.*"

"The assholes know," Tomasso told himself as he sat back down. "They're both as good as dead and dismembered. They're food for the gulls."

Rupert's voice interrupted Tomasso's vision of merciless vengeance. "You hear all th' tape, Mistah T'masso, suh?"

"Yes," Claude screeched into the speaker. Then, toning down his voice, "Yeah, Rupe. Heard it and all its implications."

Here again was The Man speaking words that Morgan didn't understand. As usual, though, he knew what Tomasso *meant*. His boss hadn't commented to any great degree about the failed Amsterdam bomb, but Rupert knew he agonized deeply about the screwup. Now Claude Tomasso would seek quick and horrible deaths for the American and Frenchwoman.

"You wants Rupe to take care o'th two foreigners, Mistah T'masso?"

"Yes," Tomasso said. "The bodies are never to be found . . . understand Rupe?"

"No ev'dence, suh. No suh, Rupe takes care o'th two in Jacksplit time."

Claude smiled. He knew the words meant Rupert would get the job done immediately. "You do just that, Rupe. Jack-split time."

* * *

Dornier had been assigned to handle the operation in St. Martin, and he wasn't handling it well at all. The second-story room of the Balmoral Hotel looked directly above the man Chief Horst DeGroot offhandedly identified as a vicious hired killer. The disfigured black man had been observed aiming his listening device at the same people Paul Dornier and his men kept under surveillance. DeGroot impassively advised Dornier there was no due cause to arrest or detain Rupert Morgan for "listening to a radio in public." The chief left.

This had happened to the team from Marseille ever since their arrival in St. Martin two days before. They had gotten little "respect" from either French or Dutch authorities on this hot little island. "These Dutch West Indies cretins don't even take French francs," Dornier grumbled at Kronstein. "Even on the French side they'd rather have American dollars," he complained, as if it were a sacrilege, " . . . and on a French *territoire*."

Due to the bilateral agreement between France and the Netherlands Antilles regarding high crimes on the island, the three French *Sûreté* officers were authorized to investigate in Philipsburg, Sint Maarten. Chief DeGroot, nevertheless, assigned three of his own officers to watch and report every move the Frenchmen made.

Dornier's great uncle was French prime minister Jean-Pierre Raffarin. The relationship was the principal reason Dornier had not been drummed out of the DST section of the *Sureté Nationale* despite pathetic scores at training school. Even with his family connections, Dornier understood the folly of hassling Abby Duchamps. After all, Jacques Chirac was French chief of *state*, while Raffarin was head of government.

Chatelaine handled the setup and technical monitoring of

the fifty thousand dollar Philips electronic parabolic listening device. When he stood against the front window through which the two-foot long "shotgun" mike was aimed, the Parisian could barely make out Rupert standing four meters below on the sidewalk. Louis Chatelaine held a postgraduate electronics engineering degree from the Sorbonne. The engineer was not about to admit to his colleagues that Morgan's forty-nine dollar "walkman"/parabolic mike was just as effective as the heavy twenty-kilogram Philips at this short distance. Truth was, the little Electronic Super Ear was probably *better* at that range since it wasn't inhibited by window glass.

It had been Kronstein who'd originally noticed Rupert Morgan "putting the ear" on Lamplighter and Duchamps. His hurried phone call to Chief DeGroot netted the DST officers *l'oeuf* . . . a goose egg . . . nothing. It was almost as though DeGroot knew everything about Tomasso/Morgan, Lamplighter/Duchamps and Maitland/Pundamaj. *He probably even knows about the Iranian connection with Colombia's drug lords.* Back in early 1995, American CIA and NSA operatives in Syria and Lebanon intercepted several highly-classified documents. The reports conclusively showed Iran's secret alliance with at least seven Colombian cocaine, heroin and cannabis drug lords. Evidently, it was Tehran that first prompted the Cali and Medellín cartels to smuggle emeralds, gold and platinum from the upland areas of the country.

Karl Kronstein held no university degree. He was, nevertheless, a mechanical and electrical wizard, and a computer hacker of no small note. Kronstein handled the DST team's video camera and its recording apparatus with the ease and creativity of a professional cinematographer.

In room 214 of the Balmoral, Kronstein used a thousand-millimeter lens on the expensive, professional Sony ES550. Handling the lens at a mere one hundred meters, the DST officer could almost smell the aroma of the coffee grounds in the five-pound bag Abby Duchamps tossed to the American. Kronstein had always admired Abby's professionalism. He'd worked with her twice in Marseille. Spying on this bright, experienced *Sûreté* officer left Karl Kronstein inwardly questioning the wisdom of their mutual administrators in France.

Horst DeGroot incessantly paced the room above Boston Baked Cameras. If possible, he was angrier at the three *Sûreté* officers holed up across the street than at Lamplighter and Duchamps. From his window, the French DST men weren't visible, but DeGroot watched Tomasso's black henchman standing on the sidewalk. *The man is too obvious and easily seen.*

Two other men sat in wobbly hard chairs in widely separated areas of the room. Both had been on the beach at Sunshine Pointe not many hours before. After retreating from the American's villa, their stolen cruiser was abandoned in Marigot harbor. Both were humiliated and infuriated that the assassination attempt fell through. The swarthy man with the thick, black mustache, however, was both outraged at his failure and frantic about his uncertain future.

"Sabri Al-Banna does not acknowledge blunders, DeGroot," the Iranian named Ahmad al-Majid screamed at Philipsburg's police chief. "I swear I will take you to the gallows with me." His bandaged leg still stung severely from the .22 caliber slug fired by the pig American.

Horst DeGroot disliked the man intensely. He also was deathly afraid of him, and especially his group . . . the international terrorist organization Abu Nidal. Chief DeGroot knew Sabri Al-Banna's alias was Abu Nidal, and he'd split from Al Fatah back in 1974. The ANO had been headquartered in Israel, Lebanon, Iraq, Libya and Syria since then. Now there were assassination elements of Abu Nidal in Iran. Rumors abounded that Ali Akbar Hashemi Rafsanjani, Iran's house Speaker, unofficially sanctioned the ANO's Iranian connection. Recent NSA documents revealed that other terrorist groups operating from Iran included Black Wednesday Brigade, Mujahideen-e-Khalq, al-Qaida, Komleh and the Islamic Jihad, to name but a few.

"Keep calm, al-Majid. We will take care of the American and Frenchwoman with little trouble." DeGroot was not as convinced as he sounded. The private investigator and DST agent were definitely more cunning than he originally thought.

"Little trouble!" the Iranian blurted out. "Tell that to Barnstable's widowed wife and children, they who no longer have a provider."

DeGroot felt no sympathy for the late French West Indies policeman's family. They were no concern of his. He *was* disturbed by the possibility of losing out on his share of the Colombian emerald and heroin smuggling. "I will explain to Al-Banna that you were lured into a trap," he lied.

"Bah! The Father of Struggle does not listen to cowardly excuses. Sabri Al-Banna speaks and his followers obey." Al-Majid stared at his muddy boots with piercing black eyes of foreboding.

"You give bad information," the Iranian yelled at DeGroot. "You say no weapons with Yankee pig and French whore. Is not truth. You lying to ANO!"

DeGroot turned and looked at the Colombian he'd worked with for so many months. *What's bothering al-Majid?* He was certain the Iranian didn't speak Spanish. *"Temor. Opina Al-Banna cortará su cabeza."*

DeGroot nodded. *Yes, he's fearful of being beheaded.*

"Si," the Colombian nodded, *"debo admitirme tiene el mismo miedo de mi jefe."* Things went so well before the Iranian terrorists got involved in our work, he thought.

Although the man from Medellín had piloted the cruiser—and was not directly involved in the bungled attack—he feared Enrique Vargas Mantilla wouldn't see it that way. *Stupid Iranian dog ran as soon as the black cop was shot.* Alfonso Garcia drummed his fingers on the side of the chair, glaring with rage at the Abu Nidal terrorist sitting on the opposite side of the small room.

"Enrique Vargas will understand the screwup," DeGroot told Garcia. The Philipsburg police chief no more believed his consoling words than did the Colombian. He also was certain that al-Majid was in for certain torture, if not beheading, from Abu Nidal.

For the first time since replacing Anders Verhouten as Philipsburg's Chief of Police, Horst DeGroot felt the fear of failure. Several months had passed after DeGroot assumed his Sint Maarten post before he began to take small, local bribes. Several prosperous Front Street retailers were allowed to increase their inventories without reporting the taxes due to Curaçao's Tax Revenue Department. Before his first year was completed, Horst DeGroot was a Sint Maarten millionaire.

It was inevitable that the Colombian drug cartel controlling emerald smuggling to St. Martin would contact DeGroot. The Medellín consortium gave Horst an offer he found irrepressible. Six months passed before the slumbering Mideast giant, Iran, involved itself in Colombian terrorist tactics. For, in truth, Iran hadn't slumbered one second after the death of the Ayatollah Khomeini. The Islamic Republic of Iran continued to be the most significant practitioner of terrorism in the world under Hojatolislam Said Ali Khamenei and Presidents Hashemi Rafsanjani and Mohammed Khatami.

Iraq, Iran's Persian Gulf neighbor, found out a fellow Muslim nation couldn't be trusted during the Persian Gulf war. After granting landing privileges to more than one-hundred fleeing Iraqi pilots who ditched in Iran to avoid annihilation, every warplane was confiscated. The American and French jet fighters were added to Iran's military machine, giving that country the fourth mightiest air force in the world.

Horst DeGroot now felt like one of the Iraqi pilots who'd unwittingly lost a multimillion dollar jet aircraft. Allied intelligence reported that all one-hundred pilots who'd landed in Iran were executed on orders of Saddam's sons upon their repatriation to Baghdad. Chief DeGroot did not relish the thought of being another messenger hanged by an irrational leader. DeGroot's pacing became more intense. *I will rid myself of Duchamps and Lamplighter*, he silently vowed.

Madeleine Cromray was no covert operative by any stretch of the imagination. Nevertheless, Maddy was curious, and that curiosity could be an asset. Marigot under-inspector Bouchard occasionally engaged the middle-aged St. Martin widow when he needed someone inconspicuous to scope-out a mark . . . or several marks.

On this splendid March morning, she had two marks to watch. After chaining her bicycle to a phone pole near the man and woman, Maddy barged into the small café as if she owned it. She found the innocuous private door two yards from the rear entrance. She retrieved a large key given to her by Henri Bouchard and quickly opened it. *Not so much a bad mon*, she mused of the *sous-inspecteur*. The two to three hours of investigating, Maddy never called it snooping, would net her fifty dollars U.S. This was handsome pay in St. Martin. She always earned every cent of her "curiosity money."

After leaning the bicycle wheel against the bottom stair step, she climbed the dusty, squawking stairs and found a small room perched above the café. She was careful not to brush against the dusty, rickety furniture with her crisp, white cotton waitress uniform. Shoes off, Madeleine Cromray edged to the window overlooking the narrow street. By adjusting the tattered, drawn window shade, she looked directly down Great Salt Pond Boulevard. Madeleine was one of the few natives on the island who remembered the original name of the little, unmarked lane. She could just see the kneeling American as he waited for his lady friend. Maddy wasn't told by under-inspector Bouchard what the French agent would probably be doing behind the East Indian's emerald shop. The policeman had assured her too much curiosity concerning the DST officer and private detective could prove hazardous to her future as a sleuth.

Maddy pulled the compact Copitar 30-power electronic binoculars from her cloth shopping bag, plus a pen and notebook. Finally, she pulled out the Minox IV micro-camera. A quick pull-push action and the device was ready to use. Since she wasn't out in public where the Minox would be hidden from view, a specially-manufactured, short telephoto lens was attached.

Focusing the binoculars, she studied the window down at the corner, and carefully described the three French *Sûreté* officers in the notebook. Next, she noted a description of the sophisticated equipment the men used, quite evident as they poked through closed Venetian blind slats. Next she photographed the men in turn, as they stared through the window. Maddy took at least a dozen shots of each.

While he stood on the sidewalk, Rupert Morgan was another subject for Madeleine Cromray's Super Minox. As the black man listened to his "Walkman," Maddy took a mere half-dozen shots of Tomasso's henchman. Marigot police files were already so littered with photos of Morgan that additional glossies were absurd. After all, every law enforcement officer on the island knew Rupert by sight and reputation. No one was really certain why the man wasn't in a prison cell in Fort-de-France or Willemstad.

Madeleine got pissed off when she noticed Bret pop the spokes on her bicycle, drag it to the high fence and use it as a stepladder. *Damn his blue 'mer'can eyes*, she mumbled. *Gonna git that mon 'rested by Mistah Bu'char'*. Maddy wrote several paragraphs about the American's actions in her notebook. Three swiftly snapped photos would convict Bret of his indiscretion. Only later, when she found the twenty dollars in a chain link, did she forgive him. Maddy's brother-in-law could repair the two spokes in a minute for free. It would be a mighty profitable day for the middle-aged investigator.

Sous-inspecteur Bouchard had earlier briefed Maddy that Chief DeGroot, the Iranian and DeGroot's Colombian colleague were surveying the scene from a window in a small room above the corner camera shop. For certain, Madeleine Cromray was an excellent natural-born spy.

Chapter Eleven

"Largest emerald of the *eighteen*?" Bret rephrased Abby's last question.

"You said the eighteen stolen emeralds totaled 2,000 carats. What size was the largest of those?" Abby asked.

"Just a second," Bret responded. "I know I have the range of emerald sizes in the robbery." He began to leaf through papers on the table in front of him.

Abby stood next to the American private detective in the living room of her villa. Glaziers were repairing the glass door and windows in Bret's suite. He sat on a sofa as he read sheets of documents taken from several file folders. He'd been taking notes on a legal pad while digesting the information in front of him. Earlier that morning, after making a phone call to Johnson, a messenger delivered a grocery bag to Bret's villa. In the bag was the item he'd requested from his St. Martin contact, a CSI-1 electronic eavesdropping detector. Developed by counter-surveillance experts, the small handheld device could pinpoint the location of any electronic bug. Bret carefully swept both his and Abby's quarters before they began to discuss their next step. As he suspected, five additional minuscule radio transmitters were found in each villa. He terminated each bug with the heel of his shoe.

Bret reached for a bright green-colored folder and flipped it open. Several sheets of bond paper bore the letterhead of Ultragem, Inc. The third sheet he came to he handed to Abby.

"Here's the list, typed in order of carat size and the amount Ultragem paid for each."

Abby took the list of stolen emeralds. "Total weight 2,022 carats. Largest emerald weighs 265 carats. Wow." She reviewed the size briefly. "How large was that emerald your lady in red bid eight hundred thou for? It looked big from where I stood."

"It *was* big, about 220 carats. That's around two ounces in weight. Size of a small matchbox or a nine-volt battery."

"Hmm, the amount Lustfield paid for his 265 carat emerald," Abby noted the price at the right of the sheet, "is one point three million. That's only 45 carats larger than the eight hundred thousand-dollar emerald."

"It's not easy for a layman to figure out an emerald's price." Bret smiled at her. "A lot depends on quality, color and other factors." He picked out another sheet from the Ultragem file and scanned it. "Listen to this: 'Flawless emeralds of good color and size are very rare and command higher prices than diamonds of equal weight'. This memo comes from Ultragem's top management."

"So Bernie had himself some really high class Green," Abby remarked.

"Ultragem stood to make a huge profit," Bret reasoned.

"Enormous, like more than double what Bernie paid Ravi," Abby said as she sat cross-legged, on a thick throw rug. She was seated at the far end of the table, with the contents of her retrieved coffee bag spread out in front of her.

"Incredible markup on natural, high-quality gemstones. The bidding today was strictly for the wholesale customers. That's why they got nervous when I butted in."

Abby nodded. She began to push small uncut emeralds to the edge of the coffee grounds. "Thought we'd find teeny little crumbs in here, Bret. But some of these emeralds are as big as the tip of my thumb." She held up a jellybean-size green stone and squinted at it. "Pretty, but definitely not usable as a gemstone," she quietly said almost to herself. "No shine to it. No translucence."

Bret took her hand and looked closely at the stone. "It varies in greenish shades throughout." He picked up several other emerald chips and noted, "They're nice, but worthless as emerald jewelry." Bret rolled them between his thumb and index finger. "*Real* green thumb," he showed the young woman. "Only value would be as a dye. Lots of black and gray shale in them." He tossed them back into the coffee grounds.

"Probably worth little more than the coffee they're mixed in with," Abby mused. "Proves our smuggling theory, though. Imagine the 'ones that got away'." They had already examined the contents of the cigarette carton. The first two cigarette packs were totally legitimate, while the next eight contained only the filter tips and loose tobacco. In with the tobacco were shards, chips and dust of emeralds.

"Also shows I've gotta take a plane to Colombia. There must be records of the smuggling transactions somewhere near the emerald digs." Bret knew that starting at the source would be the best way to find information on the eighteen missing emeralds.

"Always thought that was the answer, myself," Abby retorted. "Not so sure, now."

"We already spoke about . . ."

"I've been reading some of your State Department advisories." Abby interrupted. "Colombia's not safe. Listen to this one." Abby took a computer printout off the floor next to her. "It says 'Areas of Instability in Colombia: The entire country is currently experiencing daily and nightly power outages. Serious crimes (such as homicide, rape, assault and kidnaping) have greatly increased during these blackouts' . . ."

"A little darkness won't slow me." Bret smiled.

"Let me continue," Abby pressed on. "'The following particularly dangerous areas are off-limits to U.S. government personnel because of security concerns. In addition, U.S. government personnel are prohibited from road travel outside the Bogota metropolitan area'."

"That's for employees of the U.S. government, Abby. I don't . . ."

"Stop interrupting. *I* know you aren't DEA anymore. But others might figure you're working undercover. 'Off-limits areas include: all of Antioquia Department (state) including the city of Medellín; the northern half of Choco Department, particularly the Uraba region, except for the tourist area of Capurgan; Rural Valle de Cauca Department and most of the Cauca River valley including the cities of Cali and Buenaventura, and the road between Cali and Buenaventura; the Magdelena Medio region including western Boyacá and eastern Caldas. Americans who register with the Consular Section of the U.S. Embassy in Bogota or at the Consulate in Barranquilla can get updated informa . . .'"

"Abby," Bret barged in, "I know what's happening in Colombia. I've read reams of advisory bulletins and State Department memos and circulars. You've cherry-picked the spots I'm interested in, and I'm grateful. But I've gotta go there."

"Bret," Abby appeared quite serious, "western Boyacá of the Magdelena Medio region includes Muzo. You can't go to Colombia alone. No one will let you walk into the main office of Muzo mines and give you files on Ultragem's stolen emeralds."

"I know the problem," Bret replied. "I phoned my St. Martin contact Johnson before I met you this morning."

"I know . . . he sent the CSI over. You trust this man Johnson?"

Bret sighed. "He's done fine so far, and my bosses trust him. When I spoke with him this morning he gave me the name of someone in Colombia to help me cut through the red tape."

"Admittedly you need a Colombian contact. But you need a partner to cover your ass, too."

"I'm ex-federal government, Abby. They've surely got that data in their computers, no matter if they think I'm deep cover." He gave her his most reassuring smile. "You'd be fingered before you got off the plane at Medellín. You're a government agent of a foreign country. Talk about a millstone! National police would stick so close to you, they'd be pulling down your panties every time you took a pee."

"Don't wear panties."

"Cut the bluster, Abby. I'd love to work with you, but you'd be an albatross around my neck in Colombia."

"I'd be a good backup." She glared at him.

"Alone I've got a chance to get leads on Bernie's Caribbean Green. With you along I'd be far too conspicuous, *n'est ce pas?*"

Abby stared into the pile of worthless emeralds and coffee grounds. "Suppose my bio and photo *would* pop out of their database in a few seconds."

"We both know they would, Abby. You and I've used computers often to get the same type of information."

"This assignment isn't working out the way my section chief planned, Bret."

"The best laid plans . . ."

"Knock it off, *mon ami*," Abby growled. "DST wanted to be certain you weren't still an active American agent on the French *territoire* of St. Martin."

"So they sent their most formidable *femme fatale* to check me out." He leaned back on a soft cushion of the sofa.

Abby stretched legs out beneath the low table. Patches of blue-colored salve were visible on her scraped knees and thighs through the glass-top. "Initially, believing the reason you gave for being here was difficult, especially after, after . . ."

"After I'd been involved in the deaths of five, make that *nine*, people on the island." Bret completed her sentence.

"Don't you see the French viewpoint?"

"Sure, the American government would have done the same thing under similar circumstances."

"So I want to help you."

"Do the three DST officers on St. Martin share your feelings?"

"They're here to investigate the bombing at the Amsterdam House, since French nationals were killed and wounded."

"I'll make a little wager that you and I are on their investigation itinerary. Those bugs we found were *Sûreté* issue."

Abby closed her eyes momentarily, then opened them and stared at Bret. "You're right. I've used the same model myself."

Slowly he nodded, turning to gaze out the picture window at

the blue-green waters of the Caribbean. As he started to say something, the phone chirped. Bret reached for the instrument, lifted it from its cradle and handed it to Abby.

"*Allô*, Duchamps *ici*," she answered.

Bret studied her face and noticed it tighten as she listened to the voice on the other end of the line. Abby made short comments in French before she handed the phone back to Bret.

"Bad news?" he asked.

"The opposite, actually," Abby said. "It was *sous-inspecteur* Bouchard."

"He often represents bad news, in my biased opinion."

"He said he was sorry for any inconvenience he may have caused me, and you."

"What's he up to? Two days ago he wanted to run both of us off his little island territory."

"The bugs!?"

Bret shrugged his shoulders. "Doubt if it was his doing. Must have other sources who convinced him we're no threat to St. Martin."

Abby was momentarily silent, then said, "He told me he's already sent one of his police cars over here with my MAS."

"No shit! That's one small step for Bouchard, one giant step for the French *Sûreté*. Give you any reason?"

"Just that his forty-eight-hour weapon restriction order was finished. We've been cleared of involuntary manslaughter."

"He knows it was either the terrorists or us, indisputable self-defense. Just lucky for us Johnson slipped me the High Standard."

Abby shook her head and said, "Not every country's as lenient about killing someone and using it as a justifiable excuse as the United States is, Bret. I believe our sub-inspector has other reasons for returning my pistol."

"Guess that's true. Guilty 'til proven innocent, hunh?"

"Yes, very often." A sudden rapping on the front door halted Abby in mid-sentence. She quickly got to her feet and hurried to the door, stick mirror in hand. Angling her mirror at the opening, she peered outside at a native dressed in civilian clothes.

"Who is it?"

"D'tective Mobley, ma'am," he replied. "*Sous-'specteur* send me."

"Identification, *s'il vous plaît.*"

The husky black man pulled open his jacket lapel revealing a shoulder-holstered automatic pistol. On his shirt pocket a six-pointed badge read: St. Martin Police, Detective Lieutenant, and a three-digit I.D. number. Finally, he held up a photo I.D. card, identifying him as a St. Martin police officer.

"*Alors,*" Abby said. "You have something for me?"

Mobley nodded and showed Abby a plastic Stop 'N Shop grocery bag. He pressed it against the wooden door.

Clicking open the two front door locks, she pushed the door ajar ten or twelve inches, reached out and grasped the bag. Heavier than she'd anticipated, Abby swung it inside.

"Thank you, detective," she said and pulled the door shut before the policeman could respond.

"Grocery girl!" she announced as she lugged the bulky bag into the living room and set it amid the clutter on the coffee table. "Specialty *de la maison,*" she said. "Broiled MAS 1950 automatic, *m'sieur.*"

"Slice me a clip," Bret said, smiling. "I'll have mine on French bread." He reached over to an end table and picked up the "bug detector" supplied by his contact, switched it on and stuck it into the large bag. Nothing sounded and the dial on the small indicator panel didn't budge. "All clear, mademoiselle. No bugs, no bombs, no electronic activity whatever."

"There are several packages in here," Abby said as she reached into the bag. "I'll check the one on top, first." She pulled out a package wrapped in green and red Christmas colors. It measured about ten inches by six inches and was some two inches deep. A card taped to the top of the 'gift' read: To Abby, From Henri Bouchard. Happy Holidays.

"Looks like you have a Gallic admirer," Bret teased.

"What did I do to deserve this?" Abby joked. She ripped off the paper and pulled the lid from the box, which was imprinted with the name of a local variety store.

"*Voilà*, my own sidearm as a belated Christmas present." She removed the steel-gray MAS 1950 automatic and immediately began to check it for any missing or damaged parts. "Good as new," she proclaimed.

"What other gifts did St. Martin's Saint Nick send you?"

"Not sure. Why don't you get the next package while I reassemble my weapon."

Bret lifted the next package and set it next to him on the sofa. It was approximately the same size as the package Abby opened. A black marking pen had been used to write: 'To Whom It May Concern' on the light brown wrapping paper. "Bouchard playing little mind games with us?" Bret asked.

Abby turned to look at him. As he opened the lid of the box, Bret whistled. He stared at the High Standard Dura-Matic M-101 used to eliminate the terrorist who'd tried to kill Abby and him. "Ol' Bouchard never bought our story that this was your pistol."

"It was far-fetched now that I think about it. I doubt if any *Sûreté* officer would use a long-barreled assassination weapon as a backup. It's too hard to conceal."

"I won't look Bouchard's gift horse in the mouth, but I don't understand . . ."

"Unless . . . ," Abby broke in, "he figured you're going to Colombia."

"Figured, or heard it before I deloused our villas."

Abby shrugged her shoulders. "Moot point. Fact is, he's on to you."

Bret slowly nodded his head, eyes fixed on the .22 automatic. "And that means, I've gotta catch the first plane to Willemstad before anyone else tries to slow me down."

"Willemstad? That's in Curaçao." Abby looked puzzled.

"Johnson said I should take a commuter plane from Willemstad to Barranquilla. That's where I meet my Colombian contact."

"Doesn't that take you out of the way? Curaçao is south of here."

"It's southwest, not out of the way at all. He wants me flying in a smaller plane when I arrive in Barranquilla. Says it's less than 400 air miles from Willemstad; believes it's safer for me to land in Barranquilla than Medellín."

"Sounds as if he has better connections on the coast than inland," Abby noted. "I'm happy to see he's looking out for you. According to your State Department advisories, Barranquilla's one of several 'semi-safe' spots on Colombia's north coast."

" . . . in a hotbed of coke trafficking," Bret added.

"Un humn, I've heard the Sierra Nevadas south of Santa Marta in Magdalena department have practically no other industry but coca growing."

"Except tourism. For instance, Cartagena's a peaceful tourist stop, but some of the world's highest-grade coca thrives less than an hour's drive from the city."

"You know a lot about Colombia's narcotics without ever having been assigned there," Abby said as she arose and sat on the sofa. Johnson's little bag of tricks rested between them.

Foremost in their minds was the inescapable knowledge that they were being hunted. One group wanted to keep close track on them, while the other wanted them eliminated. The assassins, evidently, knew they were coming dangerously close to the truth about the stolen emeralds.

Do the terrorists realize I'm going to Colombia? Bret wondered. *Looks as if Bouchard knows . . . since he gave the pistol back to me.*

"Let's see what else Santa Henri sent in the last package."

Bret pulled the remaining package from the supermarket bag. This one had no card or writing on the outer wrapping. "*Pour vous, mademoiselle,*" he said as he handed the parcel to his French companion.

"Thank you," Abby responded. "You expecting a bomb in here?" She smiled at the unamused expression that came over Bret's face.

Just to be safe, Abby ripped away a side from the inner cardboard carton after she tore off the beige-hued wrapping paper. She held the box up to the light after the side was exposed.

"*Now* Bouchard writes his little note," she exclaimed. Abby carefully put her hand inside the box and withdrew a folded yellow sheet of lined legal paper. Placing the still-covered small box on the coffee table, she unfolded the note and read: "Mademoiselle Duchamps and Monsieur Lamplighter: I believe the enclosed articles will be of critical necessity in your endeavors. Beware the wolf in sheep's clothing who lurks in Sint Maarten. Trust only those who you must. Affectionately, H. Bouchard." Abby hesitated for a moment before she said, "That's all there is. Learned advice from one who knows?"

"Why wouldn't your man Henri simply say 'Watch out for Johnson' or 'Don't turn your back on Ravi'?" Bret reached over and took the note. He studied the short message for a couple of seconds. "Hmm, you know, I think Bouchard did point the finger, though indirectly."

Puzzled, Abby leaned forward and took the note back. She studied it more closely. "Aha, the island's *spelling*!"

"And here I thought I was the only master detective in the room." Bret grinned broadly at the *Sûreté* agent.

Abby pretended to totally ignore Bret's comment. "He deliberately wrote the name of the territory with its Netherlands Antilles spelling. Bouchard would never do that except to make a particular point."

"And I think that 'point' is to alert us to Chief DeGroot."

". . . or DeGroot and *other* reputable Sint Maarten nationals."

Bret lifted the cover from the box on the littered coffee table. "Better see what else the under-inspector sent us." Several other items lay on the bottom.

Bret retrieved two brown leather packets that were bound together with rubber bands. "Look like small holsters," he said, turning them in his hands. The objects had narrow straps slung over their openings and inch-long, spring-tensioned fasteners on their backs. "This one's long and slender, while the other's shorter and more squat." After several seconds a smile enveloped Bret's face and he murmured, "Henri Bouchard, you sonuvabitch."

"Scabbards for a knife and a taser?" Abby pondered. "But why . . ."

"Educated guess," Bret nodded, "but not quite correct." He set the leather items on his lap and picked up the High Standard M-101 pistol. "All I do is loosen this single screw . . ."—he twisted a nut built into the bottom of the weapon—"and, *voilà!*" In his right hand Bret held the slender, six and one-half inch barrel. His left hand clasped the 6-inch long, one-piece butt/trigger housing/slide assembly, which measured about 5 inches in width. Both parts fit into their custom-made "holsters" perfectly.

"*Magnifique.* Instead of trying to hide an eleven-inch long pistol, you can equally distribute two, six-inch metal pieces." Abby picked up the weapon parts and smiled at the ingenuity of Bouchard and his police force.

Bret barely nodded as he gawked at several other items he'd pulled from the box. "Bouchard tryin' to get me in trouble with the Colombian authorities?"

Setting down the High Standard pieces, Abby asked, "Why do you ask that?"

"Look at these." Bret handed three wallet-size articles to Abby Duchamps.

Her eyes opening wide in astonishment, the French *Sûreté* officer stared at an Air France airplane ticket. The document displayed a flight reservation leaving Sint Maarten for Medellín, Colombia later that day. "I thought *Johnson* sent you a plane ticket."

"He did. And Johnson's has *my* name on it . . . not an alias."

Abby studied the Air France ticket. "Señor Manuel Parra Vega. Why would *sous-inspecteur* Bouchard send you an airline reservation with a false identity?"

Bret handed two more articles to Abby. Half-chuckling he said, "To match this fake passport and National Police credentials, I imagine."

In disbelief, the Frenchwoman stared at a laminated card. The Colombian passport had a photograph of Bret, his description and the same name that appeared on the airline ticket.

Multicolored customs stamps appearing on its pages showed many countries visited by Señor Parra. "This is remarkable," she said.

"You want 'remarkable'? Look at the last item."

Abby opened the billfold Bret presented her. "Unbelievable!" she exclaimed. The DST agent gaped at the badge and identification card of Colonel M. Parra Vega of the *Policía nacional de Colombia*. Bret's somber visage formed part of the I.D.

Chapter Twelve

ALM Antillean Airways flight #046 left Princess Juliana Airport at 1650 hours Atlantic Standard Time. The GAF Nomad 22 was to fly the 580 miles to Curaçao in two and one-half hours. Twelve passengers boarded the twin-turboprop airplane in Sint Maarten, two less than its normal capacity. Johnson had been firm that Bret Lamplighter take the smaller aircraft to Curaçao. "Jour contact will wait for jou in Barranquilla, after jou switch to other plane near Willemstad," Johnson had said.

Abby looked on while Bret was halted at security screening. The same obese native woman as before stood near the X-ray machine. She told Bret to take the film for his small camera through the metal detector. Despite his complaint that the film would become streaked, the woman insisted. When the American walked through the detector's arches, the alarm sounded. The fat security guard and her companions cackled as Bret stalked on into the noisy waiting room. He griped loudly that the film in its metal canister had been ruined. Several nearby tourists sided with him, saying that the same trouble befell them. Abby knew one important difference. Bret strolled through the metal detector with a .22 caliber automatic and two clips of ammunition. They were fastened inside his slacks waist band, unseen beneath a shirt and light jacket.

Abby gave him a kiss on the cheek as he left the terminal to board his flight. She stood at a large window and watched Bret climb into the Nomad. In ten minutes the high-winged aircraft sped down the runway and became airborne. Abby held Bret's ticket for the Air France flight to Medellín. She'd promised to return it to Bouchard after the Curaçao flight became airborne.

As she glanced at a departure schedule monitor nearby, it showed the Air France flight #109 would leave Sint Maarten in less than an hour, reaching Medellín an hour before Bret landed in Curaçao. *Still*, she thought, *that's how Johnson wants it.* Abby couldn't fault the man for being cautious.

She hurried outside the terminal in search of a public telephone, and located a phone booth. Abby pulled the small Enos-Schnaar Burst/Scrambler phone connector from her **BYE-BYE** shopping bag, and snapped it onto the receiver. Abby dropped two U.S. quarters into a change slot and dialed police headquarters in Marigot, St. Martin.

A woman answered after two rings. "Marigot Police,"

"I wish to speak with *sous-inspecteur* Bouchard, please."

"He be mos' busy, ma'am. Is someone else can he'p you?"

"He's expecting my call," Abby said. "I am officer Duchamps of the *Sûreté Nationale français*. This is quite important."

"*Certainment*, un moment," the police dispatcher said. The line became quiet, not a note of elevator music.

Fifteen seconds later, under-inspector Bouchard answered. In French, he said, "Miss Duchamps, what a great pleasure for me that you called."

"I would like you to turn on your telephone burst/scrambler device, please."

"Scrambler and burst device?" The tone of Bouchard's voice became wary if not openly distant. "Just a second." A very low-pitched hum suddenly replaced the usual muted tones found on 'open' telephone equipment. "*Alors, mademoiselle* Duchamps. We are secure."

"Thank you. I have information regarding Bret Lamplighter. It could be dangerous if the wrong ears hear what I have to say."

"You believe I am interested in the American?" Bouchard asked.

"I know you are, Henri." The Frenchwoman decided it may relax the police official if she were less formal. "You returned his weapon . . ."

Interrupting, Bouchard said, "Your 48-hours were up. It *was* his pistol."

"Yes, it was. You knew that and you knew he was going to Colombia. Somehow, you were able to discover his plans."

"Your interest, Miss Duchamps. Is it more personal than professional?"

A note of uncertainty in her voice, Abby replied too quickly, "Of course not, *sous-inspecteur*. Mr. Lamplighter and I are both working on the emerald theft."

"You, as a member of the DST, hunt a murderer on French soil," Bouchard said. "The American, as an insurance investigator, must show whether or not the policyholder is innocent of the theft and murder." Pause. "Have I covered all points, *mademoiselle?*"

"Even a layman would understand, now." Too late, Abby hoped she hadn't offended him. "I mean, that's a good summary."

"Hmm, perhaps you should continue with the reason for this call." He sounded irate.

"Henri, Bret, um, Mr. Lamplighter, did not take the flight to Medellín. He took another route, believed safer."

"I know of his flight on ALM Antillean. He did the right thing." The under-inspector didn't seem sarcastic. "We expected him to take another flight."

He doesn't mind? "I see. Um, I have your ticket. I could send it to your office or bring it over when I have a chance."

Bouchard chuckled pleasantly. "That would be delightful, my dear. But I will have Detective Mobley drop by later to get it." The under-inspector paused for a moment. He then said, "Mobley told me you *seemed* very amicable, judging by the split-second he saw you at your door."

"Really, Henri? I'm sorry, but I am not always friendly when strangers appear at my villa entrance. That includes someone saying he is your detective."

"I don't think we need the burst scrambler on any longer, Miss Duchamps. We have covered..."

"Not yet," Abby broke in. "Will Bret be in any danger with the false documents you sent him? He took them to Colombia."

"That's excellent. The documents are genuine cover. He'll have all the police cooperation he needs. I have spoken to Major General Serrano Cadeña, director of the Colombian *Policía Nacional* about him."

"General Serrano? He's one of the most powerful officials in Colombia."

"Considered Number Three in that country, agent Duchamps. And Number One on the "hit lists" of the Colombia cartels and their new partners, the Milan Mafioso."

"You received the Mafia information from Paris, also, *sous-inspecteur?*"

"St. Martin may be what your American calls the 'boondocks'," Bouchard said, "but Paris still includes us on their mailing list."

Slightly flustered, Abby changed the subject. "Bret will be reporting to General Serrano?"

"No, no," Bouchard stressed. "He will report to the *comandante* of Antioquia department in Medellín. He is a *narc*, *mademoiselle* Duchamps, and a colonel in the P.J.R.—the anti-narcotics police."

"But he's looking for proof of an emerald theft, Henri. Why do you have him searching for *narcos*? It is very dangerous for an ex-DEA officer."

"True. However, his many years in the Drug Enforcement Administration will help support this assignment. U.S. DEA personnel are often given advisory positions in Colombia's war on drug lords and terrorism."

"His name, Henri. You gave him an alias—a Spanish name."

"Abby," Bouchard finally called the French DST agent by her first name, "in Colombia, American advisors are often given an alias with their new job."

"But, why...?"

"The drug cartels are far-reaching, *mademoiselle*," Bouchard interrupted. "Without a false identity, the families of these, er, mercenaries would be at great risk."

Abby Duchamps knew this was true. She knew a woman whose husband had taken part in a large drug bust. Their only child was kidnaped, tortured and murdered in response to the raid. "Will Bret be safe working with the Colombian police?"

Bouchard's long pause was answer enough. Finally he said, "He will have more people on his side. He will have a 'license' to conduct more inquiries. He will, nonetheless, be more exposed to the cartels, traffickers and terrorists."

"*Sous-inspecteur,*" Abby began a vastly different issue, "Is Chief DeGroot, um, involved in the emerald theft and murders?" She knew she was out of line, but the tone of Bouchard's note hinted at the Sint Maarten police official.

"You and Lamplighter read what I wrote to you," Bouchard said. "You outrank me in law enforcement, but I must let you extract your own opinions." The line was silent.

"Fair enough, *sous-inspecteur* Bouchard." Abby thought, *For now, let it be. But I am here to investigate a murder. If nothing turns up soon, Bouchard will be cited for concealing evidence.* "*Au revoir*," Sûreté Officer Duchamps said.

"*Au revoir*, Officer Duchamps." The humming stopped.

After the line went dead, Abby distractedly stared down at the phone and its attached portable scrambler. *What will happen to Bret in Colombia?* she wondered. *He wouldn't go to the emerald mine with the police, since it would cause too much suspicion.*

She pushed two blue buttons on each side of the scrambler, releasing it from the phone receiver, and dropped it into her shopping bag. Abby was startled by a young black woman holding a small child, standing outside the booth. Hurriedly, she tucked the scrambler beneath some souvenir T-shirts, next to her MAS 9mm automatic.

Abby pulled the folding door inward and stepped out, carrying the plastic bag with her. The warm air was refreshing compared to the stale heat of the confined booth. Her cotton blouse and shorts clung to her body where she had been sweating. *"Tu peux utiliser la cabine du téléfon, maintenant,"* she told the woman.

The native woman stared at Abby with a blank expression. "M'um, I don' talk no ot'er speech from Englis'."

Damn, this is the Dutch side, Abby thought. "Sorry, just said I'm through using the phone."

"I be waitin' t'talk t'*you*, m'um."

"If it's about a flight, I'm sure someone inside the terminal could . . ."

"Mistah Johns'n, he ask me to d'rect you to him."

"Johnson wants to speak with me?" *Has to be Bret's Johnson,* she thought.

The younger woman nodded as she shifted the infant on her hip. "He say is ver' 'portant you and he chat, m'um."

"Where is he?"

"He close by. Park'n place nex' t'highway," she turned her head toward the nearby Airport-Philipsburg road.

How did he know where to find me? Abby decided: "Let's see him," she said, and followed the petite native woman and child. Over the shoulder of its mother, the child curiously stared back at the darkly-tanned European woman.

Abby glanced at her watch. It was time for the Air France flight to Medellín to take off. It was fortunate Bret had taken the earlier flight. Abby reached into the shopping bag and inched the 9mm pistol closer to the top. *Don't know who to trust any more. Girl looks okay, but can't take chances.*

"There be de car, m'um," the young woman pointed a finger indicating a tiny green Subaru M-80, a fitting size for the island's narrow roads. The automobile was not in a parking slot, but sat in the middle of a main driving lane. A lone figure in the vehicle sat behind the steering wheel.

"That's Johnson?" Abby nodded toward the person in the car. She couldn't make out the person's features because of the sun's glare on the windshield.

"Ay', he be waitin fo' you t'chat wi' him in de car."

"Are you a friend of his?"

"I be his 'woman'," she declared with a big smile. "Johnson he ver' good mon."

Bret had said Johnson's okay, she thought, *but why doesn't he come out to talk with me?* Cautious, she stared at the car for several moments, and stood her ground. Friend or not, she wasn't going to walk any closer. "Go ask him to come over here," she told the young woman as she continued to gaze at the vehicle.

There was no response. Abby quickly glanced around, but there was no sign of the black woman and her child. *Merde*, she cursed herself. *I walked right up to a trap.* Abby squinted at the person in the small vehicle. *Bret had told me Johnson was short. The man in the car sits too high.* She inched backwards, her right hand reaching for the top of the bag.

"Stop," came a shout from the little car. "Do not move, anus of a she-jackal." The door began to push open.

Middle-Eastern accent, Abby recognized. *One of the Iranian terrorists helping Colombia's drug and smuggling cartels?* The door continued to move outward. Abby's hand was already slipping into the opening of the shopping bag. She continued to stare at the man in the car, hoping he wouldn't notice her slow-motion actions. His face came into view as he started to lean out of the Subaru.

Swarthy. Black mustache and hair. Seems familiar. Suddenly, his left hand appeared through the open window. He clutched a deadly Micro-Uzi submachine pistol. Abby knew the ten-inch long 9mm weapon fired an incredible 1,200 rounds per minute. The submachine gun had a 20-round clip attached, probably to help its portability.

"Revenge is mine, stinking whore," the killer screamed. He propped the weapon on the car's lower window frame. "You and the Yankee bastard die today as one!"

Abby dropped her hand into the bag and shouted, "You must trust your life to an Israeli weapon, you filthy swine!" She felt the cold steel of the MAS 1950 against her fingers.

Ahmad al-Majid was a crazed man. He shrieked with rage and wrenched himself from the car. The injured leg buckled when his foot met the asphalt. His Micro-Uzi twisted toward the sky as the unsteady Iranian terrorist squeezed its trigger.

The slugs from the Uzi snapped loudly above Abby's head as she dropped to the scorching asphalt. Her finger was on the familiar MAS trigger, although the pistol still lay within the plastic and cloth. She swung pistol and bag toward the Iranian, as he began to lower the submachine pistol toward her, and Abby pulled the trigger. A head shot. Two shots to the chest. Another to the head. The lifeless killer dropped to the pavement. And suddenly Abby knew, remembered . . . this was the man who'd survived the attack on the beach. Bret had shot him in the leg, and that was the terrorist's fatal flaw.

She slowly rose from the hot asphalt. No one had arrived at the scene, though she could hear shouts that seemed to be getting nearer.

What had the bastard yelled? *Both* Bret and I die today? "Shit," she shouted, "could he have sabotaged the Air France jet?"

She turned and raced for the terminal, a half-mile away. The flight was due to take off any moment. As she neared the drop-off area in front of the main entrance to Princess Juliana Airport, a high-pitched whine sounded at the far end of the runway. Abby shuddered with fright. She saw the familiar Air France diagonal red and blue stripes on the rudder of the swiftly-accelerating 737. The large aircraft reached speed and the nose turned toward the heavens. Air France flight #109 immediately began to bank left over the crowded beach of Simpson Bay Lagoon. As the landing gear started to retract, tiny servos hidden within the wheel wells triggered two detonators. The exploding Semtex *plastique* sounded like a thousand thunderclaps. A second fiery eruption of high octane jet fuel split both wings where they attached to the fuselage. Small portions of intact steel broke into still thousands more pieces as they struck the beach and shallow water. All forty-four passengers and crew died instantly. It took a few moments longer before seventeen sunbathers and swimmers perished.

Chapter Thirteen

"He was an Iranian terrorist, *sous-inspecteur*," Abby said in French. She sat in a small, crowded conference room Air France offered the local authorities. "He must be the 'shooter' who escaped in a speedboat from Sunshine Pointe Resort's beach."

Bouchard nodded, partly in agreement, partly from fatigue. "He profiles Middle-Eastern, Abby. Still, you and Lamplighter said both men wore masks." The under-inspector had been at the airport since 6:05 P.M., twenty minutes after he was alerted of the disaster. Chief Horst DeGroot, on whose territory the airplane crashed, had appeared at the scene briefly, then had left ashen-faced.

Abby shook her head, trying to rid it of the horrible sight of the large disintegrating aircraft. "Bret and I were certain he'd been winged. We put that in our written report to you, Henri. And, and, that *hideux* man in the car park had a fresh bullet wound in the back of his left thigh. When his leg folded, I got the jump on him." She paused briefly, then said, "He spoke of revenge, of avenging something that happened earlier. It had to be his bungled assault at Sunshine Pointe." Abby kept brushing at her soiled and slightly-torn blouse and shorts. It had been easy to kill the terrorist when she'd had no other choice, but that didn't ease the queasy feeling in her stomach.

"You may be right," Bouchard admitted. "We telexed and faxed his photo to our agents throughout the world. It won't take long." Henri had been at Princess Juliana Airport for two exhausting hours. Disaster and rescue crews from St. Martin, Sint Maarten, Anguilla and St. Barth worked feverishly to bag the dead and tend the injured. Body parts not recovered on the beach were still being found and labeled as they washed ashore. Federal airline investigators from the Netherlands, America, France and Colombia were descending on the island to join in the grim crash probe.

"You never saw the black woman and child before today?" he continued.

"Never."

"You said earlier she called herself 'Johnson's woman'. Did you ask for her I.D.?"

"It seemed pointless at the time. She knew my name. Even said she knew Johnson. I believed she'd say she brought no identification if I asked her for it." Vacantly, she uttered, "Odd how I trusted her, probably because she carried that child."

One of the Air France office staff walked through the open door and approached Henri, then leaned over and whispered into his ear. He listened attentively, then thanked the woman. He waited several seconds, forming his next sentence as well as he could. "My men picked up Horst DeGroot at Grand Case Airport a short time ago. They reported he'd just purchased a one-way plane ticket for Fort-de-France."

"Why Martinique?"

"Near by. No passport or visa needed from St. Martin." Grinning slightly he said, "Maybe a safe house there for corrupt police chiefs."

Abby smiled for the first time in hours. "That seems to clinch his involvement."

"I believe so. Probably got in over his head."

"Looks like it. He must have loved the bribes and perks in Philipsburg. But when his partners began murdering and bombing, he wanted out."

An inquiry into DeGroot's activities during his tenure as Chief would be held by Netherlands Antilles and Dutch authorities.

Abby continued to work on the stack of paperwork she was required to fill out. Her shooting in self-defense of the terrorist required completion of multiple pages of reports and statements. She had to provide an exact description of the native woman. Also, as a DST *Sûreté* agent on the scene, she was required to give a precise description of the airplane explosion and aftermath.

Two of the three 'other' *Sûreté* officers presently on the island walked into the room. Abby looked over at Paul Dornier and Louis Chatelaine. She wondered if Dornier would have Karl remain at the crash scene, photographing every grain of sand on Simpson Bay Lagoon's South Beach.

"Ah, *mademoiselle* Duchamps." Dornier affected surprise at seeing Abby typing her endless report forms in dirty and ripped clothing. "Pity you cannot be on the beach where all the excitement is."

"I've had more than my share of 'excitement' today, *m'sieur* Dornier."

"So I heard. Killed the bugger with your first shot, then continued with three more. Seems awfully like overkill, wouldn't you say?"

Fortunately, only four people in the small conference room spoke fluent French. Abby quickly stood and confronted the DST team leader. "No wonder you needed your great-uncle to bribe your way through Le Mans. You'd have no idea of the proper techniques for saving your skinny ass in a life-threatening situation."

"You can't talk to me that way, Duchamps. You're dressed like an American vagrant and speak like a Left Bank *prostituée*. When Marseille hears . . ."

" . . . when Marseille hears about what you call an investigation, they'll have you cleaning *pissoirs* in the Federal Building with your mascara brush."

"Stop this right now!" Bouchard ordered. He thrust himself between Abby and Dornier, gently pushing her back by the shoulders. "You are both professional officers. You will not act this way, in public or private." Most of the people in the room spoke only English or a few words of Dutch. A quarrel between two members of the French *Sûreté Nationale*, nevertheless, interrupted all typing, computer processing and phone conversations.

"You'll hear from . . ." Dornier began.

"Be quiet," Louis Chatelaine interrupted his supervisor. "*Allons*." He grabbed Dornier's arm and led him from the room. Only slowly did the fifteen or twenty police, media reps and officials resume their grim jobs of attending to the plane crash.

Henri Bouchard draped an arm over Abby's shoulder. "Try to forget that idiot. He'll never understand," Henri snarled, gnashing his teeth in anger.

He stood and told the agent, "It's time you go back to your villa to get some sleep. Finish the paperwork tomorrow." He took her hand, gave her the shopping bag, and led her from the room.

"Maybe I do need some sleep, Henri. I'm not thinking very well right now."

Bouchard smiled. They walked from the terminal where the under-inspector motioned to the driver of a police van.

The driver parked at the curb, got out and walked around to the passenger side.

"Mobley, you know where Officer Duchamps is staying. Drive her there as quickly as possible," Henri instructed.

"It be my pleasure, *sous-'specteur*. She some brave lady to look down Uzi barrel and kill Iran terr'ist," Mobley said.

Once Abby was seated in the van, Bouchard walked around to speak with Mobley. "Lieutenant, remain outside her villa. Make certain no harm comes to her," he ordered.

* * *

Less than fifty yards from the crash site of Air France flight #109, at Number 68 Airport Road, stood the Laguna restaurant. Usually, the Simpson Bay Lagoon setting of the Italian restaurant was serene and casually elegant. This day, rescue and cleanup workers labored feverishly only yards from two men sitting at a veranda table.

"Little ruckus on our beach, eh Rupe?" Claude Tomasso smiled.

Rupert Morgan was always on the alert around this man. "Look like mebbe big sha'k in l'goon water, Mistah T'masso. No one want go in swimmin' dees day." He tried to smile at his joke, but his disfigured face more closely resembled one of the airplane crash victims.

"Shack? Oh yes, shark. That's *très drôle*, Rupe." It reminded Claude of the scene in "Jaws" where thousands of people lingered on the beach . . . afraid to go in the water. "Which speck of sand out there is our Mr. Lamplighter?" Tomasso chuckled.

"If Lam'light on plane, he sho 'nuf parta l'goon beach, suh." Rupert took a quick swallow of the cola drink he'd ordered.

Tomasso stared hard at his hired assassin, smile now gone. "Rupert," his voice deadly, "you and the damn Arab *did* go to the Air France boarding gate, didn't you?" Tomasso sat up so straight in his chair the vertebrae in his back made a popping noise.

"Me 'n de A-rab go t'boardin' gate like you say, Mistah T'masso." Morgan's stomach immediately surged, not unlike the onset of dysentery. "You know what crowd of people be in waitin' room. Me an' al-M'jid stand nex' t'man who check boardin' pass, but we neva sees Lam'light."

Tomasso stared. Then he calmed slightly. He knew what Morgan was talking about. The waiting room of Princess Juliana Airport was built before many tourists 'discovered' Sint Maarten/St. Martin. It is about one-fifth the size suitable to handle incoming and departing passengers. There were only three boarding 'gates,' each a windowed door opening onto the tarmac.

"You didn't watch the other doors to the airfield?" Tomasso asked. The other boarding doors were usually open for anyone to walk outside. Often, scores of passengers wandered around the asphalt tarmac, searching for their planes.

"We watch close as pos'ble, Mistah T'masso. But we don' see no Lam'light."

Stupid-ass morons, Claude swore to himself. "We're going

back to the airport, Rupe," Tomasso proclaimed. "I'll make sure that sonuvabitch was on the flight."

With Claude in the lead, the two men noisily marched out of the restaurant. Tomasso threw a five-dollar bill near the cash register and continued through the front door. The *maître d'* was elated that the two men had finally gone. Now the Laguna could close for the evening.

Crossing Airport Road was a simple task. It was still closed to traffic, and several large searchlights illuminated the entire beachfront. Tomasso and Morgan tramped across the bus and taxi park and into the terminal. "We're going to the Air France ticket counter, Rupe. I know people there."

"Yas suh, Mistah T'masso," his winded companion blurted out. They'd nearly run from the restaurant into Princess Juliana Airport's terminal.

There was no doubt where the Air France ticket and information desks were. A noisy crowd of passengers, TV cameramen, police officers and men and women of the media stood around. Claude and Rupert headed straight for an Air France official speaking into a two-way radio. A St. Martin *gendarme* lieutenant, dressed in khakis and the familiar black and yellow round pillbox cap, stepped in front of Tomasso.

"No one is to go beyond our line, *monsieur*," the lieutenant said. He pointed to nearly a dozen other gendarmes and native police who formed a human barricade.

"I am a personal friend of Felix Moreaux, lieutenant." Claude nodded toward the man speaking on the portable radio. "I must ask him about the fate of a very close acquaintance of mine."

The St. Martin police officer knew Tomasso by sight and reputation, and also of the man's influence throughout the 36-square mile island. He'd read reports about Claude Tomasso's shadowy activities, mostly hidden behind the pretense of an upstanding Philipsburg businessman. The Mercedes dealership in Sint Maarten's capital city was only one of Tomasso's thinly-veiled enterprises. Finally, the gendarme decided, "Wait here, *monsieur*. I will speak with Moreaux." He spun around and walked to the airline official.

Tomasso folded his arms across his chest. He wasn't used to being told to wait. People, police included, jumped at his every command. *One day I will have Bouchard and his police force jumping through hoops for me*, he thought. Claude saw the Marigot *gendarme* turn and point to him.

The police officer strolled back to Tomasso and said, "Moreaux will see you. Your, er, friend is to stay here." The *gendarme* lieutenant knew the name and complete history of Rupert Morgan. His file at Marigot police headquarters was two inches thick.

"Stay behind the young lieutenant's police line, Rupe. I'll find out about our mutual friend." Tomasso brushed past the gendarme, 'accidentally' bumping his shoulder against one of the officer's uniform epaulets.

Rupert was proud that Mistah T'masso was so respected and so feared.

"Felix," Tomasso extended his hand to the annoyed Air France executive, "I'm so sorry this visit is held under such dreadful conditions."

"Thank you for your concern, Claude. How may I be of help to you?" Felix Moreaux owed Tomasso too many favors to suggest this was not a good time to visit. His British racing green Aston Martin 6.3 Liter was practically a gift from Claude. Perhaps he could now repay some of his dues.

"I have a good friend who was booked on flight #109, Felix. I was to see him off, but arrived here after the, er, terrible accident." Tomasso had worked out the scenario while he strode across Airport Road with Morgan.

"That is tragic, Claude. But it was not an accident. It was a sickening terrorist bombing." Felix nervously switched off the squelch as someone tried to contact him on the hand-held two-way radio.

"Beastly," Tomasso replied. There was a very brief silence before he continued. "I must relay my sentiments to Bret's dear wife, Felix. However, since I was unable to see him off, I must be absolutely certain he boarded the plane." Another short pause. "You could imagine her trauma if I phoned, er, Emma my condolences, then she found out he was alive, after all." Tomasso thought he'd handled his story remarkably well.

"Certainly, Claude. Let's check our computers."

"Thank you, Felix." Claude followed the official from Air France as he began to walk toward the rear of the ticket counters. He noted that Rupert stood next to the Marigot *gendarme* lieutenant, as ordered.

"Here we are," Moreaux said as they reached the first computer terminal on the ticket counter. "I'll pull up flight #109," Felix said. He pushed several keys. A screen popped up that read: Air France Flight No. 109, Philipsburg to Medellín. Beneath it, covering the entire width of the screen, was a bright, blinking red warning message: SECURED FLIGHT DATA. ENTER PASSWORD AND SECURITY CLEARANCE. Moreaux tapped several additional keys. A new screen appeared to show a list of flight 109's passengers.

Neither Tomasso nor Morgan noticed Bouchard escort Abby down the hall to the front entrance. The large crowd of bystanders and police had caused the area around Air France's counter to be loud and chaotic.

"Great," Claude said when he viewed the computer image. "They're in alphabetical order, so Lamplighter would probably be on the next screen." He felt his heart beat rise through his temples.

"Correct," Felix said and tapped another key. "That's odd," Felix muttered as he studied the monitor. "There's no Lamplighter listed for this flight."

"Impossible," Tomasso raised his voice louder than he intended. "I mean, that's wonderful, but I definitely know it was Air France flight #109."

"This *is* the correct day, Claude? We have a flight 109 every day but Sunday."

"Absolutely," Claude stressed, as he pulled a slip of paper

from his trousers pocket. "Here, see for yourself." He stuck the yellow sheet in front of Moreaux' face.

Sweat popped out on the airline manager's forehead. He pushed several other keys and asked, "Where is Lamplighter's home? I'll sort by city."

"Home?" *Um, home. Ah, yes*, Claude remembered. "He's from Chicago."

Felix tapped another key and then typed in the word Chicago. "Nothing," he said. "No one on the flight listed their home town as Chicago." Moreaux thought a moment. "Your friend may have taken another flight or airline, Claude. You have a hell of a lucky friend."

"Yes, yes indeed," Tomasso managed to smile as he silently tortured his informant at the Marigot police station. "Er, Felix," Claude's voice was calmer as he managed to think clearer. "What about 'no-shows'? Surely you have a list of ticketed passengers who didn't show."

"I don't see why . . . ?"

"Indulge me, Felix," Claude spoke with the slightest hint of a threat. "It would show me we've covered all areas."

"Certainly," Felix nodded. He'd already begun to type on the keyboard. "Here it is, *mon ami*," Moreaux smiled. Both men stared at a nearly empty screen.

"We had two fortunate no-shows for flight 109," the Air France representative said as he looked at the monitor. "Mrs. Elizabeth Smalley of Flagstaff, Arizona and a Señor Manuel Parra Vega from Medellín, Colombia."

Claude Tomasso looked up from the screen. "Did they *ever* show up, Felix?"

Nervously, Moreaux pushed a key that scrolled to a "Comments and Remarks" screen. He was pleasantly surprised to see notations left by diligent Air France employees. The screen showed the following messages:

> **1.** Mrs. Smalley arrived by taxi five minutes after #109 accident. She informed staff delay caused by cab

flat tire. Smalley fainted; immediately taken to Trinity Hospital, Philipsburg.

2. Señor Parra's lost ticket was found by a Marigot police officer one hour after flight 109 crash. Parra was said to be resting after hearing of his good luck.

Neither Tomasso nor Moreaux spoke as they read the data on the screen.

Claude thanked his friend and unsteadily turned away, shaking his head. Rupert and Ahmad al-Majid had managed to totally screw up a finely-tuned double assassination. He strode toward Rupe, trying to think of a suitably-ghastly punishment for the twice-failed assassin. Tomasso's eyes withdrew from Morgan long enough to study the face of the Marigot *gendarme* lieutenant. *Behind his eyes, the bastard's laughing at me*, Tomasso imagined.

In point of fact, it wasn't Claude's imagination.

Chapter Fourteen

The Milky Way is an immense band of light in our galaxy. It generates the radiance from many millions of far-off stars. Normally, the brilliant display appears when all earthly surroundings are totally dark and pollution free. Perhaps this is why Bret was surprised when he stepped from the twin-turbo Nomad. Although the moon had not yet risen, Curaçao Central Airport glowed with light from the brilliant constellation. Willemstad, twelve miles southeast, was too far away to provide ambient light.

"Colonel Parra?" a captain in American camouflage military utility garb asked as he strode up to Bret.

"Are you acquainted with Johnson?" Bret didn't give him his alias.

"I know Johnson. Also, the business you have here this evening." He hesitated momentarily. "May I examine your passport and identification, please?"

"When's my flight to Barranquilla?" Bret pulled the documents from his flight bag and handed them to the officer.

"Immediately, sir." The captain closely scrutinized the identification. "Would you care to freshen up before we leave?"

"Just a quick bathroom break and a soft drink."

The captain smiled. "Come this way, colonel. Anything for the Colombian anti-narcotics police." Finished comparing Bret's face with the photos on his passport and I.D. card, he handed them back as they walked. Bret couldn't help notice at least three other figures walking along with them, at a distance of fifteen or twenty feet.

"Don't I get to see your identification, captain . . . and those of your friends?"

"No," the man answered. "There are no friends."

By now the Nomad and its other passengers were nearly out of sight. In fact, Curaçao's airport terminal was now nothing but a misty memory. "My luggage?" Bret suddenly remembered. "I had two bags other than this . . ."

"They're safe," the captain said.

Bret squinted at the 'shadows' accompanying them. He was certain two of them held his bags. He was also certain each ghostly form held a weapon in their hand.

The only light on the airfield now came directly from the heavens. "How far . . . ?"

"Almost there, colonel."

Bret tried to look at his watch, but it was too dark to make out the time.

"Nearly twenty-hundred hours," the captain offered. "Your plane landed at nineteen-thirty-five hours. Stiff headwinds."

A gate appeared so quickly it startled him. A high fence topped with concertina wire disappeared into the darkness on either side of the gate. The captain pulled a small card from his shirt pocket and pressed it against a metallic plate. Bret heard a 'click' and the gate swung free very, *very* slowly "Something wrong with the gate?"

"Perfect condition, Colonel Parra. If someone were running from guards or dogs from the inside, they'd never have time to get out." At least two minutes passed before the captain said, "Squeeze through, now. There's enough room." As he slipped inside the gate and fence, Bret sensed his shadowy escorts slip inside, too.

"This way, colonel." The captain continued to walk at the same brisk pace as before. "There's your transportation to Colombia," he pointed to a large silhouette parked about fifty yards from them.

"I'd swear that's the outline of a DC-3."

"Good eyes, colonel. 'Cept that military version's called a C-47."

A small night light beckoned the band of travelers to a wooden front door. The captain used his 'credit card' to gain entrance. The interior was small and looked like any of the old wooden army barracks Bret occupied throughout his military days. A single, dusty light bulb hung from a cord in the middle of the room, putting out no more than twenty-five watts of illumination.

"Shades of Fort Leonard Wood," Bret mumbled. "Everything changes and nothing changes."

"You wanted to use the latrine." The officer handed Bret the little plastic card. "Use this on that door." He pointed across the room.

Bret took the card and walked across the bleached-out wooden floor. It looked as though thousands of military recruits had worn the surface down to within a fraction of its original depth. Bret heard the latrine door click as he placed the keycard against the black metallic plate.

Suddenly Bret stepped through Lewis Carroll's "Looking-Glass." "What th' hell?" were all the words he could utter when he walked into the latrine.

"Feel like you just stepped into another dimension?" the escort captain asked.

Concrete stairs began descending about ten feet in front of him. To his right was the entrance to an elevator, a gauge showed three levels. Spread out in front of him and downward, seemingly stretching off to infinity, was a huge, modernistic war room. At least, "war room" was the definition Bret gave the scene.

"The set of 'Dr. Strangelove'," Bret marveled.

The captain nodded and said, "More like Cheyenne Mountain."

Bret looked at him and nodded. "You're right. I've been there several times. That's why my first impression was 'war room'."

The headquarters of NORAD lies deep within granite Cheyenne Mountain, several miles southwest of Colorado Springs.

"Do I take it this is a Latin American version of Cheyenne Mountain?" Bret saw uniforms of dozens of Central and South American nations worn by the men and women working around him.

"Your security clearance allows me to say affirmative, Colonel Parra. Your Top Secret classification from the DEA and French *Sûreté Nationale* ranks you among the highest levels on board tonight."

Bret had wanted to avoid the question of his security level. *Somebody did lots of wheeling and dealing to get me in good with the DEA, again,* he thought. "Do you search for drug smugglers through this facility?" Bret felt the captain believed his name and rank were cover for tracking down *narcotraficantes*.

"Our secondary role," the captain nodded. "First is the same as at Cheyenne—in our case, prevent enemy military action against Latin American nations."

"Much luck in the, um, secondary function?"

"In the last five years, 37 million kilos of raw cocaine and more than six hundred thousand kilos of heroin."

Bret stared at the captain. "That's, it's unbelievable."

"When your men . . . er, excuse me. When the DEA advisors in Colombia conduct a raid, who do you think gives them precise coordinates?"

"You have that capability?"

"To within one meter. Normally, we'll also provide data on the number of *narcos* the DEA or government troops will find at the site."

"Satellites?"

"Radar sats, sonar sats, ultra hi-res video sats. Then we have AWACs, helicopters, light planes, land vehicles, you name it."

"Captain, not to change the subject . . ." Bret glanced around.

"A man in search of a restroom." The captain looked past Bret toward the left side of the landing. "Charlie, show our friend to the men's room."

A 'shadow' appeared and beckoned Bret to follow him. They walked down the steps. "A restroom's just off the next landing, Mr. Lamplighter."

Bret walked down at least four concrete steps before he realized the man he followed had called him by his real name. *Th' hell with it*, he decided. *They probably know the reason for my trip to Colombia.* The two men reached the second landing and Bret's escort turned the same direction as the wooden barracks door one flight up. There was a door, but it was remarkably thick steel entry that opened with a keycard.

As the door lock clicked open, a mechanical voice sounded from a speaker next to the metal pad: "Two small arms weapons and ammunition detected. Take necessary steps." Barely two seconds passed before the speaker began again: "Two small arms weapons . . ." Bret's companion pressed the keycard against the pad once more and the message ceased.

"We know you're carrying, Mr. Lamplighter. Disregard our tattletale alarm."

"Blabbermouth," Bret scolded the speaker as they passed by it.

"Feel like a new man," Bret said as he strolled from the bathroom into the adjoining lounge. Both his escort and the captain sat on chairs. "Think I need two escorts back?"

"Hardly, colonel. We received a message from St. Martin I believe you'll be interested in," and he handed a sheet of paper to Bret.

"Jesus Christ," Bret exclaimed as he finished reading the brief note. "One-Oh-Nine's the flight I was booked on several hours ago." He glanced at the top of the sheet. "Sent from 'S.M. Johnson' five minutes ago. Received by CENTRO. What's that?"

"The acronym for this facility, similar to NORAD at Cheyenne. No need to know the precise words . . . they're in Spanish."

Bret nodded and read through the message again. "Initial conclusion suggests plastique detonated as the landing gear began to retract. Shit! No chance for the passengers and crew with a full load of jet fuel."

"Barely made it across Airport Road," the captain said. "Killed more than a dozen people on the lagoon beach."

Bret shook his head at the captain's remarks. Suddenly, his mood changed. "Thank God," Bret said as he read the last sentence. It stated: "*Sûreté* partner of Colonel Parra safe after negating Iranian bombing suspect."

"Um, colonel," the captain hesitantly began, "in 'spook' language, does 'negating' mean what I think it does?"

Although Bret didn't smile, his face brightened barely. "Exactly what you think, captain. Even his handler wouldn't recognize him now."

"Good," the captain nodded. "Johnson never says anything about one's organization or background, colonel. He did say, though, that you seem to have a shitload of enemies . . . *really* bad actors."

"I've managed to provoke someone's anger, captain. No doubt about it."

"Take this little keychain, Mr. Lamplighter," the captain finally acknowledged Bret's real name. "The plastic portion shows a colonel's rank on one side and the Colombian flag on the other. Carrying would be appropriate for you . . . beyond suspicion." He handed Bret the novelty made of black plastic, with a short chain link attached through a hole near one corner.

"Thanks, captain. I can put my luggage keys and the key to my villa in St. Martin on it. Sorry I don't have anything for you."

The captain smiled. "It's a super-sensitive, silicon-battery radio transmitter. We'll be able to track you by satellite wherever you go. It's virtually undetectable, since there are no metallic, electronic or moving parts in it."

"You think I need constant monitoring?"

"Yes, judging from Johnson's stories about a hotel in Philipsburg and your own private beach, not to mention the plane crash."

"Even if something happened to me in Colombia, you wouldn't know about it in time to help." Bret leisurely pulled the monitoring device around the chain like a supplicant with his rosary.

"True, that's why we have a secondary use for the monitor . . . its destruction."

Bret studied the captain for several seconds. "By destroying it, my 'blip' on your screen would disappear. You'd know I managed to get myself into trouble."

"Damn, Charlie," the captain looked at his aide. "Think the colonel's caught on."

"Yeah, except who is the cavalry deep in Colombia?"

"We have operatives there who are trustworthy, Mr. Lamplighter. We'd do our utmost to get them to your last known grid coordinates. From there, well, it's finger-crossing time." The captain paused briefly, then said, "We know from experience that our men can be relied on. *Most* anti-narcotics police are okay, but *mordida*—bribery—turns too many law enforcement officials to the side of the drug lords."

The captain lifted the receiver of a phone on a table next to him. He pushed three numbers and said, "Julio, give me the coordinates on four-one-eight-seven." He listened to the response and said, "Confirming you have twelve degrees, twelve minutes north by sixty-eight degrees, fifty-nine minutes west. *Gracias, amigo.*" The captain replaced the phone and told Bret, "Your keychain fob is perfectly configured. The coordinates given by that technician are those of this facility, colonel."

"And I'm number forty-one eighty-seven. Is that how many of these gadgets are out there right now?" Bret still worried the piece of plastic and its small chain.

"Hardly. We'd be hard pressed trying to monitor that many travelers. Our numbering system is more exotic," the captain smiled. "Forty-one degrees north and eighty-seven degrees west are the longitude and latitude of your kinda town, Chicago."

The captain rocked forward and lifted himself from the chair. "Colonel Parra, it's time we cranked up those two old Wright radials on the C-47."

The last leg of the journey to Barranquilla was about to begin.

Chapter Fifteen

The pounding in Abby's head became so acute she abruptly sat up in bed, rubbing her eyes to relieve the endless rhythm. Light shown in through partially open wooden slats at the bedroom window and outer door. *So damn real*, she thought. Suddenly the rapping began again, clearly someone knocking at the front door of her villa.

Awakening slowly after the preceding night's destruction and death, she swung her legs off the sheet and staggered onto wobbly legs. Pulling her pistol from a bedside table, she made her way to the door. Standing to one side Abby stared out through a slat she'd carefully lifted several millimeters. First, she saw that Detective Mobley's car was gone from the spot it had been parked much of the night and early morning. Abby recognized her visitor as a fellow *Sûreté* officer.

"*Un moment*, Karl," Abby whispered to the Frenchman. She turned to find something to put on.

"Do not hurry, Abby," Karl Kronstein replied. He rubbed the palm of his hand through thinning hair.

She pulled on a thigh-length red T-shirt, returned to the door and unlocked it. Karl began to speak, but Abby put an index finger to her lips and motioned for her guest to follow. She led the middle-aged man out onto the patio at the rear of her villa. "We should be able to talk here," she said.

"Your place is bugged?"

"The American and I probably got all of them, but why take chances?"

Karl smiled vaguely, then nodded. "I wanted to get in touch with you earlier, but Dornier keeps a close watch on Louis and me." He dropped to his hands and knees and checked beneath the metal patio table and chairs, as if examining the bottom of furniture was a normal, everyday occurrence. He then got up and sat opposite Abby. Without skipping a beat, he continued. "Paul even has the three of us sleeping in the same room at our hotel."

Smiling, Abby said, "I'd wondered why none of you contacted me here. We do work for the same Interior Minister."

"Typically bizarre reasoning. Said we were on different assignments, so we shouldn't interfere with each other."

"Until last night." She became serious.

"Heard about it from Louis." Karl shook his head. "Behavior like that could finally get him bounced from the Bureau."

"Nice thought, but his connections got him in and should keep him in."

Karl nodded. He stretched for a brown briefcase he'd set on the table, zipped it open and reached inside, fumbling around for several seconds.

"Lunch time?" Abby joked. In France, briefcases and valises were more often used to carry bread and meat than business papers.

Karl smiled and dragged out several letter-size articles, turned them around and set them on the table in front of Abby. "Know them?"

Abby looked at four blown-up black and white photos of Claude Tomasso and Rupert Morgan. Two of the shots were taken at a restaurant table near a beach, since the angle showed sand and water. The other two photos were at a location all too familiar, the Air France counters at Princess Juliana Airport.

"Bastards," she murmured.

"Thought you might say something like that," Karl said as he stared off at the blue-green waters of Nettle Bay. "Beautiful spot you have here."

Abby grunted at his remark. "Glad you could document this, Karl." She stared at the restaurant shots for several more seconds, then said, "This café?"

"That's the Laguna. The aircraft missed the restaurant by less than ten meters as it hit the beach and lagoon. About 40 customers and staff were in there at the time."

"You know Tomasso and Morgan, Karl?" Abby wanted to crumple the photos.

"Yeah. In fact, Morgan was recording you and the American with a shotgun mike when I first saw him."

"When we were at the jewelry store?"

"Behind it. He probably heard and taped everything the two of you said when you were digging through a big trash bin."

"Dumpster, Karl. That's American for trash bin." Abby smiled slightly. "And," she added, "'the American' is named Bret Lamplighter."

"Sorry I'm acting rather Gallic. A bad trait for someone whose parents came from Germany." He had been attracted to Abby since they'd worked an assignment together on Corsica three years before, but they had parted ways after the case was closed.

"Speaking of the dumpster, Karl . . . how did you happen to see Tomasso's hit man tape-recording Bret and me?"

"That's the reason, other than the photos, that I came to talk with you." Karl was actually squirming. "Dornier had Louis and me photographing and recording you and the Am . . . , er, Lamplighter behind the Bombay." He stared at his briefcase, unable to look Abby in the eye.

"Shit, Karl!" Abby exclaimed. "We're all supposed to be on the same side."

"You and I know that. Louis Chatelaine knows it, too."

" . . . but that, that twit-in-charge wants to create conflict between us." Abby was angry with the situation, but realized things wouldn't change. "He said we're on different assignments? It all stems from the same crime, Karl . . . the murder of the emerald buyer on Anguilla. That brought me into the picture to check out Lamplighter."

"Right. Then, because he began stepping on Colombian toes, and Iranian toes, and Tomasso's toes," Karl jabbed an index finger at the photos on the table, "we were assigned to investigate the deaths of St. Martin citizens."

Abby stared at him a moment before saying, "How many French nationals were on flight one-oh-nine?"

"Unfortunately, there were eleven French St. Martin citizens and four French citizens. None of the dead on the beach were French as far as is known." Karl began to drum his fingers on the metal table top.

"Are we officially in on the aircraft bombing investigation?"

"Paris has yet to notify us either way. Dornier phoned DST headquarters when we heard of the bombing."

"Odd. We're right on the scene, yet we're being bypassed by headquarters." The apparent oversight puzzled Abby. "Could someone have neglected to report the fact that four experienced DST personnel are at the scene of a terrorist strike?"

"Impossible, Abby," Karl shook his head. "Everyone was talking about you being here to shadow the American before Dornier, Chatelaine and I were sent."

"Paris DST knows what Marseille DST is up to?"

"Almost before it happens," Karl said. "Sometimes *literally* before it happens."

Abby pondered the information, occasionally shuffling through the photographs. "We're going to begin investigating, Karl."

"My team has already been investigating."

"You know what I'm talking about. You've been eavesdropping on Lamplighter and me, for God's sake."

"Yeah. Doesn't seem right to be watching my own people, at least, *person*."

"Now you understand," Abby said. "Does Dornier know where you are?"

"I was at the lagoon until four in the morning. Got to the hotel at a quarter past four. Developed these photos until five. Set the alarm for eight, told Chatelaine I was going for breakfast." Kronstein hesitated a few moments. "Louis said he'd tell Dornier."

"Louis didn't ask when you'd be back?"

"No, but he'd realize I needed several more hours sleep. Three hours hardly does it for me any more."

"We should be finished by noon," Abby said. "Until you came here this morning, Morgan and Tomasso were suspects . . . but nothing else."

"And now?"

"Now we have these photos placing them at the scene of the bombing and at the Air France desk. Probably checking at the ticket counter to see if they killed Bret."

"You could be right, Abby."

"Then you're in?"

"*A coup sûr, mon cher.* Let's get going." *This could help my career*. He just had to be sure not to cross Dornier.

"That's wonderful, Karl. I'll be dressed in only a minute or so." She jumped from her chair and had the T-shirt off before she reached the door into her living room. "Just a few minutes," Karl heard her shout again from within the villa.

Kronstein smiled as he watched Abby's deeply-tanned figure disappear through the doorway. *If I play my cards correctly*, he thought, *I could be heading up my next assignment from Paris.*

It took 20 seconds to find the address of the only Rupert Morgan listed in the Philipsburg phone directory. Abby then asked an aloof Yvonne at the lobby desk to phone for a taxi. After calling a cab company, Yvonne coolly stated that their taxi should arrive at Sunshine Pointe within ten minutes.

Abby's attire was casually touristy . . . a white cropped halter top and a short powder blue tennis skirt. She carried a brown leather handbag with shoulder straps that held her credentials and pistol. Kronstein, on the other hand, looked out of place in the tropical sun with brown trousers and a long-sleeve white dress shirt. At Abby's insistence, he rolled up his sleeves several inches, exposing pasty white forearms. Dornier always insisted his agents be the core of professionalism, no matter how ridiculous they looked.

When the taxi van arrived, she told the driver, "Number twenty-one St. Eustatius Boulevard in Philipsburg, please."

Both DST agents saw the driver's eyebrows arch when he heard their destination. He turned and peered at his passengers. "Sure dees de address you wanta go, m'um?"

She stared at the scribbling she'd made on the note paper. She held it in front of the driver's eyes and asked, "Did I pronounce this correctly?"

"You pr'nunce c'rect," he said after looking at the writing. "D'you know dees mon you gonna visit, m'um?" He still hadn't begun moving his cab.

"Do you know the man at this address?" It was obvious the driver *did* know Morgan, or his reputation, but Abby was curious why.

"I know 'bout Mo'gan. Mos' people here know 'bout dees mon." The cabby began to drive down the resort roadway.

"What do 'people' know about him?" Abby prodded.

The driver said nothing. Karl fidgeted in his seat. The van pulled onto the main highway toward Philipsburg, mingling with the midmorning traffic.

"Is Morgan a man to be feared?" she asked, not yet ready to give up on the taxi driver. "Is he a dangerous man?"

Karl wasn't very conversant in English, but he did understand her questions. He wondered how such a visible criminal could stay out of prison, terrorizing his native islanders. Claude Tomasso was a different matter. He had kept a legitimate front with his businesses, but *he* should also be occupying a jail cell by now.

The taxi descended the narrow, winding road near Dutch Cul de Sac. They passed the only spot on the island that clearly marked the fact that two small territories shared thirty-six square miles. Overlooking Great Key in Simpson Bay Lagoon, an obelisk-shaped boundary monument marked the border. In French and English it said: 'Welcome to Dutch St. Maarten. Please come back to French St. Martin.' Traveling north, the reverse sentiment was carved into the tall stone marker. They were halfway to the home of Rupert Morgan.

Across from the boundary monument, the driver pulled onto the narrow shoulder. Pointing down to the lagoon, he said, "Dat be de place w'ere Air France jet crash."

"Terrible disaster," Abby said as she stared at the crash site. A large area of lagoon water was darkened from oil and fuel that hadn't burned. Dozens of people wearing black waders skimmed metal detectors through the hip deep, dirty water. Officials supervised from vehicles near the beach and two bobbing boats.

"Was de work of ter'rists, m'um?" the driver asked Abby.

"I couldn't know." Abby felt she'd been put on the spot.

"You be French Ter'tory police, I t'ink, m'um. You fer sure knows."

How the hell? she asked herself.

"I looks in mirror an' sees big pistol of your partner."

Looking at Karl, she saw the shoulder holster and butt of his MAS semiautomatic. His cotton shirt was so wet with perspiration it was transparent. Abby said, "Put the pistol in your trouser waist band. Give me the holster."

As they sat by the edge of a sheer drop, Karl pulled off his sweat-soaked shirt. The shoulder holster rested on a sweaty undershirt. He pulled the holster over his head, and slid the pistol from its niche.

"Sorry, Abby," Karl apologized in French. "Didn't think I'd get so hot and sweaty." He handed the soggy holster to Abby, who dumped it into her handbag.

An amused smile replaced the driver's somber look. *Mon soun' French aw'right, but lady soun' an' axe like 'mer'can. She be sure piss 'd off.*

"Driver," Abby said, "it's time we visited Morgan, *n'est ce pas?*"

"*Oui,* m'um," he said with one of the few French words he could handle.

As the taxi stopped near Rupert's little house on St. Eustatius Boulevard, a dog began barking. The brown mutt was tied to a nearly-dead coconut tree, one of a half-dozen growing in the weed-infested front yard.

"Not what I imagined," Abby said. "Somehow I expected Claude's henchman to be rolling in money." She stepped out of the van.

"Mos' fo'k say Mo'gan be ver' rich," the driver said, as Karl dragged himself from the stifling van. "He live wif his mother. This be de house she bo'n in."

"Front door's open," Abby said, as she removed the pistol from her handbag.

"Some folks leaves doors op'n, m'um. Mos' folks with air c'dition leaves 'em closed." He pointed to a room air-conditioner that snarled and vibrated as it dripped water from the condenser.

Karl understood much of what was being said by watching Abby and the taxi driver. In French he asked her, "Should I check the rear of the house?"

"Without probable cause, it could be trespassing. We'll knock on the front door."

They approached the entrance. Karl held his pistol now, low at his side. Two rickety steps led to a sagging porch.

The lower step squawked as Karl put his weight on it, startling the dog. The howling mutt dashed around the tree trunk, as other neighborhood dogs began to wail.

"Dammit, Karl," Abby admonished, "we'll have people showing up to check out the barking dogs."

"The damn step squeaks."

She regretted her rebuke. Of all the DST officers she'd worked with in the past decade, Karl was the most professional. He had never gone into a situation half-cocked, nor had he ever looked down on her because of her gender. The only other man she'd worked with who had treated her as an equal was Bret. *Must be why I'm kinda fascinated with him*, she thought.

"Sorry, Karl," Abby whispered. "You stand to the left of the door. I'll go to the right side."

He nodded, scuttled across the porch, and stared in the partially-open door. It was too dark inside to see any details. He nodded and Abby bounded to the porch on sandaled feet. She crossed to the side opposite Karl, and peered around the door jamb. Her view was less than Karl's. The door was hinged on the right, giving him a clearer, more open view inside.

He indicated he was going to rush in. Abby realized this was the only way to gain access. Right or wrong, there was no choice, and she nodded. Karl pulled back the slide on his semiautomatic and rushed into the dark building.

No sound came from within. *I'm going in in three seconds*, she decided.

There was no need to count. From inside, she heard a single muted gunshot. She dashed inside the house, pistol cocked and ready to fire. Halfway down a hallway she spotted a body lying in a pool of blood, a very tiny body.

Looks like an old woman, Abby noted. "Karl," she yelled. "Are you all right?"

"In here." His voice bellowed from a room to the right of the hall.

Reaching the doorway, she dropped to her knees and swung the pistol into the room. Karl stood in a bedroom staring at the remains of a full-length mirror. It had been secured to a wall directly across from the door. Very little glass remained inside the wooden frame, but a chest-high bullet hole told the story.

Getting to her feet, Abby stared at the 9mm hole, then at Karl. "You killed the shit out of that mirror, Karl,"

"Walked into the dark room, saw a guy aiming a gun at me . . . and fired."

"It could happen to anyone."

Karl stood still and shook his head.

"The old woman in the hall. Rupert's mother?"

"Probably. Cab driver said they lived together."

"Let's check the place before we call the police."

It took less than five minutes to search the entire house, closets and a crawl space above the kitchen. It was empty.

"You see a phone anywhere, Karl?"

"Living room. I'll call the Philipsburg police." He hesitated, then asked, "Okay with you?"

"Get on the horn." She knelt next to the old woman. The

blood was congealed, cold to the touch, red-brown in color. Her throat had been slit from ear to ear . . . severing the carotid artery. Mrs. Morgan had died very quickly. Abby wondered how a son, even a deviant like Rupert, could so cruelly kill his mother. She stood and faced the kitchen window. Outside, the brilliant sun shown on an odd structure in the back yard. *I'd better check out there.*

"Karl," she shouted, "don't call the police yet."

"Too late. They're on their way." She heard him approach from the hall.

As he appeared in the kitchen, Abby beckoned for him to come by the window. "Look. We didn't check that."

"Large sailboat, two-masts. Some of the planking looks new. Maybe Rupert was renovating her."

"We'd better check it out," she said. "The murderer could be hiding there."

"Ketch," Karl remarked.

"*Pardon?*"

"That size boat with two masts is called a ketch." He stared at it. "Mainmast in the center, mizzenmast aft and a jib, if I remember my nautical terms."

"Those are sails?"

"No, they're where sails are hung. I was in the Boy Sea Guides centuries ago."

She stared at the boat. "Is there a 'hold' where somebody could hide?"

"In a ketch that size, yes. Also, they could hide in the trunk cabin, that portion raised above the hull, between masts."

"Let's get out there. The *gendarmes* will soon be here." She placed several kitchen towels over the body since it was beginning to attract flies. Then she walked to the back door, opened it and stepped down two broken steps. Karl was on her heels.

"What's hanging from that mast?" she said, stopping in her tracks.

"Could be a bag holding the sails," Karl offered "Or, it could be someone at the boom aiming at us." They dropped onto their knees.

"Bad thought." Abby checked that her pistol was cocked, then moved in a crouch toward the back of the old boat.

Karl headed toward the bow, where he'd try to get the drop on anyone waiting in ambush. Abby moved alongside the sailboat, then beneath the rotted bowsprit.

Abby figured if no one 'made' her yet, they must be looking some other direction. The form hanging onto the beam was no longer visible, the side of the sailboat hiding it from view. She realized the dogs had stopped barking. *Now it's too quiet.* She crawled along the sand of Rupert's back yard, her favorite casual attire soiled by dragging herself across the ground. None of this discomfort registered in her brain, as her instincts for survival overcame all else. Pistol in her right hand, a spare ammo clip in the left, Abby pulled herself forward. She reached the edge of the sailboat's rearmost portion.

She'd come to the point that soldiers, police, explorers, adventurers had reached uncounted times before, exposing oneself to death. Abby knew she could die, but she was doing her job. She rolled into clear view of the long boom, both hands clutching her weapon, aiming it forward and above. She gasped and stared in horror at the sight on the mainmast's boom.

"Mon Dieu," she cried. *"C'est Rupert!"* Abby stood on trembling legs, staring at the obscenity atop the boat.

Karl rushed over to her, saw the revulsion on her face and turned toward the boat. "Holy Mother of God," he uttered.

Stripped naked, Rupert Morgan hung from the boom. His large arms encircled the wooden beam, bloody wrists bound above it. His disfigured face was twisted in a grimace of inhuman torment. Impaled deep within his barrel chest was one knifelike fluke of a large, rusted anchor. The ring end hung down to his thighs, mingling with dried blood.

Karl lowered his eyes from the grisly scene and stared at Abby. "Who would have ever thought . . . ?"

She knew this had been Tomasso's revenge for one failure too many, not a ritual conducted by a Colombian terror squad. In the distance she heard sirens, as the local police rushed to Rupert's house.

Abby walked from the site of the execution, skirting the small cottage. As she reached the waiting taxi, she studied the driver's face. He looked like a man from whom a great burden had been lifted. Instinctively he knew.

Chapter Sixteen

It was almost midnight in Fort-de-France, Martinique. The telephone rang in Bertrand Hough's lavish apartment, a hotel penthouse suite two blocks from the U.S. Consulate General at 14 Rue Blenac. He flinched at the harsh *briing-briing* of the instrument. He'd been three-quarters asleep at the moment, so he sat for several moments to get his bearings. Shaking his head to awaken, he grabbed the instrument.

"Hough" he said.

"Yo, this is your captain speaking." It was a familiar voice.

"Why are you calling me this time of night?" He had pulled off his watch while changing clothes, so he had no idea what time it was.

"Only midnight, but maybe it'll wait 'til tomorrow."

"No, no, Freddie. Stay on," Hough insisted. "You secure?"

"As much as possible, partner. "

"Hold on, I'll grab the safe phone." He pushed 'hold' on the cradle and hung up. Reaching inside an end table cabinet, he removed a square, blue-colored box. He pressed five buttons on a ten-digit keypad. Opening the steel box, he pulled a phone from inside, its cord trailing behind. Bertrand plugged the cord into a wall jack, pushed a red button and picked up the receiver.

"What's up?" he said.

"Just flew your buddy Bret to Colombia."

Stunned, he didn't know how to reply. "You can't be right."

"Too right. The Iranian and Tomasso blew it. Lamplighter's alive and well, posing as a Colombian narc."

"How do you know?"

"Told you, I flew him to Barranquilla."

"No, how do you know he's playin' narc again? He was kicked out of the DEA, Wilson. I helped nurse him through his last days in St. Martin."

"His cover's anti-narcotics police. He's got Colombia's blessing, at least that of General Serrano."

"Serrano? Damn, I figured Bret was here to investigate the emerald theft. If he's working for Serrano, he has DEA sanction."

Wilson grunted. It could have meant agreement, it could have meant anything.

"Why Barranquilla?"

"Don't know, but it's a safe city for anyone undercover."

"Who's his control? Did he mention where he was headed?" With all his contacts in Colombia, Bertrand hated getting this news from Wilson.

"You know the drill. I drop someone on the military side, then get my ass out."

"Lamplighter didn't mention . . . ?"

"He's a professional. CIA and NSA freelance braggarts end up in body bags, but your buddy will come marchin' home again."

Bertrand wanted to curse the wise-ass black American pilot, but knew he was too valuable. "He and I are *not* buddies. He could wreck our lucrative arrangement. You're involved in this as much as I am. If he lives much longer, my bosses will get rid of me . . . and you. It's a wonder Claude and the Iranian are alive since they were ordered to kill Bret and the French bitch."

"Tomasso iced Rupe. The bitch offed al-Majid."

A frigid hand gripped Bertrand's stomach. His throat constricted and he felt bile begin to rise. He swallowed to keep from retching, and his heart pounded within his chest. *This is all an awful dream*, he thought. Hough managed to ask, "Is DeGroot keeping his mouth shut?"

"We have another problem there."

Good God, he thought. *What else can go wrong?* "Wha, what kind of problem, for crissake?"

"DeGroot made a run for your island. Cops caught him at Grand Case airport."

"They have him in the Philipsburg lockup?" Maybe there was still hope.

"No, Bouchard's actin' chief under the island's bilateral security agreement. Both police forces are working together on the plane crash, Rupert's death, the dead Iranian, you name it." He continued, "Netherlands Antilles have to name a successor for DeGroot. Until then, both French and Dutch territorial police are working under Bouchard."

"I got word of the plane crash yesterday afternoon. Thought Lamplighter was out of our hair." Hough waited, but there was no response from the pilot. "Why didn't I hear about DeGroot's arrest?"

"Wasn't arrested. Collared and now being kept under house detention. Cops and *gendarmes* inside and outside his place."

"His wife?"

"At an unnamed hotel, home, hostel . . . nobody really knows." Wilson asked, "Did she know about her husband's extracurricular affairs?"

Bertrand pondered the question. "He always told me Vera knew nothing, but Horst has a big mouth. I'm betting he let her in on it."

"Broad spent money like an A-rab princess," Wilson said. "From the day DeGroot replaced Verhouten."

"Yeah, at least we know Bouchard's location. He's dangerous, but like a circus bear, he can be watched while kept in his cage." *Supervising the two main police departments on St. Martin will keep Henri busy*, Hough understood. "Our old friend Horst must be eliminated. Use one of our local assets, Wilson."

"Suppose the island cops and French *flics* are watching likely suspects?"

Why did I ever bring Wilson into my program? Hough thought, but he knew the answer. Wilson had the perfect method of smuggling emeralds and other "product" into Martinique, his unhampered aircraft. Traveling from Martinique to St. Martin, Bertrand enjoyed the *second* best smuggling method, a large valise and diplomatic immunity.

"The Iranian and Colombian terrorists are experts at their craft, Fred."

"Lamplighter and the French broad are still alive."

"Tomasso's idiot 'hitman' screwed up!" Bertrand shouted.

"Bertrand, keep cool. We'll get things back on line real soon. Can't let dead ole Rupe and one dead A-rab get you so tense." He didn't want Bertrand to lose it when they made fortunes off his connections.

"Sorry I might have sounded upset at you, Wilson. We are an unstoppable team, you know." Hough knew you didn't get rid of a goose who's layin' golden eggs.

"Could it be my top-secret security clearance, Bertrand? Or the way they trust me here at Cheyenne Mountain South?"

"Both, Wilson, and more. I may have many contacts in high places, but your own acquaintances in less-lofty neighborhoods are most necessary."

He sure loves to run off at the mouth, Wilson thought. "Seems like I got better cards in my hand than you got in yours, Bertrand."

"Not better, Wilson. We're like two canny bridge partners who realize their collective bids will bring a Grand Slam if played properly."

"Coexistence, huh?"

"Uh, cooperation to achieve enormous mutual wealth."

"Like the sound of that, Bertrand," he replied. "I'll speak with, how'd you put it?, my 'less-lofty' contacts regarding the DeGroots."

"Wonderful, Frederick, and I'll speak with friends in high places in Colombia. Lamplighter's getting too close to the source of our emerald trade."

" . . . and the French bitch?"

"Yes, Frederick. I'll handle her. Believe I'll set off on a short trip to St. Martin. It's time to tie up that loose end."

"Like your style, man. *Bon voyage.*"

Bertrand concealed the secure telephone in its small box and put it away. As he shut the instrument in its hiding place, he thought about the future, *his* carefully mapped-out future in Brazil.

Fifty million dollars U.S. in Rio de Janeiro would last him a long lifetime, especially with careful investments. And what if someone ever got enough evidence to convict him of theft, smuggling or accessory to murder? Many others had faced the problem and easily overcame it. Brazil will not extradite anyone for *any* crime if they have a dependant child by a Brazilian woman. *Ah*, thought Bertrand, *how easy to arrange for a young lady who wishes to have the child of an American millionaire.*

Hough began to hum the old tune about flying down to Rio as he prepared for a relaxing night's sleep.

Chapter Seventeen

The shadow called Charlie stood at the edge of the runway. He and Bret had exited the old C-47 on the military side of Barranquilla's world-class airport. They'd barely trotted off the concrete before the pilot had gunned the engines, spun the plane around and roared off into the still-dark eastern skies.

"Captain got a hot date back in Curaçao?"

"Standing orders. Land, unload, fly. Don't waste time."

"Nice arrangement."

Charlie nodded, then lifted his right hand. He'd seen a small automobile approaching. It halted on the tarmac about ten feet away. "Get in," Charlie said.

"'Nother spook, Charles?" the driver asked.

"Colombian Colonel," Charlie answered. He pulled up the trunk lid and tossed Bret's luggage inside. He motioned Bret to get in back, as he crammed into the small front passenger seat.

The husky blond crew-cut driver looked Bret over and said, "Fat chance. He's standard issue American narc."

"Drive," Charlie said.

"What kinda piece you packin'?" the driver asked Bret.

Before he could think of an answer, Charlie again said, "Drive."

Crew Cut drove without asking any more questions. It took five minutes driving with the headlights off before the car stopped in front of a modern building. An etched message over the wide front entrance read *Bienvenido a Barranquilla, Atlántico*, but there was no hint of the structure's function.

"Please wait inside for your guide, Colonel Parra," Charlie said. Bret and Charlie left the car and retrieved the luggage. "Good luck," Charlie wished him. "I must prepare for return transportation."

"How do I know my, uh, guide, Charlie?"

As he slipped into the rear seat, Charlie answered, "The guide will come to you, Colonel. Wait in the terminal." The car drove away, still without its headlights lit.

He walked to the terminal entrance, where an armed national policeman politely asked for identification. Bret showed him the passport and National Police credentials of Colonel Manuel Parra Vega. The guard bowed as he handed the credentials back. In passably good English, the police officer asked if Bret needed to use a restroom, would like a hot dinner, wanted a drink, or wished to rest on a comfortable sofa or chair.

"Think I'll just sit and enjoy a few quiet moments," he said, smiling. *Damn pilot kept that C-47 about a foot above the Caribbean the whole flight.* Captain Wilson *had* stayed below five hundred feet for most of the 300-mile flight.

The police officer took his two bags and led him to a lounge area with deep carpeting and subdued lighting. "This is a place of comfort for *Señor*," he said. He saluted and quickly walked away.

The air-conditioned lounge was welcome relief for Bret after the sweltering C-47 and warm-humid early morning of Barranquilla. He snuggled his luggage against his legs and shoes to make certain they weren't snatched. Abruptly, he noticed a man sitting on a sofa across from him.

"Mornin'," the stranger spoke, since the distance between them was no more than ten or twelve feet.

"Morning," Bret said. "Didn't see you right away."

He nodded. Dressed in tan slacks and a light blue shirt, he was probably in his early forties. Medium short brown hair framed a pleasant if not handsome face. Like Bret, his single piece of luggage touched his right leg. He looked across and asked, "Arriving or departing?"

"I just arrived."

"DEA?"

Bret didn't answer. He stared at the man.

"I'm NSA," the man continued. "Ft. Meade assigned me back to Puerto Rico."

"Wise to tell a stranger?"

He smiled broadly. "Only spooks in and out of this terminal. This your first time in Barranquilla?"

"First time." Bret knew that undercover agents were occasionally tested to see if they were good risks. This stranger could be more than a coincidence. "Sounds like you've been here before."

"Name's Russell, and I've been here before."

"Why's NSA in Colombia?"

"Why not? Every other U.S. intelligence group is here, including you narcs."

"An American national security agent in Colombia is ludicrous," Bret replied. "Drug cartels, poverty and leveling the rain forests don't come under any NSA agenda I've heard of."

Russell said, "Any place where America's national security is compromised . . ."

" . . . far as I know, Bogotá doesn't have a Welcome Wagon for American spies."

"I seem to note some anxiety," Russell said, his smile replaced by a grin. "Also a great deal of naïvety regarding U.S. intelligence and counterespionage."

"You may be NSA, but the Colombian government never invited you. At least *my* presence here is known by the PJR!"

"If I were you I'd feel much safer if the anti-narcotics police had no idea of my presence in Colombia. *Los narcotraficantes* kill cops here the way we kill pesky gnats"

Russell paused, then asked, "What's your name?"

He did tell me his name, or his alias, Bret thought. "George. George Princeton, from Chicago."

Russell nodded and said, "Guess that's as good as any." He leaned forward and zipped open the soft-sided bag at his feet. "Let me show you some of State's latest advisories, George. Picked 'em up here at the Barranquilla consulate two days ago."

"I've seen enough of State's Highlights and Advisories to last a lifetime."

Ignoring Bret's remark, Russell dug into his bag and retrieved a handful of State Department Bulletins. "Don't even know which ones I pulled out, George, but I'm sure they're typical." He walked to Bret and handed him the bundle of sheets. "Look for yourself, might learn somethin'."

He scanned the papers Russell'd given him. One sheet included a paragraph entitled "Guerrilla Activity." He read, "With the breakup of peace negotiations with the Colombian government, the country's remaining insurgency groups have focused on taking their war to the cities, using urban terrorism. Both the Colombian Revolutionary Armed Forces (FARC) and the National Liberation Army (ELN), united with the Simon Bolivar Guerrilla Coordinator (CGSB), have made efforts to increase their presence and infrastructure in urban areas, particularly in and around Bogota. The capital and other major Colombian cities—including Barranquilla, site of the U.S. Consulate—have been hit by sporadic terrorist attacks . . . including the burning of buses and attacks on police stations. Meanwhile, rural insurgent fronts have continued their terrorism against the country's economic infrastructure. The ELN, in particular, continues to target the petroleum industry, including U.S. interests."

"Interesting, huh, George?"

"Enlightening."

Russell said, "I'm surprised your control gave you a Colombian assignment without a proper briefing."

He didn't answer, since he was more or less freelancing his journey to Muzo.

"Remember to cover your ass at all times, in the cities, country or jungle."

"Okay, let's assume I'm here on a mission, but I'm being

monitored," he said. "Secondly, my cover will help me complete my objective."

"Shit, George," Russell choked a reply, "that's the worst explanation of illegal entry into a foreign nation I ever heard." He shook his head.

They suddenly saw a darkened automobile drive by the building's bulletproof windows. They lost sight of it as it drove on, presumably stopping at the entrance to the restricted terminal.

"Another spy," Russell stated.

This my contact? Bret wondered.

Soon, from the reflection of a window pane, Bret saw two men near the lounge.

The same police officer who'd brought Bret to the lounge area appeared. He escorted a short Hispanic man wearing a beige suit and carrying an attorney's brief valise. The shorter man stopped and regarded the two Americans.

Both Bret and Russell looked on in disbelief. Simultaneously, they jumped up and shouted, "Johnson!"

Russell stared at Bret. He asked, "Johnson's *your* control, too?"

"No, not really, but he's handled many vital parts of my job."

"Then he's your damn control, George." Russell shook his head in irritation.

Johnson approached them. "Ees good to see both of jou at this time," he said. "Mr. Russell, jou please come with me into conference room." Johnson glanced at Bret and said, "Colonel Parra, here jou can wait until Russell and I end our talk."

"Sure, Johnson," he said. *Guess he's gotta get Russell off to Puerto Rico.*

Gently, Johnson shook Bret's shoulders with both hands. "Maybe I speak to Russell longer than I think he is to be. Jou were sleeping."

"How long . . . ?"

"We speak for two hours, until now," Johnson explained.

Bret focused tired eyes on Johnson. Russell eased himself

into a chair four or five feet from Bret's and also looked at their Control.

"Mr. Russell, jou mus' be good friend with Mr. Lamplighter," Johnson said.

"I'm supposed to have an alias." Bret frowned when he heard his real name.

"Jou trus' me, Lamplighter. Russell, he trus' me from our long confrence."

"What does he have to do with me, Johnson? He's off for San Juan or Ponce or somewhere in Puerto Rico."

Johnson stood in front of them. "Plans change," he said.

"Johnson," Bret said, "I've come this far, so I'm going all the way to the site."

Johnson set his leather valise on a chair seat, unlocked it, and began rifling through the contents of the bag. He removed several documents with light-blue paper covers, handed a copy to each man, and kept one copy.

"Shit, Johnson," Russell swore, "if this's my Last Will and Testament . . ."

"Trus' me, is not Will, Mr. Russell. Please, jou open to page *numero uno*."

"Trust, after you just conned me?"

Damn, Bret thought, *did Johnson just pull the rug from under Russell's leave?*

"Mr. Russell," Johnson began, "it is not the fact jou are in neighborhood, it is because jou are bes' man for this duty. I tell jou in confrence, jou get double normal field pay. Jou agree." He hesitated, then said, "Please open orders to page *uno*." Johnson flipped over the blank blue cover page.

Bret noticed Russell said nothing more after Johnson had reminded him of double pay for some new assignment. Bret turned the cover page of his packet.

"*Primero*, I mus' read Colombia 'sclaimer for jou two," Johnson declared. "The Department of State warns U.S. citizens to exercise extreme caution when traveling in Colombia," Johnson read the first line of paragraph one of the first page. "Nex', State give

'Major City Snapshots' report, but we stay away from Bogotá, Cartagena, Cali and Medellín. We are in Barranquilla, also on lis', but we sidestep downtown." He glanced over the sheet of paper from which he read. Johnson then asserted, "State report say: Violence outside Barranquilla remains high. Insurgent bombings of electric towers and highway banditry by various criminal elements in areas surrounding Barranquilla are common occurrences. Nighttime travel outside the city is not advisable." Johnson turned to the next sheet of flimsy paper. "Now to importan' . . ."

" . . . Johnson," Bret interrupted, "on all the maps I went over with Abby Duchamps, we noted that it's impossible to drive to Muzo without going to Medellín using the Western Trunk Highway. There are no other roads passable by automobiles heading south, then southeast."

"Mr. Russell, what do you say to that?" Johnson asked. He fixed two dark brown eyes on him.

"I spent lotsa time around the DeMares Oilfields, east of Medellín. Could only get there by DeMares company helicopter. Think Lamplighter's right."

"Jou are both right. But jou will not have to go to Medellín, Mr. Lamplighter."

"Awful railroads or another puddle-jumping plane ride?" Bret asked.

"Not either," Johnson answered. "And not by helicopter, also. I will read more of papers jou hold."

"Muzo's a little less than five hundred miles south of Barranquilla, Johnson. Can't hike that distance in three days."

Johnson stared at the Bret for a three-count, then began to read from the papers he held. "Memo from chief of DEA in Colombia say 'Regarding your report channeled to me through Washington, Colonel Parra's assignment is acknowledged and respected. Field officers in the outer regions will be notified to afford all reasonable aid to the Colonel.' Jou see it is signed by head of Drug Enforcement Administration in Bogotá, no?" He looked at Bret.

"Yes," he replied. "I appreciate you got the DEA to see I'm still alive and well. Let's get the show on the road."

"Here is translates of notice to me from good fren' General Serrano. He say: 'I am most happy to invite Mister Lamplighter to my country on his important mission in the name of justice. In the role of Colonel Parra, your American ally will enjoy the full cooperation of all *la policía nacional de* Colombia.'

"'I have received word,'" Johnson continued, "'that the American and his French ally executed two enemies of Colombia on St. Martin.'"

"Whoa, Lamplighter," Russell broke in, "Didn't know you been whackin' some of Serrano's opponents in the Caribbean."

Johnson continued reading his monologue: "'These heroic actions make the National Police proud to help him in his visit to Muzo in Boyacá department. He will make a visit to Comandante of PJR in Chiquinquira upon his arrival.'" Pausing, Johnson said, "Jou mus' for certain report to El Comandante when jou are near Muzo mines, gentlemens."

"*Momentito*, Johnson," Bret spoke up. "You made a mistake. You included your friend Mr. Russell in *my* investigation."

"Meester Lamplighter," Johnson said, "jou do not know Colombia. Mr. Russell ees spending two years in thees country, much of eet in the Magdelena Medio region between Cordillera Occidental *y* Cordillera Oriental."

"DeMares Oilfields is about a hundred miles north of Chiquinquira in Boyacá," Russell volunteered.

"Johnson, I don't care if Russell lived deep *inside* a mine at Muzo . . ."

"Meester Lam'light'," Johnson continued, "thees ees decided by DEA, Colombian National Police and American NSA. Jou are here, also, because *sous-'specteur* Bouchard gives you good recommends." Johnson paused for effect. "Jou would not have CENTRO monitor if I do not say okay to includes Russell, *¿Entiendes?*"

"No choice?"

"*Nada*."

"Look," Russell said, "I'm not happy about stayin' in Colombia, either. But Johnson says Ft. Meade doubled my ante. It's too much to refuse." He let the words sink in, then continued: "I hate having a partner, too. The only good partner I ever had is buried under six-feet of Colombian *llanos*. Still, Johnson told me this's the only way you get to travel to the Muzo mines, period."

"Did Johnson outline what I'm looking for at Muzo?"

"He never said a word about why you're going there. Emeralds, I suppose."

"Looks like I've got a traveling companion."

"*Bueno*, chentlemen," Johnson beamed with a paternal smile. "Now we get jou on the superhighway to Muzo."

Chapter Eighteen

Detective Mobley was one of nine police officers and territorial *gendarmes* guarding Horst DeGroot at his residence north of Philipsburg. He was officer-in-charge of the Midnight to eight detail. His men were divided along the lines of French and Netherlands Antilles government police. He'd always liked his north side, the French region, better than the southern Dutch division. Now that the island police were working together, though, the two separate island departments hadn't seemed as important as they once did.

"Yas, LaRue," Detective Mobley said to his partner in the police van, "we gots de start of a 'mer'can-style gang showdown."

"*Je ne sais pas*, Mobley," *gendarme* sergeant Robert LaRue said. "Smuggling is a part of the *histoire* of St. Martin for centuries."

"Sure, de smugglin' is known fer hundreds years, sargen'. But it do not stop like de ole slave trade in de Caribbean. It hang in here mo' den ev'before."

"Umm, I suppose eet is true. And with eet come more crime, more murder than we ever see before on St. Martin."

"Fer sure, sargen'. I don' fancy watchin' to the safety of DeGroot. He bad mon. It be he wha' bring mos' drug, dimon' an' em'rald smugglin' here." Out of the side of one eye, Mobley saw LaRue nod at his comment. "An' now he sit like de cat wha' et de sugar bird, all so comf'ble in his big, fancy house here on Williams Hill."

Williams Hill was about one mile due north of Philipsburg's Great Salt Pond. It included a fancy subdivision where many of Sint Maarten's more prominent citizens lived. It was only a half-hour's drive from Philipsburg on the blacktop running through Dutch Cul De Sac. The house owned by Horst DeGroot was precisely situated at 18°07'24" longitude and 63°18'43" latitude, a fact unknown even to ex-Chief DeGroot or his real estate attorney. In fact, only a cartographer, surveyor or ballistic missile expert would be interested in the long/lat coordinates of Horst and Ana DeGroot's home.

Aboard the yacht *Queen Lizzie*, anchored off the northeast coast of St. Martin and forty miles east of little Pinel Island, Professor Ladislaz Moriclav was just one such interested man. Dr. Moriclav had learned much about missiles when he had interned with Dr. Wernher Von Braun at Peenemünde on the Baltic Sea. Moriclav, in fact, had been Von Braun's prize pupil, an important fact for the allies when Germany had surrendered. In a bizarre "deal" between Stalin's NKVD secret police and Truman's Office of Strategic Services, Von Braun had gone with the Americans and Moriclav had gone to the Soviets.

Years and politics change, and eventually Professor Moriclav found himself working for the Iraqis. It was his knowledge of missiles, begun with the German V-1 and V-2 "vengeance" weapons, that brought him to Baghdad. Saddam Hussein had wanted a gun with a quarter-mile-long barrel, mostly concealed in the earth. The huge cannon would shoot missiles a thousand miles away. Moriclav's work on the V-2 ballistic missile was just what the Iraqi despot needed. The V-2 had reached an altitude of about 70 miles and had an overall range of 200 miles, this in the mid-1940s. Unfortunately for the expatriate German, only days after Iraq's defeat in the 1991 Persian Gulf War, the gargantuan artillery piece had been discovered and dismantled. As if the professor had personally pointed out the location of the monster gun to U.N. representatives, Saddam threatened to execute Ladislaz for being a traitor to Iraq.

Meanwhile, 500 miles east-northeast in Tehran, functional leader of Iran, Ayatollah Ali Hoseini-Khamenei, and president Ali Akbar Hashemi-Rafsanjani had been briefed by secret police about Moriclav's dilemma. Their neighbor Iraq had been in enormous disorder after losing one-half million military personnel in the "Mother of All Wars." It had been decided that Iranian secret police and Abu Nidal agents would bring the disgraced professor to the Islamic Republic of Iran. Only four days after the decision was made, Dr. Ladislaz Moriclav had sat in the same Tehran palace suite with Ayatollah Khamenei and president Rafsanjani. The agents had not only sneaked Moriclav out of Iraq, they had brought along several dozen missiles that were highly prized by the professor.

First and foremost among Ladislaz' missile collection were three American Tomahawk air-breathing cruise missiles. The eccentric missile expert refused to budge from Iraq until he'd received a promise that his strategic delivery systems would accompany him across the border. The Tomahawks had been in the experimental stage at the time of the Persian Gulf conflict. A tiny percentage of the hundreds that had been launched from U.S. warships, dropped to sandy earth without detonating. Three relatively undamaged Tomahawks had been requisitioned by Moriclav, and had been dutifully brought to his suburban Baghdad laboratory. Several years later, the Tomahawks, complete with ultra high-explosive warheads, had come to Tehran. Moriclav had held a complex kinship with the three cruise missiles, since they had been refined modern versions of the professor's original V-1 "buzz bomb."

Aboard the large American-flagged yacht, Dr. Moriclav puttered around the launching platform, the twenty foot-long Tomahawk resting on movable metal rails. It looked much like a large Fourth of July skyrocket lying on a big Erector Set stand. "For many years my *drei wunderkinder* wait to fulfil their duty," he beamed. The Iranian agent standing across from him smiled at the old man.

"Some say you invent this type of missile." The Iranian barely made out the features of the old German in the morning darkness.

"Von Braun, three others and myself," the professor proclaimed. "V-1 was the first truly aerodynamic *guided* missile!"

"The V-2 was not?" The tall Iranian had been a physics and electronics engineer at graduate school until he joined Sabri al-Banna's ANO three year's before.

"Ach, *nein*. Remember ze two words "pulse jet," my friend. *Das* is ze difference. A missile with a pulse jet, like *mein* V-1, is a schmardt missile. No pulse jet engine *und* it is UP, OVER, DOWN, Boom! *Nicht* so schmardt."

"I see, *Herr* Doctor. And the American Tomahawk is a smart missile."

"Vor certain. In fact, I call it *sehr* schmardt, *mit* high intelligence." He glanced approvingly back to the dull gray missile on its launcher. He said, "For its time, ze V-1 was *sehr gut*. It had a compass and altimeter, so it got to its target most times." Again, he began to hum the little melody. From somewhere in the Iranian's deepest-brain data banks he identified the tune as the "Horst Wessel Lied."

"This, er, Tomahawk will fly nearly one hundred kilometers and hit its target precisely?" The Iranian had always been warned about the untruths of American science and technology at Tehran's Technical University.

"*Mit* no problem, my *jung* friend." Moriclav finally turned back to the curious man. "You see here ze ultimate schmardt bomb, a seeing-eye missile." His eyes sparkled when he spoke.

"Smarter than the Sidewinder, Shrike, Exocet or the B Durandal?"

"Imbecile missiles," he shot back. "You stand next to ze next best thing to a flying man carrying a map and tons of TNT."

"I remember a CNN cameraman catching a ten-second shot of one during the Western Alliance War against Iraq."

"Precisely," he said, nearly weeping with joy. "Millions of people saw that Tomahawk missile video years ago, long before it was 100% perfected."

" . . . and during the Bosnian Serb patriotic war for independence . . ."

" . . . and ze recent incursion uf Venezuela, uf course. *Ja, das ist wunderbar, junge.*" Moriclav didn't care that his audience spoke no German.

The Iranian looked down at his wrist watch, and twisted it several directions until he found enough ambient light to see the time. "*Herr* Professor, time to launch."

Moriclav nodded. He'd already known that the launch was imminent. The launching platform was quite professionally-made, despite the fact it was built from parts for other American and Russian missile launchers.

"In here go your brains, little Tomahawk," Moriclav mumbled to the inanimate weapon. He placed a gray box the size of a bread loaf into the recesses of the missile. The Iranian helped him load the heavy and cumbersome pack. Together they secured it with steel straps and wingnuts. "Now, chust place ze two cables onto their matching colored connections," Moriclav instructed.

The Iranian did as he was told, under the watchful eyes of the elderly German expatriate.

"*Sehr gut*," he nodded, examining the results. With trembling hands, he pushed shut the door on the side of the missile. With a screwdriver, he tightened the door securely over the Tomahawk's delicate sensors.

"We'd better go below, *Herr* Professor," the Iranian said as he again glanced at his watch. Abu Nidal did not condone tardiness.

"Always ze vorld iss fill uf hurry, hurry. *Nicht war, junge?*" He feigned agitation, 'though his heart beat with anticipation.

Inside the yacht, Ladislaz Moriclav placed his right index finger on a black button. The word 'launch' had been typed on a piece of paper and then affixed with transparent tape next to the button. "For the fatherland," he quietly said in the hushed cabin. He pressed the button and a closed circuit television screen showed the missile leap from its launcher. From inside the yacht the only sound anyone heard was a long whoosh that soon ended. Another much fainter whoosh was barely audible, but that was the last Tomahawk breath heard from within the *Queen Lizzie*.

A technician aboard the ship kept the television camera aimed at the missile, keeping it within sight with the telephoto lens. After a brief spurt to about one hundred feet altitude the Tomahawk intuitively dove to within eight or ten feet of the low swells of the Atlantic. Cruising at less than 600 miles per hour, it maintained that height as it flew the fifty miles toward the St. Martin mainland. What the Tomahawk lacked in great speed, it possessed in determination and unparalleled accuracy. The cruise missile slowly pulled away from the furthest range of the camera's zoom lens.

"Incredible," the Iranian said as he stared at the monitor. He still stood next to Moriclav. "It flies no more than two or three meters above the ocean."

"Invisible to all radar," the Moriclav replied. His thoughts had gone back to Peenemünde, where he'd loved to watch the V-1's and V-2's streak into the clear, gray skies above the Baltic Sea. *"Wunderschoen vogel!"*

The Iranian silently added: . . . *flying its mighty cargo of death.* He fingered the small remote device in the pocket of his light jacket. Once word came from the small radio of the team's spotter crouched two miles from ground zero, the Iranian would press his *own* black button. This, he'd been briefed, would send a signal to a submarine off the coast of Colombia that the mission was a success. The sub, in return, would use its more powerful burst-transmission radio to announce the triumph to listeners in Cartagena.

The crew prepared the yacht for a fast voyage to a safe haven in St. Lucia. Smiles shown in abundance. The passengers and crew were proud of the important role they'd played in their incessant battle against repressive and brutal authority.

The Tomahawk sped across the Caribbean at five hundred, fifty miles per hour. Five minutes later, Moriclav's "bird" rushed over Orient Beach, trees, buildings and a slightly rising terrain. This presented no problem. The smart missile's gray-box brains anticipated variations in land contours, and instantly rose or dove to keep its now-twenty-foot height on an even keel. Every three or four seconds the Tomahawk took a deep breath of clean St. Martin oxygen, exhaling it in a kind of wheeze. This was similar to the sound made by its older V-1 cousin many decades before, and frequently described as an unearthly "buzz."

Searching out and following landmarks with its electronic sensing devices, the missile found its final navigational approach. The blacktop highway running from Etang Aux Poissons to Williams Hill is practically arrow-straight, an oddity on the small island. The land at this northeastern end of the island is fairly flat, with nothing more than a few rolling hills. The higher volcanic "mountains" lie on the southerly Dutch side and the northwest corner of the French *côte*. This mission was almost too simple for a proud Tomahawk cruise missile.

Then, the flying weapon smelled the blood of its target. Somewhere between the two small hamlets of Maho Well and French Quarter, the Tomahawk's navigational system urged it to rise to about two hundred meters above Williams Hill. It scanned the early morning scene below it with unerring electronic eyes. It calculated millions of pieces of data in one second, then, rolling out to 'dodge incoming enemy fire', the missile dove nearly vertically. Its "brain" calculated longitude, latitude, range, township, section and specific subdivision lot number down to within six inches. It relished the thrill of the last seconds before it struck the roof above the master bedroom.

Sergeant Robert LaRue was wide awake as he peered from the passenger's window of the van. Detective Mobley stood by the front door exchanging small talk with a *gendarme* corporal from Marigot. The slightest hint of a cool breeze wafted across the grassy, spacious lawn this early hour before dawn. LaRue may have seen something plunge from the sky toward the mansion. Or perhaps Mobley, Prentice, Duvalier or Goodman had noticed a streak of light, or was it some reflection? No one would ever know if any human saw the final plunge of the Tomahawk.

* * *

Sadaq Mahdavi-Karubi gaped in awe beneath an ancient tamarack tree trunk nearly two miles southeast of Williams Hill. The sudden hypnotic blinding light and rumbling explosion had caught him off-guard, although he'd been expecting it for three boring hours. At that moment the dark early morning became so bright it left an imprint on Mahdavi's irises. He'd been instructed to report the detonation immediately after it had happened, but he was struck temporarily immobile. The ultrahigh explosive warhead on the Tomahawk leveled Horst DeGroot's home plus two other neighboring houses near the impact. The structures were gone, wiped from Williams Hill as if they'd never existed. Everyone who'd been in or near the DeGroot house was vaporized in the split-second the cruise missile detonated.

The side of one nearby home burst into flames as Mahdavi stared at the incredible destruction. *The radio*, he thought. *At least twenty seconds have passed and I have neglected my sacred duty.* Sadaq heaved the portable transmitter from his small knapsack and held it against his face. Ambient light illuminated the device. Hastily, he turned a protruding round knob to ON, then placed his slightly unsteady right index finger on the single white button. Taking a deep breath, the swarthy man pressed the button four times, three short pulses and a final long pulse. Sadaq Mahdavi-Karubi slowly let out his breath, knowing he'd correctly tapped the Morse Code for the letter "V." As chilly as it was on the little hill, Sadaq was flushed with the knowledge he'd just proclaimed another glorious Victory over Western imperialism. He recalled how tears of joy filled his eyes years ago on Long Island. Mahdavi-Karubi had tapped out the same code after witnessing TWA flight 800 explode high above him.

Just 81 kilometers northeast of St. Martin, the crew of *Queen Lizzie* prepared to sail the short haul to St. Lucia. The Iranian had checked the amount of elapsed time from the moment the Tomahawk darted from the launch pad. He had glanced around the luxurious, crowded stateroom and had realized that every crew member was aware of the length of time that had gone by. If successful, the signal from the lookout on the island would soon be coming.

Several loudspeakers suddenly crackled with static, then a hiss. And the sounds came loudly, slowly, three dots and a dash, and the hissing ceased. It had been Morse code for "V." Victory, and Vengeance, were theirs! Everyone aboard the yacht stood and shouted. Some shook hands, all smiled. The Iranian felt intense personal pride, and relief. It was time to press his own radio tone transmittal device to alert the waiting submarine.

He pulled the transmitter from his jacket pocket and pressed the black button. Its tone activated the detonator on a nuclear warhead hidden far behind the yacht's powerful engine. No one would ever find as much as a tiny trace of *Queen Lizzie*. Certainly, geiger counters would have shown a trace amount of enriched plutonium atoms in the region where fishermen would later puzzle over thousands of dead fish. But why would anyone ever take a geiger counter into this peaceful stretch of the Atlantic Ocean?

Chapter Nineteen

"It's the freakin' African Queen," Bret exclaimed. He stared at the unsightly boat bobbing on the Rio Magdalena.

"Johnson," Russell spoke as he eyed the large craft, "The ante's gotta go up. I'm riskin' my life just climbin' aboard that scow."

Johnson peered sideways at the vessel, then gazed at its full length. He did a lousy job of pretending he didn't know what they were talking about. "Iss *muy* seaworth vessel, I theenk, *mi amigos*."

Johnson, Bret and Russell had left the military side of Barranquilla's huge airport in an unmarked Colombian police car. The driver, although clothed in civvies, was addressed as 'Captain' by Johnson. He whispered that only senior Colombian military officers were considered reliable these days.

"You guarantee he won't turn around and shoot us right here on the street?" Russell had asked, not wholly tongue-in-cheek. He and Bret had seen the fully-loaded Armalite-15 with grenade launcher hugging the captain's right thigh.

"Ees good man. I work weeth him before."

"Guy can be a great *amigo* 'til a better paycheck comes along."

"Cynical attitude, Russell," Bret had said. "Johnson's gotta trust someone."

As Russell had begun to reply, the streetlights of downtown Barranquilla had dimmed, then died. Dawn had broken over the grimy port city, producing an orangish haze to the business district.

In Spanish, Johnson had told the captain to pull over. "We get out here," he'd said. "We find jou taxi for driving rest of travel."

"Captain got a boundary he can't cross?" Russell had asked.

Johnson had frowned and said, "No, *pero* we must be careful."

Bret had seen more people on the street than he would have imagined for five A.M. The captain had turned around and sped back the way he'd come, leaving them standing on a street corner next to a small bakery.

"I didn't see a cab all the way from the airport, Johnson," Bret said.

"Is that what I think it is?" Russell had pointed at an approaching taxi. The Ford sedan stopped next to the three visiting *"turistas."*

"We get in luck, no *Señor* Lamplight, *Señor* Russell? Now we go to *supercarretera*," Johnson told them, smiling.

After they'd entered the car, Bret thought the driver looked familiar.

"Still not packin', *gringo*?" It was blond Crew Cut from the airfield. He'd turned and spoken to Bret in his mid-South twang.

Shaking his head and smiling at the young man, Bret said, "Remember, Charlie told you not to ask me that."

"A'ways been a curious down-home type, ole narc buddy." Crew Cut had turned his head about ninety degrees and asked, "How's my little *amigo, Señor* Johnson?"

"Neffer better," Johnson said. "*¿Y usted?*"

"Great, *hombre*. You never seem to change . . . even the same suit."

"Iss not same suit, yust same color," Johnson said. "No more talkings. We continue driving, sergeant."

Sergeant? In whose military? Bret wondered.

"We drive as I telling jou on *telefono*, sergeant," Johnson stated.

"Gotcha, no sweat." He hesitated, then asked, "Who's the other dude?" He'd hitched his head backward in Russell's direction.

"You keepin' a diary, Sparky?" Russell asked.

"Another spook with attitude, hunh Johnson."

"No *problema*, sergeant. We chust keep many things to us only."

Crew Cut had continued through the early morning traffic without any more questions. Several miles had passed when the sergeant said, "Okay *turistas*, we've arrived at beautiful downtown Soledad." He'd pulled to the curb.

"'Alone', 'lonely' . . . right, Johnson?" Bret had asked.

"Not bad, colonel. *Pero*, we are more happy with English word 'solitude'."

Johnson had then said, "Ees good seeing again jour face, sergeant. Ees time we are going. *Vamos, amigos*."

"Ohfer here," Johnson had said to them when they'd dragged themselves and their luggage from the taxi. "Chust one plock eass from thees street, *hombres*. We walk to Calle del Embarcadero."

"Hell of a nerve of Johnson to correct my English translation," Bret said, then smiled. "I have to guess what he means mosta th' time."

"Yeah," Russell said, "but he's got allies like a goddam ambassador. Sprung me from a grubby Bogotá jail cell once, before State knew I was in it." Russell had gazed at the little man in the lightweight suit. "Still owe 'im fer that."

"Saved my ass, too." Bret had recalled Johnson's 'gift' pistol.

"'*Embarcadero*'" Bret had read a street sign on a lamp post. "Means 'dock', doesn't it?"

"Yeah, or 'wharf' if you like precise translations like Johnson does. Gettin' a strange feelin' about our superhighway."

They rounded a corner and Johnson had folded his arms across his chest. He had cheerfully looked at a long wharf and a muddy, wide river filled with boats and ships of every size and description.

"A thousand miles of mud, human waste and rotten vegetation" Russell had muttered. "The Magdalena River."

"*This* is Johnson's super*carretera*?" Bret had asked. Deep inside, however, he knew he stared at the world's muddiest highway.

"Chentlemens, now I chow jou the fine boat jou will take to Muzo *minas*." He'd beckoned them to follow, as he had gotten closer to the banks of the river.

They'd picked their way along the wide street until they had come to a wooden wharf of rotting and loose timbers. They'd stepped between gaping crevices, gingerly edging to the end of the dock. The stench of the brown-black water had nearly been overwhelming.

"Now jou see the transportate I get for jou, *señors*," Johnson said. Ees eet not for certain a sore eyes sighting?"

"Seaworthy my ass!" Russell exclaimed, after Johnson praised the transportation he'd arranged. "Look how low it sits in the water? We'll be on the bottom of the Magdalena five minutes after casting off."

Johnson looked like a puppy that'd just been kicked. "I theenk I do good."

"Wait," Bret said, "we know you did your best, *always* do your best. We both like you, trust you, owe you a hell of a lot."

"George's right," Russell said. "God knows, I'd still be in a Bogotá slammer if you didn't pull strings." Russell glared at the dark boat, then back at Bret. "But I'm a shitty swimmer, *amigo*. I'd sure as hell get terminal dysentery after bein' in that slime."

"Time's wasting, Russell," Bret said. "I've gotta get to Chiquinquira, fast." He thought he'd figured out Russell's mind set: "With a good map I'm sure I'll be able to manage that river alone."

Johnson said, "I haf the ver bes' map of Rio Magdalena in Colombia, Lamplighter. Jou make no mistaking if jou follow eet to Chiquinquira. *No es un problema*."

"Excellent, *amigo*. Now if you'll just show me . . ."

"Bullshit, Lamplighter," Russell exclaimed. "I'm damn near a Colombian native and *I* could get lost on that grungy stream."

"Doubt that I'll have any trouble, Russell," Bret said. He picked up the baggage he'd set on the mildewed dock planks. "I've done a fair amount of boating myself on Lake Michigan, and if Johnson's map's anywhere . . ."

" . . . a lake's just another freakin' *lake*. This here river runs a goddam thousand miles through jungle, around boulders . . ."

" . . . sounds like a terrific challenge, huh Johnson? Think Russell forgot I'm travelin' less than five hundred of those thousand miles."

"*Si*, Lamplighter. Jou mus' drive and study map."

"*Loco*," Russell rasped, shaking his head. "There's river pirates, there's the goddam *policía* patrols. Tributaries look like the Magdalena, but . . ."

"What's he sayin' about pirates, Johnson?" Bret asked.

"Ees *nada*, Lam'lighter." Johnson glanced at the craft. It was a rather roomy launch, at least thirty-two feet long. A small cabin and hatch suggested it had sleeping and living areas. "Pirate iss old word," Johnson said. "Sometime guerrilla or *bandito* stop boat, Lam'lighter."

"Shit, Russell's telling the truth? I could get hijacked or shanghaied?"

"Eet ees *problema* in all Colombia. Bandit, guerrilla, assassin who protect drug lord. Jou find this on *carreterra*, on *calle*, in city, in yungle. Iss *nuestra enfermedad nacional* say *el presidente*."

"Colombia's national sickness," Russell said, glancing at the homely boat. *Sits low in the water, but looks sturdy*, he thought. "Okay, I'll go, since I promised Johnson I'd take care of you."

"Hey, don't do me favors just 'cause you want your blood money." He turned his back to Russell and winked at Johnson. "The harder the job, the better I love . . ."

"Cut the bullshit. Johnson, show us your cruise ship. I gotta check out th' First Class dining room." He hoisted his duffle bag to his shoulder.

"Follow me," Johnson directed. They hopped over holes and

cracks in the spongy dock, and reached the bobbing boat in fifteen seconds. Lashed to a dock support by a single threadbare rope, the craft looked forlorn in the early morning fog.

"Surprised it didn't break away from that rope," Russell said, as he began to haul the boat closer to the quay. "Funny, rope's cruddy lookin', but strong."

"Not funny," Johnson said, grinning. "Camouflages hide many thing."

"I'll pull the boat parallel to the dock," Bret said, and grabbed a section of the bow. It inched closer until the left side thumped against the rotting wharf timbers. "Doesn't look all that bad," he observed.

Russell grunted a doubtful snort.

Johnson hunched down on the dock, taking in the surroundings. "Eet look hokay for us. Seenk we make it to *embarcadero* wiss no escorts."

"Yeah, been checkin' the scenery ever since we left the terminal," Russell said. He gazed across the river and asked, "How wide's this cesspool?"

Johnson tested the question like someone tasting unfamiliar food. "Rio Magdalena iss maybe one mile wideness at this place." He added, "Thees iss close to mouss of river, where eet go into sea."

"How far downriver is Chiquinquira?" Bret asked.

"*Primero*, eet iss *up* river, Lamplighter. He run from souse to norse, thees one. No like jour Mississips."

"Okay, it runs uphill," he said, smiling. "So, how many miles to Chiquinquira?"

Johnson answered, "As jou *yanquis* say, 'jou no can get there from here'."

"Wait, you're my damn travel agent. You said this muddy river was my superhighway to Chiquinquira, and to the Muzo mines."

"Lamplighter, the *segundo* part of my answer iss coming." Johnson stared at a group of longshoremen some eighty or ninety feet away. "*Si*," Johnson said, evidently preoccupied, "I say superhighway to *Muzo*, no to Chiquinquira. And," he added, "no directs to one or other."

"The Magdalena doesn't go all the way to either place?" Bret also began to gaze around the wharf, to satisfy himself that everything was satisfactory.

"Jes, jou mus' stopping at Honda on Rio Magdalena, then drive to Chiquinquira, then Muzo *minas*."

"Dammit," Bret said, "You tossed another monkey wrench into the machinery."

"We get on boat, now," Johnson said. "I show jou 'portant, um, pieces jou mus' know." Johnson hopped over the side of the cruiser as agilely as possible, stumbling against the closed hatch.

"You okay, little buddy?" Russell asked with genuine concern.

"Hokay," Johnson grumbled. "Jou two come here now."

Bret tossed his two bags onto the deck and quickly followed them, landing on both feet. Russell let go of the rope, put his hands on the side and vaulted into the boat. The cruiser slowly drifted to the rope's limit, while Johnson began his tour. Even as he pointed to various portions of the cruiser's anatomy, Johnson glanced at workers on the dock. He trusted no one.

"Wood planking on the rails above these bulwarks," Bret said, pressing his hand against the pitted, dark plank, "looks intentionally stressed." He rubbed his hands along the planking of the high bulwark.

Russell stared closely at the dark brown wood. "He's right, Johnson. Resembles some furniture when it's supposed to look antique." Looking closer he said, "Hell yes, this is pretty good planking, just *looks* old and rotted."

Johnson smiled at them. "I theenk jou make the good *policía*," he said. "Ees camouflages, thees boat. Look here." He walked to the starboard bulwark where it met the raised deck cabin. He poked at some top rail, then pulled it upward. A small block of the wooden rail pulled off the bulwark. "Jou see what ees under the wood?"

"Sonuvabitch!" Bret exclaimed. "Looks like heavy steel plating."

"Don't just *look* like it," Russell said, "it's goddam half-inch armor plate. We got more armor'n an Abrams tank. This steel all the way around, Johnson?"

"All hull, all keel, all cabin. Both rudder, Russell. Only deck ees wood." He thumped the deck with one foot to let them hear the sound of heavy wooden planks.

With increasing enthusiasm for the upcoming journey, Bret asked, "Did you say 'both rudders', she's got twin-screws?"

"*Si*, and eet mean twin-engine."

"Shit, Russell, Johnson's got us on some badass craft." He looked aft where the engine hatch would be. "What make are your engines?"

"Don' know. Neffer ask. Eet one time belong to Colombia navy." He dug around in his small, tattered briefcase. Pulling a ream of stapled papers out, he looked them over. "Ees be call PB *boat in navy. Policía Nacional* impound heem, cut off, um, five meter from back side."

"Hell yeah," Bret said, nodding, "PB stands for Patrol Battle. Should be runnin' twin Cummins 12-cylinder marines under her aft deck. Most PBs were built at Newport News about twenty years ago."

"Good for catch *el narcotraficante* when he run 'caine on river or open sea," Johnson said, reading from one of the sheets of papers. He put the wooden block back over its steel edge.

Russell said, "This one's been chopped, channeled and given a disguise its architect wouldn't recognize. With all its steel plate, no wonder it sits so low in the water."

"Considerin' these were built for hot pursuit with fifteen additional feet of steel aft, I bet it's quite the racer," Bret speculated.

"I show jou cabin," Johnson interrupted. "More surprise for jou an' anyone who geeve jou *problema*." Johnson cast one last glance toward the docks, especially at five or six men standing together in a small group. He walked to the hatch.

Both Americans gazed at the men Johnson had been watching, thinking that he might have justifiable cause for suspicion. "Aren't makin' moves, yet," Bret said.

"Portholes downstairs?" Russell asked.

"*Si*, two each side. Bulletproof Plexiglas."

"You leavin' that key with us?" Bret asked. Johnson opened a heavy Schlage deadbolt lock with a key he took from his valise, then handed it to Bret. He stuck it into a pocket of his denim jeans. "*Gracias, amigo.*"

The cabin was spacious for a Class 2-size cruiser, and featured an elevated skipper's control sector with a broad front windscreen. Whereas the exterior of the craft appeared neglected and rotted, the cabin was tidy and clean. Throttles for both engines looked shiny new and recently oiled. Four settees that could be converted to beds were spaced along both sides of the interior.

"Now I show jou secret," Johnson said. He turned to one of the settee/bunks, leaned over and, gripping the mattress, pulled it forward. Its sturdy wooden support inclined forward as well, leaving an opening that resembled a coffin. A pillow, some sheets and several blankets lay in the open well. Two yellow life vests were in each corner.

Johnson kneeled in front of the bunk well, and began to pull the contents out, setting them beside him. "Jou help," he told Russell.

"You betcha," Russell said, pulling a life vest and the last blanket from the opening. He tossed them on the pile and said, "That's it, Johnson. You want me to make the bed, now?"

Johnson ignored his sarcasm and leaned forward into the opening. He held his left hand against the rear wooden support, then placed several fingers of his other hand into the uppermost right corner. He pushed forward and then to the right until a loud click got everyone's attention. Suddenly Johnson had trouble holding the rear wooden frame from coming forward. Bret and Russell kneeled down and pushed their hands against the straining wood support.

"Let eet come down not so ver' fast," Johnson said, panting.

The heavy rear panel folded down to the inner cabin deck. The two Americans looked on in astonishment. Lying on the padded side of the panel were several sections of a Stinger missile launcher and two, five-foot Stinger missiles/launch tubes. Further inside Johnson's "big secret" were a variety of small arms and submachine guns, a cache large enough to be the envy of most firearms dealers.

"Damn," Bret exclaimed. "It's a full Stinger package: infrared homing guidance, IFF positive hostile I.D. seeker, gripstock tracking unit, the whole 50-pound lot."

"Look in there," Russell said, pointing to an automatic rifle. "My favorite weapon . . . a Colt Commando."

"Yeah, that's a beaut. All the AR-15 features, but only 28 inches long. Army Special Ops and Brit SAS use it."

"Man, what other goodies you got in here, Johnson?" Russell had a Christmas morning gleam in his eyes.

"More 'gooties' under osser beds, chentlemens. Jou check out after jou begin journey down Rio Magdalena."

"Yeah," Bret agreed. "We've gotta move out right now, with some six hundred miles against the river current."

Johnson set a map of the route on a navigator's table, along with several other sheets of paper in a file folder. Then they approached the hatch, Johnson in the lead. He turned the latch and began to climb the three steps to the main deck. As his left foot touched the deck, an explosion broke the morning silence.

Johnson fell back into Bret's arms. He half dragged, half-carried Johnson into the cabin. "You okay, Johnson?" he yelled, as he held back the sudden panic.

"Hokay, I theenk. *Pero*, choulder hurt." Johnson's suit jacket was ripped away at the right shoulder. Beneath it, a small piece of metal was lodged in a gray, woven material.

"Damn, Johnson," Bret shouted in relief, "you're wearin' a flak jacket."

"Kevlar vest kept his shoulder attached to his frame," Russell said. He raced to the still-open bedding-well filled with arms and ammo. Grabbing a 5.56mm Colt Commando and a 20-round magazine, he raced back toward the hatch.

"Too many of them," Bret shouted. Through a porthole he counted at least six armed men spread forty to fifty yards around the boat. They carried M-16A2 assault rifles with M203 40mm grenade launchers. "Johnson musta got clipped with shrapnel from a grenade that hit the side of the cabin."

Then, Bret saw another grenade leave the launcher of the point man in the group. It struck the port side directly beneath the cabin. The blast rocked the boat slightly, but there seemed to be no damage. Russell shouldered the loaded Armalite and grabbed one of several machetes he'd noticed in a corner of the cabin. He flung the hatch open and headed toward the single rope holding the PB boat.

They all knew that chopping the rope away was their only hope. An assault against them may cost the enemy some lives, but the odds were too high at such close range. They had to get away from the wharf and the six guerrillas. Russell crawled across the top of the cabin to the rope attached to the fore bow. He kept the guerrillas lying low with quick bursts from the AR-15. Another grenade struck near the stern water line, intended to be a fatal blow to the "ancient"craft. The grenade merely knocked the wooden rind from the steel bulwark, like peeling bark from a sturdy birch tree.

Russell yelled, "Start engines, Lamplighter, if we have *gasolina*."

"When was the last time this boat ran?"

"No *sé*," Johnson shrugged.

"You don't know? When did it arrive in Barranquilla?"

"Whan week, maybe tsen day."

"Then somebody *drove* it here!"

"Maybe pulled here by other *barco*."

"Shit!" Bret knew if a grungy-looking boat was pulled into the dock, few thieves or vandals would give it a second thought. They'd think it was probably due for dismantling soon. "These the starters?" he asked, pointing at two key slots next to the throttles.

"*Si*. Here are jour keys." He handed the starter keys to Bret. "Jou put een an' turn key."

"Yeah, yeah." He heard the chatter of Russell's Armalite between noisy chops from his machete. Then he heard him thumping on the cabin roof.

"Russell cut rope. Now theenk we maybe go mos' fas.'"

"If this sonuvabitch starts," Bret shouted. He put both keys in their slots and turned them simultaneously. The two large engines bellowed to life with a roar that must have awakened anyone still slumbering in the town of Soledad.

"Damn," he whooped, "the big bastard's screamin'. He jammed the two gear shifts into reverse and pulled both throttles all the way down to 'high' rev. The old stallion bucked like a young mustang, swiftly backing straight into the busy Rio Magdalena.

"Ee-iiii," Johnson screeched. "Eef *barco* in jour way, we seenk heem fer chure."

Through the windscreen, Bret saw Russell lying prone, hanging onto the line ring. He was swinging the Colt in the air with his free hand and bellowing at the rapidly receding guerrillas. Their last salvo of bullets and grenades missed the Patrol Battle vessel by twenty feet. Bret, Russell and Johnson had stared a death squad in its eyes, and it was the death squad that blinked.

Chapter Twenty

She kicked her ash-covered work boot at a shiny object. Abby picked up the shard of heavy glass, probably once part of a crystal goblet. She examined it, then tossed it back into the incredible destruction. *Nothing here larger than a fifty-franc coin*, she reckoned, *except that item in my pocket.* She waded through the ruins of Horst DeGroot's home, hardly expecting to discover anything new. Abby gazed across the impact site to where eleven larger pieces of metal were recovered earlier. Fragments in the debris were parts of an American-manufactured Tomahawk missile.

"Duchamps, *venez ici*," a man's voice broke the silence. She looked toward an expanse that used to divide DeGroot's home from his neighbor's. She saw one of Sint Maarten's newest arrivals, a police inspector from Martinique.

A short time before she was the only French law enforcement officer conducting official business on St. Martin. Now, the island's two police forces were reporting to a French *sous-inspecteur*. The Amsterdam House bombing in Philipsburg had brought in the Gang of Three as Abby had labeled Dornier, Chatelaine and Kronstein of the *Sûreté Nationale*'s DST. Yesterday, the horrible terrorist plane bombing had prompted Paris to send six more *Sûreté* agents. Finally, this morning's missile strike to the home of the former Sint Maarten police chief had brought a squad of French territorial police from Martinique. She counted the French arrivals, but Dutch and Netherlands Antilles' police officials were also poring in from Curaçao and Aruba. *Merde*, Abby thought as she walked toward the Fort-de-France police inspector, *what does that man want now?*

"Mademoiselle Duchamps," Herve Toubon said as she approached him, "you will find nothing new. We have been here for many hours."

"Always the chance, inspector," she replied in French. "Perhaps another centimeter and I'll hit the mother lode."

Toubon grunted his doubt. He was not used to women police officers, having none on investigative duty for him in Fort-de-France. This woman member of the highly-regarded *Sûreté Nationale* believed she was his superior. "We checked everywhere with the finest metal detectors available, mademoiselle."

"Call me 'Officer', inspector Toubon," Abby said, "or 'Agent'." Abby's I.D. and shield were in evidence on her outfit. The plane bombing and then the missile blast, coupled with finding the body of Rupert Morgan, left her with little enthusiasm after her exciting days with Bret. She'd used Bret's key to enter his villa and found the 'work clothes' she needed. A pair of tawdry Bermuda shorts fell halfway between her knees and ankles. A garish Hawaiian-style short-sleeve shirt was buttoned to her chin, its sleeves reaching within three inches of her wrists. The shorts, with their 36-inch-waist, were drawn and overlapped to fit her 24-inch waist with one of Abby's own belts. Her holstered Walther P-38 was nearly hidden in the folds of the shirt and shorts. Her I.D./shield billfold were on the shirt pocket, nearly down to her waist. Only the grimy hiking boots and socks were owned by Abby.

"You do not dress as an officer. Also, you do not carry your issued weapon."

"Inspector, you *will* hear from the Director of the *Sûreté* if you disregard my rank and station on St. Martin." Never before had she used her capacity with one of the world's foremost law enforcement agencies to shake up anyone. *Still, this is different,* she told herself. "Metal detectors do not find plastic, glass, paper or wood. You and your men may have missed many important fragments."

Toubon's ebony face revealed a tinge of crimson as he fought back his rage. "We sifted through the sand and ash, *mademoi . . . officer* Duchamps. Nothing escaped us."

"Compact discs are made of plastic polymers, inspector." She pulled a blackened clump from a pants pocket. It was round, about five inches in diameter and a half-inch thick. From the side it was evident this had been a stack of five user-recordable CD's. She held it out to Toubon. "The top one has handwriting on it I can't make out, but I'm certain the right equipment should reveal it."

"Hmm," he murmured, "they're fused together, an unusual item. Could show that DeGroot owned a CD player or a personal computer." He flipped the item several times in the palm of his hand. He handed the disks back. "I'm not impressed."

"I *am*, inspector," Abby said. "I'll have it analyzed."

"Of course. That's your call."

"I will be meeting with my DST associates, inspector. *Au revoir*."

"Only with three of the other DST members on St. Martin, mademoiselle."

The inspector from Martinique was correct. Abby and her 'Gang of Three' had been contacted by telephone from Marseille earlier that morning. Dornier, Chatelaine and Kronstein would continue their investigation of the Amsterdam House bombing and the death of Rupert Morgan. Abby was told her only assignment would be Bret and the missing emeralds. Martinique's team led by Toubon would investigate the missile strike. The half-dozen *Sûreté* personnel who arrived yesterday were to handle the terrorist-caused plane crash.

"I hope we can stay out of each other's way," she said. *Asshole thinks women's work is being the meek little housewife*, Abby thought. Her fellow students at Wellesley had taught their French classmate much useful American slang.

Toubon turned and walked toward several of his men

operating powerful metal detectors. He spoke with them briefly, then continued toward his car. Two of the Martinique police officers began to probe the ruins and ashes on hands and knees, sifting debris through their fingers. Abby smiled, hoping Herve Toubon would look in her direction. The inspector never turned back.

As she neared Bret's rented Subaru M-80, Abby pulled the car keys from an oversized pocket. She'd left all the windows ajar, just far enough to allow some of the sun's heat to escape. She saw a scrap of paper inside, teetering on the edge of the driver's seat. Someone had used the narrow window opening as a mail slot, delivering a message directly to her. *Why not phone, or speak to me in person?*

She unlocked the door, cranked down the windows and sat in the driver's seat. She loosened the top three buttons of Bret's shirt, since the temperature was already in the mid-eighties. Abby rolled the sleeves and shorts legs as far as they would go. Inside the Subaru, it felt like a blast furnace. The sheet of paper was folded twice. Her name was printed on the outer fold: "Miss Abby Duchamps." Obviously, the drop wasn't a case of mistaken identity.

Unfolding the note, she read the message: "Dear Miss Duchamps. I'm in St. Martin on consular business regarding two Americans injured on the beach in the Air France disaster." *Must be Bret's friend from Fort-de-France.* "You were speaking with inspector Toubon when I arrived, so I chose not to interrupt. I would like to talk with you about the 'case' Mr. Lamplighter is working on for Multistate Insurance. Please call me at the Club Le Grand St. Martin in Marigot, telephone 85.57.91. Regards, Bertrand Hough."

"Suppose I should speak with Hough since he's here," she murmured. A breeze had stirred up tiny whirlwinds on the ashen acre of devastated Williams Hill real estate. The same breeze cleared out the sizzling heat from the tiny car. Abby twisted the ignition key, revved the small engine and dropped the shifter into Drive.

Less than a half-hour later Abby arrived at her villa on Pointe des Pierres a Chaux. She was happy to be 'home' at Sunshine Pointe, and smiled at Yvonne. She seemed infatuated with Lamplighter and let it show in her manner toward the female DST agent.

"You have one message, Madame," Yvonne said. She handed Abby a small, beige envelope.

"*Merci*, Yvonne," Abby replied. " . . . and, for the record, it's '*mademoiselle*'."

Yvonne nodded and picked up the telephone. She pressed a phone button, shutting off the hold light. "You were saying, Nicole?" she spoke.

Ah, to be young and testy, Abby thought as she walked back toward the car. As she strode, she ripped open the envelope and pulled out a small sheet of paper. It read: "Abby. Please give me a ring at headquarters when you return. I have information about our mutual friend, Colonel Parra. Henri Bouchard."

Abby was alarmed for a moment, but then realized that the note was—if not upbeat—at least neutral in tone. *He shouldn't have gone on such a ridiculous trek*, she thought. She felt personally responsible for the American's safety . . . after all, she'd been assigned to him by Marseille. *I'll phone Henri right after I get in touch with Bret's friend from the U.S. consulate.*

Abby parked the car rented by Bret on the street in front of her villa. She bounded from the vehicle, dragging the **BYE·BYE** shopping bag with her. The bag now held her hiking boots and socks, DST credentials, 'emergency' cosmetics and the P-38 automatic pistol and holster. She reached into the bag, shoved her arm past Hough's note and Bouchard's message, and felt the door key to her villa. She also removed a remote transmitter disarm unit for the portable silent security system she'd set up in her villa. The ultra-sensitive wireless device detected any movement within a forty-foot arc. It took a photograph every two seconds on infrared 35mm film if its sensor detected movement within its range. Karl's electronic donation to his fellow

DST agent came shortly after they'd discovered Rupert and his mother murdered.

"These *bâtards* mean business, Abby," he'd said. "This will help protect you when you're away from your villa."

Pressing a button on the tiny remote, Abby noted the yellow LED turn to green. The device hadn't been activated while she'd been gone. If anyone had entered her rooms, the LED would have turned red . . . *blinking* red if the person was still there.

"Handy gadget," she mumbled, putting the key into the front door. Once inside, she double-checked the five by two inch device hanging on the living room wall. Her remote proved reliable . . . the high resolution camera hadn't discharged.

She pulled off the oversize shirt, dropping it to the floor. Then, Abby applied more of the blue-colored ointment to her scuffed nipples, areolae and knees.

Discarding the ill-fitting Bermuda shorts, she sat on the sofa next to the telephone. She glanced at the assistant consul's note, then punched the phone number for his hotel. A female voice answered, *"Bon jour,* Club Le Grand St. Martin."

"Allô. Monsieur Hough, *s'il vous plaît."*

"Merci. Un moment." French elevator music reached Abby's ears.

The serenade lasted no more than one or two seconds before she heard, "Hello, this is Hough."

"Hello, Mr. Hough. This is Abby Duchamps. You left a note in my car to give you a call."

"Ah, Miss Duchamps," Hough declared. "I'm glad you phoned me so quickly."

"Really? Is there something wrong, Mr. Hough?" Abby wasn't sure if Hough knew about Bret's trip to Colombia.

"No, no. Not at all," he assured her, sounding amused. "I simply wished to speak with you about, umm, Bret's most recent excursion."

He does know. "I'm not certain what you mean Mr. Hough. He and I have been working together on an emerald theft. I believe he's still working on it."

"We really should not talk of this business over the phone,

Miss Duchamps. Perhaps we could talk over a drink, or dinner. How about this evening?"

She ignored the invitation. "Why did you leave your note in my car, Mr. Hough? It seems like more trouble than simply phoning me at my residence. Bret said he'd informed you that he and I stayed at the same resort."

"Ever the police officer, *mademoiselle*," Hough joked. "I spoke with *sous-inspecteur* Bouchard this morning. He said he believed you were at the remains of Chief DeGroot's home."

I suppose Henri would tell the assistant American consul general my whereabouts, since Hough's a friend of Bret's. "You could have talked to me at Williams Hill, Mr. Hough. Your credentials would allow you to visit the scene."

"Quite true, Miss Duchamps. However, *Inspecteur* Toubon and Martinique's U.S. consulate are not on the best of terms."

"You knew the car I was driving?"

"I recognized it as the one Bret Lamplighter drove last week at Grand Case."

"Look, Mr. Hough, I'm really tired from investigating all the incidents we've had on St. Martin." She thought about a way to relax *and* speak with the American.

"I understand," he said. "In one short week St. Martin has seen more trouble than the devastating hurricane caused several years ago. I realize even the finest officers in the *Sûreté Nationale* must take a break occasionally." He paused. "Call me Bertrand."

Abby smiled at Hough's attempt to flatter her. She stared out the floor-to-ceiling picture window, noticing several sunbathers by the swimming pool. "Do you swim, Bertrand, or at least get a little sun?" She added, "And call me Abby."

"I used to be on my university's swim team, but now I spend my pool time lying under a beach umbrella. What did you have in mind?"

"Some sun and fresh air should help me unwind, Bertrand. Why don't I meet you by the swimming pool next to my villa? We will talk and relax at the same time."

"Sounds splendid. Been keeping my nose to the grindstone

myself. Going from a car air conditioner to an office air conditioner isn't very healthful."

"You left out 'an apartment air conditioner' in your daily schedule." Bret had mentioned Hough's unusually posh apartment for a federal government civil servant.

"That's true, Abby," Bertrand laughed. "My one grand extravagance in life . . . trying to live like a king on a pauper's wages."

Abby thought she detected a slight edge to his chuckle. "See you about two o'clock?"

"Two o'clock it is, officer Duchamps. *Au revoir.*"

She hung up the receiver and thought, *I remember pondering how odd for Bret to get here on an important case, then go straight to the pool.* Abby now understood how stressed-out and tense one could get juggling many difficult chores. She shrugged, pulled on the bikini bottom, and applied another coat of blue salve to her mild abrasions.

Now to see if Henri's at the station. Abby dialed the Marigot police station although, officially, Philipsburg was the interim island headquarters. At the second ring, the police dispatcher answered: "Mar'got police. May I he'p you?"

"*Sous-inspecteur Bouchard*, please. This is . . ."

"Dees be officer Duchamps?" the native woman interrupted.

"Uh, why yes. I'd like to . . ."

"I gets de *sous-'specteur* right away, ma'am," she again interrupted. "You jis hang on where you be an' I patch him in t' you, 'toot sweet'."

Abby set the Enos-Schnaar Burst/Scrambler on her left thigh, ready to attach it if Bouchard thought it was necessary. The DST agent heard three clicking sounds, then an echo-effect came to her ears. She'd been transferred to a scrambled telephone, so she clamped the scrambler over her phone's speaker.

She gazed at the French family from the adjacent villa, as they marched toward the beach. Mother led the way, with two children trying to step in her sand-prints. Five-year-old Daughter wore a swim suit with both bottom *and* top. Next came three-year-old Son, not wearing a stitch of clothing. All three waved to Abby, who smiled and waved back through the floor-to-ceiling picture window. Taking up the rear, wearing vulgar red Speedo swim trunks, came Father. He stared straight ahead, loaded down with blankets, towels and assorted beach toys.

"Hello, Abby. I see you got my message." Henri Bouchard's voice penetrated the line. He sounded as if he were speaking from the bottom of a well. "Is your scrambler in place and activated?" Bouchard asked.

"Ready to go, Henri. Do you have news of Bret . . . Mr. Lamplighter?"

"Some news about him, some news about your visitor at the scene of the missile strike. Let me get to Hough first."

"Fine with me. How did you know . . . ?"

"Toubon. He contacted me after one of his men noticed Hough near your car."

"I see. Hough told me he and Toubon weren't on very good terms."

"Toubon's a professional—quite knowledgeable." Abby noticed that the *sous-inspecteur* hesitated. "Abby, I'm going to give you some classified information. Knowing it before wasn't necessary, but Hough's appearance on St. Martin changes things."

"Sounds sinister, Henri."

Henri grunted. "Bertrand Hough is known to be a principal smuggler of contraband into Martinique and then on to St. Martin and Anguilla."

"I'll be meeting him in a couple of hours . . ."

"Meet him at the pool as planned, Abby. Enough tourists and resort help should be around at two o'clock for him not to try anything."

"Damn it, Henri!" she exclaimed. "You know my plans. The least you could do is *tell* me you're still bugging my phone." She hadn't checked the instrument for hidden mikes in two days.

"Believe me, Abby," Bouchard answered, "it's for your own good. We couldn't have known Hough was going to contact you if we didn't have your phone line tapped."

"I'm a professional law enforcement officer. I can handle a smuggler like Bertrand Hough. I even received a commendation from Marseille for my handling of the Iranian terrorist at the airport."

"Abby," Henri Bouchard said in his most considerate voice, "no one on this island or in the Caribbean—or back home in Marseille—is more aware of your bravery and professionalism than I. However, the man you see as a sensitive, gentlemanly smuggler of gemstones, is a cold-blooded killer and a terrorist!"

"Why is he still running around killing people and smuggling?" Abby retorted. "If he's so dangerous, lock him up."

"That's my personal top priority. Right now, though, my hands are tied. Interpol, the F.B.I., MI-5 and SDECE are all watching him. There's ample film and video footage linking him to many violent crimes, but larger countries want to get more on him."

"DeGroot's murder?"

"Almost certainly. We believe Horst and Bertrand Hough were accomplices. When DeGroot bolted, an order went out to silence him."

"Hough has the power to issue such an order?"

"Yes, with the authorization of his Colombian and Iranian associates. Do you remember an American Airlines jet crash quite a few years ago near Cali, Colombia?"

"Flight 965 . . . Miami to Cali. Flew off-course and crashed into a mountain," she recalled. "Are you suggesting the flight's crash was sabotage?"

"Two influential Colombian drug dealers who'd 'flip-flopped' to U.S. federal authorities were on the airplane. All published reports said the flight recorder showed a computer error. CIA technical analysts confirm sabotage to the computer which was activated when the 767 descended to the Cali flight pattern."

"And Hough . . . ?" Abby thought she knew the answer to her question.

" . . . was at Cali Municipal Airport at the time of the crash. Also in Cali that day was one late-Rupert Morgan and one Sabri al-Banna of ANO renown. Our assistant U.S. consulate general deals in vast quantities of precious gemstones."

"Cocaine, heroin, hemp and synthetic narcotics, too?"

"No, never, Abby. The Colombia drug cartels are extremely jealous of their product. Outsiders are absolutely not allowed in . . . at any price."

"Umm, I see," Abby remarked. "Do you believe Hough was responsible for the Air France bombing?"

"Probably not, although he may have been told it was going down. The Iranian terrorist you nullified—Ahmad al-Majid—and Rupert Morgan evidently planted the servos, detonators and Semtex plastique." A beeping noise sounded. "Time to sign off, Abby. Oh, Lamplighter's okay. I'll be in touch and update you on him." In an electronic age when all security devices could be overridden, the scrambler's 'secure time limit' had been reached. Sophisticated descramblers, if started at the phone conversation's onset, could decode all signals. Solution: take no chances.

"My best to your wife, Henri. *Au revoir*." She set the receiver in its cradle.

"Shit," Abby cursed aloud. *Wanted to tell him about the fused CD's. They might help prove Hough's involvement with DeGroot's illegal activities. I'll put them in my safe*, she decided.

Bouchard's hunch proved correct, as eight other residents of the resort sunbathed or swam in the pool nearest her villa. Four of the people at the pool were Abby's French next-door neighbors. The children noisily splashed in the pool. Mama read a magazine. Papa dozed.

A young man and woman lay in loungers pulled tight against each other. Initially, upon arriving alone at the pool, the young woman glanced at Abby's blue salve-tinted bosom. Right fist clenched, she smiled and said, "Cool statement, sister." Now, however, they patted lotion onto each other in the torrid sun, curious causes forgotten. *What the hell statement am I making with maimed, blue-smeared boobs?* Abby wondered.

A good-looking young man and an attractive middle-aged woman periodically checked each other out across three empty chaise lounges. Periodically, the woman strutted to the edge of the pool and splashed water onto yet-untanned legs, stomach and breasts.

Looking around Abby decided, *God's in His heaven, All's right with the world!*

At what Abby calculated to be exactly two o'clock, a shadow passed over her closed eyes. *Has to be Hough*, she figured. Opening her eyes and pushing herself up slightly with her elbows, she saw a man pulling a lounger close to her.

"Bertrand Hough," he said, extending his right hand. He'd pulled the reclining chair close to Abby, but not so close as to appear intimidating.

"Good to meet you, Bertrand." Abby shook his hand. "Bret mentioned your name before he . . . the last time I saw him."

"Good man, Bret. Regrettable mess he got himself into a couple of years ago here on St. Martin. Not his fault, of course." He smiled, then glanced at Abby's chest and knees. "*Guérisseur Bleu*," he said, nodding at the daubs of blue ointment. "Blue Healer for all maladies, eh? I've used it for everything from chigger bites to gunshot wounds."

"Really? I don't see any scars." Abby grinned. Hough wore green swim trunks and leather sandals. He'd set a cotton shirt and beach towel on the chaise next to him.

Hough said, "The chigger bites were me—the gunshot wounds were an American tourist in Fort-de-France." He paused, getting no reaction from the pretty Frenchwoman. "Even the civilized Caribbean has its share of street crime."

"Perhaps *more* than its share, Bertrand?" She swung her legs off the lounger and sat up straight. "Why did you get in touch with me?"

"As I wrote in my message, I was sent here to check the condition of two Air France victims." He clasped hands around one knee and leaned back. "The families are preparing law suits, and I'm their American conduit for police and hospital reports." He smiled and said, "It's my job."

"Also, you said you wished to talk about Mr. Lamplighter's Multistate Insurance case. Is that part of an assistant U.S. consulate general's job description?" It was now Abby's turn to clasp a knee with her hands and lean back slightly on the pool lounger.

Hough continued to smile. He picked a tube of suntan lotion from among the folds of his towel and opened it very deliberately. "As with your job description, Abby," he spread some lotion on his arms and legs, "mine tends to change from day to day. If career government employees relied on written outlines of their work, nothing would ever get finished. This is true for myself and you, *officier* Duchamps."

"Your note said you wanted to discuss the emerald theft with me."

"True. First, I'm a friend of Bret's." He wiped his hands on the towel. "Secondly, the consulate general in Martinique represents all American citizens on the Caribbean's French possessions."

"Right, Bertrand," Abby said. "Then why weren't you here to help him after he nearly got killed at the Amsterdam House?"

"Philipsburg's on the Dutch side, as you know, so it wouldn't have been an official act of the Martinique consulate general. Nonetheless, I personally visited him two days later. We had dinner at the Alabama restaurant in Grand Case."

"That was after we both were nearly killed right on this beach."

"He told me the story . . . including the fact he'd suspected you of the Amsterdam House bombing."

Abby smiled at Hough's assured poise and easily-delivered answers. "Bret told me he had a few suspicions about me at first, but quickly discarded them." She studied Hough's face. "Tell me, Bertrand, why did you give Bret a photo and bio of me?"

"A simple matter of identification, Abby. I wanted Bret to be certain you *were* who you said you were." He said, "again, it's part of my job."

"To show an insurance investigator the photo of a French law enforcement officer?"

"I told you . . . to verify your identity."

"Where's Bret now?" Her sudden change of subject took Hough aback. He stared at her, puzzled.

"How should I know?" Hough answered. "He's been on St. Martin with you. I'd think you'd keep close tabs on him; after all, he's your special DST assignment."

Abby grinned and dug into her shopping bag. She removed a raw carrot and slowly chomped on it. "I *do* know, Bertrand," Abby replied. "So do you."

"I don't see how . . . ?"

"You're acquainted with an American army pilot named Frederick Wilson," Abby stated. "Interpol has a file on Captain Wilson that his commanding officer at Southern Command would love to see." She stared at a now-sullen civil servant.

Hough wiped sweat from his face with a beach towel. He looked at the other people by the pool, and scanned the sky—seemingly hopeful that a helicopter would whisk him away. He said, "Wilson's an American; you're French. There's no way . . ."

"You've been nodding off, I fear. The operative word I used was Interpol . . . the International police agency." Abby bit into her carrot, producing a crunch of superb grandeur. Hough teetered on his lounger.

"What sort of evidence does Interpol have on Wilson?"

"Thousands of videos, moving pictures, optical camera CD's, still photos and slides, Polaroids . . . probably even floppy disks. There's so much photographic evidence, in fact, their Willemstad office had to buy two large file cabinets to hold it all."

"Sounds like he's in deep shit." Hough looked out onto Nettle Bay.

Abby nodded, stared into eyes focused far beyond her, and said, "Steve Janicek of Interpol Caribbean showed me several photos of Wilson yesterday."

"Good."

"I brought two high-res, color glossies with me. Look at them." She put her hand into the shopping bag again, pulling out a beige file folder. Abby withdrew the photos from the folder and handed them to Hough.

"Uh-hunh," he looked with interest at the photos. "You're right, Abby, these are very high-quality." He paused, then said, "Sorry I didn't bring my family album along for you to look at." Hough slid back the photos.

Abby said, "I particularly enjoy the happy smiles on your faces in this interior setting." She studied the images much as a visitor to an art museum studies an Old Master. "Interesting idea, Bertrand . . . quite creative." It was taken in the living room of Hough's apartment in Fort-de-France. Bertrand Hough sat in a plush chair at a stunning mahogany or dark oak table. Across from Hough sat a black man in his late-thirties or early-forties. Captain Wilson had his fingers on an exceptionally large emerald, ready to "checkmate" his opponent.

"The scenario was Freddie's idea, the chess game using thirty-two exquisite emeralds." Hough said, "The magnificent stone he's holding fetched us seven-hundred fifty thousand dollars. The dealer's markup probably more than doubled."

Abby slowly shook her head. "Good recall. You must have had thousands of emeralds to dispose of."

Hough gazed at the photograph on Abby's lap. "They're like children. You never forget them, no matter how many you have." Hough gathered his towel and other belongings together, evidently preparing to leave.

"Mr. Hough, we have to talk," Abby said, deftly pulling a T-shirt over her head. She placed the photographs back in their folder and began to slip them into the bag.

"Bad idea," Hough whispered, swiftly pulling the bag over to his lounger. He reached inside and removed Abby's automatic pistol. He held the large towel at the opening to the shopping bag, slipping the weapon behind it. "You really are quite the bag lady, Abby. Something in here for every occasion."

"Bertrand," Abby said, "Janicek presented a tradeoff. Smuggling charges dropped in exchange for names in Colombia and Curaçao. No one would know it was you . . ."

"Are you crazy? A fucking idiot would know I informed.

Wilson and the others in prison, Bertrand Hough free as a frigate bird." He snickered.

"Then we could work something else out. Keep some of the smugglers in business, but put them under surveillance. There's always a way, Bertrand." Abby didn't tell Hough she was aware of his appalling crimes. They knew the witness protection program didn't apply to mass murderers.

"I'm leaving," he sputtered. Standing, Bertrand Hough beckoned to the young woman. "So are you, Abby, as far as your villa. Afraid that's the end of your journey. You should have stayed on the *côte d'azure*. Nice is lovely this time of year." Hough grabbed Abby's shoulder and pulled her toward him.

"Take your hands off me, you bastard," Abby shouted. The two children in the shallow part of the pool watched them, expressionless. Everyone else pretended they hadn't heard the argument.

"Come, come, Abby dear." Hough soothed his troubled young lady friend, just loud enough for all to hear. "We'll sit in the villa and talk out our little problem." He consoled Abby as the sunbathers around the heated pool knew he should . . . as Bertrand Hough knew was expected of him. Hough had an arm draped over Abby's shoulder as he led her off the soothing pool tiles. His right hand held the towel and P-38 pistol.

Stepping onto the sun bleached sand, Abby felt the heat burn her feet. *Not much chance*, she thought. Suddenly she shouted, "Sand's scalding my feet!" She abruptly sprinted toward her villa, pulling away from Hough's grasp. *Must get to my MAS*, she realized, remembering her government-issue sidearm.

"Goddam it, Abby—stop," he shouted. Off balance, Hough slipped in the sand down to his knees. "I'll shoot, you bitch," he growled, dropping the towel and aiming the powerful pistol at Abby's back.

A deafening blast spoiled the serenity of the resort. Seagulls and sugar birds gave flight and squawked in startled fright. Abby's wild dash ended twenty feet from the rear patio of her villa, where she'd fallen in the unstable sand. She turned toward Hough, who'd dropped the weapon and was staring in dazed disbelief at his mangled, bloody arm. Standing ten feet from him, smoking Beretta 92S automatic cradled in his hand, stood the single young man from the pool. Several feet from him, also aiming a sinister-looking Beretta at Hough, was the young woman who'd saluted Abby's 'cause.' She jumped from her kneeling position and ran to Hough, kicking the P-38 away from his reach.

"Interpol," the young man said to Abby and Hough. He pulled a credentials billfold from the waistband of his swim trunks and held it for viewing. "You're under arrest, Mr. Hough." In shock, Bertrand stared at his wound.

"How could you know . . . ?" Abby began.

"You have Inspector Toubon to thank, agent Duchamps," the young woman divulged. "He knew Hough's background from a stack of files on Martinique. When he found out Hough contacted you at Williams Hill, well . . . here we are."

Still sitting on the uncomfortably hot sand, Abby could finally smile. She jubilantly raised a clenched fist and declared, "Right on, sister."

Chapter Twenty-One

"You wanted to see me, Mr. Gruener?" George Princeton's question was purely one of formality, since Henry's secretary summoned him less than three minutes before. He stood in the frame of Gruener's door, looking at his boss. *Time to get my ass chewed out*, George thought.

"Yeah, yeah," Gruener motioned his subordinate in. "Sit here," he mumbled, pointing at the chair closest to his desk.

"Fog and rain finally lifting," George said, glancing through one of Henry's 46th floor corner office windows. He never knew what the weather was doing from his windowless cubicle two floors below. It was getting dark.

"Assassinations, George," Henry said, as he lifted a slip of paper from his desk, "are the easiest crimes to commit . . . at least if the assassin doesn't mind getting caught."

"Bernie Lustfield's killer wasn't caught, Henry . . ."

"Not Lustfield," Henry affected disgust. "They just gave me this information about another killing on St. Martin." He held the small yellow note in both hands, propped up in the center of his immense desk.

"I hadn't heard . . ."

"Not your place to hear about these matters." Henry peered above bifocals at the claims adjustment manager sitting in front of him.

He thought, *Tell me, you shithead. Who was it this time?* "Not Bret, I hope," George said, practically imploring his boss to give him the bad news.

"Mrs. Douglas and the Colonel spoke with me at The Citadel, George. They heard of it from Director Fitzpatrick of DEA. He said he'd keep us abreast of any further developments."

"We were notified about another killing?"

Gruener grunted and leaned back further in his five thousand dollar chair. "The chief of police of Fredricksberg was killed . . ."

"The capital of Sint Maarten is *Philips*burg, Mr. Gruener," George corrected. "Sorry for the interruption." *Someone snuffed DeGroot*, he pondered.

Henry nodded at George's apology, then continued with, " . . . killed with an American Tomahawk missile, fer crissake."

"America's involved in another . . . ?"

"Ordnance experts flown in from the U.S. Virgin Islands say it's an old model," Henry said, ignoring the man seated across from him. "Markings on some debris show it was used during the Persian Gulf war years ago. Apparently some missiles failed to explode on their Iraqi targets."

"The Iraqis killed Chief DeGroot with a goddam missile?" George realized he'd spoken his thoughts out loud. "I mean," he fumbled, "it looks that way."

"Possible, according to Fitzpatrick, but not probable. He seems to think their next-door neighbors, the Iranians, are more likely candidates," Gruener replied.

"Lamplighter could be overwhelmed, if that's true," George said. "Is there any way we can get him outta Colombia?"

"Mrs. Douglas, the Colonel . . . and I," Gruener said, "are *not* unhappy about this." He inspected his fingernails for several seconds. "Haste makes waste, we've all come to learn. We won't be hasty with Lamplighter."

"He could be in danger, Mr. Gruener."

"It was Lamplighter's call," he replied. "He's gonna learn to live with that decision, now."

George Princeton was so disgusted with his boss he decided

to change the subject. *No sense in getting fired. I'll check on Bret myself.* "How was the Tomahawk launched? Wouldn't a missile catapult be hard to hide on St. Martin?"

"Fitzpatrick hedged on that question when I asked him. He hinted that an NSA spy satellite picked up the whole incident. Won't say any more than it came from a ship off the island's north coast."

"They identify the ship? Sink it? Capture it?"

"That's all he told me, said the rest was top secret." Henry drummed his fingers on the note that lay on his desk. "Didn't want to pester him about it. Government buys a huge volume of personnel, vehicle and materiel insurance from the private sector."

That explains Henry's indifference, George realized. *The top Board members smell an insurance premium windfall from the federal government.*

"Fitzpatrick did tell me, George, that Johnson arranged for a field agent to travel with Lamplighter."

"He's workin' with a spy in Colombia? What agency is he with?"

Henry looked at another yellow slip of paper, one of many that covered his desktop. He checked its content before speaking. Gruener replied, "His exact words were: 'Your observer has a first-rate detection-collection asset escorting him.' To me that *does* mean, as you put it, that he's working with a covert operative."

"Still doesn't say what country he's from or the organization paying his salary."

"I was led to believe Fitzpatrick's information came from State."

"State's Bureau of Intelligence and Research, then?" George Princeton asked.

"Wouldn't care to guess, George. You shouldn't waste your time on that subject, either," Henry Gruener spoke slowly. "We don't want to ruffle feathers."

I've been ordered to forget Bret's spy partner, George understood. "No, Mr. Gruener. I realize the federal government's the largest client . . ."

Gruener's intercom buzzed like an irate cicada, interrupting George in mid-sentence. "Yeah, Diane?" Gruener rasped, as he pressed a button on the gray instrument.

"A Miss Duchamps on line four from St. Martin. Says she's been working with Mr. Lamplighter on the Ultragem emerald claim." The voice was firm and efficient.

"*La femme* Duchamps," Henry said, speaking his version of a French accent. "I'll take it, Diane. No interruptions."

Before Henry could press the line four button, George leaned forward. "Her father's a close friend of President Chirac. She's a Wellesley grad and has a postgraduate degree from Harvard."

Gruener brushed his hand in the air as if whisking away a pesky fruit fly. He pressed the phone button and said, "It's a pleasure getting a call from you, agent Duchamps."

"It is my pleasure, as well, Mr. Gruener," Abby replied. "I telephoned George Princeton initially, but was told he was in a meeting with you. Bret Lamplighter gave me Mr. Princeton's name if there was ever any reason to contact Multistate."

"I'll switch on the speaker phone, agent Duchamps," Gruener said while pressing a button labeled 'monitor'.

"Good afternoon, Abby," Princeton informally remarked. "It's delightful speaking with you after hearing Bret rave about his marvelous *Sûreté* partner."

"I'm very flattered, George. Mr. Lamplighter's a real gentleman and a splendid investigator." Abby hesitated, then said, "He saved my life at our resort, you know." Although this was an open telephone line, she saw no reason to hold back such a well-known fact.

"I recall Bret telling me you returned the favor in full, Abby." George was also well aware that electronic ears could be listening to their words. "You two seem to make a good team."

"*Merci*, George. I think so, too." A brief lull was evident before the Frenchwoman said, "I believe Bret may be in serious danger."

"According to reports we've received," Henry Gruener countered, "he's been in danger ever since he set foot on that island. The hotel bombing and the attempted assassination at his, um, villa."

"There's been more, Mr. Gruener..."

Cutting the French DST agent off, Gruener said, "Don't you think it may be associated with the massacre of several years ago?"

"There's no evidence pointing in that direction. It's been discussed and dismissed. Everything seems based on Bret's, er, assignment by your firm." Abby hesitated a moment, then said, "You heard about the Air France bombing here, didn't you?"

"Of course," Henry said. "Tragic incident. No Americans died, thank God."

"No, just pathetic French nationals and territorials," Abby countered.

George expressed an apology of sorts. He said, "We realize how terrible it was that so many died—of any nationality. Mr. Gruener meant that our investigator wasn't on that flight."

Even without being in Chicago, Abby felt tension over the phone as thick as the Marseille midsummer humidity. "I understand, gentlemen. My remark was a reflection of my anxiety. Too many deaths, too many assassination attempts."

"Now, now, young lady, George and I understand." Gruener thought he was soothing the young DST agent. "You see yourself in the middle of a battle, while here we are back at headquarters, all safe and secure.

"Mr. Lamplighter told me you were sent to St. Martin to check his credentials. Unfortunately, Abby, you acquired the same enemies he has, by association."

It was becoming difficult for the young DST agent to stay on the line. She'd called Princeton because he was a friend of Bret's. She realized Gruener cared little about the insurance investigator's safety. To him, Bret was a tool sent to recover large company losses. "The latest incident, perhaps news of it hasn't reached you yet, is the murder of Sint Maarten's police chief."

Both Gruener and Princeton pondered her information.

George said, "That would be Chief DeGroot. We've been notified of the assassination. Iranians?"

"The media here is blaming Saddam Hussein."

"How the hell do they explain Iraq's leader killing a small-town police chief?" Henry Gruener probed.

"It does sound far-fetched, Mr. Gruener," Abby answered. "Most of the local police laugh at such rumors." She didn't want to mention the Iranian connection over the phone while Bertrand Hough was still being questioned. "It may be related to Bret's search for the Caribbean Green," Abby added. She knew this was how Bret often referred to the emerald theft to George Princeton in open phone conversations.

Henry Gruener said, "What are you . . . ," then he was cut off. Abby detected whispering in the background, then more silence.

"We understand," George spoke again in a normal tone, "but, we don't see that matter associated with the Chief's murder."

"At the time of his death, Horst DeGroot was being held under house arrest. He'd been trying to flee Sint Maarten after the flight 109 bombing."

"The missile hit was to keep him quiet about the emeralds?" George asked.

"We believe so."

"Any proof?"

"Yes, George." Thirty minutes prior to her phone call, Abby spoke with DST agent Karl Kronstein. The electronics and computer expert had successfully run data he found on three of DeGroot's fused compact disks. Most of the retrieved information included spread sheets and a massive data base. Both applications included names of contacts in Muzo, Colombia; Fort-de-France, Curacao; and Philipsburg, Sint Maarten. "There's a direct connection to Bret Lamplighter's Caribbean Green."

Henry sighed. "I think you'll be happy to hear some information we received from the Pentagon, agent Duchamps. Our insurance investigator is being helped with his assignment by a knowledgeable, um, guide."

"What kind of guide?" The news alarmed Abby.

Gruener looked around the top of his desk. Spotting the slip of yellow paper Henry searched for, he picked it up. Gruener said, "According to the head of the DEA, Lamplighter's guide is a first rate detection-collection asset."

Merde, Abby thought, *Bret's being led through Colombia by a damned spy.*

Chapter Twenty-Two

"Last I saw my control, he gave me a *new* set of State's directives," Russell said. "Tells me guerrilla operations are on the increase in and around Cundinamarca Department." They wore government-issue khaki shorts and lightweight short sleeve shirts. Hiking boots and heavy socks rounded out their clothing.

"The oil fields are near there?"

"De Mares Oilfields are eighty, ninety miles north of Cundinamarca, but I was still relieved when I got reassignment orders to Puerto Rico."

"What's your point, Russell?"

"Point is, the Muzo *mines* extend into Cundinamarca. Town of Muzo is just over the border in Boyacá Department." He smiled at the last portion of his 'briefing'.

"Why the big grin? Thought this gave you severe depression." Bret glanced at him, taking his eyes from the Magdalena River for a moment or two.

Russell sat on a narrow bunk while Lamplighter manned the helm. The NSA operative had scattered an arsenal of machineguns, small arms, missiles, launchers and ammunition around the floor in front of him. He'd examined the weapons to be sure they were operable. He also checked out the variety of visual and sound detection devices stored aboard the cruiser. Most items were in surprisingly good condition considering the humidity and heat they'd withstood. "Laughed at the word 'town,' *amigo*. You ever been to Cripple Creek, Colorado?"

"Sorry, never had the pleasure."

"It's as close to a still-inhabited old gold mining town as one can find, at least in the States."

"You're comparing Cripple Creek to Muzo, I suppose." Bret again faced straight ahead watching for river traffic through the windscreen. The port of Barranquilla boasts 51 shipping companies, a suspiciously-abundant number compared with normal commercial river traffic for Colombia. Very few water craft that Bret met or overtook obeyed the "steer right" or whistle sounding rules of river navigation. It was virtually a matter of King of the Hill rather than International Rules of the Road.

"Damn right, pardner, 'cept they got laws in Cripple Creek. In Muzo, ya make up yer own laws." He applied light gun oil to the barrel of an aged but powerful .45 caliber Thompson submachine gun.

"That one reason you balked at coming back here?"

"Bet yer ass, narc." He looked at Bret's silhouette in the brilliant sunlight. "Assumed I finally convinced Defense I was due an unconditional transfer." He set the glistening Tommy Gun down and sized up a plastic-wrapped Glock automatic pistol.

"Sorry, Russell," Bret said. "Thought I could do Muzo on my own. Didn't know Johnson would pull you back in." He suddenly spun the wheel to the right and swore, "Stupid shit!" The pilot of a small steam-powered launch had pulled directly into the path of Bret's camouflaged cruiser, seemingly unconcerned for his own safety. "You run into me, you'll sink like a damn anvil," Bret continued to shout.

"Keep drivin' like this, *amigo*, might just hail me a taxi." It was at least the sixth time Bret had to avoid a near-collision on the busy river. Before Johnson waved *adios* to them from shore near Sabanalarga village, he'd warned Bret and Russell about *chóferes malos en el río*. Bret believed the little man's warning, but never imagined *this*. "Hope Johnson made it outta that swamp we dropped him in."

"Insisted his associates knew his precise location," he reminded Russell. "Showed me a contraption that pinpointed his position." Bret studied the river as it made a wide bend through a valley.

"Saw it, tracking/homing transmitter. Powerful bugger. My company uses them. Johnson's people can spot him on a small cathode ray tube as far away as ten miles at ground level, twenty miles from a plane or helicopter." Russell paused, then continued, "It's like your 'homer'."

Bret started to ask how he knew of the keychain electronic tracking device, but decided against it. *Probably has one of his own.* He studied the riverbanks whenever he felt he wouldn't run aground or collide with a floating object. "Vegetation gettin' mighty green on the western shore. Haven't seen a village or human being in a half-hour."

More than four hours had passed since Johnson had told Lamplighter to steer toward an *embarcadero* on the west bank. He'd ordered Bret to halt about two hundred yards from the wharf as he had scanned the perimeter with binoculars. "Ees good," the small man had finally pronounced. "My frens wafe for us to come een."

"Not a setup, Johnson?" Russell asked. The ambush at Soledad had seemed well planned. The armor-plated cruiser and automatic weapon had surprised the enemy. If that was any indication, it wouldn't be a pleasure cruise up the Magdalena.

Bret had remained at the helm, both engines running at high idle. Russell had warily escorted Johnson to the deck, an AR-15 assault rifle at the ready. However, the eight people on shore were Johnson's associates, and had joyfully welcomed him 'home'. They had related a story of clashing with two cars occupied by armed guerrillas one kilometer south of Soledad. No one had mentioned the fate of the aggressor force, nor did they have to.

Russell began to store the arsenal and equipment back behind the four bunks, having determined most of it was in excellent working order. "Keepin' this Colt Commando and Sigma 380 for m'self, George," Russell shouted over the engine roar. The Smith & Wesson .38 caliber automatic fired powerful .380 ACP ammunition from its small 14-ounce frame. "MAC-10 okay for you?"

"Sounds good. Couple of clips, too. And don't call me George."

Russell looked up at Bret's back and smiled. *Narc sounds like he might get testy about me usin' that name.* "What'll it be, then? Colonel Parra?"

Bret sighed, then settled onto the pilot's seat. "I know you heard Johnson. What he called me is acceptable."

Russell closed the last compartment on the weapons, then adjusted the bunk. He put the .45 caliber Ingram MAC-10 on the bunk closest to Bret, then sat on a bunk against the opposite side. Russell buckled the leg holster of the loaded SW380 directly above his right ankle, setting the Colt Commando next to him. "How many miles are we from Barranquilla?" he asked.

"Gauge here says we've cruised 58 miles in three hours," Bret said, glancing to the left of the wheel. His loaded .22 magnum sat atop the console. "Makin' bad time, but we were holed up over a half-hour at Sabanalarga. Should start to average at least 25, 30 miles an hour, from now on."

"Shit, we *gotta* do better'n that. Can't move at night, from what I know of this river." He stared out a porthole at the polluted, rushing waters. "You an' me gotta get to Muzo as fast as possible, then leave Colombia far behind." *Thought no amount of money'd bring me back here*, Russell thought.

"How much *dinero* you got, Russell?"

He read my mind? "Johnson gave a couple thousand when I agreed to return," Russell shouted. "Should be enough for necessities like bribes."

"Not if it's in Colombian pesos, at the going rate of about a thousand pesos to one U.S. dollar."

"Naw, genuine greenbacks, Lamplighter. That's about all the natives trust."

"Good. I've got two thousand that Multistate shelled out for expenses."

The mid-afternoon sun pummeled the armor of the old PB boat, penetrating the craft as no assault rifle slugs had managed to do. A large air-conditioning unit in the engine compartment shunted some air to the enclosed cabin. Bret perspired as he manhandled the wheel, partially from the heat, mostly from an intensity he couldn't escape. The channel of the Magdalena changed often, and river traffic weaved recklessly from one side to the other. Bret began to recognize sand bars and shallows from their lighter shades of muddy brown. Still, the endless throttling up and down, coupled with swift spins of the craft's wheel, had nearly hypnotized the intense pilot.

"Lamplighter, you've had the wheel five hours. That's more'n enough to drive the youngest, toughest pilot on the Magdalena off the deep end." Russell took hold of the wheel. "Get some rest. Sit on a bunk and relax." Bret nodded, and moved away.

"I spent some time on the Mekong drivin' one of th'army's shitty gunboats," Russell said. "No heavy armor on those coffins, plywood and cardboard." He reached to his ankle and unholstered the .38. He tossed it on the console next to the .22 automatic.

Bret flopped onto a bunk on the port side of the cruiser. He peered through a porthole with bleary eyes, noticing that the east river bank appeared less desolate than before. "That a town over there, Russell?" he mumbled through parched lips.

"Yo. Should be Plato, accordin' to Johnson's high-tech map." Included in the CARE package he'd left with them was a Pemcol oil company road map. He swore this was as good a map as could be found in the country. They believed this was probably true. "You ready for some lunch?" It was well past two p.m. and neither man had eaten since leaving Barranquilla's airport.

"I'm starved and thirsty. Hope the natives tolerate *gringos*."

"Hang on, narc," Russell shouted. "I'm makin' a run for it." At this spot, the Magdalena was more than a mile wide. The river traffic, mostly long strings of barges, was dense. Bret had been holding as close to the west bank as possible, but Plato was on the east bank. Russell thrust the dual throttles all the way forward and swung the wheel counterclockwise. The large cruiser lunged forward, then easterly like a jungle animal impetuously intent on its prey . . . disregarding everything in its path but the quarry.

"You're gonna get us killed," Bret yelled over the roar of the powerful diesels. Russell decided not to hear his analysis of the new direction the cruiser was headed. "Only piranhas will ever know we were here!"

Dodging. Lunging. Sliding into harms way, slipping away from a freighter. The PB boat leaped from one obstacle into the path of another. "No freakin' piranhas in this slime bog," Russell screamed. "Outta m'way scumbag," he added as a ten-barge tug pilot blasted his air horns at the unwieldy, strange-looking craft. "Nothin' lives in this cess pool 'cept man-eatin' bacteria," Russell continued his biology lesson. Skidding and parrying, Russell managed to bring the cruiser close to the east bank of the scudding Magdalena.

"Think we survived the crossing," Bret declared. "Lotsa pissed-off captains and pilots," he said, swallowing as he looked back at the receding scene of chaos.

"Plato dead ahead!"

"Back-off those damn throttles. We'll end up *beneath* the dock." Bret pulled the throttle knobs rearward and down as Russell fought to steer the ironclad into more stable water closer to shore.

"Shit," Russell said. "No wonder the Monitor an' Merrimac didn't catch on for decades. This is about as easy as steering a slab o'steel through a typhoon."

It seemed that the cruiser was now under some semblance of control, with a slower speed, calmer water and time to react to danger. "That *embarcadero* doesn't look much more inviting than the wharf at Barranquilla." Bret stared at rotted pilings, and sagging, dun-colored timbers. Garbage and waste of indescribable filth slurped and slogged around the pilings that were still in one piece. "Ripe goddam place, Russell." Bret looked down the length of the pier and exclaimed, "Think the town packed up and ran away. Don't see a soul."

"It's siesta time, *amigo*," Russell explained. "We're gonna have to wake someone to get food." He wrestled the cruiser closer to the wharf. "Toss that rope over a piling when I run into it."

"Don't run into it. Just reverse the . . ." The bow of the boat slammed into a rotting piling. The sound was little more than a muffled 'cruuunch' as the piling yielded inwardly nearly a foot. Still, it was so rotted and waterlogged it didn't snap, acting much like a spongy bumper. "You learn to dock a craft by the braille method, Russell?" Bret growled, staring at his shipmate with disgust.

"Hey, we're docked, admiral." Russell switched off the engines.

"Just lucky this pier's ready to sink into the stinkin' river." Bret went topside and tossed the looped end of the rope over the piling. He pulled the cruiser's bow snugly up against the wharf, then wrapped the line tight around the bow cleat. "Gas masks should be standard issue for anybody traveling the Magdalena," he said, wrinkling his nose at the stench.

Four other boats of varying sizes and degrees of infirmity were tied to the pier. None of them appeared to have run in months. A ketch's bow pointed skyward at a perilous angle, presumably ready to sink any minute. Bret heard Russell exit the cabin and slam the hatch shut. Turning, he saw that Russell had slung the Colt Commando and Ingram weapons over his shoulders. Hatch locked and key shoved deep within a pocket, Russell walked across the bow.

"Let's climb up on that rubble," Russell suggested. "Get away from this septic tank. My bowels wanta move, think I'm sittin' on a damn latrine."

Bret shook his head in disgust. He pulled the MAC-10 from Russell's shoulder and slung it over his own. "Locals gonna call the *federales* when they see two *gringos* totin' assault weapons through town."

"Doubt it," Russell said as he hopped over to the pothole infested dock. "Probably all packin' themselves."

"You okay? Didn't fall through the dryrot?" Bret studied Russell from the deck as he warily shifted about on the blackened timbers.

"Fine, *amigo*. Thanks fer your concern."

The wobbly pier was an extension of Plato's main street, *Calle de Muerte*. They gaped at the street sign, then at each other. Nowhere had either remembered seeing a thoroughfare named "Death Street." Neither spoke as they walked along the dusty path.

"You must be right, Russell. Not a livin' soul in sight." Bret lowered the Ingram machine pistol parallel to the ground and pulled back its bolt. "Seeing nobody in a town this size is more ominous than seeing a mob." They halted.

A scruffy dog staggered from behind a tumbledown shed, briefly stared at the two strangers, then sat in the center of the dirt *calle*. It began to scratch idly for fleas, ticks, mange, gonorrhea, who knows? There were no other sounds than the heavy breathing, slurping sounds of the brown mongrel.

"Siesta, you say?" Bret darted his eyes at his companion.

"Siesta."

They began to walk down the dusty path again. Each man spread apart till Bret walked on the far left of the road . . . Russell to the far right. Twelve to fifteen feet separated them. The dog didn't raise an eye as the men slowly passed it, one on either side. Now it was Russell's turn to lower his weapon, arming it by manipulating the bolt. The dog's head jerked up as the bolt made a harsh noise in the hot sun of the village. Maybe the mutt knew the sound from other times. It rose and wandered away toward the river bank.

Retail and commercial buildings were the first structures to appear on *Calle de Muerte*. A small grocery store, a cantina, and a boat and ship supplies store were among the varied assortment that comprised downtown Plato. Russell pointed his Colt Commando's muzzle toward the modest building bearing a hand-painted sign that read *Supermercado*.

"I don't know about 'super', but it claims to be a market," Bret noted.

They walked up to a sagging screen door. A small sign bearing the name *Dos Equis* had a sliding panel that proclaimed *CERRADO*, closed. Next to the word, someone had scribbled: *hasta que las tres.*

"Siesta all right," Russell murmured, "but it's nearly three o'clock." He pulled the rusted handle and the screeching screen door swung open. "Trusting souls."

Sweat poured off their bodies as Bret and Russell entered the sweltering wooden building. A strange assortment of odors greeted them . . . a mélange of spice, must, breads, citrus, fish, others indescribable. The aroma wasn't unpleasant, only different. An interior door opened slowly as they stood inside the doorway, aiming assault rifles at boxes of taco meal and flour. They stared as a figure emerged from some secret inner sanctum. The form stepped into the ambient light cast by the still-brilliant sun, the form of a pretty girl no more than thirteen or fourteen years old.

She stood with hands on hips, head cocked slightly, as she sized up her customers. "*¿Quieres comprar comestibleses, señores?*" she asked in a voice more mature than her adolescent years. Her faded print dress was tight around full hips and pubescent breasts.

"Um, why, yes . . . *si, señorita,*" Russell blurted. He suddenly realized the Colt Commando pointed directly at the girl's midsection, so he instantly let the barrel drop. "*Mis apologías acerca del fusil.*"

She smiled at Russell's embarrassment. "Is hokay, *señor*. All days I see many guns in my father's store. It is a way here. I am called Noori."

"*Estamos aquí comprar comestibleses*," Bret said. Yes, indeed, they needed to buy lots of groceries. "Russell, let's buy enough food for the rest of our trip and take it back to Ole Ironsides. We'll cook it in the galley's microwave." Frozen dinners, canned fruit and vegetables, even bottled soft drinks and water were available.

"Do you accept American dollars, *senorita?*" Bret asked.

Apparently the question was humorous, for the child-woman burst out in laughter. "For *dolares estados unidos* we give you special price on all *comestibleses*."

Abruptly, the orangish light in the grocery store dimmed, as if a dark cloud passed in front of the sun. From the corner of their eyes, Bret and Russell saw they were no longer the only visitors. A loud voice proclaimed, "*Ésta es la policía. Pon tus fusiles en el suelo.*" Before the words might be misunderstood, the same voice demanded in English, "Put your weapons down, *señores*. We are of the National Police. My name is Captain Camargo."

Turning around, they saw that three men dressed in military-style uniforms stood just within the front entrance. At the inner door where Noori had first appeared, three more national police officers were fanned out. All of the uniformed officers held American-manufactured M-16A2 assault rifles at the ready. Further inside the darkened interior, back against the dusty counter, stood a tall Colombian officer. He held a 9mm Beretta automatic pistol in his right hand, and his uniform shirt collars were indeed trimmed with the rank of a Colombian National Police captain.

Bret noticed the young woman quickly dart into the back room from where she'd first appeared. He let the MAC-10's sling slide down his shoulder until the compact weapon lay on the floor. *Looks like Noori was a decoy for the policía*, Bret thought. "I'd like to see your identification, captain," he said to the squad's leader.

"That is a proper request in these times of serious deceptions," the tall Colombian replied. He pulled out a billfold and held it in an open hand. Bret slowly walked to the man and took his leather wallet.

"You speak English as well as many Americans," Bret remarked, smiling as he opened and examined the billfold. "Thank you, Captain," he said, returning the wallet.

"That is a marvelous compliment, *señor*. I spent my university graduate years at Georgetown . . . then six months at Camp Peary, Virginia."

Bret hoped he showed no surprise that Captain Camargo had trained at the hush-hush CIA facility on the York River. "Oh, yes, right outside Newport News."

The captain's lips parted in a thin smile. "You mean, of course, two kilometers north of Williamsburg, don't you?" The clarification confirmed that the Colombian captain was familiar with the location of Camp Peary. Camargo continued, "I will now examine your credentials, *señores*." He stuffed his own wallet back into a hip pocket. The Beretta pistol never wavered in his right hand.

Bret unbuttoned a pocket in his shorts and reached inside. "Here's my I.D." he said, extracting his passport and a billfold. He watched Camargo's face become expressionless as the police captain examined the passport. "Hmmm," was the only sound Camargo made. The Colombian official flipped open the slim billfold and glared at its contents. Even from eight feet away, Bret could read the inscription on the badge: "Colonel, Policía Nacional de Colombia." The companion documentation card was too far away to read, but Bret knew it identified him as Colonel Manuel Parra Vega of Colombia's National Police. The captain raised his eyes from the documents and squinted at Bret, a squint that seemed to last an eternity.

Camargo threw the credentials onto the grocery counter. "You're next," he shouted at Russell as he turned and glared at the NSA operative.

"Be my guest, *herr kapitan*," Russell stated. He tossed his I.D. next to Bret's on the filthy counter.

"I have the hunch you could be most uncooperative, *señor*." Captain Camargo sneered at Russell. "Perhaps I will test my theory some other time." He lifted the cocky American's passport from the counter and glanced at it. Camargo then picked up a slim billfold similar to Bret's, but much older and discolored. The captain studied it for a moment, sighed, then flipped it onto the counter next to its mate. Once more he glared at Russell. "You," Captain Camargo said as he turned toward Bret, "follow me." He nodded at a national police sergeant.

The sergeant planted the barrel of his weapon into Bret's lower back and shoved him behind the fast-walking captain. The three men entered the same door from which Noori had first appeared and then disappeared back within. Bret noticed they'd walked into a nondescript warehouse/storeroom. Across the large chamber sat Noori, with an older man and woman. Their faces were stoic like most of the *mestizos* he'd seen in Colombia. "Noori," Bret shouted across the room, "how many pieces of silver did you earn for two *yanquis*?" The only answer was the press of steel in Lamplighter's lower back.

"In here, *gringo*," the captain said as he pointed at a half-opened door at the far left of the room. Walking between bays of foodstuffs, the three reached the entrance. "After you," Camargo said, smiling, as he stood aside for Bret to enter the room.

Once inside, the captain followed and flicked a loud switch that turned on a single dim lightbulb. Captain Camargo turned, nodded at the sergeant, then shut and locked the portal with an enormous, old key. Turning back to the American, the Colombian captain pointed at a dusty chair—its cracked back pushed against a wall—and said, "Sit." Camargo followed him and stood directly in front of Bret. His stomach hurt with hunger pangs and apprehension.

Captain Camargo holstered his Beretta and swung his right arm toward Bret. It ended near Bret's right hand, which the captain then grasped. "It is a pleasure to meet you, Mr. Lamplighter."

The American was uncertain whether he should make a grab for the weapon, pull Camargo off balance and attempt to escape, or return the Colombian's handshake. Sweat from Bret's brow slithered down through a fine layer of dust. "I, I'm not sure what you're talking about, captain. You saw my identification."

"I would not blame you for being pissed-off at me, Mr. Lamplighter. However, there was no other way to speak with you alone without causing suspicion."

"Suspicion from whom?"

The captain sighed through flared nostrils. "I am ashamed to say this, but I cannot trust my own handpicked men." He tossed his head in the direction of the door. "Bribes are . . ."—he briefly searched for the right words—" . . . insidious, er, roadblocks for honest law enforcement officers."

"That's you, Captain? An honest cop?"

"Yes, Mr. Lamplighter, and, therefore, penniless compared to any of my men who take the *mordida*." Camargo grabbed a rickety, wooden chair from a small side table and pulled it near Bret. Sitting, he leaned forward and said, "You were in the DEA many years. You cannot be so naïve about how drug money turns honest people corrupt. It is most true in Colombia, where the average household wage is less than $2,000 a year."

Bret looked Camargo in the eyes, then brushed the perspiration aside with the back of his hand. His face was smudged with wet dirt and dust. "Yes, Captain. I've seen the effects of bribery in Mexico, Puerto Rico, the U.S. Virgin Islands . . . even St. Martin."

Captain Camargo merely nodded.

"Bribery. Is this why you're harassing my partner and me?"

Camargo smiled and sat back in his chair. "Is it your little joke, Mr. Lamplighter? Neither of you would be in perfect fitness at this time if we truly 'harassed' you."

"Tough *hombres*, huh Captain?"

Camargo shrugged off the remark and said, "You have a friend in Johnson."

Bret tried to hide his surprise by saying, "Who?"

"Interpol's Johnson. Your Johnson. Everybody's Johnson."

Bret dully shook his head, as if he didn't understand.

The Colombian disregarded Bret's look of bewilderment. "The camouflaged government boat you take up the Magdalena comes from Johnson. Two of my own men travel with Johnson's team as we speak. Do you not recall dropping him off near the village called Sabanalarga?"

"Okay, Captain. Russell and I have a friend in Johnson," Bret agreed. "Why do you bring up his name?"

"I have a message for you from him. He knows I could get it to you without compromising your mission to Honda." The captain reached into a pocket of his uniform shirt and removed an envelope, which he passed to the American.

"How did you know . . . ?"

" . . . where you could be found?" Camargo said. "I have no

less than three homing devices to choose from, Mr. Lamplighter. My squad has access to the personal radio transmitters you and Russell carry, through satellites used by a secret facility on Curaçao . . ."

"CENTRO, Captain Camargo. I've been there."

The Colombian sat straighter in his decrepit chair. "That surprises me. They allow very few civilians into the facility."

"You forget, I'm a full colonel in the *policía nacional de Colombia*. What's the third way you track us?"

"A high-powered radio beacon on the boat you sail. We, and I assume several other federal agencies, know its coded-data modem frequency."

"The range?"

"Practically infinite, I have been told. Whatever, on the ground our portable monitor shows the shape of the cruiser and its precise location. It gives us exact coordinates and such incidentals as town plots and names, water depth and more."

Bret lifted the flap of the unsealed envelope, while he said, "Looks like you know everything about us except when we take a pee." He pulled a single sheet of blue paper from its unmarked lodging.

"Would you believe . . . ?"

"No, no. Don't say it. I hate to think Big Brother's alive and well . . . and catching me with my fly open." He unfolded the paper and slowly began to read Johnson's scrawl. "Kee-rist," he blurted. "Unbelievable bullshit since I left St. Martin."

"I hope this won't interfere with your journey to the interior."

"No, it's more like trimming some assets. Sint Maarten's police chief was being held in custody for suspected smuggling. Then, one of the few men I trusted, an American consular officer on Martinique, had Chief DeGroot killed."

Captain Camargo shook his head. "I'm sorry your friend turned. I assume he did it for money."

"Yeah, he was involved in emerald smuggling . . ." Bret stopped speaking and snapped his fingers. "Shit, that's what was bothering me!" he said.

"I don't understand," Camargo said.

"The sonuvabitch knew *too damn much* about precious gems, especially emeralds," Bret spoke, almost to himself.

"How did you decide that?"

"Bastard gave me the number of carats, weights of gemstones in ounces, stuff that even an emerald dealer had to calculate electronically. How did I miss it?"

"Often, something that appears normal, from someone you trust, slips past, like important pieces of evidence in a police investigation."

"Damn it," Bret grumbled again, hardly hearing the captain's consoling words. "I recall Ravi at the Bombay shop chastising me because I used a 'deli weighing standard for precious gems'. He had to pull out a calculator to give me the exact weight in ounces. Even called it my 'antiquated system'." Bret stared at the far wall and shook his head.

Camargo glanced at his watch. "You and Russell have been ashore quite a while, Mr. Lamplighter. You should . . ."

"Goddam Wilson," Bret swore, looking at the note once more. "Johnson says he's almost certainly Hough's accomplice. Writes he's been under surveillance for several months." Bret rose from his chair and said, "That asshole has top secret clearance for CENTRO headquarters, and flies his C-47 from Martinique to Colombia with impunity. No wonder Hough teamed up with him; he can smuggle in anything he wants."

"Please do not speak aloud the names of people on Johnson's list to anyone else. In Colombia, less is best." He stared around him at the walls, door, ceiling, floor, even the wobbly furnishings. "As I learned at Camp Peary, 'the walls have ears'. I survive because I always remember those words."

Bret scrutinized the tall, trim captain. "Sorry, Camargo. I was too hasty to complain to someone. Only, my partner on St. Martin was put in danger because I didn't see through one of these fools." He folded the note and stuck it into a shirt pocket. He burned the envelope, though there was no writing on it, tossed it to the floor and crumpled the ashes. "You're right, Camargo. Walls could have ears . . . and eyes."

The captain unlocked and opened the door, pushed Bret out of the room for the sergeant's benefit, and ordered, "*Vamos!*"

The tiny parade reversed its previous path. Bret understood that Noori only did what a captain in the national police had asked her to do. Nonetheless, he shook his fist at the forlorn-looking young woman. He received another humiliating poke in the back from the sergeant's rifle barrel. "Watch that damn M-16, you moron," he said over his shoulder. *No prod this time*, Bret thought. *Glad he doesn't speak English.*

The three men reverted to the locations they'd occupied before, as if they were in a stage play and must return to their exact chalk marks. Russell and the other police officers gaped at Bret. "What'd he do to you, man?" Russell asked. "Y'look like shit."

He remembered the heat of the small room and the dust on his face and body. Except it was no longer dust. He'd wiped the perspiration across his face and brow several times. *I probably look as bad as Russell says*, he thought. *Face must really be a muddy mess.* A glance at Camargo revealed a hint of humor in his eyes. "I'll be okay, Russell. Don't worry about me."

"You are free to go, *señores*," Captain Camargo declared. He spoke to one of the junior non-coms in Spanish. The young police officer studied the Americans and picked up their weapons. He snapped the clips from both guns, then looked at his Captain. Camargo nodded. The young man gave his commander the ammunition clips and returned the MAC-10 to Bret, the AR-15 to Russell.

"*Los acompañaremos a su barco*," the captain told his squad. They would escort the Americans to their boat. Bret and Russell grabbed some groceries and left more than enough money in greenbacks on the counter. Most of the young *policía nacional* officers stared at the American currency with covetous expressions.

The captain walked ahead with Bret and Russell, his men following closely behind. "You are not to leave your craft until you reach the oilfields," Captain Camargo loudly advised the

Americans. "Weapons are not illegal here," he said, eying the two powerful firearms, "but ammunition for them is against *my* law." He punctuated this paradox by flinging the loaded clips far into the adjacent jungle and deep brush. His men laughed at the performance their captain accorded the two smartass *yanquis*.

"Shit, Captain," Bret groaned. "What if we're attacked by guerrillas or *banditos*? We won't have a chance without ammunition."

"Get onto your boat," Camargo ordered, "before I take you to our local *prisíon*."

The police officers found it hard not to cackle when they heard the Spanish word for prison. They leveled their assault rifles at the Americans and Camargo said, "Go!"

Bret and Russell tediously trudged along the pitted pier, then leaped to the deck of their "ironclad." Only a few items spilled from the grocery bags. In a matter of seconds Russell unlocked the heavy hatch, Bret cast off the line and they entered the decrepit-looking cruiser.

"You sure you're okay, ole buddy?" a truly-concerned Russell asked.

"Never better, Russell. Think I'll wash some of this grime off my face and hands." Bret walked toward the head while Russell started the mighty V-12 engines.

As Russell backed away from the pier and the laughing national police officers, he thought, *Hicks'd go nuts if they knew we had enough spare ammo here to start, and win, a freakin' war.*

On shore, Captain Camargo silently wished the Americans: *Vaya con dios*.

Chapter Twenty-Three

The driver of the blue Subaru sat motionlessly, watching the luxury automobile dealership through powerful night-vision binoculars. Parked more than two blocks away, Abby was certain no one had spotted the little car. It was dark and even millions of stars failed to emit enough light to set the vehicle apart from dozens of others parked near it. Island Luxury Imports Ltd. occupied a block of Marigot's downtown business district.

Claude Tomasso boasted of never having spent a moment in an island jail cell. His criminal files in the Marigot and Philipsburg police stations, however, were several inches thick. Claude was a killer, and the hirer of killers, but he was very, very careful. Abby knew his background in St. Martin and his police record in Coral Gables, Florida, where he'd begun the business of selling luxury automobiles. In that upscale community south of Miami, Claude quickly learned about the extraordinary profit in selling smuggled heroin and cocaine. He'd also learned that the Colombia cartels travel to the ends of the earth, and Coral Gables, to assure their absolute monopoly of the illicit drug trade.

If Medellín's drug kingpins saw potential for someone—even an uneducated Italian-American—they cultivated him. Of course, they had burned Claude's house to the foundation, with his wife bound and gagged inside it. Claude had been in New Jersey that day, arranging a deal for Cadillacs and Mercedes Benzes, when he'd received a phone call of his wife's death. Four minutes before the fact!

The fiery episode had confirmed Claude's rebirth and religious conversion. Claude had become a *bonafide* member of a Medellín sub-cartel, and had been relocated to prime territory on the island of St. Martin. Of course, as an American, he'd had to vow never to engage in Colombia's trillion dollar drug trade. On the flip side of the coin, Claude's association with top-volume drug dealers did establish his value as a master trader of tempting merchandise. Claude became the first American director of Medellín drug cartel's billion dollar emerald subdivision. A major coup was bringing Bertrand Hough into the fold.

Married a rich widow from Galveston, Texas, Abby recalled from her profuse reading of Tomasso's files. *Not for money,* she concluded. Ellen Yeager had been a Las Vegas "showgirl" when she'd met her first husband, a Tulsa oil baron forty-two years her senior. Now, as Mrs. Ellen Tomasso, she was twenty-two years younger than Claude, and nearly as shrewd, especially concerning unrivaled Caribbean Green. *She and her hubby fly tourist class on their twice-monthly jaunts to the States,* Abby knew.

At first, she considered bringing one of her fellow DST officers along on her visit to Island Luxury Imports. "An imbecile," she muttered about Dornier. "Competent, but an egghead," Abby judged Chatelaine. "Sincere, but no balls," she rated Kronstein. *Wish Bret were here,* she thought as she stared through the windshield.

She knew Henri Bouchard and his colonial police officers would never approve of her venture. She wasn't familiar with the additional *Sûreté* and SDECE officers who'd come to St. Martin after the Air France plane crash. The Interpol agents kept to strict national guidelines and would certainly obstruct her plan. "Nope," Abby spoke to her rearview mirror, "the only person you could really trust is cruising through Colombia."

She shifted her left wrist until the dial was visible from the glow of a distant mercury vapor street lamp. *Two-thirty,* she thought. *Time for a respectable French girl to be home in bed.* It was also time for her to leave her car and walk to Claude's dealership.

Four hours earlier, *sous-inspecteur* Bouchard's phone call woke Abby from a fitful sleep at her Sunshine Pointe villa. Henri said he had received a coded message from Johnson in Colombia. He'd assured the police inspector that Bret was aware of all the incidents on St. Martin since he left. Johnson advised Bouchard that he detailed Wilson's probable involvement to the American insurance investigator.

"Did Johnson tell Bret that Claude's been out of touch for nearly a week?" Abby asked. "He may be in the States, but he could be in Colombia."

"Informants for Interpol believe he's in the Miami area, Abby."

"*Merde!* When snitches say 'believe', they're usually on the take, Henri."

"I personally spoke with Medellín's airport security chief," Bouchard said, the pitch of his voice rising appreciably. "He and his men know Claude. They watch for him and other suspected cartel members. The *antinarcotraficantes* and *policía nacional* are immediately notified any time known criminals travel through Medellín Airport."

"I see. Couldn't Claude have gone by another route, or airport, or country?"

Abby knew that Bret was suspicious of Claude and his dealings. Bret distrusted him and his cronies, ever since he ran into Claude more than a week ago on the flight to Sint Maarten. *I think Henri's upset about losing track of him,* Abby thought.

"Of course, that is possible," Inspector Bouchard answered the agent's question. "Claude would rather delegate his dirty work, nevertheless."

"Even when he realized Bret outsmarted him in several assassination attempts by Rupert?" Abby only heard breathing for a few seconds.

"Abby," Bouchard said, "the fact that Rupert worked for Claude does not prove that he'd hired him to eliminate Lamplighter . . ."

It seemed that Henri Bouchard was going to repeat his tired theory that Claude couldn't be in Colombia. Abby interrupted him by saying, "Sorry I've kept you listening to my theories about Claude, Henri. Thanks for keeping me informed of Bret's situation."

Bouchard and Duchamps finished their conversation. Abby realized only one place existed where a businessman like Claude would keep his agenda, his records, his financial dealings—at his office. Although his wife was probably involved in Claude's illegal transactions, he'd protect all his important papers at work. She had to get into his luxury auto dealership. Once inside, Abby'd have to find proof of what Claude was involved in and where he was right now.

Bret would approve of my haute couture, Abby judged. She wore navy blue slacks, a black blouse and a lightweight dark blue jacket. Over the jacket, a medium-size dark backpack was adjusted high enough to afford Abby quick access to either weapon. She also wore black three-quarter Wilson sneakers with no socks. Her Walther P-38 was tightly bound beneath the jacket in a shoulder holster. The MAS 1950 was in a belt holster at the small of her back. Her swarthy tan, combined with the dark clothing, allowed her to slink along the gloomy sidewalk like a furtive shadow.

Less than 100 meters from the large two-story building, she noticed a dim light through several windows in the upstairs offices. *Claude's security,* she figured. During several sessions with under-inspector Bouchard, his lieutenants and patrol officers on the street, Abby'd learned much about Claude's dealership. She also learned that he and his wife owned a spacious, well-guarded home in the hills above Marigot. Although filled with an army of housekeeping personnel, Claude's pretty wife was usually the only member of the Tomasso family in residence. Often, two weeks would pass with no sight of Claude. He showed up without fail, it was known, for his biweekly flight to the American mainland, nearly always accompanied by wife Ellen.

"Circumstantial," she murmured under her breath, shaking her head. To nearly every law enforcement official on St. Martin, there was no doubt about Claude's involvement in a variety of crimes. A few visitors representing a variety of powerful, and unlawful, groups ended up in Philipsburg or Marigot's morgues. Two highly-placed members of the Russian mafia, who'd spent several hours at a meeting with Tomasso, were never heard from again after returning to their resort hotel. The airtight briefcase belonging to one of the visitors popped out of Great Salt Pond three days after their disappearance. It was presumed that somewhere beneath the briny water, two ex-KGB agents' remains lay in their own lonely purgatory.

For an hour the previous afternoon, Abby had been disguised—absurd as it seemed, as a man—had driven and walked around Island Imports. She had watched for security cameras and alarms, and had searched for faulty front and rear entrances and fire exits. She'd checked overhead doors at service entrances for signs of wear, tear, rust or rot. Lastly, she had explored the presence of security guards. Claude's security, according to *gendarme* lieutenant LaDue, consisted of thieves, thugs and suspected killers. Abby was sure no one suspected what she was up to.

Now, in the darkness of morning, she checked the small map she'd made of the premises. A small elevator took customers and office personnel to the second floor. She moved closer to the building. She saw that the main showroom was dimly lighted, as was the outer lobby where a security officer was visible behind a small table. He was dressed in street clothes, wore a baseball cap and carried a 9mm Micro-Uzi. In front of him sat an array of color monitors, evidently displaying scenes televised by closed circuit TV cameras. Abby knew there were at least two other guards at Island Imports.

She'd seen CCTV cameras hidden in smoke detectors, clocks, lamps, even microchips and lenses embedded within mirror glass, not simply placed behind a see-through mirror. Abby's earlier inspection of the luxury car premises showed six *obvious* surveillance cameras scanning the exterior. This, she speculated, should be multiplied by at least 50 percent, making a total of about nine outside closed circuit TV cameras.

During Abby's earlier survey of the car dealership, she'd noticed an overhead-opening door near the Service Department dented at the bottom. *Possible*, she decided. The Service area was the farthest point from the upstairs offices. *Bad news, it's an extremely long way to Claude's office; good news, it would probably have the least amount of security or surveillance due to that fact.* Like most outside security cameras, the one at Service was attached to the building, affording almost no view of its outer walls and Service Department doors. She slunk along the whitewashed cinder block wall to the wide overhead vehicle door, kneeling down by a dent near its center. The gouge was about two feet wide and two or three inches high, with a dull point in the middle.

Abby leaned against the door, again putting the night-vision binoculars to her eyes. Very slowly and very meticulously, Abby scanned the perimeter in front of her for possible surveillance cameras. Three trees near the street, two electric utility poles, the dark recesses of the utility transformer, a telephone pole, the top of the steel wire boundary fence. Finally, she was ninety-percent certain no hidden closed circuit television cameras transmitted her movements to within. She set the binoculars down and pulled the backpack from her body, affording her instant additional mobility to shoulders and arms. As Abby unzipped the pack, she estimated the distance from the dent to the far edge of the door. *Three meters should do it*, she calculated.

Abby withdrew several items from the backpack. She set a titanium-steel rod, about the diameter of an anglers' fishing rod, on the oil and grease-stained pavement. Holding the end with a black, rectangular box attached, Abby began to slide out the far, somewhat-smaller, end. Like a retractable lectern pointer, the metal cylinder was lengthened until the DST agent pulled it to about nine feet in length. She next slipped all but three or four inches of the rod beneath the dent at the bottom of the door. A small brown connector wire from the rod was plugged into a compact, powerful battery-transformer. A green wire was inserted into the rectangular box at the end of the metal rod. Abby took a pair of ordinary-appearing sunglasses from her pack. She plugged the other end of the green wire into a hole at the bottom of the left eyeglass frame. She flipped a toggle switch on the transformer and put the glasses on.

Abby stared at two color LED television screens, each showing the same scene. A small image offset between the red and green lenses produced a three-dimensional effect. She picked up the lightweight rod and swung it to the right, then back toward the left. The visual her eyes detected was the interior of the Service Department. The 2mm fiber optic f-1.4 auto-iris lens at the end of the rod boasts a 0.012 Lux low-light sensitivity and 550 lines of resolution. Its 400,000 pixels and extreme infrared sensitivity gave her the sensation of being inside the building, with a powerful searchlight illuminating everything. *No one there*, she noted. *Presumably no surveillance cameras.*

Gently, quietly Abby set the camera rod and 'glasses' on the concrete. She picked up a similar-looking rod of titanium alloy, except it had no rectangular electronic box at its widest end. The tip of the rod, rather than holding a camera lens, had a short hook screwed into it. Again, she pulled the metallic sections out to three meters in length. The heavy steel latch she'd seen at the door's edge slipped through a two-inch high by one-half inch wide rectangular opening in a steel door frame. The latch was padlocked shut on the other side of the steel frame, so it couldn't be pulled inward to free itself.

Abby reached into the backpack and felt the plastic canister she needed. She pulled it from the pack and reeled off two, four-inch strips of a round, black-coated substance. Haley & Weller Dartcord is about 3/8-inch in diameter, made of magnesium and phosphorous, and has a crosshatched outer casing designed for maximum instantaneous cutting. Abby bent one of the short strips in half, then set it onto her second rod's hook. She shook the rod to test the stability, but the Dartcord just swayed back and forth.

Next, she inserted a primer with detonator into the outer end of the cord. She cut off a ten-foot double wire leading from the detonator and wrapped short end portions around two bolt threads affixed to the battery. Abby screwed on the bolts. *All set*, she told herself.

With the short length of folded Dartcord gently rocking on the hook, Abby manipulated both rods through the small opening. She lay flat on her stomach, forearms and hands on the inside of the service shop. Like a puppeteer, Abby manipulated each rod closer and closer to the door latch, sweat dripping from her brow. The camera eye on the left hand's shaft skillfully allowed the DST agent to guide the hook and cord on the metallic rod maneuvered by her right hand. Wrists now aching from the strain of holding and twisting the light, metallic poles, Abby moved the Dartcord above the sturdy latch. She lowered the rod and saw the far side of circular cord disappear behind the tempered steel that secured the large door. *Got it*, she exulted. *Now rotate rod . . . get Dartcord off hook.*

She heard voices behind an interior door, opening it. Hackles rose on Abby's neck at the sudden intrusion. She inched the rod holding the camera lens to her right. *There*, she saw in brilliant full-color LED pixels, *two men coming in.* Instincts said that the guards could see her as clearly as she saw them; knowledge of the light-sensitive camera lens reminded Abby she was in a near pitch-black area of the large room. Both men were white, while the guard she'd seen in the dealership's lobby was black. *Merde*, Abby thought, *they're the three I'd figured on.*

"Turn th' light on, Rick," one of the two said in American English.

"Hold yer shit, asshole." A beam of light suddenly shown in the room.

Damn, Abby agonized. Normal flashlight illumination became compounded hundreds of times through the super-sensitive television camera lens, briefly blinding her. The lens' iris automatically closed as far as it could, still allowing far more brilliance than Abby's eyes could take. She shut her eyelids as tightly as possible, holding the two metal rods still despite desperately-aching wrists and forearms.

One of the men held a small plastic "wand," looking much like a mini-flashlight. He placed one end against a metal button-shaped electronic chip just inside the door on the frame. A red LED flashed as the wand beeped. Later, a computer printout would show that this area of the building had been inspected, and the exact time. The guard with the electronic wand crossed the inside of the Service department while the man named Rick shown the flashlight beam at the far customer service entrance.

Don't look over here, Abby thought. She'd opened her eyes slightly to see where the men were.

"Beep," went the small device as it met the button chip by the other door. "All's secure," the guard yelled, crossing toward his partner.

Rick swept the flashlight across the room in one final gesture of surveillance. "All right, sucker," he chortled. "Time you lose your ass at pinochle." He waited for the first man, held the door open for him and they walked out, still bickering.

Abby breathed. Her body was drenched with sweat. The inside "screens" of her glasses glistened with perspiration. Her wrists throbbed from holding the two rods. *"Mon dieu,"* she mumbled. *One month on holiday and I'm out of shape.* Abby twisted the left rod and the Dartcord edged off the hook, now hanging on the door latch. *Let the rod down slowly*, she ordered her brain. Abby set it on the concrete floor, then grabbed the metallic pole with the television lens with her left hand. She made another complete sweep of the room, then set that rod down as well. She pulled both titanium alloy devices outside next to her, then pulled the eyeglasses from her sweat-soaked face. For a few seconds, she lay still, giving herself a needed rest . . . letting the guards walk away from the service room.

"It's time," she mumbled, getting to her hands and knees. Eyes still smarting from the intensified flashlight beam, Abby checked the battery, then pressed a red button on its side. Her peripheral vision noted an intense flash from the dent at the bottom of the door, which she'd hidden from outside view with her body. A brief sputter was all the sound the Dartcord detonation made, barely heard even by Abby. Inside the room, the portion of metal latch touched by the vaporized crosshatched cord disappeared. Dartcord, like cordite, is smokeless and practically odorless. It was doubtful if anyone in the building could have heard the detonation or detected its scent.

Without waiting another moment, Abby dropped back to her stomach, grabbed the rod with the television lens and pushed it back through the bottom opening. She adjusted the glasses over her eyes and swung the pole toward the latch. It had been sliced through like butter with a hot knife. Nothing held the door closed on that side any more. *How about the other side?* Abby wondered. She quickly swept the rod 180 degrees to her right. *"Merveilleux,"* she uttered. There was no locking latch on the far side of the overhead door. Another pass of the tiny television lens from one side of the room to the other still revealed no telltale surveillance cameras. *Now to pump iron*, Abby thought. The overhead door was normally lifted and closed with cables from an electric winch. Cables would not prevent the door from being lifted manually, she knew, but there was no counterbalance to make the hoisting easier.

With all her tools and appliances crammed into the backpack, Abby knelt with her torso against the door. She put her hands into the dented depression and clenched the door bottom tightly. Abby pulled up on the portal, raising her body as she lifted, using leg muscles plus the strength of her arms. The door rose to a height of two feet. Abby used one leg and foot to shove the backpack inside, then lowered her body while she held the door up with chest and arm strength. She swung her upper body, head and legs beneath the wide gateway. With remarkable intensity, Abby allowed the door to settle back against the concrete floor with quivering arms.

"Sonuvabitch," she gasped. "Heavy bastard." She pulled the jacket off, rolled it up and put it in the backpack. *Wet with damn sweat*, she thought. The jacket hid any portions of her weapons from catching ambient light while outside, giving away her position.

Abby stood, swinging the pack onto her back again. She held a small infrared flashlight and wore infrared goggles. Both pistols were within easy reach. She psyched herself to face the perils central to all espionage operations.

Chapter Twenty-Four

The lovely blue-green waters of the Bay of Buenaventura spread to the horizon—an imposing view for an important visitor to Casa Bella Vista. Partially situated on Cascajal Island, Buenaventura is the chief Pacific port city of Colombia. It is an hour's drive from Cali, on a newly-constructed concrete ribbon locally dubbed *El Camino de los Narcóticos*. The Pacific seacoast city, with its population of 200,000, is one of the world's busiest export centers for illicit drugs. Emeralds, platinum and gold are its three other important exports.

Wealthy industrialist Fabio Guillermo and his family of five moved out of their superb hacienda twelve hours after receiving a phone call from his acquaintance in Medellín. He'd done it before and he'd gladly do it anytime *Señor* Vargas asked. Besides, hadn't Fabio already promised his family a two-week vacation in Rio de Janeiro?

Enrique Vargas Mantilla was a prominent and powerful man in Colombia. Many people, including Fabio, were aware that Vargas had practically singlehandedly put *el presidente* into office. Saying no to Señor Vargas would have been impudent. On occasion, saying no to *Señor* Vargas was suicidal.

Sitting on the estate's beautifully landscaped patio, Claude Tomasso gazed down through terraced gardens at the clutter of cruise ships and transports. *Wonder what's on Enrique's mind?* Claude thought as he sipped a cool glass of mineral water. *Couldn't be upset over the emerald business. Net profits up 32 percent this year over last.* He'd been here several times before, usually with Ellen. Claude paid dearly to make certain no one ever reported his arrival at Buenaventura's airport. He swirled the tall glass of water, ice cubes making a tinkling sound like wind chimes.

"*Hóla*, Claude," a loud voice shattered his thoughts. It came from only several yards away, and startled him.

"Damn!" Claude griped. "Piss m'jeans you keep that up, *Señor* Vargas." He managed a wide smile, although he'd have chewed out anyone else.

Enrique Vargas flashed an amused smile, knowing he'd alarmed Claude. Three bodyguards stood directly behind and to the side of the drug lord. Many more guards spread out among the grounds, gardens and rooms of the hacienda. The sixteen-foot high steel mesh fence surrounding Casa Bella Vista literally buzzed with more than 100,000 volts of electricity flowing through it. Dozens of exotic, multicolored birds lay at its base, electrocuted when they'd perched on the fence. Only when *Señor* Vargas stayed at the large estate were the large generators for the electrified fence activated. On these occasions, warning signs were posted along the outer fence perimeter.

"Sorry, Claude," Vargas said.

"*No problema.*" Claude realized any additional remarks would only alienate himself with the Colombians. "Your view is as beautiful as ever," Claude continued, gesturing at the scenic bay and white-painted ships sailing by in front of him.

"It is a scene to remind one of this tranquil nation I live in," Vargas answered.

"Yes, *Señor* Vargas . . . Colombia, the gem of the ocean."

Vargas turned toward the American and studied his face for signs of cynicism, but detected none. "Hmm, *si*. As your American song goes, Colombia *and* gems, no?"

For a moment Claude didn't understand. When he finally connected the dots, though, he smiled and said, "Very well put, sir."

"You give ver' good opening for me, Claude." Vargas nodded

to one of his burly bodyguards. He brought a pillowed lounge chair for his boss and placed it facing Claude. Another nod and his bodyguards walked far enough away to be out of hearing range.

"Emeralds, Claude." Vargas paused. "Rarer than many diamonds, no?"

Claude nodded. "I have been truly blessed by you, *Señor* Vargas. You've entrusted me with the honor of handling your superb emeralds." *Vargas wouldn't let someone else take over his emerald market, would he?* Claude wondered.

"Yes, Claude. Cali cartel entrust you with a responsibility mos' men would kill their grandmothers for."

Claude didn't like the sound of this, especially not the grandmother part, since Vargas was right. The reference to other men chilled Claude's blood. *Why would Vargas even consider others? Haven't I shown a huge profit every year since I've handled his emerald business?* "And, and I've served you skillfully, *Señor* Vargas."

Before a stern-faced Enrique Vargas answered, the sudden chlump-chlump-chlump of helicopter rotors drowned out the song birds, cicadas and tree frogs. Bewildered, Claude jerked his head toward the sky, sighting a large camouflaged, military-looking helicopter. The American-manufactured Sikorsky MH-53H/J helicopter banked and swung low over the hacienda, both 4,000 horsepower engines drowning out any other sound on the estate. Vargas' security forces and bodyguards searched for any possible assassin's hiding place, since no gunshot would ever be heard. As quickly as it began, the din subsided. *Bastard landed on the other side of the house*, Claude knew. His two other visits to this beautiful hacienda had been quiet. True, he'd seen the helipad at the side of the main house, but it hadn't been used. *Too much shit goin' on. Who're the visitors?* The warm late morning was heating up. Claude felt a few drops of perspiration on his face and a trickle of cold sweat dribbling from his arm pits.

The bodyguards returned to their posts, nervously twitching their heads in every direction. Vargas rose and rapidly walked toward the entrance from which he'd recently appeared, heading toward the helicopter and its occupants. Abruptly, the wine Claude had been sipping tasted like vinegar. *Why didn't Enrique take me along to see his visitors?* Claude worried.

Barely audible helicopter rotor blades phit-phit-phited slower and slower somewhere on the far side of the *hacienda*. More muted than the winding-down rotors, voices could be heard in the distance. Unnatural speech, louder than normal, to be understood over the mechanical uproar, still was indecipherable. Claude wondered what was being discussed by Vargas and his guests.

More time, perhaps five minutes, passed. The bodyguards stood in one place and swung their heads about or nervously paced, like heavily-armed expectant fathers. Claude sipped the vinegar in his wine glass simply to do something. Male voices speaking Spanish became louder. Vargas and his company were nearing the door to the veranda that overlooked the gardens that overlooked *Bahía de Buenaventura*. Vargas described the scenery as he and one other man accompanied four, uniformed men armed with lethal 12 gauge Armsel Striker revolving-magazine shotguns. The South African semiautomatic, 12-round drum 'Protector' now finds a secure home with a host of antiterrorist groups. Unfortunately, the Striker is notably popular with the same kind of terrorist and guerrilla organizations they were originally conceived to eliminate in Rhodesia.

Look like military uniforms, Claude observed. *No markings, no rank, no name tags. Blue berets, like some American infantry troops wear, but these guys look like Colombian mestizos*, he reckoned. The small detachment of troops fanned out in a much tighter inner perimeter than Vargas' bodyguards.

"*Te darás cuenta de, patrón, ésta es una vista bella de Buenaventura,*" Enrique Vargas Mantilla spoke to his regal guest. The weapons and questionable uniforms of the guards were unusual, but the VIP's own attire was downright bizarre. He wore a yellow one-piece flight suit, as fighter pilots employ. Over his head, exposing only eyes and mouth, the tall man wore a yellow mask. Claude decided it was similar to those worn in the high Andes of Peru. The guest, probably a high-ranking government official, since Enrique addressed him *patrón*, nodded at Vargas. He then leaned sideways toward the drug czar and loudly asked, "So this one is your *yanqui*?" Intense, dark brown eyes dissected the American. Claude shivered in the northern coastal heat.

"My esteemed *patrón*," Vargas addressed Colombia's Minister of Mines and Energy, "I would like you to meet Claude Tomasso, Cali cartel's Director of Emerald Marketing and Merchandising."

Minister Rodrigo Gomez smiled at the showy title bestowed on one he knew as a thief, a smuggler, a *gringo* assassin of some repute. "How long have you been Enrique's merchandiser of splendid emeralds?" Gomez settled into an easy chair carried to him by two men employed by the estate's owner.

"Four years, *patrón*. But I've been associated with *Señor* Vargas for five years."

"You appreciate your employment with Cali cartel?"

"You bet, sir. An' I know," looking toward and nodding at Vargas, "he is most pleased with my work."

"You are certain, Claude?"

"Sir, if there's a problem with my car dealership on St. Martin, I'll gladly . . ."

This time it was Vargas who interrupted the perspiring American. "No, no, Claude. It's a perfect front. *El patrón* speaks of other troubling questions."

I'm dead, Claude knew. *Somehow found out I'm still pushing 'caine and poppy*. "Then I'm at a loss . . ."

Another interruption from the Minister. "Profits from my emeralds, Claude. They are down compared to two years ago, no?"

Claude nearly swallowed his tongue with exultation when he heard the question. *Yes, there is a God*, he assured himself. "Only by t-two p-points, *patrón*," he stuttered with happiness. *They don't know*, he beamed.

"Enrique," the scowling minister from Bogotá said to his host, "explain to him that my losses are not funny."

Although the Muzo and Chivor emerald mines are government owned and operated, they definitely aren't the property of the Minister of Mines and Energy. Rodrigo Gomez was concerned only with those emeralds brought out of the pits by his handpicked mine managers and their henchmen. When the emeralds were smuggled into the hands of Claude's trusted intermediaries, they faxed cryptic data about them to St. Martin. Claude then auctioned the Caribbean Green, sight unseen, to 'suitable' jewelers and gemologists world wide by phone, cable, radio and—primarily— the Internet. The NSAs best intelligence readers and listeners seldom knew they were privy to multimillion dollar emerald transactions while in slang-filled cyberspace chat rooms.

"*El patrón* thinks your preoccupation with the American insurance detective and the French *Sûreté* agent keep you from tending to business."

"I was only thinking of *el patrón*," Claude blurted, looking into Gomez' eyes, "when I attempted to take care of those two."

"You have bungled too often," Vargas raised his voice. "Many others died, so foreign police investigate," he continued, referring to the Air France plane crash.

"When French and American officials check plane accidents, they look into other crimes that could point fingers our way," the Colombian Minister said.

"They couldn't know it was Lamplighter I was trying to snuff."

"They are not stupid!" Vargas exclaimed. "They make connections. The hotel bombing, your bungled raid at the American's resort, then the *plane bombing*!" Vargas sat back in his chair unexpectedly, glaring at Claude.

"I appreciate you looking after my emerald interests, Claude," Minister Gomez said with less irritation in his voice. "However, you spend too much time on your personal vendetta and too little time marketing our emeralds."

Claude was heartened. *Colombian bigwig used the word 'our'*, he thought, *rather than 'my'*. "You're right, *patrón*. Sometimes I can be too protective of your merchandise. I get carried away." Now Claude felt he was on a roll. "It's like this insurance dick was tryin' to steal one of your children, sir. It just tore me up to have him—and the French bimbo—snoopin' around our island."

Vargas closed his eyes, then opened them and stared sightlessly toward the sky. Gomez was one of few men he feared. He was the Cartel's most powerful advocate in the Colombian government. *Will he blame me for Claude's stupidity?*

Rodrigo Gomez Gaviria stared at Claude. Slowly, he began to nod his yellow head. "Enrique," Gomez turned his gaze toward his host, "I agree with your man's reasoning—very much. However," again looking at Claude, "you must forget outside threats to my *esmeraldas*. I will deal with such problems. *¿Entiendes?*"

"Yes—*si, patrón*, I understand," Claude said. "Your emerald profits will be up 50 percent by next year at this time, *señor*."

"Enrique, tell him."

"Our profits will be up by *100 percent* next year at this time, Claude."

Claude paled. "How could, I mean, certainly, *patrón*."

Mines and Energy Minister Gomez rose to his feet and said, "I dislike such a short visit. I will, perhaps, speak with you longer next time, Claude."

Swallowing, Claude stood, shook the Minister's hand and said, "I hope so, patrón. I really hope so." He'd become attached to his gonads. *If I don't show a hundred-percent profit in twelve months, I lose my balls . . . and probably my head.*

Claude walked behind the Colombians up to the thundering bedlam of eight thousand horses ready to thrust the helicopter off the ground.

Minister Gomez boarded the aircraft and prepared for Round Two of his Buenaventura obligations. He would visit the managers of the people who processed his platinum and his gold and his silver. They, too, would be told to increase profits. They, too, would worry if they would still have their *huevos* next year at this time.

Next week, Gomez thought, *I go to my oil and gas fields. A Minister's work is never done*, he sighed.

Chapter Twenty-Five

"Bitchin' *siesta* time back in Plato." Bret remarked.

"It woulda made sense, dammit. How'd I know the gestapo was in town?"

They'd been motoring up the Magdalena for a half-hour at the fastest speed Russell could manage without ramming any other shipping. On calm water with no other traffic, the powerful, armored cruiser may have been capable of ninety knots. Dodging everything from flimsy canoes holding Kogi Indian families to gigantic oceangoing transports, though, prevented Russell from exceeding twenty-five knots.

"Got us pinpointed, the Captain said," Bret shouted over the engines.

"Shoulda known. They were waitin' for us."

Bret nodded, although Russell was concentrating on the foaming brown water ahead of them. "Something about a powerful radio transmitter on board." He briefly scanned the interior of the cabin. "Our own homing devices, too," Bret added.

"Makes sense. Probably in contact with the CENTRO facility."

"You and our arresting officer seemed to get pretty chummy in that back room. Find out you were fraternity brothers?"

"The 'abuse' was for the benefit of his men. Can't trust them, he admitted."

Russell nodded. "Don't blame him. Used to hear stories about high-ranking cops going to *mágicos* like Pablo Escobar Gaviria to plead for certain assignments. Give him five years' salary to be chief of Antioquia, or Miraflores . . . coke-processing centers. Make up their contributions to Escobar in one week."

"No wonder our DEA guys come back to D.C. stressed-out, disillusioned. Sounds like a no-win situation."

"This hemisphere's Vietnam, Lamplighter. Russia's Afghanistan. Colombia, Peru and Ecuador, for that matter, base their economic growth on cocaine. Been that way here since the first millennium A.D., fer crissake."

"Since when did you become the NSA's Alan Greenspan?"

"Spend two years in Hell, Lamplighter, you learn a lot about the Devil."

Bret studied Russell's back from the bunk on which he sat. "Guess I'm lucky it's emeralds brought me here . . . not drugs."

Taking his eyes from the swiftly-flowing Magdalena, Russell turned and glanced at Bret. "Coke, heroin and THC may head their economy, but Colombia's mighty selfish with their emeralds. Technically, all emeralds are government property . . . the mines are all government owned and operated. Anyone involved with cutting and selling emeralds has to register with the government."

"So I've heard. Ninety-five percent of the world's highest-quality emeralds come from here." Bret swung around and stared out a port hole. "A chunk of chromium beryl going for as much as $50,000 a carat—mind boggling."

"That's what you want to track down near Muzo . . . some *specific* emeralds?"

"Not the gems, themselves," Bret decided to reveal. "The beginning of their paper trail. How did they get out of Colombia? Who sent them—should I say 'smuggled them'—in coffee bags and cigarette boxes to a jeweler in Sint Maarten?"

"How's that gonna help you recover them? Since you're an insurance PI that has to be why you were hired."

"Follows, doesn't it?" Bret answered. "Look, everyone keeps records. They could be receipts or computer tapes, handwritten or typed. The mine bosses have to keep records for Bogotá, unless they're the ones who ripped-off the 'green'."

"I'd put my money on the mine managers. It would fit into the Colombian work ethic I've come to distrust after bein' here two years."

"Don't you think a few bad incidents have clouded your judgment?" Bret asked with a sheepish grin on his face.

"Conventional wisdom says the Muzo managers paid a small fortune to get their jobs and now make humongous fortunes from grabbing the superior emeralds."

"Your 'clouded' judgment sounds feasible," Bret agreed. "They'd still hand over enough excellent emeralds for the government inspectors to stay satisfied."

Russell nodded, then said, "Agreed, narc-man. An arrangement that keeps many people happy and rich."

"... and the emerald miners workin' for peanuts—or is it coffee beans?"

"I've been told by many people who know that the emerald *paisas* earn the equivalent of about five dollars a day. It's the little extra, a hard-labor perk, that keeps them comin' back ... coca."

"The government provides this?"

"Yep, but don't think of a white powder. They chaw the leaves like baseball players chaw chewin' tobacco ... more like suckin' than chewin', really. Get a new hit every two hours from their bosses."

"This's legal? You said their bosses are the Colombian government."

"It's legal. Processed 'caine ain't."

For nearly an hour, they had gazed at the banks of the river for possible landing sites. The sun, dropping low in the west, was totally eclipsed by the hills and low mountains. The Magdalena, for many hours the dazzling grabber and reflector of the blazing sun, became subdued. Muddy waters rendered the valley torrent dark and thick as pitch. Boats and ships without running lights or sounding horns leaped into view like jaguars springing from the brush. Dusk was a dangerous time, although the ironclad now showed all her running lights.

"Throttlin' down. Shadows across the river. Can't make out shit."

"Checking our translocator, Russell," Bret said as he scrolled a real-time satellite map across the screen. "Shows us about halfway between Mompós and El Banco. No highways of any size shown by this gadget near here."

"Sounds right. El Banco's where the César River breaks off from the Magdalena. There'll be an east-west highway, but nothing heading north and south."

"Gas gauge shows we're nearly empty, Russell. Let's put in over there," Bret said, pointing at the west bank. "Looks secluded enough for our purposes."

Russell turned to stare at the west bank, nodded and said, "Enough forest on the river for us to . . ."

"Jeezus, man! It's the goddam Titanic!" Bret bellowed. He pointed directly in front of their cruiser.

"Holy shit!" Russell yelped as he swung his head back toward the river.

An immense transport ship bore down on the small armored gun boat. There were running lights high on the bridge, but they were of no help since the ship dwarfed the Americans' craft.

"Swing to the right," Bret shrieked. The enormous ship was nearly on the cruiser, no more than fifty yards from a head on collision. No danger horn sounded from the transport . . . the helmsman hadn't even noticed the small boat in the shadowy Magdalena.

Russell thrust both throttles to their limit, swinging the wheel hard on the starboard beam. No time to even consider a drogue anchor, and the cruiser was almost instantly rolling and yawing simultaneously. Russell remained standing only because he held a vice grip on the wheel. Bret grabbed a handle on one of the lockers holding munitions and supplies, keeping him from being thrown to the top of the cabin.

The fake starboard planking that covered the armor plate suddenly became the bottom of the cruiser. The small vessel had rolled to its side. Both engines howled like scorched banshees as the port propeller revved in dry air. Fortunately the starboard prop remained beneath the water, and the craft continued to scoot out of the way of the great vessel, barely. Russell, eyes wide with terror, saw the gigantic steel bow pass within inches of the little ironclad. A resounding clang pounded the ears of the two Americans, and they felt a jarring sensation that shoved the cruiser further from the wake of the ship.

Filthy water cascaded into the cabin from the edges of the hatch, although it wasn't at a rate to fear sinking. Bret let loose of the locker handle, stood on the inside starboard frame and grabbed the wheel.

"What're you . . . ?" Russell yelled.

"Pull port—left—dammit! Only way we'll correct ourselves."

The two men barely glimpsed the large transport ship pass by them. The heavily armored vessel slowly began to right itself in millimeter-by-millimeter increments. They pressed themselves as close to the port cabin walls as possible, although it was unlikely that their combined near-four hundred pounds would help right the unwieldy craft. Suddenly, the deafening roar of the powerful Cummins marine diesels lessened by half. Evidently, one of the engines quit.

"We lost the port engine," Bret shouted. Still, the cruiser continued to right itself, until, with a lurch, it was floating properly. "Cut power," Bret yelled at Russell. The single starboard engine was rotating the boat clockwise, since it no longer had the port diesel to keep the cruiser on an even keel.

"Shit, man," Russell bellowed. "Can't believe we're back upright." He swung the wheel counterclockwise to offset the still-operating engine's pivoting effect. Brackish water sloshed around their bare feet.

"Compass! Which way're we goin'?" Bret asked, staring at the still whirling and lighted instrument. "Damn. South."

"Okay, okay, Lamplighter. I see the west bank." Again, Russell spun the wheel until the vessel headed westerly. "Damn iron coffin," he muttered.

"Don't knock it. Armor plate kept that ship from caving us in."

"Hunh? Yeah . . . maybe. Look for an inlet, a cove, anywhere we can pull in."

A tree-covered, swampy looking riverbank leaped into view. "Damn! Cut power. We're nearly on shore."

Russell quickly slapped both throttle controls downward, 'though only one engine was operational. Bret shoved the hatch open, allowing another inflow of Magdalena mud and water. "Hope there's a comfy Holiday Inn so we can get a good meal and a cold shower," Bret said, as he sloshed up to the deck.

For the first time in many hours Russell laughed. "Now there's a man with an active imagination." He stared out the windscreen at the lush underbrush and dense trees.

"Mighta lucked out. Little stream over there." Bret pointed twenty or thirty yards away. "With our shallow draft, we can probably move our asses outta this marsh next to dry land." He tossed the main anchor overboard. Skittish, shrieking birds leaped from their roosts at the sudden commotion. "I'm gonna check the stern. See if that monster ship did us some bad damage." Bret padded toward the boat's rear-end on the sodden, slimy deck. With bare feet nearly slipping out from under him several times, the private detective made his way aft. Mosquitoes and horse flies already swarmed around his bare head, chest and legs in the muggy, torrid late-afternoon heat. *Won't last another half-hour without insect repellent.*

The rushing river was loud, but not so loud that it drowned out the agitation of wild animals and birds lingering nearby. A noisy human contraption had invaded their private sanctuary, and they weren't happy about the intrusion.

Having reached the stern of the armored cruiser, Bret leaned over the port bulwark, tossed away a soggy, half-eaten sandwich and stared down at the waterline. A section of camouflage wood about two feet by three feet was missing, apparently snipped from the boat by the huge, seagoing vessel. Dark gray armor plate shown in the dusk.

Leaning over the bulwark again, he stared at the large "scar" near the waterline. *Doesn't look like any damage other than our bark getting peeled off.*

Russell appeared on deck. "I'll look at the diesels. See if there's anything screwed up." He noisily splatted over to the sturdy engine hatch. "Give me a hand. This looks double-thick an' heavy."

Four large, sturdy spin clips held the hatch tightly against the aft deck. The hatch cover weighed at least one hundred fifty pounds, having been designed to be lifted by cranes at army and navy shipyards. They wrestled it up until they'd leaned it against the armored aft cabin housing. With the hatch removed, several high-intensity lamps automatically lighted the engine compartment from within.

Bret crouched on all fours while Russell lay on his chest and belly—both men surveying the huge Cummins KTA38-M2 diesel engines for some sign of damage. Two large fuel tanks hung above and forward of the engines hard against the inner planking.

"No fuel pumps," Russell mumbled.

"Gravity flow."

"Yep, fuel pumps would just be more equipment to break down in this climate."

"Then we should be ready to jam, Mr. NSA-man," Bret said, sitting back.

"Right on. It figures our sudden rollover starved the left-side engine of fuel. Never did try to crank it back up."

"Keep your hands outta the hole," Bret said, rising. "I'll give the ignition for the—we call it 'port' engine, landlubber—a twist." Slight pause. "Shall we pray?" He slogged forward on the damp deck to the cabin hatch and disappeared inside.

The sound of the starter motor ticked and the port marine engine came to life. The 1,300 roaring horses unnerved every living animal, bird, reptile, and Russell, within the area of a square mile. Birds of all sizes, from tiny hummingbirds to hulking condors, took to the air as one huge mass of avians. Tapir, red deer, anteaters and spider monkeys stampeded for the foothills. A nosy gator slammed its mighty tail in the swamp water, yowled "shiiisss-hhshaaw-shiiisss," and swam for the small rivulet in which it made its home. Russell leaned back against the bulwark shaking demons from his head.

Bret let the engine run only long enough to satisfy himself that it worked perfectly. Turning the ignition switch off, he left the cabin, reached the deck and told Russell, "The damn thing's in excellent condition, far as I can tell."

" . . . an' I got the busted ear drums to prove it!" Russell sat hunkered over on the wet deck. Head in hands, he stared with wild, reddened eyes at his companion.

"Shit," Bret uttered, becoming annoyed at the other American, "it wasn't a secret I was starting the engine."

Nodding slowly at Bret's words, Russell stood . . . shaking his head. "Let's get the hatch locked back down. It muffles those thundering diesels."

"Yeah, gettin' darker every moment. We won't be able to see that little inlet much longer, and we gotta get out of sight." River traffic still sailed by, no more than a hundred yards from the quiet armored cruiser. With their running lights extinguished, it wasn't likely the American's vessel would be seen, but there was no use in taking chances.

Engine hatch secured, they hoisted the anchor and switched the engines on at dead low idle. Slowly they inched backward through the marshy shore until they entered the small brook that trickled down from the Andes. Upon reaching relatively solid land, they tied two of the cruiser's docking lines, bow and stern, to two sturdy balsam trees.

For the next hour, they mopped up excess water from inside the cabin, chests, head and galley. Pumps emptied additional Magdalena river water from the vessel's shallow, normally-watertight bilge.

Once the craft was dry and moderately livable, they wandered for miles, setting booby traps on either side of the brook. Neither man would ever be convinced that mere secrecy and stealth could keep any determined enemy from finding them. It was nearly eleven P.M. when the exhausted men finally lay down to fitful sleep.

Bret awoke from a dream where his head was aching from the sound of a high-pitched buzzing. "What's that, Russell?" he shouted.

Russell awakened. He heard the noise, too. "What the hell?"

"There it is." Bret pointed toward the craft's front console. "The ARPAM detected weapons out there." For the two Americans, 'out there' meant a complete 360° detection capability of the early-warning device. Its low intensity imaging picks up new on-scene base metal devices as small as a hand gun, then warns of the threat by emitting an audible or visual signal. Bret had set the range finder to detect incoming mobile or human-carried metallic objects at a distance of 2,000 meters.

"Whoever it is can't be much closer than a mile," Russell reasoned. "You woke up less than a minute ago." He shone the flashlight at the floor to reduce its glare. "Gonna grab two Arwens."

The Arwen 37, Mark 6, originally designed by the British for riot control, fires a variety of rounds. Johnson had equipped the boat's munitions lockers with high explosive and H.E. airburst "grenades" for the Arwens. Evidently, Johnson didn't think highly of non-lethal rubber shot, teargas or smoke rounds. The '37' in Arwen 37 is its caliber in millimeters—approximately one and one-half inches in diameter. The rounds are about six inches in length. The lethal weapon holds six rounds inside a quickly-revolving cylinder located in front of its trigger guard.

Bret scurried to the console. Having served its purpose, he set the plastic boxed early-warning ARPAM on the floor and switched the battery-operated device off. Next, he pulled the Life Finder LP-5, IR4 infrared detector into position at the windscreen. The LP-5 detects, through measured heat, any animal, vegetable or mineral within 5,000 yards. A seven-inch monitor screen folds up from the base of the detector—much like a lap top computer. Upon its base are dials for on/off, auto-sensing, motion detection, gain and squelch. Included also is a brightness switch, a dial to designate LED or audio signals, with earphones, if desired, and a computerized distance guide.

"About a two seventy-degree direction, Russell?" The Life Finder scanned a thirty-degree swing from the point it was aimed toward. Directed due-west—two hundred, seventy degrees—the detector picked up all infrared activity from about two hundred, fifty-five degrees through two hundred, eighty-five degrees. The closer the target to the LP-5, the more precise the setting of direction would have to be.

"Yeah," Russell estimated, as he gathered weapons and ammunition. "Set it for three thousand. We should pinpoint a bogey somewhere in those parameters." Russell had used the LP-5 often before with his NSA eavesdropping cronies. Bret had some classroom knowledge of the instrument, but no field experience with it.

Bret punched in the compass degrees and range on a numeric keypad. The screen remained blank, although the LP-5 was fully-charged and switched on. "Shit," he muttered, "I have to choose a screen or audio signal." The private investigator shunted a toggle to 'screen'. Immediately, the LED screen was lighted. Grids in dark grey overlay a misty green scene. Near the right edge of the screen, shown as 280°, bright green 'amoebae' pulsated. The computer distance guide showed that section of grid to be at 1,712 yards. *Count them*, Bret told himself. He tried to find a separation between the intense green splotch of light in a jungle of hundreds of tiny green-white lights. *Zoom in*, he thought.

"Got a fix yet?" Russell dragged weapons and ammo boxes along the cabin floor.

"Yeah. Hafta zoom in, though. I'll see how many there are." Bret punched in 280 degrees, entered it and then punched in 1,800 yards. He entered the data and the hostile assets instantly became some 30 percent closer and sharper.

"Damn, yeah. Six of them, Russell. Almost human shapes, fer crissake." At this closer range, some slight movement was noticeable, since the spread narrowed down to 270 degrees left, 290 degrees right.

"Hope it ain't some Boy Scout troop doin' night maneuvers." Russell glanced at the screen and noisily hauled the Arwens and several boxes of rounds to the main deck.

"At two in the morning?" Bret scoffed. ". . . and they got us locked in, Russell. Heading straight for our location through pitch black forest."

"Where'd we set up the first line of wires?"

"About three-quarters of a mile out . . . around 4,000 feet. Should show as approximately thirteen-hundred yards on this screen."

"Okay, they're crossing fifteen hundred yards and headin' straight for us." Russell studied the screen, green light painting his face into a jack 'o' lantern. "You're right, they got our image straight from some spy satellite." He looked skyward, as if he could spot the orbiting object. "Be a shame if was a squad of nuns out on a survival test," Russell continued.

"Dammit, Russell," Bret spat out. "Wait here." He turned toward the munitions storage lockers.

In less than fifteen seconds, Bret stepped back on deck. He held an M-16A2 assault rifle with attached M209 40mm grenade launcher and carried two 40mm concussion grenades. Bret quickly loaded one of the grenades into the M-16's launcher.

"Maximum range about a thousand yards?"

"Well, um, sure. Give or take . . ."

"Nothing we have's gonna penetrate that damn jungle. I'm lobbing a grenade toward your Boy Scouts—or are they nuns?" Bret aimed the rifle/grenade launcher at a 35-degree upward angle, high enough to clear the nearest tall trees.

"Think that's a good idea . . . ?" Russell barely managed to ask.

Bret pulled the launcher's trigger and both men listened to the hollow "thunk" of the grenade being propelled about 280 degrees west-northwest. "Yeah, great idea. Shouldn't take too long," Bret said. Both men turned their gaze upon the green-glowing Life Finder LP-5 screen.

An eternity of eight or nine seconds passed until an explosion sounded. Light from the concussion grenade was visible out of the corner of the men's eyes, but it was the small screen that lit up like a searchlight.

"Grid shows 980 yards at a direction of 279 degrees," Russell noted.

The echo of the grenade blast hardly died away before another brilliant green flash erupted on the LP-5's screen. Its epicenter was at fourteen hundred, forty yards and 280 degrees from the cruiser. Suddenly, a noise like an insane animal rushing through the jungle was evident to Bret and Russell. Several hundred yards from the ironclad vessel, another mighty explosion pierced the jungle. Birds and animals screeched and howled about them. Shrapnel thumped through leaves, branches and foliage.

"No missile . . . not enough heat here," Russell muttered.

"Antitank rocket, I'd guess. Seldom carried by your average nun."

Russell glanced at Bret, then shrugged. "Didn't want innocents hurt."

"Understood." Staring at the screen of the infrared detector, Bret said, "They've spread out. Moving faster. Should be nearing our . . ." A muffled triple explosion again unsettled the jungle birds and beasts. It was far less bright than the two previous blasts. On the Life Finder screen, they'd detonated at the twelve hundred, forty-yard grid.

"Came to a trip-wire. Set off three Claymores."

"The detector shows one down. Others stopped . . . know it was booby-trapped." The remaining five eerie green forms slowly neared each other, but didn't venture forward of the area they knew contained menacing land mines.

"Zooming closer . . . thirteen hundred yards," Bret said while he tapped new data into the alphanumeric keypad. The screen appeared to blink, and then the forms were definitely human, with arms, legs and heads attached to green bodies. Hundreds of tiny green images surrounded the five attackers . . . birds, monkeys, tapirs and other dwellers of the dense jungle. Many images darted back and forth.

"Notice the form stretched out," Russell pointed at the fallen enemy on the screen. "Already getting cold." The dead foe was several shades lighter in color than its comrades, now emitting less detectable heat.

"Doesn't take long, even in this temperature?" Bret looked down from the screen at the keypad. He punched in several more numbers. "Gonna look at the whole area around us. Don't need more surprises."

The screen faded into a panorama of the perimeter surrounding the craft. The Life Finder itself was located directly in the middle of the luminescent screen by a red LED dot. The grid showed that Bret now searched for any possible entrapment up to 2,000 yards in every direction. On the right side of the screen, green-lit vessels on the Magdalena sailed past in both directions, but none neared the ironclad cruiser.

"Our trackers are still at 279 degrees and about a half-mile from us," Russell said. He noted that the "unfriendly amoeba" undulated but didn't move closer to them.

"Can't make out any other 'hostiles'," Bret noted, carefully scanning every grid line on the screen.

"Hey, cool. Guess it's time to prepare for our guests." They started to plan their welcome.

* * *

Alonso Hernandez fumed. He stared at the corpse of his cousin, twisted as only a contortionist or a cadaver could be. Pedro Marin had stumbled over the trip wire, but it was Alonso's close relative who lay dead, blown apart by a *yanqui* Claymore mine.

"Marin," Hernandez quietly ordered, "bury him, but be quick. Just deep enough so the jungle animals don't find him." *Pedro will not make it back to headquarters.*

The guerrilla named Pedro began to dig in the soft humus of the river valley. He used his hands, his boots and the butt of his M-16 assault rifle. Also, he used one of the rocket launchers supplied to his brigade by the chief of Bolívar state's Revolutionary Armed Forces of Colombia. The Russian-made 75mm RPG-18 was sturdy, and, at 4.97 pounds, easily wielded as a shovel. *Commander Hernandez blames me for the death of his cousin*, Marin knew. *I must watch my back while we return to headquarters.*

The Iranian "advisor" noted the hatred between the two

Colombians. Sadaq Mahdavi-Karubi arrived in Cartagena just in time to be sent with the guerrilla killing team. Hadn't he been on a Long Island beach to immediately report the death of TWA 800? Had he not recently witnessed a Tomahawk missile destroy nearly an entire block of homes? Truly, he felt, it was beneath him to accompany these filthy *banditos* on a mission of assassination. *Ah, but still it is the will of Allah*, Mahdavi-Karubi rationalized.

The dwarf César Serpa carried the portable satellite multi-spectral imager. The equipment bounced laser beams off a CENTRO-controlled surveillance satellite, then instantly beamed three-dimensional images back to earth. CENTRO re-orbited the spy satellite to track the two Americans up the Magdalena on orders of General Serrano. He'd been assured that the ultra-secret project could not be compromised. Yet, a deep-cover 'mole' at CIA-operated National Reconnaissance Office mailed the highly-restricted imager to Colombia in a crate marked "personal computer with monitor." The NRO espionage asset held one of the highest security clearances at the Reston, Virginia facility. Consequently, a Colombian guerrilla team viewed images from the MILSTAR 26 recce satellite, newly lofted into orbit by an American Titan IV launch vehicle.

"*Rápidamente, idiota*," Hernandez urged his underling. "We have two *yanqui* spies to butcher for our cause."

Chapter Twenty-Six

"No, no, slimeball. His *name* is Tomasso," Wilson shouted into the phone's mouthpiece. "Claude Tomasso. He's a, um, *invitado norteamericano de* Enrique Vargas Mantilla."

The name Vargas Mantilla caught the attention of the man who'd answered the phone. He stopped misdirecting Frederick Wilson. *Tomasso must be the yanqui who meets with El Patrón*, he reasoned. "*Un momento.*" The bodyguard dropped the receiver onto a small end table, and left to find his security chief.

Wilson fretted while the security chief was sought out. Fully ten minutes passed before Vargas was found. Enrique gave his security chief permission to tell Claude he was wanted on the telephone. The phone call would be monitored and recorded from a basement command center.

"Claude Tomasso. What is it?" He hadn't been told who was phoning him.

"Shee-it, man. I be waitin' fo' you a half-hour, dude."

"Wilson? Cut the homeboy jive . . . you're no good at it. What's the problem?" Claude seldom spoke with the army captain when things were going smoothly. It had usually been the same when Hough sought him out.

"Hough's in the St. Martin slammer."

Claude's life rushed past him. *What the hell . . . ?* "Shit, Wilson. How secure's your end?" *If Bertrand starts talkin' poppies, 'caine . . . .*

267

"The best. CENTRO scrambler. All alone in their White Room."

Ten feet from Claude, a Colombian security man leaned back in a wooden chair, staring at him. *Probably speaks better English than William F. Buckley.* "Just the opposite here." So many clicks echoed on the phone line, Claude imagined he was broadcasting the afternoon news live on Radio Bogotá.

"A helluva lot of static . . ."

"Okay, okay. Let it be, Frederick. He been charged, yet?"

"Attempted murder . . . French DST agent."

"Nothing more?" *Maybe I'm still safe.* "Who, the broad?"

"Yeah. Lucy says that's the only charge, so far." Lucy was a trusted male computer operator at police headquarters who was on Claude's payroll.

"Mention 'sugar' and 'spice'?" Claude used their code for cocaine and heroin.

"Nothing. Lots of talk about gummy bears, though."

Claude nearly dropped the telephone, bringing a puzzled frown to the security man's face. Gummy bears was the code word for emeralds. "This, this . . . um, talk. How *specific* did it get?" The sweat on Claude's forehead dribbled to the luxurious carpeting.

"*Very* specific, even to telling many different gummy bear sizes." Wilson took a breath, then said, "It also included possibly turning state's evidence—particularly the names of sugar and spice traders in exchange for the fed's WPR program."

"He, he wouldn't . . . couldn't spill. Would he, Frederick?"

Vargas' security man wrinkled his nose in disgust as the *yanqui* soiled his pants. He watched sweat pour in rivulets from Claude's chin and nose, adding to the stench.

"Never liked the candy-ass little motherfucker," Wilson answered.

"Any inside connections at Marigot Country Club?" Lucy was good for leaking information from the St. Martin jail, but he wasn't an assassin.

"No more." Wilson's veiled reference was to Barnstable, the

rogue Marigot police officer who'd been killed in Bret's villa. He'd committed several murders for Claude, two inside police station cells orchestrated to look like suicides.

"Wha—what about Huckleberry and Tom?" Claude asked.

"Spotted on the banks of the ole Miss. CENTRO television. 'Friends' on the way as we speak."

"We better talk face-to-face, Wilson. Iron some things out, fast."

"My place or yours?"

"Be at my office in Marigot day after tomorrow, around noon. Okay?"

"Noon . . . two days." Wilson hung up. The static ceased.

The security chief switched the Nagra tape recorder off. Both he and Vargas had held speakers to their ears while they listened to the double-talk.

"This Hough they mention is assistant U.S. consulate general in Martinique," Vargas explained, " . . . or, apparently."

"It's clear they'd like to eliminate their 'friend', but it's most difficult when the man is in a jail cell."

"One would wish to eliminate someone who is a threat, eh Jaime?"

"*Sin duda, señor* Vargas. Of that there is no doubt."

"My emerald director . . ." Vargas stopped speaking when the security man who sat near Tomasso gently tapped at the partially-open door. "Come in, come in."

Entering the room, the husky young Colombian said, "A thousand pardons for disturbing you, *patron*." He also searched the eyes of his security chief.

"It's all right," Vargas said. "Did the American act suspicious as you watched him speak on the telephone?"

The security man spoke of the gushing perspiration, fearful eyes and the releasing of his bowels at one point.

"Do you recall the conversation when he shit his pants?"

"The *yanqui* had just asked if someone would 'spill'. It is usually a short way to say the American phrase 'spill the beans,' which means 'Will he tell what he knows?'"

"Hmm, I see. Jaime," Vargas pointed at the small Nagra.

The security chief turned to the tape recorder and began

rewinding it. After several seconds, he pushed the pause button, then switched on the room's interior Bose speakers. The younger security man shut the door until the latch clicked.

"It was at about this point, Senor Vargas," Jaime said. He pushed 'play'. The two American voices resounded clearly in the small room.

TOMASSO: "This, this . . . um, talk. How specific did it get?"

WILSON: "Very specific, even to mentioning many different gummy bear sizes. It also included possibly turning state's evidence—particularly the names of sugar and spice traders in exchange for the fed's WPR."

TOMASSO: "He, he wouldn't . . . couldn't spill. Would he, Frederick?"

"So, my young friend," Enrique Vargas Mantilla said, as he smiled at the American-educated Colombian lawyer. "You now have heard *both* sides of the phone conversation. What can you tell me about the 'fed's WPR'?"

He smiled at the powerful drug and gem czar. "*Patrón*, I fear you have placed great trust with one who may be a *yanqui* traitor." He went on to explain the theory and history of the U.S. federal witness protection program.

"So," Vargas mused, "sugar and spice and, er, gummy bears are something that Tomasso is smuggling from our country."

"*Si*, with the help of Wilson and Hough," the security man-lawyer said. "I suspect emeralds, of course, since that is his primary interest."

"*Naturalmente*, but also we must consider hard drugs, cannabis, coffee, gold, platinum—all major Colombian exports."

"Of course, *Patrón*," the security chief spoke.

"Tomasso will trap himself, Jaime. Watch him carefully."

"*Si, Señor* Vargas." *This assignment is better than winning the national lottery*, as far as the security chief was concerned.

* * *

Abby Duchamps was afraid her heart sounded like a marching band. *They'll hear it throughout the dealership*, she thought.

From the maintenance area to the upstairs hallway lasted less than five minutes. Her homemade map was accurate. She'd climbed the narrow stairway, since the small elevator would have been noisy in the quiet of the morning. As she neared an office door with MR. TOMASSO stenciled on it, Abby heard the elevator door open downstairs. Perspiring, she darted through a door that said CONFERENCE ROOM, and walked around a long, wooden table to a folding double door. Stepping inside, she nearly stumbled over several slide projectors and other audiovisual equipment, then pulled the door closed behind her.

"You're mullet bait if Boss finds you been sniffin' 'round his old lady," a voice broke the silence. The sound of two of Claude's security men grew louder with each second. Abby heard the latch squeak as the conference room door opened.

"Hey, all I be doin's givin' her 'howdy do's' when I drive her to de jew'ry store or mall, mon. No harm in bein' sociable."

"Sociable, shit . . ." Silence cut off the man's banter. "Joseph, you leave this door unlocked again?"

"Oh, shit. Man, you got no call t'write me up on that, hear? You leaves Payroll office wide-open jis las' night, 'member? An I say nuffin to Bergen, you recalls?" Both men were walking around the large room, Abby knew. She slipped behind a table-mounted overhead projector. The equipment room door rattled.

"Look, dickhead. The expensive shit's locked up in there. No reason t'lock that door." Abby assumed the man pointed to the conference room entrance.

"Rules be rules, asshole."

"Next time, man . . ."

"Up yours." The conference room door slammed, and was noisily locked.

"*Merde*," Abby murmured, using her hand to wipe the sweat from her brow.

Two sales offices were on the opposite side of the hallway

and Claude's office at the end. Those door latches were shaken, then additional quarreling followed as the two men made their way back to the elevator. At last, the irritating squabbling ceased.

She leaned back against a wall, using her backpack as a pillow. *Thirty seconds*, she thought. *Then I'm hitting Claude's office.*

Time's up, she told herself, after inspecting the watch. Abby slowly inched her way back toward the conference room's main door. The slightest squeak of a loose floor board would tip off the guards. In the hall, she decided to leave the door unlocked, in case she were on her way out and suddenly had to duck back inside. She removed the Walther P-38 from the shoulder holster, cocked it, and held it at the ready.

Photographs of Claude with some of his more affluent automobile purchasers, covered the walls. As she slowly moved in the dimmed hall, Abby casually glanced at smiling men and women staring into a camera lens.

What the hell? she thought, and stopped. Three men posed in front of a blue-gray SL Mercedes coupe/roadster. Claude stood at the far left; a tall, distinguished-looking man commanded the center; and to the right posed Bertrand Hough.

"Small world," Abby murmured. *A Tomasso-Hough connection. I shouldn't be surprised.*

Walking the last ten feet to Claude's office door, she probed the edges of the frame for telltale alarm wires or magnetic blocks. *Clean*, she decided. Next she kneeled down, set the pistol on the floor and studied the lock for a moment or two. *Too sophisticated for ordinary lock-pick tools*, she realized.

She swung her backpack onto the floor and unzipped a compartment. She pulled out an instrument resembling a fat fountain pen, with a red slide switch near one end. Another peek at the lock, then she selected the correct raking and tension tools from a small cloth packet. She stuck the raking pick into the front of the "pen," and tightened it with a set screw. The pick was inserted into the lock along with a tiny tension tool, then the battery-operated device was switched on. At 100 rakes per second, the tumblers quickly opened the lock. *Forget modern deadbolt technical advances.*

Abby entered. No motion detector red lights blinked on the walls. No alarms blared. A hall night-light glowed enough that she didn't take out her penlight. She grabbed the backpack and the automatic, and pulled them through the doorway. Abby replaced the lock pick. She closed and locked the door, and switched on her penlight.

She remembered to be tidy, organized, unhurried, careful. Take nothing for granted. The absence of a motion detector could mean the presence of a hidden video camera. Tiny electronic bugs could broadcast the mere sound of breathing to a listener. These were but a few of the lessons learned at LeMans, the art of staying alive.

First, ingress and egress . . . are there other exits from the office? A small, private bathroom had no other door and no window. The office windows . . . is escape available, if necessary? No, she saw that they were made of a thick acrylic, unbreakable Plexiglas-like material. *So much for leaping through a window two stories above the pavement*, she thought. *Only happens successfully in movies and comic books*. She recalled Bret correctly saying, 'Sam Spade is dead.'

A fast but efficient sweep showed the room was clean. Now for the computer. She pulled on thin, latex gloves. It wouldn't look good for police to find her fingerprints at the scene.

A new Savant LX personal computer sat atop a small desk across the large office, in a cubicle whose entrance was hidden from the main door. It was one of the new super-PC's . . . 986 microprocessor, 50 gigahertz of power, and complete with a read-write compact disk device. Oddly, the full tower CPU held a 5-¼ inch floppy diskette drive, plus the usual 5-inch, 3-½ inch and 1-¾ inch CD drives. Since there was no way to determine the hard drive capacity, Abby guessed about two-hundred gigabytes.

At the huge walnut desk near the center of the room, Abby ran a finger around the edges of the top center drawer, but felt nothing. She pulled. It was unlocked, and the key sat there. She picked it up, thinking, *Why do people lock a computer, then put the key where anyone can find it?*

She inserted the stubby key and twisted it. She punched the CPUs toggle switch ON, hit "Enter" and waited for text to appear. When Abby saw words on the screen giving system data, she pushed the SHIFT, CONTROL and F7 keys simultaneously. She knew the Savant 9-2000 wouldn't emit a beep using this command. The screen went blank for several seconds until a "menu" appeared. *Need user I.D. and password*, she noted.

Abby was familiar with personal computers. Computer science had been one of her minors at Wellesley, and she had done her homework before 'attacking' Island Imports. She'd gone into a computer shop and asked a clerk if she could "rent" one of his PC's for a short while. She said a fifty-dollar bill was his for the rental, and he let her use any software she'd need. She sat in the shop's small office and entered variables into the latest version of Quattro Pro. Abby quickly listed the most likely possibilities that Claude would use in forming his user I.D. and his password. This "what if?" analysis gave the DST officer a projection of possible words and numbers Claude would be most likely to use. She requested a ranking for ten words each, according to Claude's socioeconomics, personality and profession, legal and "sideline."

The computer's choice for Claude's user I.D. was "CTomasso," given that it was limited to eight letters. She typed in the letters and pushed Enter. An error message told her this was not a valid I.D. The computer's second choice was simply "Claude," so she typed it. This was correct, and the cursor dropped to the slot for Password. Abby sensed this part would be more difficult.

A throbbing noise sounded in the distance. She'd heard the commotion several times in the last few minutes. Tempting fate was offensive to her. She was uncomfortable and perspiring in the muggy building.

"First password," Abby spoke in a whisper, peering down at her notes. 'Luxury1.' She typed in the letters and number, then hit the 'enter' key. The computer beeped, sounding like a sonic boom. *Merde!* she thought. She sat still, expecting to hear shouts.

She noticed a slight quivering of her fingers as they rested on the keyboard. Since the letters and number she'd typed in were incorrect, a small rectangle appeared. Inside, Abby read: 'ERROR. You have not entered a correct password. Please remember that the password is case sensitive.' *So I have to worry about caps and lower case letters, too,* she thought.

Abby deleted the prior six letters and single digit. Cursor blinking, she pushed SHIFT, CONTROL and the *F2 key* simultaneously. This command would eliminate the dreadful beep if a second error resulted.

The computer software chose the second password possibility as 'emerald1', logical with Claude's real occupation. Again, the rectangle appeared in the center of the screen. There was no beep sound. She tried the same letters and digit with the first 'e' capitalized. Error screen. Her blouse and slacks were plastered to her skin with sweat.

She typed the remaining eight computer-generated passwords, and got eight error messages. Abby stared at the CPU. Staring back, the CPU seemed to offer its name and model, microprocessor, number: Savant 9. *Oh, no,* Abby thought, *Claude wouldn't.* She typed the word *Savant*; the SHIFT key and dash, usually used as a *space*; and the digit *9*. She tapped the 'enter' key. A 'C-prompt' appeared in the upper left corner of the screen. Even Claude couldn't forget the password.

Abby sighed. Had she been holding her breath during the entire wrestling match with the computer?

What's on the C-drive? she thought. *Can't waste a second. Directory?* She opened the hard drive's directory, which proved to consist of only five subjects: OS, ENET88, EZWRITE7, ISLLXINV, and WINDOWS. She checked to see the files in ISLLXINV, which proved to be an inventory of vehicles at Island Luxury Imports.

EZWRITE7 was a popular word processor, while OS and WINDOWS were self-explanatory to any computer user. That left ENET88, the directory for Earth Net version 8.8. *Claude's a net surfer?* Abby wondered. *No browser directory.* Most people on the NET use any one of many powerful, fast browsers to supplement ENET88. *Why would Claude 'surf' with the NET's own, less sophisticated, browser?*

Abby dared not boot the ENET88 directory because of its music, sound effects and speech distractions. However, she could get plenty of data through the 'back door'. She opened 'Dosshell', OS's own data utility, and highlighted the ENET88 directory. She clicked the "[+]" portion and immediately saw the subdirectories of ENET88. Abby checked DOWNLOAD. Only some upgrade, temp and read files were in the subdirectory. *That leaves chats and mail*, she realized. *Where does he keep it?* Two seconds sped by. *His writeable CD player. Just like DeGroot had at his home.* Abby'd remembered the fused-together clump of CD's she picked up where the Tomahawk missile struck. She exited Dosshell.

Change to D—no, E—prompt, she thought, typing furiously. An 'E' appeared where the 'C' had been. *Directory*, she typed. The screen flashed on two directories, named INCOMING and OUTGOING.

Back at the 'E' prompt she typed INCOMING, then DIR for the directory of files. The screen was filled with cryptic file names. APLSTRD2.CAL was one of the first file names Abby noticed. *California apple strudel? What the hell?* She went into the file's contents through Dosshell. The file was a straight download, or copy and paste, from Claude's Earthnet e-mail. It showed:

> Subj: Apple Strudel Two
> Date: Aug 14 (previous year) 20:44:30 EDT
> From: CalColo001
> To: ClaudeTLux
>
> Mr. Tomasso: Rif call to say add 30 tbs sugar and 35 cup flour to recipe for applestrudel. That can make him 500% more better taste. 12 green flavor gummy bear to make pretty decoration on top. Good sounds to it?
>
> Sr. J. Velasco

Code from Claude's source. CalColo? Cali, Colombia, I'll bet. Abby was sure the words sugar, flour and gummy bear stood for some goods Claude smuggled from Colombia. *Why does this sound like more than gems?* she thought. The 'green' gummy bears were probably emeralds, a dozen of them. 'Sugar' and 'flour' were condiments used to create something, but gummy bears were a finished product.

"Would Claude be foolhardy enough to risk his life by smuggling the cartel's drugs out of Colombia?" Abby speculated. *If he's that reckless, this Señor Velasco isn't with a drug cartel ... he's working with Tomasso.*

Loud 'thumps' sounded somewhere down the hallway. Abby's heart leaped. She pushed the OPEN button on the CD player/writer and grabbed the compact disk. Other disks in plastic "caddies" were stacked on a shelf above the keyboard and monitor. She swept them from the desk, stuffing them in her backpack. She heard the sounds of running, keys jingling, weapon bolts snapping shut on rounds. No shouts yet.

Where'd I screw up? Abby wondered. She pulled back the slide on the automatic, then released it, slamming a 9mm shell into the barrel. *Not time to die. No panic*, she told herself. She heard a key go into the lock of the door. Abby flipped off the master switch to the PC. She moved with catlike stealth in the semi-dark room.

The door burst inward with violent force. Two security guards darted inside, one on either side of the entrance, submachine guns ready. The computer finished turning itself off, speakers emitting an eerie *ding* and "Goodbye."

"Waste him, man!" a guard screeched. "In that computer cage." They let loose an intense barrage of deadly 9mm Parabellum ammunition, ripping apart the metal and cloth cubicle. Small parts of the computer soared in every direction. Firing at 1,200 rounds per minute, the 20-bullet magazines emptied in seconds.

Slapping in loaded magazines, they ran to the remains of the cubicle. Cordite hung low in the room, creating eye-stinging mist. The two guards stared at the carnage.

"Sucker ain't here!" the guard called Joseph yelled.

"Gotta be. Ain't no ghost." Rick rummaged through the remains of the cubicle.

"Drop your weapons," Abby ordered from behind Claude's desk. "Move and you're dead." The dim hall light silhouetted the men standing twenty feet away. She had scuttled to the desk while the guards riddled the cubicle. To Rick and Joseph, Abby was an unseen voice across a narrow expanse of darkness.

Slowly, Rick turned his body toward Abby's voice.

"T'ink mebbe she gots de gun, Rick."

"Naw. Real pro woulda wasted us by now." Hoping he'd aggravated the intruder, Rick abruptly dropped to the floor and aimed the Micro-Uzi toward the spot from which she'd spoken. He depressed the grip safety and his index finger jerked the trigger back to its guard. Again, the office resounded with eardrum-shattering blasts of gunfire. Sixteen or so high muzzle-energy slugs from the Uzi splintered the right side of Claude's desk.

From the left end of the desk, where Abby had slithered, she accurately emptied her Walther automatic. Rick died instantly, having no time to scream.

In his haste to rearm in the dark, Joseph stuck his second Micro-Uzi magazine backward into the grip bottom. It had barely entered, since the front is rounded, while the rear is squared. He'd pounded so hard it was jammed in tightly. While his partner was firing and being shot, Joseph smacked the magazine against the floor, wriggling it free. He reversed the magazine and hit it home with the palm of his hand. Raising the Uzi chest high, he aimed where he now knew Abby kneeled. He heard her automatic click several times, his luck had changed. The bitch had spent her load.

With the second click, Abby knew the Walther was out of ammunition. She'd expended all seven rounds in less than three seconds, with deadly accuracy. The black security guard, however, wasn't scratched and he pointed the miniature Uzi toward her with one hand. He began laughing.

"You wasted ole Rick, lady."

It's time, Abby knew. She hurled the P-38 at Joseph with all her strength, then lurched back and down toward the shattered portion of the desk. The weapon hit his right arm, enraging him. It also slowed his trigger finger by a split second.

Abby dove and rolled into the pile of splinters. She slid on her stomach while snatching the French MAS 1950 automatic from the holster at her lower back. She saw the room light up and heard bullets smash into the spot she'd just vacated. A quick snap of her left leg flipped Abby onto her back. While propelling herself across the slick wooden floor on her back, she gripped the MAS and aimed it at Joseph. *Déjà vu. An airport parking lot. A head shot . . . two slugs to the chest . . . another shot to the head.*

His body lay near the door, the muted hall light casting its glow across a torn ear and missing mouth. Rick's corpse was partially slumped across the mutilated computer partitions. Vast rivulets of murky blood soaked into the hardwood floor.

Abby reached between the bodies to retrieve the Walther pistol. She lifted the backpack, checked the dozen or so compact disks, and slung it across one shoulder. She used her penlight to check the scene for any forgotten or misplaced items, then she abandoned the carnage.

What's the light for? As Abby stepped over Joseph's remains, she'd seen a yellow LED light flash. Leaning down, she saw it came from the top of a two-way radio attached to the security man's belt. *The third guard. These* two men had turned the radios down when they neared this office. Abby rotated the volume control.

" . . . sounded like Nam during Tet. What's your status? Over."

Abby pressed the TALK switch twice. *Let's see what happens.*

"That mean you're okay? Over."

Another double-click.

"Ten-four. Get back here and report, ASAP. Over." The lead guard would believe his men had terminated the intruder. Two-way radios can be heard by anyone tuned to their frequency. Claude's security men wouldn't want to risk the police or anyone else hearing any part of the incident.

Abby inserted the radio back into its leather holder on Joseph's belt. She took his handcuffs, and put them into one of her trousers pockets. *Degnan, Berkin? Bergen... that's the name the guards called their security lead.* She would pay him a visit.

As she walked down the hall, Abby breathed deeply to try to regulate her wildly-beating heart. Her legs felt steadier, now, and she detected only faint quivering in her fingers. Pure adrenaline had pumped wildly through the bodies of three people in Claude's office. The atmosphere had been electric. Now, all was curiously, yes, deathly, quiet.

Abby pushed the elevator's down button. In a few seconds the small hydraulic elevator door opened. She entered and poked the button marked "1."

On the main level, Abby remained near the wall. The guard at the security desk sat with his back to Abby, evidently absorbed in reading a magazine. She approached the guard without really trying to be silent . . . since he expected his men to return soon.

"Sounded like a firefight upstairs. You guys waste the bastard?"

Abby placed the muzzle of the pistol against his neck. "Stare straight ahead, Bergen . . . and *you'll* survive."

"Who're you?"

"You don't want to know. Head on the desk."

The big security officer leaned his forehead against the steel of the desk top. "Rick, Joseph. Where . . . ?"

"Dead. Gave them a chance to drop their weapons."

"Jesus, lady. When Mr. Tomasso hears this, you're a dead bitch."

She smacked the automatic against Bergen's skull. It wasn't hard enough to draw blood, but the guard shut up. "Where's Tomasso?" she asked.

"Don't know."

A second, harder, bash above Bergen's left ear brought a gasp. "Does that jog your memory?"

"Shit, lady. The Man leaves, tells us he'll be back in several days. Don't say when. Don't say where he goes."

"When's he due back?"

"Three—no, *two* days, now."

"Hands behind your back, *lentement,* slowly."

"Y'ain't gonna kill me, lady. I can't finger ya."

"Cooperate and you live."

He cooperated. Abby put handcuffs on his wrists and ankles. She put duct tape over his eyes, and wrapped the handcuffs about the metal desk legs bolted to the concrete floor. He wouldn't be able to reach a phone or two-way radio.

"Cuffs killin' my ankles, lady."

"But you'll survive, won't you?"

Bergen grunted, but said nothing.

She walked toward the front door. She realized it was probably alarmed, but the car was just a minute away. She'd have plenty of time before any alarm service personnel would arrive. She looked at Bergen and asked, "How did you know I was in Claude's office? I checked it for bugs and alarms."

Bergen thought about the two painful raps to his head, and said, "The Man's computer, lady. Whenever he goes outta town, he sets it so a red light flashes on this console if anyone turns the thing on."

Merde, she thought. *So many space-age gadgets, and Claude hot-wires an LED to the PC's lock.*

"So long, Bergen." Abby pushed open the lobby door and jogged up the street.

Chapter Twenty-Seven

Bret pushed the goggles to his forehead and stared at the Life Finder LP-5. The detector showed five silhouettes within one hundred yards of the cruiser. Except for small detours to sidestep booby traps, the guerrillas unerringly moved toward the boat and its American crew. They had to be following directions from a spy satellite.

" . . . but, whose?" Bret mumbled.

"Say something?" Russell fussed at wiping dew from his Armalite-15. The British Arwen 37, loaded with six high explosive rounds, lay next to him on a tarp.

"Wondering what Spy Sat's got us pinpointed."

"All of ours are NRO's responsibility. Think your C-47 pilot has a buddy at the National Reconnaissance Office?"

"That sonuvabitch Wilson. Gotta be him at CENTRO. Musta faked priorities for satellite target spotting, so only *these* shits," Bret pointed at the monitor screen, "are watching us."

"Yeah, you said that Hough and Wilson had a foolproof smuggling scheme between several countries."

"High-security clearance at CENTRO and unrestricted use of his C-47. No customs checks at all . . . anywhere."

"Damn-near perfect smuggling setup. They sure don't want us snooping around your emerald digs."

The detector's screen showed the guerrillas again moving

forward. "I'll try to blast their satellite imager before they trip over us," Bret murmured.

They'd assumed that the hit squad could see their own images plus that of the boat. The cruiser's armor wouldn't have cooled off enough to reduce its image completely. Bret and Russell's body temperatures would show up on the imager like two Dutch ovens. Johnson, while not knowing how they would be tracked during their voyage, had provided for most eventualities.

The FIM-92C Stinger would have been perfect if the enemy were in vehicles that provided heat for the missile to seek. No vehicles. Stingers were out.

An M206 40mm Grenade Launcher attached to Russell's favored Armalite-15 could provide an excellent high explosive airburst. Except there were far too many trees to aim the weapon with accuracy. Grenade launchers were out.

The Arwen 37 would be very lethal once the guerrillas could be flushed out. This was why Russell patted the Arwen's adjustable butt.

Bret had found the weapon he hoped would destroy the tattletale satellite imager. Only three feet, four inches long, the British-manufactured LAW80 was a portable light antitank weapon. It penetrated more than 2-½ inches of armor at 500 yards, an impressive "super bullet." Bret learned to trust the LAW80 during a covert mission training session at Camp Peary, Virginia six years before.

The antitank system now lay on the tarp extended to its full five-foot length. British Royal Marines and SAS special operations teams often used it for anything but an antitank weapon. The LAW80's strong suits are portability, high penetration and deadly accuracy with its 3.7-inch diameter HEAT, High Explosive Anti-Tank, warheads.

Russell whispered, "Full zoom shows those dipshits at seventy-five yards. Better do your thing." He checked the Life Finder again, and said, "Point man probably holding the sat readout." He directed Bret to the estimated area of trees and brush ahead of them where the point man would be.

He raised the LAW80 to his right shoulder, comfortable with his elbows pushed against the soft earth at the rim of the stream bed. He spotted the target in the scope of the attached 9mm sniper's rifle, then loaded the projectile and five 9mm tracer bullets. Bret aimed where the target should be and fired the rifle.

"Hit a yard to the right of the target," Russell said. "No flash head. Another, narc-man." On the Life Finder LP-5's screen, the tracer shown as a bright white line barely missing the point man's ghostly white silhouette. The tracer line would not totally disappear for some time.

"One blond hair to the left," Bret mumbled, slowly pulling the trigger. The 9mm round was eerily quiet as it sprang from the smaller weapon's muzzle. He watched the tracer flash away from them.

Russell saw a white line reach the forward-moving enemy, then produce a flash head, a solid hit. A shriek came from a distant point. "Right on. Launch!" Russell yelled.

"Missile launch," Bret said. He pulled the trigger for the main projectile. In less time than one can think about the process, a percussion cap in the launcher connected by a flash tube to the igniter fired the lethal missile. "Away," he said as the four-finned, high explosive projectile sped off at 900 feet per second.

A terrifying explosion lighted the night. The point man and his satellite monitor vaporized, as the two men directly behind him died instantly from shrapnel and shock. Birds and animals of the jungle fluttered, screeched and bolted toward safety.

"Outstanding!" Russell shouted. "Life Finder shows one disappeared, two down and images fading, two retreated north. Taking up a new position."

Bret pushed himself to slipping feet, grabbing his MAC-10. "I'll take the left flank. You go right. Can't give 'em time to use the rocket launcher."

Mahdavi-Karubi and Hernandez stumbled in their withdrawal. Hernandez clutched the remaining RPG-18 rocket launcher and an M-16. Mahdavi-Karubi fled with his AKM-74 assault rifle and holstered 9mm Makarov SL. The dwarf and his satellite imager no longer existed after the *yanqui* pig's direct hit. The other dead Colombians shielded the survivors from the warhead. Their "eyes" were gone, but the two men knew they could not return to headquarters. In a few seconds, the hounds became the hares.

We will suffer great humiliation if we do not kill the yanquis, Hernandez knew.

If the Zionist swine are not eliminated, they will execute us without delay, the Iranian reminded himself. Sadaq Mahdavi-Karubi cursed the eyes of the Colombian FARC commander who sent him on this foray.

Hernandez shined a penlight on a small compass. He and the filthy Middle Eastern terrorist still headed north, away from the Americans.

"We halt here," Mahdavi-Karubi hissed. "Americans follow and we slice them down like wheat." His Spanish was nearly unintelligible to Hernandez.

Sweat and blood mixed and formed puddles at the feet of the guerrillas. Many of their wounds were created by the bursting projectile. During their race through the jungle, tree branches, bushes and fallen logs added cuts, bruises and gashes to tormented bodies.

"Where are bandages and morphine?" the Iranian asked.

"Gone," Hernandez muttered. "Smashed by the missile."

"Imbecile! You were leader. It was your job to keep the medicine." His voice was much too loud for one attempting an escape.

"Shut your mouth, son of a whore," Hernandez raged. "I am *still* leader. You are not clever enough to herd camels." He jammed the muzzle of his M-16 beneath Mahdavi-Karubi's sternum.

"Alonso," the Iranian gasped. "It is—as you—say, you are—in truth—*el jefe*." He dropped his AKM-74 rifle.

A smile came to Hernandez' blood-caked face. "*Si*, placenta of a sow. I *am* the boss!" He pulled the trigger, bellowing into the darkness. The corpse at the end of the assault rifle danced like a puppeteer's doll as a dozen 5.56mm rounds punctured its chest and mid-section. *"Está verdadero. Soy el jefe!"*

Russell and Bret dropped to the ground at the first sound of loud voices. Bret motioned his partner to meet him. Russell navigated the short distance in a crouch.

"Sounds like an argument," he whispered. Russell held the Life Finder so both men could view the screen.

"More than that," he said. "Those assholes," he nodded at the images on the monitor, "are really pissed."

A dozen muffled shots ended the shouting. Laughter echoed through the jungle, punctuating the gunfire.

"Damn," Russell said as he stared at the Life Finder screen. "Guy wasted the other guerrilla." The M-16 displayed brighter than the man holding it, while the image to the left of its superheated barrel crumpled to the ground.

"Musta squabbled about stayin' here after the sat imager got snuffed."

"Bet on it. We got us one bonafide lunatic." Bret rose from the prone position he and Russell shared. "Time to take him."

Russell pushed himself up with his riot control weapon. "No more'n fifty yards north," he noted.

"We'll hit his right flank. He's not movin'." Having the LP-5 was far superior to tracking someone in broad daylight, Bret realized.

They stepped over logs, between bushes and around vines. They slipped around tall mahogany, balsam, oak and cedar trees. Occasionally, a large insect or small rodent would dart from their path.

The thermal imager showed that the assassin stood in the same place as before. The likeness of his automatic weapon had dimmed, having cooled nearly as quickly as the cadaver stretched out four feet away.

"Almost on him," Russell warned. They stepped into a small clearing. A sneering man in a tattered camouflage outfit stood at the far end of the open area of glade grass and shrubs. In his right hand he held a weapon at a slight downward angle. His head was cocked to the right to increase his night vision. The clearing caught enough starlight to make the smallest objects distinguishable

Turning toward the terrorist, Bret said, "He looks dazed, maybe in shock."

"Never think that way," Russell said. "Sizin' us up."

Bret stared at the remaining guerrilla. He saw what Russell meant. The assassin's head bent downward, but attentive eyes focused on them.

Bret said, "Drop your weapon. You'll be okay. The fight's over, *amigo.*"

Alonso Hernandez' eyes bore deeply into Bret's eyes, hatred evident even at the thirty-foot distance. He said nothing. His weapon was locked and loaded.

Russell said, "*Coloca tu fusil en la tierra, hombre,*" speaking in proficient Colombian Spanish. He added that no harm would come to the man if he put down the weapon.

The Colombian's eyes darted to Russell. There was no movement of his body.

Cautiously, Bret began to step forward, glancing nervously at his adversary. Again, the Colombian's eyes riveted on him.

It was the tiniest of twitches of a minor vein in Hernandez' hand closest to the trigger. The shooter's index finger began to pull back, seen by Russell as the tensing of a minor muscle in the Colombian's right wrist.

"Drop!" Russell shouted, watching the assassin's assault rifle swing parallel to the ground. The bloodied man decided that Bret, the man who'd begun to advance, would be his first victim.

Diving sideways, Bret hit the soft, sandy ground on his left shoulder and upper arm. The .45 caliber MAC-10, aimed closer to Russell's position than the guerrilla's, was useless at this time. As he landed and rolled, the crack of M-16 slugs ripped into the patch of space he'd just vacated.

In less than the split-second Hernandez fired twenty 5.56mm

rounds at Bret, Russell sighted his Arwen on the Colombian and pulled the trigger.

Bret heard the powerful anti-personnel weapon roar. Its large high-explosive projectile bridged the thirty-foot gap at supersonic velocity. The assassin was dissected at the chest, allowing no time to emit a last scream.

Again, the disoriented animals and birds of the jungle raced in frenzied circles, having nowhere to go. Bret pulled his homing device from a pocket and smashed it against a tree trunk. Then, all was quiet.

* * *

Wilson dialed an extension within the facility. He'd botched the number on the ancient rotary-dial phone three times before he got a connection. Somewhere within the bowels of CENTRO command, a woman's voice answered.

"Yes, Captain Wilson?" Airman Second Class Bartlett said.

"Um, hello Rita. I just received word from Triptych at NRO. Advised me to adjourn the reconnaissance training exercise on MILSTAR 26."

"Unusual the order didn't come to me, captain. They always have before."

Wilson nearly lost it, but said, "Airman, I'm sure the order came to me because I was monitoring MILSTAR 26 alone." He thought for a moment. "Since it's early in the morning, I guess Triptych's aide decided to phone *this* extension."

"Yes, sir," the Airman said, unwilling to debate the issue with a captain. "Are we to return MILSTAR 26 to its original orbital coordinates and altitude?"

"Affirmative, Rita. With the exercise aborted, '26' reverts to Southern Command's primary orbit." The deplorable job done by the FARC team kept playing in Wilson's mind. *Goddam Lamplighter*, he thought. *I shoulda had him killed in Barranquilla.*

"Do I notify the OIC of the revised orbit, captain?"

"Shit, no! I mean that's a negative, Rita."

"But, I always . . ."

"Airman Bartlett," Wilson interrupted. "CENTRO operations memos say if an NRO senior exec doesn't wish to log a training exercise, it's a black operation. Triptych wants it kept black, understand?" *Bitch's tryin' to play games with me.*

"No report, sir. Original orbital coordinates, sir. Just leave it to me."

"Very well, Airman. Been a long day, huh?" Wilson hung up.

Wilson looked at the enormous monitor built into the far wall. The location at the upper left corner read Bolivar state, Colombia and showed longitude, latitude and satellite altitude. Adjusting his keypad, he watched the two Americans examine the dead guerrillas' pockets. Next, they smashed the weapons of the Iranian and Colombian against a nearby tree trunk.

"Hough, Claude, now these assholes," Wilson muttered.

Suddenly, the clearing shook violently, then swiftly receded. In thirty seconds the recce satellite camera surveyed an area identified as a secret rebel camp in Venezuela. Airman Second Class Bartlett had deftly placed MILSTAR 26 back in its original orbit.

Another revolution brewing in Latin America, Wilson noticed. He turned off the monitor. He truly had *important* matters to attend to.

Chapter Twenty-Eight

The chirping telephone awoke Abby in her villa. She'd fallen asleep only an hour before. She felt like someone whose mouth was stuffed with cotton balls. She wasn't surprised to hear the voice of a Marigot detective. The young man said that officer Duchamps' presence was requested with *sous-inspecteur* Bouchard.

"An' that would be . . . how shoon, detective?"

"*Sous-'specteur* say *neuf heures*, ma'am. That be nine o'clock."

She smiled at his attempt to help her with the translation. She looked at her bed table alarm clock, and saw it was already eight-ten A.M. "Tell *'specteur* Bouchard I'll be there *tout suite*." She pronounced the words 'toot sweet', the local native enunciation.

Smoothing her colorful skirt, Abby sat back in the chair Henri Bouchard had pointed to. *Nine thirty*, she thought as she glanced at her watch. *Didn't think I could make it here until ten*. It wasn't the showering and dressing that would take time, she knew. The problem was concealing bruises and small scrapes. Her acrobatics in Claude's office had not been performed without some aches of the trade. The result was an uncharacteristically shrouded Abby Duchamps, peasant skirt falling to her ankles and blouse demurely buttoned to her neck.

"*Alors*, officer Duchamps," under-inspector Bouchard

remarked, "you remind me of the pretty farm girls one often sees in Dordogne."

"Such a refreshing comparison, Henri, and I thought you wished to talk shop."

"Then shop it is," he said. "What do you make of these?" He handed her a bundle of photographs.

"This appears to be a dead man, security guard by the looks of the uniform." She set the photo on the chief's desk and looked at the next glossy.

"I would say this is another dead security guard, with a Micro-Uzi," she remarked, scanning the second photo. She quickly shuffled through the pictures, as one would with playing cards when adding up their score. "Who are they?"

"I was going to ask you the same question. No idea?"

"Never saw either of them, I'm certain."

"Really?" Bouchard grunted. "Do you recognize this person?" he asked, holding out one more glossy photograph.

"To the best of my knowledge, I would guess this is a *live* security guard." She looked at the photo of the security officer she'd hogtied to the reception desk.

"Live because it was God's will to spare one who is pure and innocent," Henri added, taking back the package of photos.

"Pure? . . . of what? I don't understand . . ."

"I paraphrased security officer Walter Bergen's written statement. He's the live security guard you just looked at. Got a bump on the head, but figures he was spared because of clean living."

"Where did this, this monstrous crime occur?"

Sous-inspecteur Bouchard picked a sheet of paper from his desk as he said, "At Claude Tomasso's automobile dealership."

"Someone killed those poor guards to steal automobiles?"

Henri Bouchard stared at Abby. The edge of one lip almost rose—as if a smile wished to appear. "*Merde*," Henri muttered. "I still have many years before retirement." He paused, then sighed. "No, no cars were stolen."

"A safe, then. A criminal like Claude probably keeps

thousands of dollars at his dealership . . . legitimate and illicit money." Abby sat forward.

"As far as we know," Henri sighed, "nothing was stolen."

Abby leaned back in the chair. "Then why would they kill the two guards?"

"'They' was a 'she', Abby. The surviving guard identified the killer as a woman, one who fits your description."

"Impossible," Abby said with a grin. "*I* wouldn't give him a chance to see me. *I* would have a mask on, or a hood over my head . . . or *I'd* make certain he didn't have *time* to look at me. What is his description of the criminal?"

"Bergen said it was a woman about your height and build." Bouchard consulted his notes. "He also said she spoke American English with a slight French accent."

"That 'description' would fit half the women on the northern side of this island, Henri. He didn't see the murderer, in other words."

"'See' is an indefinite verb, in Bergen's case. He claims he saw the woman's reflection in the window and door glass at the lobby."

"Reflection? What time are we talking about?"

"Early morning . . . about four a.m. Darkness outside, night lights inside. Said the woman wore dark pants, dark jacket, carried a backpack or knapsack. Thinks her hair was brunette and cut short."

"You call me in here, a good friend and fellow law enforcement officer, to accuse me of, of breaking and entering, and, and committing a double homicide . . ." Abby managed to extricate a delicate little handkerchief from among her attire. She dabbed it at a rather too-dry eye.

Henri sat at the desk with his chin resting on intertwined fingers. His facial expression was neutral. "Abby," the under-inspector said after taking a deep breath, "I haven't accused you of anything."

"True, but why am I your first . . . ?"

"All the men Claude hires to guard his buildings and home are criminals, ex-cons, the dregs of society."

"What about the three at his import car company?"

"The two Americans—one dead, one alive—most-recently served as mercenaries in Venezuela. These days, *mercenary* is another word for assassin, hit man, hired gun, whatever so-called 'respectable' work a fugitive can get."

"They were outlaws, on the run?" Abby casually stuffed the unused handkerchief down the neck of her blouse.

Watching the disappearing 'prop', Bouchard stifled a smile and said, "Both Americans were wanted for murdering two armored car guards and armed robbery. We will be extraditing Mr. Bergen to Connecticut USA within the week."

"... and the background of the black Caribbean guard?" *Merde*, Abby thought when the words left her mouth.

Bouchard stiffened noticeably. After studying various *objets d'art* on his desktop, Henri leaned back in his chair. "Never mentioned what citizenship the black man held, Abby. Now you know why you were the first person I questioned about the, um, *monstrous* crime."

"You were so certain...?"

"Quite certain. You are the only young woman I know who could have gotten out of there alive."

Looking down at her sandals, Abby said, "That almost sounds like a compliment."

Sous-inspecteur Bouchard arose and slowly paced behind the desk, arms folded across his chest. "Almost. I don't condone criminal acts, especially those committed within my jurisdiction." Henri pondered his next words. "Nevertheless, I was at Island Luxury Imports four or five hours ago. I saw the arsenal Tomasso's hired killers used against, against one brave woman."

"Henri, I did not wish to harm anyone. It was only..."

"Enough," Bouchard interrupted. "The, um, vermin used automatic weapons. They had enough firepower to defeat the Vietminh rebels at Dien Bien Phu." Lowering his voice, Henri said, "And all those scum exterminated was a computer and large desk."

"I considered asking for your help, Henri," Abby said,

standing. "I realized I couldn't do that without jeopardizing you and your position."

Bouchard stared out an office window.

"Other members of the DST, Interpol, they had to be discounted. It was, in truth, a covert operation. I didn't dare put others at risk."

Bouchard watched two of his men walk by the window into the police station. They had a cursing, handcuffed teenager in tow. Henri turned to Abby. *Merde!*" he exclaimed. He sank heavily to his chair. Abby remained standing. "The president. The goddam president of France phoned me the day after you and, and that American were ambushed at his villa."

"But, why . . . I didn't know. I hope he was cordial, Henri."

"*Mais, oui*. He was cordial. He told me that the wonderful daughter of his best friend Antoine Duchamps should never have to worry about assassins."

"I'm sorry. All my life my father has 'sent me' on paths he deems suitable."

"I concluded that fact from the 'presidential decree' I obtained from his high-ranking comrade," the under-inspector replied.

"Papa was very angry when I chose to attend an American university, and I refused to back off. Eventually, he and *maman* came to the graduation exercises."

Bouchard nodded. "So you believed his interfering in your life had stopped?"

Shaking her head, Abby said, "Not really. He was sincerely happy when I went to Harvard for graduate studies. I recall he once said, 'Harvard cannot be *all* that terrible. John F. Kennedy graduated from there'."

Henri Bouchard smiled. "The Bouvier roots of Kennedy's wife."

"You understand, of course." Abby sighed. "Not even DeGaulle was as intense a Francophile as *monsieur* Duchamps of Grenoble."

The *sous-inspecteur* drummed his fingers on the desk for a

few seconds. "*Alors, mademoiselle.* Back to *small* matters, murder and intrigue on a tiny island."

"It was very important that I find proof of Claude's emerald smuggling. It was reasonable he would keep records of his dealings on his computer."

Bouchard nodded. "And were you correct?"

"Absolutely . . . and then some. He also is involved with smuggling illicit drugs from Cali, Colombia."

"*Mon dieu,*" Henri uttered. "For this, a foreigner will not live five seconds after that fact is discovered. The cartels are most protective of their coca and poppy plants." He stared out the office window again. "Is there enough data from the computer files to find the emeralds Lamplighter is searching for?"

No reason remained for Abby to hedge about her Island Luxury Imports invasion. "I only got a brief glimpse of the contents of one 3-½ inch CD disk. The file I checked was a recipe sent over the Internet."

"Claude doesn't impress me as being an epicure. Was it a coded message?"

"Yes, I'm certain. It said: 'add 30 tablespoons of sugar and 35 cups of flour' to the original recipe . . . whatever that was."

"Very large pie," Bouchard said. "Sugar could be cocaine, flour could be heroin, or vice versa. Did you find any decrypt sheets?"

"Unfortunately, no. It was becoming most uncomfortable for me by that time."

The *sous-inspecteur* shook his head at the thought of two killers with assault weapons attacking Abby in the small office. "Um, did you manage to, er, liberate any other CD's that may help implicate Tomasso?"

"Fourteen others of the same size. However, I don't know if all of them hold data downloaded from Tomasso's e-mail."

Nodding, Bouchard said, "We'll look at the other CD's as soon as you can bring them here."

"I found another part of the 'recipe' interesting. The Cali contact, he signed the e-mail *señor* J. Velasco, wrote about green gummy bears."

Bouchard stared at the *Sûreté* officer with a blank expression. "I don't..."

Abby smiled and explained, "Gummy bears are a small chewy candy, with a consistency similar to gum drops. Children, and I, love them."

"You believe 'gummy bears' is another code for illicit drugs?"

"*Mot du code, oui. Drogues, non.* I'm certain a green gummy bear is an emerald, one of the exquisite emeralds Claude deals in."

"But of course. That is his only accepted tie-in with the drug czars. No matter how profitable the drug portion is, he must spend maximum time buying, smuggling, stealing, concealing Colombian emeralds."

"*C'est vrai.* He cannot afford to arouse suspicion... or he'll be belly-up on the bottom of Great Salt Pond."

"*Oui*, Abby." Bouchard gently tapped a letter opener against his desk lamp. "It would be a pity if any of your evidence reached Cali cartel's drug chief."

"Without doubt, Henri. Unfortunately, in these days of insane crime and terror, one can never know when a CD or two may fall into the 'wrong' hands."

They nodded several times regarding a world turned upside-down. Henri took a sheet of paper from a file and handed it across the desk to Abby.

"This is a copy of a report that will be leaked to the news media regarding the incident at Claude's car dealership. The original is with our *Sûreté Nationale Français* team in St. Martin. Interpol and the U.S. State Department received copies, as well."

Abby unfolded the sheet and began reading:

CONFIDENTIAL. FOR EYES ONLY.

Marigot, St. Martin, French West Indies.
Acting Chief of Police of combined St. Martin, French West Indies and Sint Maarten, Netherlands Antilles—*sous-inspecteur* Henri J. Bouchard—revealed

that reliable informants and a first-hand description place an international terrorist at the scene of a double homicide. The murder of two security officers employed at Island Luxury Imports of Marigot was evidently the work of a notorious female assassin and provocateur, known as *El Gato Negro*.

Often said to be the female equivalent of the infamous terrorist Carlos, The Black Cat was seen and identified by the only surviving security officer at Claude Tomasso's automobile dealership. Her description by Walter Bergen is as follows: Hispanic, light complexion, shoulder-length black hair, very slim, 5' 9" tall, weight approximately one hundred pounds. The killer wore dark trousers, shoes and jacket, and carried burglary tools in a black valise. Her facial features were partially obscured by a cloth mask. *El Gato Negro* spoke what the surviving security man described as poor English with a thick Spanish accent.

Claude Tomasso's three security guards all have outstanding arrest warrants, two from the U.S. Federal Bureau of Investigation. Among crimes described in the American federal warrants are murder and grand larceny. Richard Tucker's remains and Walter J. Bergen will be extradited to the U.S. this week. A British warrant for Joseph Ragsdale (deceased), a citizen of Anguilla, include crimes of homicide, rape and armed theft. His body will be given over to U.K. authorities this week.

Very unpleasant backgrounds," Abby said as she handed the flimsy sheet back to under-inspector Bouchard.

"A gross understatement, officer Duchamps," Henri said, nodding.

"Bergen's description of the female intruder in your bulletin is much different from his rather accurate description of me. May I ask . . . ?"

"I had a long phone conversation with high-ranking members

of the American Department of Justice several hours ago. I explained that you were working deep cover for my organization, and you would be in great peril if compromised."

"They bought your story?"

"Absolutely. After all, they want criminals like Tomasso behind bars as much as we. Seems the crimes I attributed to Claude were more accurate than I realized. I said we suspected him of being a major player in emerald and drug smuggling."

"Had you any idea of that before I told you about the CD's?"

"We'd been led to believe he *dabbled* in Colombian drugs. But only your findings prove it. We simply didn't believe he'd risk certain death by crossing the criminal cartels."

"What will the Justice Department do with Bergen? He could still give my description to the wrong people." Abby leaned forward in the wooden chair.

"Justice and I made a deal with Bergen," Bouchard revealed.

"Not the witness protection program . . . he's a murderer and thief."

"No, no," Henri said. "While he helped the Americans and us, he still *didn't* aid in incriminating any high-ranking suspected criminals."

"You can't simply trust his word, Henri."

"No, his sentence will stipulate confinement at Marion federal penitentiary."

"Total lockdown," Abby remarked in hushed tones. "He won't have anyone to talk with, even if he wanted it."

"That was our deal with Bergen. In fact, he suggested it." Bouchard picked up another sheet of paper. "He volunteered to put it in writing, as well," the under-inspector said, waving the agreement over the desk top.

"Exceptional that anyone would ask to be totally isolated from other people."

"Normally, yes," Henri nodded. "Bergen admitted that before he fled America, the Brooklyn mafioso put out a contract on him."

"The FBI and Mob wanted him? *Mon dieu*, that's a dead man's hand. What did he do to arouse the wrath of the mafia?"

"Bergen didn't volunteer that information, and neither the Justice officers nor I tried to force it out of him," Bouchard noted. "He did mention that he'd 'stepped on a few toes' of members of the Brooklyn Cosa Nostra before heading to Venezuela."

"Even in Marion, I wouldn't bet on a long life for Walter Bergen."

Henri Bouchard nodded at Abby's comment, laid Bergen's agreement down and looked long and hard at the attractive *Sûreté* operative.

"*Maintenant, jeune dame* . . . it is time to check the contents of the CD's that recently fell into your hands."

"Agreed. I'll go get them from a little hiding place . . ."

The intercom squawked an interruption, halting Abby in mid-sentence.

"Yes, Selma?" Bouchard asked while pressing an intercom button.

"Ver' 'portant phone call for you, suh . . . line three," the police dispatcher told the under-inspector.

"Bouchard *ici*," he spoke after punching another button. "*Comment est-ce que je peux vous servir?*" He pressed a switch allowing Abby to listen to the call.

"Bouchard, *mon ami*. It is here I am Johnson."

"*Señor* Johnson, it is a pleasure. How may I be of assistance?"

"That is question of this week, *sous-'specteur*." Johnson's command of the English language was not much better than Henri's. He knew practically no French and Bouchard was not very conversant in Spanish. "It might be that I here am to make you the help. First you are to please turn on your scrambler."

"The sound of it is that you need help?" the *sous-inspecteur* probed, as he started the scrambler toggle located inside his top desk drawer.

"No, no, Henri," Abby broke in. Speaking louder, she said, "Johnson, *amigo*, this is Abby Duchamps of the *Sûreté français*." She leaned forward slightly and asked, "Am I correct to presume you have information that may help us?"

A long pause revealed Johnson spoke through a satellite

hookup. "It is for *verdad*, officer Duchamps. I have the phone talkings with General Serrano."

"Yes, Johnson," Abby interrupted. "We know the person you speak of."

"*Bueno, mademoiselle*. What I say is not information top secretly," Johnson clarified. "*El general* Serrano sent note to all *Policía nacional* garrisons this morning. It tell to all *comandantes* of guerrilla attack by *rio* Magdalena on Lam'lighter *y* Russell."

"Hold it. Slow down . . . not so fast," Abby shouted. "Guerrillas attacked Bret and Russell? Are they okay, dammit?"

"*Muchas* hokay, *señorita*. *Es* guerrillas what make widows of *esposas*."

"Are you saying that they destroyed their attackers?" Abby asked.

"Is the truth, *señorita* Abby," Johnson answered.

"That's wonderful news, *señor* Johnson. Where did this happen?" Abby hoped the information wouldn't further endanger Bret, since a vast number of police and military higher-ups were on the take.

"In morning dark *a las cuatro*," Johnson answered.

"Um, thank you, but where . . . not when," Abby rephrased her question.

"Ah, jes; attack by *rio* Magdalena north of El Banco, *departamento de* Boivár."

"You are truly a good friend and ally to tell us this," Bouchard interjected. "We were worried about them."

"Company of Lam'lighter pay good *dinero* to help him find *esmeraldas*. General Serrano say to me in confidence that *el Policía Judicial Anti-narcoticos de* Buenaventura make *telefono* tappings of most high importance."

"Any information you have is welcome, I'm sure."

"Ees many, how jou say, *eventos extraños* to occur een that city."

"What 'strange' things, *señor* Johnson?"

"Jou and I know a man of St. Martin named Claude Tomasso. *También*, we know U.S. army flyer named Wilson."

"Wilson?" Abby tried to place the name. "I recall that Bertrand Hough knows a man called Wilson."

"Ees same *hombre, señorita.*"

Sous-inspecteur Bouchard jumped to his feet just as Abby rose from her chair. "Are you saying that one or both men are in Colombia?" Henri grumbled.

"*Si*, Claude Tomasso is in Buenaventura . . ."

Bouchard said, "With all our assets, how the hell did Tomasso get into Colombia? We were told he went to Florida."

"Claude has mos' customs people of Colombia in his pocket, *sous-'specteur.*"

"How did General Serrano discover where Claude is staying?" Abby asked.

"*Policía* informants finger Colombian *narcotraficante mágico* who borrow *hacienda grande* from a businessman."

"'Finger'?" Bouchard asked Abby.

"Implicate, uncover," Abby answered in French.

"'*Mágico*'?" Bouchard asked Abby.

In French, Abby explained it was the Spanish word for 'magician'. "Bret once explained that *mágico* is what coca and poppy growers, *paisas*, call the powerful drug traffickers. They are considered 'untouchable', so they display near-magical powers.

"Most of the magic being deep pockets of money," Henri noted.

"Pablo Escobar Gaviria was beloved by his *mestizo* drug growers," Abby continued. "He spent millions of pesos on new homes for the *paisas*. In return, they provided him with billions of pesos worth of coca, marijuana, poppies, coffee, emeralds . . . everything that reaps a huge profit after smuggling."

"*Si, señorita*," Johnson joined in, knowing enough French to get the gist of the conversation. "*Señor* Lam'lighter tell jou right. Ees why *puerto* of Buenaventura ees *muy importante*. Escobar ees no more, *pero* if other Cali or Medellín cartel boss come for visit, *policía* stop all other investigations."

"A drug lord came to the home of a Buenaventura businessman?" Abby asked.

"Enrique Vargas Mantilla ees one *patrón*, boss, of Cali cartel *de la droga*. Eet ees Vargas who come to *hacienda*."

"So both Tomasso and, and this Vargas stayed at the same *hacienda*. Did the Buenaventura police find out why they were there?"

"*Si*, officer Duchamps. Eet is long story, but one you and *sous-'specteur* will have much interest in hearing."

Abby and under-inspector Bouchard were spellbound by the events that happened at industrialist Fabio Guillermo's magnificent estate two days before. The arrival of Colombia's Minister of Mines and Energy had been recorded by federal police telephoto cameras and high-frequency parabolic microphones.

Police suspicions of Minister Rodrigo Gomez' complicity with the crime cartels in mineral smuggling and bribe-taking had finally been confirmed. Gomez' demand that Claude raise emerald profits by 100 percent during the next year was transmitted by one of the many hidden bugs. It was so audible, the authorities swore they heard sweat dripping from the American's armpits.

Finally, the entire conversation between Claude Tomasso and Captain Frederick Wilson had been taped by Colombian federal agents.

"Excellent, Johnson," Henri Bouchard shouted toward the speaker phone. "You say the words Wilson and Tomasso spoke were 'sugar', 'gummy bears' and 'spice'?"

"*Si, sous-'specteur. Policía* say for sure these words are code for *drogas*."

"We believe you're right," Abby said with a slight grin. "From information we obtained through reliable sources, *sous-inspecteur* Bouchard and I already came to the same conclusion."

Chapter Twenty-Nine

The armored cruiser edged into the Magdalena. "Still not light enough to see well," Bret said, as he pushed the two throttles well forward. "We can't risk hanging around, though."

"Don't know who saw us on 'candid satellite'," Russell said. "Whoever at NRO authorized the Spy Sat recon of our trip's gonna end up like Aldrich Ames, Harold Nicholson or Robert Hanssen. Turncoat's gotta pay for his treason."

"Hope the sonuvabitch had a coronary watching his hit squad get wasted," Bret yelled over the diesel engines.

After eliminating the guerillas, they knew they could no longer wait out the darkness. They'd rigged up two, one and one-half million-candlepower spotlights at either side of the cabin superstructure. The lights were among various items found in one of the vessel's stowage cabinets. Aimed about two hundred yards in front of them, the "headlights" would allow them continuous sailing. Any more thoughts of resting because of river traffic or darkness seemed ludicrous at this point. They'd been pinpointed by the enemy, now it was important to speed to Muzo. By now they admitted that Johnson's converted military craft was the only game in town. One man would sleep while the other piloted, a dangerous plan on the busy river, but the only practical plan.

"Fuel gauges say we're running on fumes. How far to El Banco?"

"Has to be around this bend," Russell said. He pointed to a tight curve in the Magdalena, while checking a navigation map left in the cruiser. "Look for docks on the east side of the river."

"East bank it is." Bret paused. "That must be it," he said, pointing to a wharf with a few small fishing boats tied to it. He swung the wheel until they headed toward the docks. He pulled the throttles forward once they'd crossed river traffic, slowing to four or six knots. Like the other *embarcaderos* they'd seen along the Magdalena, this one was in horrendous condition.

Over the rumbling engines, Russell yelled, "There's a gas pump, near the end of the wharf. Slower, still slower. 'Nother thirty feet."

Bret pulled the throttles back tight, then disengaged the propellers, engines growling but no longer driving the heavy craft. The port flanking bumped the rotting wood. Russell stood and grabbed part of the soggy pier. He easily edged the cruiser forward to within five feet of the Pemcol diesel fuel pump.

"Douse one of those lights," Russell said. "Shut off the diesels and get on deck. I need a hand."

Half the glare and all the sound of the engines ceased. Russell lobbed two lines onto the dock, then followed them over the slippery log footing. Bret held several dry-rotted pilings, keeping the craft from drifting or slapping against the *embarcadero*.

"Ropes are fastened," Russell called out.

Several street lights could be seen along a road that paralleled the river. Bret reentered the cabin, switched off the remaining spotlight, and came back on deck with two, powerful Mag-Lites. He handed one of them to Russell.

"We need the key to this padlock," Russell grumbled. The rusty old lock he fumbled with kept the diesel fuel pump from being switched on.

"No dock keeper?" Bret's beam of light slowly swept past a rotting pile of lumber. Almost immediately, he turned back the Mag-Lite's beam toward the wood pile. What at first glance may be a heap of old planks now proved to be a ramshackle little hut built at the edge of the *embarcadero*. "Think we found *la casa* for our keeper of the fuel pump keys."

They walked toward the shack. Bret pulled his pistol from his waistband, holding it at the ready. Russell clutched the flashlight in one hand, .38 caliber Sigma automatic in the other. The Mag-Lite was still needed, although the dawn was breaking.

Bret rapped against the sagging plank. Each thump was doubled, since whenever his knuckles met the door, it pushed inward slightly, banging against an inner frame. "Should wake the dead," he judged.

Russell said, "No answer, but I hear snoring." He lifted the rusted latch, but the door was locked from inside.

"What's the sign say?" Bret asked, pointing to a scrawl on the door frame.

After shining his light on the words, Russell said "We're at the office of Mr. Boniz, the Harbor Master."

"Master of a harbor that doesn't exist," Bret said, looking back at the waters rushing past the neglected wharf. "Guess titles are important wherever you live."

"Look at the door hinges." Russell shone the bright light at the hinges holding the door to the hut. They easily looked through cracks in the wooden slats.

"The two door hinges just slide down into round plates on the frame," Bret said. "Shall we?"

Russell handed Bret the Mag-Lite and the pistol. "I'll lift it off. Shoulda noticed it right away." He stuck the fingers of both hands through two prominent cracks. Lifting the dry-rotted, featherweight door from its hinges, he pushed it inside against the wall and set it down.

"Yon sprawls our harbor master." Bret pointed to a filthy bunk measuring nearly the same length as the shack. "Smells like he died a week ago," he said of the bearded, mustachioed form of an elderly *mestizo* gentleman. The 'corpse' snored and grumbled, caressing an empty rum bottle to his chest.

Russell walked to the bunk, breathing as shallowly as possible. "This is one odor I'll recollect the rest of my days." He shook the man, shouting, "*Arriba, arriba, hombre. Vamos, señor Boniz.*" He may as well have been shaking Raggedy Andy.

"I admire your determination, but he's gonna be comatose a lot longer."

Russell let the body fall back to the bunk. The bottle popped loose of the old man's vice grip and clinked to the hard packed dirt floor. Another sound jangled against the bottle. "It's his damn keys."

"A bottle and the keys to his domain," Bret said. "All any man really needs."

Russell grabbed the ring of keys and stumbled for the doorway. He almost knocked Bret over as he sprinted outside, gasping for fresh air. Snatching back his pistol and flashlight, Russell walked toward the fuel pumps.

Bret turned and looked toward the street that ended next to the dock. "We've got company." A car stopped twenty feet from where he and Russell stood, bright headlights centered on them.

"Local police," Russell said. A bar held four red and blue emergency lights to the roof. "Quiet Colombian cops frighten me more than the loud, reckless types."

Both front doors swung open simultaneously, one armed, uniformed man emerging from each side. The officers held 9mm Uzi submachine guns. The driver's weapon was aimed at the Americans, while the passenger let his Uzi sway back and forth from a shoulder sling. They walked toward Bret and Russell.

"Got sidearms, too," Bret noted. "Aren't here to rattle doorknobs." They held their pistols, although they were pointed at the ground.

"*Policía,*" said the officer who'd emerged from the passenger side of the vehicle. "*Pones su armas a la tierra,*" he ordered.

"*No problema,*" Russell said. They dropped their weapons, as told.

The police officer then told them to drop their flashlights. After complying, he told them to put their hands on their heads.

In Spanish, the older officer asked, "What are you doing here?"

Russell said, "My superior officer," nodding toward Bret, "landed here to buy gasoline for our government cruiser." He turned and pointed to their moored craft.

Bret stood straighter, put hands on hips and managed an officious look of tolerance. He knew enough Spanish to realize Russell was using him for his official Colombian credentials. He reached deep into a large pocket of his khaki shorts. Although the younger policeman briskly swung the Uzi directly toward him, Bret simply scowled as if the man held a child's toy. He pulled out the passport, billfold with badge and identification—and, finally—the letter written by General Serrano.

"*Aqui*, Russell," he spoke loudly. "*Dale estos al jefe.*" He wasn't sure he said 'Give these to the chief' in correct Spanish, but precision wasn't necessary. He held out the documents to his 'subordinate'.

Neither of El Banco's police officers knew what was happening, but they seemed less hostile. The older man, in fact, smiled as Bret called him *el jefe*. Julio Cruz was a police sergeant. 'Chief' did sound more fitting.

Russell jogged over to Bret, gave a half-bow, and took his credentials. The two policemen didn't see him wink at his shipmate.

"This will explain what we are doing here," Russell said in Spanish, as he approached the older town policeman and handed him the fistful of documents.

The officer accepted the papers and billfold. He stared back and forth at the two Americans. Then, in the dawn of an ever-brightening sky, Sergeant Cruz read the information. His eyes widened, his face paled.

"*Maricon del idiota pendejo,*" Cruz swore at his patrolman. "Don't point your gun at these gentlemen," he snapped, striking the barrel of the Uzi SMG down toward the ground with one hand. "We are in the honored presence of *el Coronel* M. Parra Vega of the *Policía nacional de Colombia.*" He ran to Bret and returned his credentials.

Quickly becoming green at the gills, the younger policeman

said, "*Un millón perdones, señor Coronel.*" He darted to Bret and Russell's handguns and picked them up. Dusting the weapons off on his uniform blouse, he handed them back.

"We ask that you tell no one about our presence, chief," Russell said as he stuck the automatic in his waistband. "General Serrano would be furious if our mission against *los narcotraficantes* were discovered before we reached Medellín."

"Upon the grave of my departed mother, *mi amigos norteamericanos*, I swear that no one in El Banco will hear of your secret purpose." Sergeant Cruz stared sternly at his subordinate. "Pacho, swear on your honor that these brave American *anti-narcoticos* may rest assured no harm befalls them."

"*Si, sargen—jefe* Cruz," the youth sputtered. "I swear it on my sacred honor as a member of *el policía judicial.*"

That and ten pesos will buy a ride on an El Banco autobús, Bret thought.

"So," Sergeant Cruz said, "the great and honored General of all Colombian *policía* and military entrusts you with a great responsibility. You must surely be proud."

No, Cruz, Bret thought, *I'm not telling you what we're up to*. "*Si, una muy gran responsabilidad*" Bret replied in what he felt was impeccable Spanish.

"*Jefe*," Russell interrupted, "you will excuse us while the colonel and I fill the boat's tanks with fuel."

The older police officer glanced at his deputy and ordered, "Pacho, you will put diesel fuel in the men's cruiser. *Vamos.*" To Bret and Russell, he said, "This is the least we can do in the service of the honorable General Serrano."

"I have the Harbor Master's keys to the fuel pumps, *señor*. I'll help him," Russell said, pulling the key chain from a pocket of his shorts. "We would not appreciate Pacho putting fuel in the wrong hole," he said, smiling and winking at the sergeant. *Don't want the little shit inspecting our boat*, Russell thought.

Eyeing the keys Russell displayed, the police sergeant looked toward the shack of the elderly, unconscious harbor master. "*¿Dónde está señor* Boniz?"

"*Duerme por demasiado ron,*" Bret spoke. Not knowing the idiom for "He's drunk," he'd said, "He sleeps from having too much rum."

Apparently, his oblique explanation satisfied Sergeant Cruz. The police officer grinned and nodded. Then more seriously: "Jou, ah, break him *puerta?*"

"Oh no, no," he said, laughing too-uproariously. *What's the penalty in Colombia for breaking and entering?* he wondered. "*Vienes conmigo.* I show you." He pulled the officer's arm, leading him to the little shanty.

The town police sergeant wasn't happy being dragged across the wharf. However, the *norteamericano* was on a special assignment for Colombia's third most powerful official. It was said by some that Serrano was the *most* powerful man in the country. Whatever, Sergeant Cruz wouldn't displease the general's personal representatives while they were on a covert assignment.

Bret pointed out the crocked harbor master and his empty rum bottle. He also pointed to the hoisted, but not broken, door to the hut. Cruz examined the hinges and simply shook his head. It seemed as if the police sergeant made a mental note to check his own doors when he returned home. Bret lifted the door and set it back into the hinge holes from where it came. Later, he or Russell would toss the keys through a crack so they'd be near the *capitán del puerto.*

"*Vámanos al embarcadero, ahora,* Bret suggested. He led the sergeant to where Russell and the younger police officer stood by a rusty diesel fuel pump.

"Tanks filled yet?"

"Yes, Colonel Parra," Russell said. "The patrolman has been very helpful." Turning to the young man, Russell said, "*Se agradece su asistencia grandemente.*" Pacho had been a big help in fueling the cruiser.

"*Bueno,* my friend," Bret said to Pacho, nodding his head. He pulled out an American five-dollar bill and handed it to the young man. "*Para usted Pacho, con nuestras gracias . . . y las gracias de General Serrano.*" Equivalent to about 5,000 Colombian pesos, the "tip" equaled an 8-hour day's wages for the young police officer after taxes. Pacho stared in wonder at the portrait of Abraham Lincoln.

"*Muchas gracias, coronel* Parra," the young officer uttered, hesitantly shaking Bret's hand. "*Vaya con dios.*"

"*Gracias*, Pacho." Bret then turned to look at Sergeant Cruz' inscrutable face, asking, "How much *dinero* do we owe *señor* Boniz for the fuel?"

Looking at the fuel pump gauge, Cruz said in Spanish, "The boat's two tanks took a total of 359.06 liters of diesel fuel." He then stared at the price per liter listed on an adjacent sign. "At this time, one liter costs 1,550 pesos, *señores.*"

Bit more'n a buck and a half a liter, Bret thought. *Whew, about six dollars a gallon!*

Russell provided a pencil and scrap of paper for the police sergeant. Cruz took them and calculated, talking aloud: "Three hundred, fifty-nine-point oh six," he said. Multiply that times fifteen hundred, fifty-five, and, umm, we come to a total of five hundred, fifty-six thousand, five hundred forty-three Colombian pesos, *señores.*"

Shit, Russell thought, *we just bought more'n five hundred, fifty bucks of freakin' diesel fuel.* "You'll take that in U.S. dollars, won't you, *jefe*?" Russell asked, knowing the answer full well.

"*Por supuesto, mi amigo*," Cruz smiled. "Your dollar carries more weight than our poor peso."

"I know there's a daily fluctuation of your peso's value, but I believe 1,000 to one is the fair exchange rate, now. Am I not right, *mi amigo*?"

"That is quite correct, *señor*. Thus, the fuel comes to five hundred, fifty-six dollars and forty-three cents." Cruz grinned as if he'd won the national lottery.

Russell pulled a tattered wallet from one of his pockets. Opening it, he extracted five, one-hundred dollar bills, a fifty and a ten. "Here's five hundred, sixty dollars, *jefe*. Your harbor master can keep the change." *Fat chance*, Russell thought.

Harbor master'll never see one cent of that money, Bret said to himself.

"It is most pleasant doing the business with you," Cruz said, shaking Bret's hand. *Americans and their ready cash are such fools*, the sergeant thought.

"Take the fuel pump keys, *por favor*," Bret said, handing the keys to the sergeant.

"We have to leave immediately to continue our mission."

They walked to the pier's edge and eased onto the cruiser. The police sergeant and his young assistant were right behind the Americans and bade them a safe journey. Cruz and Pacho unfastened the lines when Bret started the engines. Russell retrieved the lines and waved to the small town police officers. The swift current of the Magdalena quickly pulled the craft into its waters. Bret engaged the twin propeller shafts, throttled up and moved southwest across the river. Dawn promised another torrid, humid day for the Magdalena River Valley. "What the hell happened to all the boats and barges?" he asked. "Holiday or something?"

Russell thought about Bret's question. The number of large and small craft was inexplicably less than the previous day. "Wait just a minute, narc-man." Russell checked a calendar taped on a panel near the head. After a moment, he said, "Must be psychic. Today's St. Joseph's Day, a national holiday in Colombia."

"*Bueno*," Bret shouted, thrusting the throttles far forward. The cruiser jumped ahead until its speed showed 55 knots on the console. "*Vamos. Arriba.*"

Russell glanced back at El Banco, but it was already disappearing in the early morning river haze. "Not so sure the town's in the safest hands with Sergeant Cruz handling law and order." He knew Bret probably couldn't hear him over the mighty, rumbling diesels. He shrugged off the experiences at the refueling stop and went to turn on the spotlights. *At this speed, I want everyone to see us comin'.*

Pacho smiled to himself as he rolled the American greenback in the palm of one hand. Cruz smiled as well; he'd just earned a small fortune in U.S. currency. The two police officers were certain it had been God's will that they were on the hated graveyard shift this blessed morning. No one in El Banco would be told about their good fortune on this holy March morning of *el día de San José*.

When Cruz stepped out of the six-year-old Chevrolet police sedan, he said, "Pacho, spell the desk sergeant while he goes for breakfast."

The young officer nodded and replied, "*Sí, sargento. Inmediatamente.*"

Cruz sauntered across the pothole-pitted asphalt and gravel street. He greeted a few citizens who opted to open gray, decaying shops this national religious holiday. But the sergeant seemed oblivious to the squalor surrounding him. Like the two *yanquis*, Sergeant Cruz was on an important mission.

Julio Cruz stepped into a decrepit telephone booth that sagged as badly as many surrounding buildings. Since the thick plastic windows were unbreakable, there was sufficient privacy to conduct a private conversation. Even the paneled door managed to pull closed when yanked by the police officer. The new, push-button phone would be a surprise to anyone daring to enter the 'private' police phone booth.

Cruz took the receiver from its cradle, deposited ten pesos and punched in thirteen digits permanently etched on his brain. An impersonal voice answered after a minute's wait. "*¿Sí?*" was the only word Cruz heard.

"This is Sergeant Julio Cruz of El Banco department of police. I wish to speak with *El Patrón, por favor*."

"*Uno momento.*" Two words this time.

The sergeant waited in the rickety phone booth for five minutes. He was used to such long waits, so he hummed a meaningless tune and fingered the coveted American banknotes crumpled in a uniform pocket.

"Cruz, you are on The List," the same voice abruptly spoke. The police officer was given another thirteen-digit number. "This is where *El Patrón* stays." Dial tone.

Cruz punched in the new digits. After another minute, a voice said, *"Hóla."*

"I wish to speak with *El Patrón*. I am Sergeant Cruz of El Banco police. I h-have very important information about t-two *norteamericanos*," the sergeant explained.

"¿Qué es el información?" the impersonal voice asked.

"One *norteamericano* has the identification and p-passport of a colonel in the Colombian *policía nacional*. He is under orders from General S-Serrano. The two men are, er, *anti-narcoticos, señor*. They t-travel on a s-secret duty up the Magdalena River."

Silence filled the earpiece. Cruz dared not utter another word to the person at the end of the telephone cable. *"Uno momento,"* the man murmured.

Another minute passed. Then, in a voice that intimidated presidents and cabinet ministers, Enrique Vargas Mantilla said, "Julio, *amigo*, how good it is to hear from you."

Chapter Thirty

"My old stompin' grounds, De Mares Oilfields," Russell shouted above the rumble of the huge Cummins V-12 diesels. He pointed across the eastern bank of the Magdalena. "Not much output of crude anymore. Larger fields all over the country, now . . . including huge offshore reserves."

Bret took his eyes from the river long enough to regard the shore. Several oil derricks still stood, but mostly he saw scores of large black crude oil pumps. Their massive steel walking beams, mounted on center pivots, endlessly bobbed up and down. "No oil workers, Russell."

"St. Joseph's Day. Even the riggers an' drivers take off on national holidays."

Bret nodded. "Okay, what's the town five, six miles ahead. I can just make out the roofs of some buildings."

"Don't have to look at a map for that one. Puerto Berrio's the name; De Mares oil workers brought it fame."

"Old hangout?"

"You betcha." Russell stared at the buildings and large wharf as if reliving ancient memories. "This's as far west as we went into Antioquia Department. Sixty-five miles from here is Colombia's Orchid City."

"Medellín . . . this close?" He stared at the odometer, then agreed. "Hard to believe we've gone two hundred, fifty miles since beautiful El Banco."

With Magdalena River traffic nearly idle because of the late-March holiday, the powerful Cummins diesels drove the cruiser at speeds up to sixty knots. Some hairpin bends and narrow passages forced them to go slower. Still, they averaged about fifty miles per hour since leaving El Banco. Each man piloted the big craft about fifty miles at a stretch, giving the other time to catch some badly-needed sleep.

Abruptly, the early-warning ARPAM began to whine, while its LED light flashed. Bret had set its detection pickup to a 200-degree arc from the instrument, to cover the vessel's forward, leeward and windward sides. He'd adjusted the range finder to detect all mobile and portable weapons up to 1,000 meters away. Its low intensity imaging exposed base metal objects or weapons within a close proximity of the boat.

"Shit," he blurted. "Could ARPAM be picking up those oil rigs?" He jerked the throttles back. The cruiser abruptly rocked forward as it slowed to ten knots.

"Shouldn't be. Didn't detect 'em for the last coupla miles." Russell raced to a storage locker and jerked out the Life Finder LP-5, IR4 infrared detector. Within ten seconds, he'd set it on the console against the windscreen and switched it on. He stared at the seven-inch monitor screen, while adjusting its various dials. Since the ARPAM detected probable weapons at 1,000 yards, Russell fixed the LP-5 for the same distance and a 270-degree perimeter. Green moving images appeared. The screen *filled* with images.

"Sonuvabitch."

"Which side? How many?" Bret didn't like the fact that Russell wasn't screaming and swearing. With him, not bitching was a bad omen.

"Both sides, man."

"Jeezus." Bret adjusted the throttles back and forth, wildly swinging the wheel from port to starboard. The oncoming strong flow of the river wavered in intensity, and also its cross currents. Keeping the heavy, overpowered craft in some semblance of forward motion tested every ounce of his seamanship. Higher speeds would reduce the problems of fighting the swirling torrent, but trying to move ahead at five or ten knots was a draining chore. "We gotta run for it."

Russell scanned the high ridge of the west bank with binoculars. "See 'em on that plateau," he said. "Whoever wants us outta the picture's taking no chances this time. Life Finder shows at least twenty-five people up there."

"Dammit. What about the other side . . . over to the left?"

"Not as many. Maybe ten or twelve."

Wrestling with the controls, Bret said, "You're talkin' at least thirty-five enemy, probably armed to the hilt."

Suddenly, a colossal explosion off the starboard bow boosted a ton of brown Magdalena River water into the air, then down on the bucking craft.

Russell stared at the LP-5's screen, still able to see the greenish-white streak where the superheated exhaust of the rocket had sped from 900 yards away.

Bullets from assault weapons and rifles began clinking against the cabin's armor and bulletproof windows. At this range, they probably wouldn't have broken *normal* tempered glass.

Two more rockets exploded near the rolling craft. Bret had reduced the speed of the engines to where there was no forward motion at all. The river's current, probably about fifteen erratic knots, jerked around the heavy craft worse than ever.

"Gotta head for the far shore," Bret shouted. "Can't hold us neutral any longer." Another rocket exploded nearby, again spraying the cruiser with filthy water.

"Saw that last rocket before it exploded," Russell yelled. "Conical warhead's from an RPG-16 AT the Russkies sold when the Soviet Union went belly-up. We're at twice their effective range, but they could get lucky." He began putting pocket items into a large waterproof pouch. "Gimme your ID's, wallet, papers," then began removing items from Bret's pockets himself.

"Goin' across to the oil fields, Russell. Fewer enemy." He slammed the throttles forward and swung the wheel left. The mighty diesels nearly lifted the boat as it skidded on the tricky current and headed toward the eastern shore.

Russell poked his and Bret's sidearms into a holster and waistbands. He put on a life vest and helped Bret put one on while he raced the ironclad for land. Next, he slung a MAC-10 over Bret's shoulder and the Colt Commando over his own.

Squinting at the Life Finder, Russell saw several more rockets coming their way. One of them behaved erratically, not following a natural arcing trajectory toward its target. It rose, fell, even veered to the sides. Russell peered back through a porthole, fearing what he would see.

"Jeezus. Gotta swim for our lives! Stinger's on our ass." The FIM-92C Stinger man-portable missile is a heat-seeking IR-homing weapon. The Afghan mujahideen defeated the Soviet army with hundreds of Stingers smuggled into their country by the CIA and American special forces. It now is the most coveted weapon of choice for guerrillas, terrorists and civil dissidents the world over.

Originally, the FIM-92A Stinger was called a portable *air-defense* missile system. Eventually, it proved effective on *any* vehicle producing moderate to high heat from its power plant. The two Cummins V-12, 1300-horsepower engines on Johnson's gunboat developed more than enough heat to whet a Stinger's destructive appetite.

Bret didn't say a word when he heard Russell's warning. He shut off all power and followed Russell onto the forward deck of the twisting boat. His heart leaped as he saw the missile begin its final dive from a hundred feet up. The projectile seemed to taste the heat of the powerful engines.

The cruiser was fifty yards from the eastern shore. Russell leaped feet first into the putrid Magdalena. Bret also jumped in on the upstream side, since the current was carrying the unpowered craft downstream. Both men summoned all the strength in their bodies to hustle from the missile's quarry, and swam for land.

The five-foot Stinger struck to the extreme. Its high explosive warhead entered the engine compartment through the deck hatch, expending incredible destruction through the entire length of the vessel. There was very little residual devastation since the fuel tanks were nearly empty. The only burning fuel settling on the river quickly flowed north, along with the small amount of wreckage that didn't immediately sink.

The short distance to shore took ten minutes of exhausting strokes, since they were clothed and carried weapons. Their life vests kept the Americans from sinking like anchors. Stumbling on pebbles and driftwood, Bret took the plastic pouch from Russell.

"Thanks, Russell," he panted. "Seeing—Stinger saved—us." He spat out river water that tasted like it came from a septic tank.

"My—pleasure," Russell said between gasping and vomiting up a pint of the Magdalena. "Move into—oil fields. Still in—rocket—range." Assault rifle lying on the pebbly shore, Russell pulled off the bulky life vest, then helped Bret shrug out of his.

More rockets exploded in the water, edging closer to the east side of the river with each salvo. It was obvious the guerrillas weren't very familiar with the old Soviet RPG-16 AT rocket launcher, but they were learning quickly.

"Assholes—firing—another Stinger," Russell said. The missile went straight away for several hundred feet, then rose, fell and finally veered south, upriver. Some fifteen seconds elapsed before a loud explosion erupted from about where the town of Puerto Berrio was located.

"Think the Stinger found a target at your old stompin' grounds, Russell." Bret pulled the MAC-10 sling over his shoulder. "Come on, rockets are getting closer." With squishing boots, they trudged from the river's shore, away from the ever-present noise of rushing water.

"Dickheads are tryin' again," Russell shouted, as he peered behind his back. "Looks like the Stinger's sniffin' out an oil pump engine." After rising to about one hundred feet, the Stinger's IR components found enough heat to interest it. The five-foot HEAT missile headed straight for a diesel engine that kept its walking beam moving like a giant teeter-totter. The missile, having descended to a ten-foot altitude, streaked above their heads and exploded several hundred yards away. The entire pump, walking beam, engine, pump jack and sucker-rod piping separated into thousands of pieces of shrapnel. The pump's stock tank—holding crude oil and natural gas—ignited, filling the air with fire and black smoke.

"Doubt they'll try that again," Bret said from his prone position. "It's a beautiful smoke screen for us."

At that instant, six smaller explosions burst ninety to a hundred yards away. With binoculars pulled from the waterproof satchel, Russell saw the dozen guerrillas on the east bank closing in. They were firing M-16A2, 40mm rifle grenades at the *yanquis*, although they were still too far away for accuracy.

"At least the odds are somewhat in our favor."

"Don't think so. It's nearly a mile across the river, but I think I see trouble."

Russell swung his binoculars out over the Magdalena, below the bluffs where the rockets and missiles had been launched. He worried the focus knob until he said, "Good eye, narc-man. They're jumping into Zodiacs, three, no, four of 'em."

"Heavy action. That's gear your average drug-running guerrillas don't have."

"*Policía* sergeant in El Banco?"

"That's my guess. Musta phoned a drug lord that two *antinarcotico gringos* were heading into prime coca, poppy and *cannabis* country."

"Wilson wouldn't have the local clout to assemble this kind of army."

"Nor would he want to make waves with the drug cartels. Remember, Claude can only deal with emeralds . . . not drugs. Otherwise, he disappears."

". . . and Wilson works real tight with Claude." Russell got up and took another look across the river. "First Zodiac movin' out. Better head north."

After three more rifle grenades and a Zodiac-launched rocket exploded, Bret said, "Let's get behind a pump without a moving walking beam. I gotta dry out my weapons." The heat of midday was torrid, and the humidity along the river approached 100 percent. Sweat mingled with the foul stench of the river as they sprinted toward the nearest motionless pump.

"Good choice," Russell said, as they reached an unmoving, quiet pump. "No diesel engine or oil stock tank. Sign on the beam says it's a dry hole."

Rifle grenades exploded around the oil pumps, and a fusillade of rifle and assault weapon bullets made incessant snapping sounds. The river was still close enough to add its rushing thunder, while the working pumps shrieked from the giant walking beams and diesel engines. The result was a cacophony of sounds that roared around them.

"Bastards are halfway 'cross the river," Bret yelled. He was using the binoculars Russell had lugged along.

"Yeah, I can hear the engines on the Zodiacs."

Bret gawked at his companion. "Impossible. They're still a half-mile away and it's so noisy I can't hear myself think."

"Ain't shittin' you. Hear something different." Clutching the AR-15 rifle, he rose and leaned against the immense steel rig. Nervously, he glanced around the perimeter. *"They sneaking' up on us from another direction?"* he wondered

From one of the Zodiacs, another Stinger leaped into the air. It headed due north, straight down the Magdalena, like a hawk streaking toward a certain kill.

"Idiots fired the wrong way," Bret shouted, turning his head in the direction the high explosive missile charged.

"Omigod," Russell blurted. "Think the guerrillas spotted the same thing I see flying this way."

Jumping up, Bret pressed the binoculars against his eyes, staring down river. "It's a goddam Stealth helicopter. Comanche's following the Magdalena from the north."

"Shit," Russell shrieked. "They really came for us."

The Boeing-Sikorski RAH-66D Comanche's passive long-range, high resolution sensors flashed "Missile Lock" on the pilot's helmet-mounted display. The short missile-to-target distance of two miles posed no problem for the reconnaissance/attack stealth helicopter. Its two T800-LHTEC-801 turboshaft engines are shrouded in low-observable graphite/composite skin. Immediately, however, they received intense fluorinated hydrocarbon-like bursts that sent their external temperatures to extreme lows. "Missile Lock" warnings disappeared from the helmet displays of the two crew members. The aircraft's fully-retractable missile armament system automatically deployed.

The approaching Stinger missile's electronic brain was stymied. The high-profile target disappeared to its internal IR sensors, leaving it with nothing to demolish.

"Stealth's anti-missile defenses kicked in," Bret exulted.

"Damn Stinger's gonna be lookin' at the rocker arm diesel engines, now."

As if the Stinger missile heard Russell's reproach, it leaped to a higher altitude, quickly sensing multiple smaller targets to the west. Left with a variety of alternative targets, the missile's IR homing sensors ordered it to attack and destroy. The deadly, high explosive, 26-pound missile dove toward its selected engine heat source a half-mile north of Bret and Russell. At a speed now nearing Mach 1.2, the IR homing electronics led the missile to the intense heat of the diesel engine. Since the engine was operating, the pump had nearly filled the stock tank with crude oil and natural gas. The high explosive detonation as the missile's warhead struck the crankcase was brutally destructive. A second plume of acrid, black smoke and raging flame rose from the field.

At a distance of 3,000 yards, the Comanche's pilot fired two of the Stealth's eight outboard Hydra 70 rockets toward the bouncing Zodiacs. The anti-personnel weapons were outfitted with unitary warheads and fuses set for impact detonation.

The chief warrant officer piloting the RAH-66D thought, *Shit, shoulda had support chief install airburst-range warheads.* The army CWO was too hard on himself, since there'd been no way he could have foreseen targets on rafts in a raging river. Both Hydra 70's barely splashed as they sliced through the swift current, exploding ineffectually in the river's silt bottom.

"Orphans ahead at ten o'clock, Pulsar One," the Stealth's

navigator advised. The sergeant first class spotted Russell's homing transponder blinking from the onboard diagnostic system. "Both assets at oil rig closest to river," the SFC told his pilot, bringing their images up on the 30mm gun pod's zoom sight. The display now appeared on the pilot's helmet shield, as well as the navigator's.

"Impressive grab, Pulsar Two. Any aggressors east side of the river?"

The sergeant raised the sights less than one degree before he responded, "Affirmative Pulsar One. Sensors show fifteen enemy closing on foot at seven-two-eight meters distance southeast. AK-74 Kalashnikovs with grenade launchers identified. Also, sensors show two rocket launchers evaluated as Soviet RPG-16's."

"Put two Hydras in the guerrilla force, Pulsar Two. I'm going down to give our friends the big volleyball." The army pilot banked his Comanche sharply and dropped sideways toward the two grounded Americans. He kept the fire-control radar stalk aimed in the direction of the aggressors. The navigator sighted the steadily-advancing guerrillas, then fired two Hydra 70 rockets at a four-second interval. The anti-personnel rockets sped at Mach one velocity toward targets for which they were designed.

"Rockets heading for that FARC squad," Bret yelled above the din of diesel engines, tottering walking beams and small arms fire.

"Getting within range," Russell shouted as he stared through the binoculars. "Hope that 'copter stops the bastards . . ."

The first exploding rocket abused Russell's words and thoughts. It detonated upon impact with the loamy shore of the river, sweeping white phosphorous and heavy shrapnel through the aggressors' ranks. Within seconds, both Hydra 70 rockets exploded on target, obliterating the fifteen guerrillas and destroying their weapons.

"Kee-riiist," Bret said. Russell nodded in disbelief, swallowing bile that had surged up his throat.

Bret watched the descent of the matte black helicopter. "Comanche's only about a hundred feet over us, Russell," Bret shouted.

Unlike most helicopters, the RAH-66's "low-observables" include radar, infrared and—discovered by Bret and Russell—acoustical. The five-bladed bearingless primary rotor "whooshed" above them, rather than "phit-phit-phited."

"The navigator's holding something out his door." Rockets and rifle slugs from the four Zodiacs continued to explode around the Americans.

"Hovering at ten yards," Bret hollered. "Here comes some luggage."

Hurtling down toward the men was a dark blue ball with three bright fluorescent yellow bands encircling it. The globe, about twice as large as a basketball, missed the immobile walking beam by several yards, bounced once and came to rest. The navigator, well aware of the pounding rockets and small arms fire around him, gave a thumbs up. The Comanche's pilot gunned his T800 turboshaft engines, shooting upward like a St. Joseph's Day skyrocket.

Hunkering down as low as possible, Bret ran twenty feet to the large ball. He kicked it back to the relative safety of the steel oil pump rig.

"Kinda hard on our present, hunh Pélé?"

"Built to withstand a two-hundred-foot fall without cracking an egg inside it." The U.S. government's M2A2 All-purpose Supply Sphere is usually called by its acronym, ASS. Built of composite materials, plastics and resins, an ASS drop is far handier and quicker than parachuting supplies to downed airmen or ground troops.

A few twists on three partially imbedded latches, and the ball literally popped open into two hemispheres. The interior—a polystyrene-like material—had been custom trimmed to accept its load . . . in this case, a two-way Nextel digital radio with a separate power pack.

Bret plugged the end of the battery pack cord into the small radiophone and pushed the ON/OFF button. He and Russell heard, ". . . when you copy my transmission. Pulsar over."

Bret keyed the radio and replied, "Pulsar, got your present. Receive you loud and clear. Do you copy? Over."

"Orphan One, Pulsar Two. Good copy. Any personnel casualties?"

"Pulsar Two, um, Orphan One. Negative casualties. Aggressors in Zodiacs approaching, estimate 400 yards. Over."

"Ten-four Orphan One, we copy. Beowulf, this is Pulsar One. What is your twenty? Over."

"Pulsar, this is Beowulf One. Just rounded bend in river. We spot four craft in water dead ahead. Is this our target? Over."

Both Bret and Russell spun around. North of them, less than a mile down river, an AH-64B Apache Longbow helicopter sped toward them. "A Longbow," Bret shouted as much to himself as to his companion. They edged further from their large steel shelter, until a greater volley of bullets and another rocket forced them back.

"Shit, saw where that last rocket came from," Russell said. He grabbed the radio and keyed the mike. "Pulsar and Beowulf, this is Orphan Two. Four Zodiacs are *most* of the aggressor force. At least one rocket position is on the high bluff of the western riverbank. Possible transport trucks beyond that bluff, as well. Do you copy? Over"

"Orphan Two, Beowulf One. Ten four and many thanks. Pulsar reported Stinger missiles before you got radio. Do you have *that* location? Over"

"Beowulf One, Orphan Two. Saw two FIM-92C missiles, both launched from Zodiacs, both attracted by oil pump engines. Over."

"Ten-four Orphan Two. We have two RPG-16A rocket launchers centered on TADS. Beowulf One out." The Apache Longbow features a Target Acquisition and Designation Sight that supplements its fire-control radar (FCR). Once locked onto this assemblage of sophisticated electronic gear, few targets have a chance of survival.

The self-activating Fire Control Computer for the Longbow's

Hellfire missile system commenced launch as the Hellfire neared its 500-meter minimum safe range. The hundred-pound missile's laser seeker and guidance section carried the shaped charge warhead to its target. The resulting eruption purged the bluff of personnel and weapons, not surprising for a missile that can defeat the armor of any known tank or armored vehicle in the world.

"Orphan Two, Beowulf One. Enemy eliminated. Don't move, Orphans," the Apache pilot advised. "Bulldog Foxtrot, this is Beowulf One. Status? Over."

"This is Bulldog Foxtrot. Holding over river two miles north of your position. Monitoring your progress. Over."

"Ten four, Bulldog Foxtrot. Hold position. Got more targets. Over" The Apache pilot paused. "Orphans, hold cover. We're going for the Zodiacs. Out"

Neither man needed to confirm the message. The four boats were now no more than 150 yards from the eastern shore, several hundred feet south of them. The FARC guerrillas continued their intense weapons fire on their position.

"Other side of the rig," Bret shouted, scampering on all fours toward the end of the large oil pump. Russell was behind him, dragging the waterproof pouch and his weapons. Abruptly, Bret saw him ball up his fist and pound it into the soft loam of the field. "You okay?"

"Sonuvabitch," he yelled. "My foot." He turned and checked his left boot, now sporting a 7.62mm hole below the ankle. Blood began to seep through the break.

Bret tossed his weapons behind the steel structure, and raced to Russell. He grabbed him under the armpits. "Hold the pouch and weapons." He dragged him until they lay on the east side of the oil rig. Bret began to untie his left boot lace.

The radiophone squawked to life from where Bret had left it against the rig. "Bulldog Foxtrot, go to primary debark zone. You know the drill. Beowulf over."

"Ten four Beowulf. Bulldog Foxtrot beginning D.Z. approach. Over."

Bret grabbed the radiophone and shouted for the

reconnaissance aircraft, "Pulsar, this is Orphan One. We have one casualty, repeat one casualty. Over."

"Orphan One, Pulsar One. Roger. Stand by," the Stealth's pilot advised. "Bulldog Foxtrot, Pulsar One. Did you monitor Orphan One? Over."

"Affirmative Pulsar One. Bulldog Foxtrot has Medic. Copy? Over."

Before Bret heard any answer, he saw the Apache attack helicopter streak by him for the river. It rumbled as a sudden barrage of 30mm rounds spat forth from its M230 Chain Gun automatic cannon. Thirty to forty 1.2-inch diameter shells smashed into the four rubber and plastic Zodiacs within five seconds. Apaches carry 1,200 rounds of lethal 30mm ammunition for its M230 cannon.

The surviving twenty guerrillas of the Revolutionary Armed Forces of Colombia brigade leaped from the onslaught into the river. Two Zodiacs sank immediately, while the other two were swept downstream with their cargo of dead. The Apache paused above the battle site, then streaked toward the trucks beyond the bluff.

"Pulsar, Bulldog Foxtrot. Reached landing zone. Relay coordinates. Over."

Bret swung his head one hundred-eighty degrees. A huge Sikorsky MH-53H/J Pave Low helicopter hovered over the oil field, well away from the burning wells. The twin-turbine engine, heavy-lift aircraft can carry more than two tons of troops and/or materiel. Bret heard the RAH-66 Comanche rattling off coordinates to the big Pave Low, as it prepared to set down nearby.

The Comanche helicopter can 'memorize' an entire firefight landing zone in two seconds. When it pinpointed the right spot to land, "Bulldog" dropped between oil rigs, wells, pipelines and storage tanks. Seconds before the MH-53H/J's landing gear touched earth, the wide doors slid open. Upon touchdown, heavily armed troops leaped to the field and began to fire at the armed FARC guerrillas who'd swum to shore.

"Twenty Special Ops troops," Bret told Russell. "Guerrillas dropping weapons."

"Yeah," Russell said. "Suckers know how we felt with real bad odds." The appearance of a score of American soldiers armed with Colt Commandos and M60 machine guns ended their resolve to have a showdown. Kalashnikovs and other small arms were hastily thrown down. Only seven guerrillas remained alive.

Across the river, nearly a mile away, a deafening double-explosion erupted. A spume of black and yellow smoke rose into the torrid air. The Apache gunship had found and destroyed the trucks that brought the guerrillas to this killing ground.

"Casualty here?" A young woman ran up to Bret and Russell. Dressed in camouflage fatigues and steel helmet, she carried a 9mm sidearm and a medic's first aid kit.

"AK-74 slug just below his left ankle."

The corporal dropped to her knees and inspected the ankle. She pulled down the sock that Bret had kept tight around the wound. "Clean hit, entry but no exit," she said matter-of-factly. "Heavy boot kept the slug from doing any major damage, sir."

"So I can continue the mission, corporal?"

"Whatever the mission, sir, you're not included anymore. Let's get you over to the Pave Low." She finished wrapping a sterile bandage around the wound.

"Hold on now, girlie. The colonel needs me. I feel fine." He began to rise, but was caught by the medic and Bret as he slipped back down with a moan.

"Couldn't have proved the point better," Bret said, patting him on the shoulder.

"Um, colonel sir, you hold him up on the left side, I'll hold him up on the right. We'll remove the bullet when we reach Southern Command headquarters."

Russell grumbled and cursed as the corporal and Bret helped him to the multipurpose, special operations helicopter. As they reached the wide rear door of the aircraft, two crew members helped Russell in and lay him on an air-evac cot.

A few feet inside the helicopter, a familiar voice said, "Jou seenk my boat."

"Oh my God," Russell said. "It's our little tour director."

Bret walked to Johnson and hugged the slight man, lifting him a foot off the floor. "Shit, Johnson," he said, dropping him to the steel plating. "Your boat couldn't even stand up to a Stinger missile."

"Jou keed me, Lam'lighter. A Stinker end jour ride on *el* super*carretera*?"

"Only weapon made that could stop your river-tank, Johnson."

"Yeah," Russell said, "That was the meanest mother of boats on the Magdalena."

Johnson stared at Russell's ankle, then looked at Bret. "Now, jou need new partner, meester Lam'lighter."

Bret said, "Johnson, I always figured you'd make a better partner than that sorry excuse for a National Security agent."

"Ees not so bad the idea, *amigo*," Johnson said, "but I have 'nother plan, *mucho* better, I theenk."

"Better than you? . . ."

"Who could be better than your St. Martin partner?" came a disarming, female voice from inside the helicopter. Abby Duchamps walked from the interior, prettier than Bret could remember.

Chapter Thirty-One

A vast green canopy of jungle swept beneath the Stealth chopper at nearly 200 miles per hour. The RAH-66 neared the beginnings of foothills, so tree cover appeared less dense. Flying due south, the aircraft had already flown over the Carare River on its journey to provincial Chiquinquira. As the Stealth helicopter flies, the distance from De Mares Oilfields to Chiquinquira is seventy miles. At Comanche speed, that distance is covered in twenty minutes.

"Five minutes to touchdown," the pilot shouted.

"We hear ya," Bret yelled back. Abby sat facing Bret on a jerry-rigged jump seat hastily constructed at Southern Command headquarters. Initially built for either Bret or Russell, it just missed pressing against the co-pilot/navigator joystick. As claustrophobic as the small space was for Bret and Abby, having two *men* jammed into the area would almost have been comical.

"I think five more minutes are about all this bod can take," Abby said. Her head was tilted slightly to avoid bumping against the top of the Plexiglas canopy. Her cotton skirt-covered legs were propped on the edges of Bret's seat. Her hands pressed into the sides of the Stealth's narrow 'back seat.'

"Thanks again for the clean clothes, Abby." She'd impetuously bought men's underwear, slacks, shirt, socks and shoes when told she could accompany Johnson.

"*Está nada,*" she replied, smiling. "I knew you'd be grimy after that first firefight in the jungle." She paused, then said, "I can't sympathize with the guerillas' cause. FARC and other Colombian terrorist groups are literally the enforcers for the drug czars."

"Yeah, FARC and the National Liberation Army alone are known to have murdered some 10,000 police, soldiers, politicians, judges and innocent civilians in the last five years. They eliminate anyone they believe is standing in the way of the drug traffickers and corrupt civilians who pay them millions of dollars a year in protection money."

"Prepare to debark," the pilot shouted. The helicopter, barely skimming trees and hilltops, slowed and began to drop toward a small meadow.

"Nothing around," Bret said, scanning the terrain.

"Car at the edge of the clearing," Abby noted, pointing through the trees. "See a dirt road winding through the jungle." A young man stood by the vehicle.

"Emerald and 'caine smugglers use this spot to pick up their product," the pilot said. "They don't know NSA and NRO have watched 'em by satellite for over two years."

"He on our side?" Bret hollered. An assault rifle was slung over his shoulder.

"Supposed to be, colonel. Have your identification ready to show and don't aim a weapon at 'im." The pilot settled the Stealth onto the grassy meadow, switching the engines off immediately.

"Mighty quiet for battle-weary Colombia," Abby said. The swishing rotor blades were the only sound to be heard.

"Not always this way, ma'am," the pilot said. "I've made fifty, sixty drops like this. Some get noisy and nasty." He flicked a latch and the Plexiglas canopy raised.

"You waitin' for our return, warrant officer?" Bret asked.

"I'll be here. Hang onto your radiotelephone. We'll stay on the same frequency we used at the river . . . it's silent."

"Silent?" Bret halted as he swung one leg over the side of the Comanche. It was a four-foot drop to the ground.

"Silent to others," the army pilot said. "Got a wavelength band so ultra-low no other known radios can pick up the frequency."

Bret dropped to the ground, and lost his balance slightly. He tumbled backward and landed on his rear. He still held the Nextel phone in one hand and his Ingram MAC-10 in the other. "Broke my ass, but the important items are okay," he griped.

Abby's knapsack landed next to him. "Heads up," she called, then dropped to the other side of Bret.

The warrant officer gave a thumbs up, then began speaking into his radio. The 39-foot diameter, five-bladed rotor smoothly continued to slow its whirling. The wooded area around the clearing was quiet, all birds and animals having sped off at the sudden appearance of the giant grey-black beast.

"Our chauffeur's not coming to us," Abby said. The young man leaned against the '82 Chevrolet, smoking a brown cigarette. He watched every movement of the helicopter pilot and the two *yanquis* on the ground.

"Tired," Bret muttered as he hauled himself to his feet. He slung the MAC-10 over a shoulder and hooked the radio and battery pack over his belt. The .22 caliber pistol was inside his waistband, concealed by the white *camisa* worn outside his trousers.

Abby nodded. "Should be. I saw the shootout you and Russell had with the five guerillas." She paused. "Too intense."

"How could you have possibly seen . . . ?"

"I'll explain on our drive into town. We'd better go." She grabbed her knapsack and strode toward the car.

Bret trudged behind her, noting she wore garb suited to rural Colombians. The hem of her cotton skirt fell several inches beneath her knees, and a print, short-sleeve blouse was tucked into the skirt. She wore cloth and rubber sandals.

"*Hóla*," she greeted the young man. "Are you Che?"

"*Si*," the young man replied, ignoring her outstretched hand of greeting. "Johnson tell me to expect *dos hombres* . . . and jou are a *mujer*. How ees thees so?"

Approaching them, Bret said, "My friend, *señor* Russell, was shot by a death squad of FARC guerillas," He stepped closer to their Colombian contact. "The *señorita* replaces him . . . *¿Comprende 'substituye'?*"

"I understand 'replace'," Che said. Pointing to Bret's MAC-10 and the backpack, he said, "Put weapon and packet to the ground. I must search jou . . . and, and her." A 9mm Parabellum Heckler & Koch P7M8 pistol in his trousers waistband supplemented the slung M-16.

As Che began to search Bret, he reached down and lifted the P7 from the young man's belt. "Lift your arms," he ordered, and pointed the powerful automatic at Che.

"*Señor*, I was to think jou are friends," he grumbled, raising his arms.

"Friends don't frisk friends," Bret said. Then, he reached over and stuck the pistol back into the young man's waistband. "I have this automatic," Bret said, raising his *camisa* far enough for Che to see the weapon.

"*Gracias*, colonel Parra. I only follow orders." He squirmed, but finally said, "The lady, colonel. I must . . ."

Abby said, "This lady is packing, also." She lifted her skirt until the MAS 1950 pistol was evident in a breakaway holster strapped to her right thigh.

Despite his deep tan and naturally swarthy complexion, the young man blushed. "Thank jou for showing me the, the, um, weapon."

"*No problema*, Che," she replied, skirt falling back below her knees. "Also, I have this," she said, opening her backpack. She held up the lethal Walther P-38, then put the weapon back into the pack.

Smiling, Bret said, "See you still come loaded for bear."

"Wherever there are bears, I come loaded."

"Friends," Che said, "I am, um, told to check all I.D.'s." He glanced back and forth at them.

After examining Bret's bogus credentials that identified him as a colonel of the national police of Colombia, Che checked Abby's identification. Satisfied that he'd met the correct infiltrators, he put a magnetized sign that read "Taxi" on the car's roof.

Johnson had briefed Bret and Abby prior to their departure. He had told them that the local office for Muzo *minas* was in downtown Chiquinquira. This meant there was no need to venture to the mine region. He'd told them that security at Muzo was greater than at Fort Knox. This was understandable given the importance and rarity of the region's famous emeralds.

Seated in the old Chevrolet, Bret turned to Abby and said, "You mentioned you'd seen the firefight."

Nodding, she replied, "I was shown digital video tape the National Reconnaissance Office uploaded to Marigot police headquarters. It'd been made from the spy satellite Wilson used to direct the attackers against you and Russell."

"The sonuvabitch," Bret grumbled. "We knew we were being watched by an I.R. 'bird.' Didn't know Wilson had the pull to get NRO to divert it to our location." Bret paused. "I thought the Latin America recce sats were secure from other governments. How'd the NRO get a tape of it?"

"You're right. Only Latin American countries, and American possessions in Latin America, can use the CENTRO facilities on Curaçao."

Bret said, "That disclaimer clarifies it. Puerto Rico and the U.S. Virgin Islands."

". . . and?"

"No more Canal Zone . . . oh shit, how'd I forget Gitmo?"

"*Oui*. Guantanamo Bay, Cuba. Prison for terrorists and United States leasehold *in perpetuity*."

"The spy sat's downlink is right under Fidel's nose?"

"An NRO ultra secret facility. You're one of very few who know about it."

If Che'd heard the conversation, he wasn't letting on. In fact, the raucous South American music from a Bogotá radio station he was playing would have drowned out a nearby nuclear explosion.

"Why'd they check that tape? There must be thousands of

reconnaissance satellite video tapes made every day."

"Exactly, and only a random selection of tapes are examined. Still, an alert technician at CENTRO was suspicious. She wondered how an army captain, Wilson, had a clearance so high he could personally divert a billion-dollar spy satellite."

"Wilson! Bastard did seem to have *carte blanche* to a highly sensitive operation." Bret stared out a rear window. "Strange I didn't suspect he was a traitor."

"When Wilson told the satellite technician to restore the 'bird' to its previous overview, she phoned the NRO duty officer in Reston, Virginia."

"The duty officer agreed with her suspicions?"

"Totally. MILSTAR 26—the spy sat Wilson shifted—is the newest of the NRO's military reconnaissance satellites, I was told. It was to be diverted from its unique surveillance coordinates *only* with special permission from Reston."

"Obviously, Wilson hadn't been advised about that qualification."

"Neither did the mole at Reston who'd given Wilson his top security status. He'd been a part of Hough, Tomasso and Wilson's smuggling activities."

"Didn't take long to nab him," Bret said, thinking about the jungle shootout. He and Russell knew they were being watched by satellite. Now the Judas who'd assigned Wilson to CENTRO was in federal custody.

The brown dirt road seemed as hard as concrete, as the big American car jarred its occupants with bad or missing shock absorbers. It looked as if rain seldom fell in this region of Colombia. Settled only five degrees north of the equator, Chiquinquira's setting in low foothills subdued the intense rays of the sun. The reduced humidity and moderate elevation combined to make the early-afternoon heat bearable, breathable.

"So then we were saved by the cavalry—and Johnson," Bret said. "Seldom happens these days."

"They did an outstanding job, your American special operations forces."

"Some of the finest soldiers in the world. Israeli Zahal are good as well. Can't leave out the British SAS or the Russian Spetsnaz, either."

"... or the French 13th Dragoons Parachute Regiment."

"Right, Abby ... the 13th Dragoons, of course." Bret took a deep breath and said, "Speaking of France, did your, er, father play any role in my rescue?"

"Certainly you don't think I would ..."

"You're my partner. I know I'd have done anything possible to help you if the circumstances were reversed."

It was Abby's turn to stare out the dingy window at the landscape of thinning jungle and brilliant, tropical wildflowers. "I watched you and Russell fight for your lives against guerillas who outnumbered you and could 'see' you in the dark."

Bret nodded. "We were petrified."

"So was I, goddammit." She turned and faced him. "*Oui*, I used my, my clout ... for the first time in my career."

"Your father ... ?"

"Yes," she interrupted. "My father. He phoned the French president, who contacted your president Mackenzie ..."

"... who had Secretary of Defense Tannenbaum get hold of Southern Command sub-station in Puerto Rico."

"Precisely," she confirmed, nodding her head. "They notified the chief of Colombia's armed forces they were crossing the Panamanian border just north of Jurado. Then, Colombia's Minister of National Defense Botero Zea, ordered his air force to stand down during the American three-aircraft 'anti-narcotics' operation."

"You and Johnson. How'd you ... ?"

"Inspector Bouchard thought you and Russell would require proper liaison with the American Commandos and a briefing. *Voilá*, Johnson and I flew to Medellín's military airfield where the Pave Low picked us up."

Bret paused for a moment, then said, "A hell of a lot of high-ranking politicians and military got involved, thanks to you, Abby. I owe you one."

"*Merde*," she exclaimed, punching a fist into the side of her backpack. "Is that all you can say to me?" She punched the sturdy backpack again.

A large green and white sign welcomed the trio to Chiquinquira, population 75,000. A smaller sign informed *turistas* and other travelers that the city was the most important sanctuary of the Holy Virgin in Colombia. The sign spoke of an earlier visit to Chiquinquira by Pope "Juan Pablo II."

"*Es una ciudad muy bella*," Bret told Che as they drove down a palm tree-lined main street. The buildings were larger, newer and far more imposing than he would have imagined. "It looks quite modern."

"She ees settle first een sixteen century, colonel Parra." "*Pero*, even these times, Chiquinquira ees well known to host the tournaments of tennis."

The sidewalks were filled with merrymakers, many spilling into the street. Che kept his speed down to avoid maiming or killing large numbers of people. The farther he drove into the city center, the more people wore costumes and masks. The dominant theme of the holiday attire, Abby noted, was skull masks and other articles dealing with death and dying.

"This is St. Joseph's Day, isn't it, Che?" she asked.

"*Si, señorita* Abby," he answered, smiling. Che believed he knew what she was getting at.

"This, this fascination with, um, death." She paused to word her sentence in a way that wouldn't offend any religious beliefs. "I see skulls, death's heads, blood—I hope *fake* blood—gravestones and . . ."

"San José, St. Joseph, is patron of the dying, *señorita*."

"Dying? I always thought he was the patron saint of fathers and workers. I recall *Soeur* Marie Luc trying to teach me that in *école élémentaire* religion class."

"Jou are correct, also. San José ees patron for *dos* feast days, *señorita*—March 19, patron of dying *y* May 1, patron for working." Che smiled, believing he'd simplified the subject for his *visitadores extranjeros*.

Bret had been watching the growing crowd of shouting, dancing, drinking, festival-goers. "Anyway," he said, "we know there are a hell of a lot of people out there with great disguises." He scanned the robust crowd.

"We near the Muzo *minas* offices," Che said. He pointed to a modern ten-floor office building diagonally across *carrera santafé de Bogotá* from a large plaza. "I mus' find parking for my mule." He advanced into the mass of strollers pressing around the plaza, shaking his fists and shouting impolite oaths at the throng.

"Thank God for the black windows," Abby said. "I don't think those 'pilgrims' with tequila bottles would take Che's gestures lightly." Most vehicles driven this close to the Equator have windows tinted so darkly it's impossible to see in and hard to see out. The windshield of Che's Chevy was dirty and had such a dark tint it might filter out the flash of a lightning strike.

"He's leaving, Che," Bret yelled to his driver, pointing toward the curb forty or fifty feet ahead.

"*Gracias*, colonel," Che whooped, and gunned the big engine. A half-dozen jaywalkers dove from Che's path when they heard his engine roar and horn blare. Several objects were hurled at the car, not the least of which seemed to be a wooden cross. Che aimed his Chevy at the parking space just as a spanking-new BMW 940Si began to back into the opening.

Cutting the angle to perfection, Che squeezed the front one-third of his vehicle into the opening. The driver of the bimmer mashed his brakes violently. He stopped several centimeters from scraping rust off the Chevy's left front fender. The rear two-thirds of Che's car stuck out into the lane of traffic.

"*Merde!*" Abby exclaimed.

"Jesus Christ!" Bret blasphemed.

"Ees good parking, no?" Che said, turning in his seat to receive praise from them.

"Yow," Bret gasped. "Coulda fooled *me* you'd make it." He asked Abby, "Did my hair just turn grey?"

The driver's side door opened on the BMW and a large,

affluent-looking man of fortysomething flung himself from the car. His face was crimson with rage. From the passenger's door another man of nearly the same size and age jumped out. They approached the Chevy shouting oaths and shaking their fists.

Che and Bret stepped out of their respective front and rear doors. The men from the BMW must have seen Che's M-16 and H&K P-7 about the same time they saw Bret's MAC-10 submachine pistol and large .22 Dura-Matic. The frenzied crowd also saw the collection of automatic weapons.

Pandemonium broke out. Very quiet pandemonium. Bret was amazed at the acceleration of the large bimmer.

"I think you made your point," Abby scolded from the back seat. "Che, why don't you park the car just *two* tiny *meters* closer to the curb?"

Chapter Thirty-Two

Despite their display of weapons, no police or *guardia nacional* stopped the trio during their walk. When they arrived at the office building housing Muzo Mine's corporate headquarters, the elevator wasn't operating. Very few businesses were open on this religious feast day. A business locator panel in the lobby pinpointed Muzo Properties, Ltd. at suite 906. No mention of mining, no mention of emeralds. The locked stairwell was no problem for Abby's automatic LPG-1 lock-picking device.

"You haven't slept in days," she said. "Nine flights are going to be a hard climb."

"Had catnaps. I'll be fine."

"We rest every two floors," Che said. "Eet will be more easy for us all."

"What about building security?" Abby asked. "Did you have time to check for guards, alarm systems, surveillance cameras?"

As they began climbing the concrete stairs, Che pulled some paper from a shirt pocket. He unfolded it and held it for all to see.

"When building has lock-down like today, only one *guardo* has duty. He stay een, um, underfloor . . ." Che pointed downward.

" . . . basement," Bret said. "Are there monitors for surveillance cameras in the security room?"

"Montars? Serveysants?"

"Sorry, *amigo*," Bret said. "Do *el guardos* watch television that comes from cameras on each floor?"

"*Ahora comprendo*," Che said, grinning. "*Cada piso tiene una cámara, colocó cerca del elevador.*"

"One camera per floor, mounted above the elevator. Right?"

"Perfect, *señor* colonel. Jou make the mos' great translate."

Abby said, "Che could be a very good diplomat."

Bret nodded, and they began to climb the stairs. "How do we bypass that ninth floor camera?"

"We keel heem, *señor* colonel, cut hees cable," Che answered.

"Too obvious," Abby said, as they passed the fifth floor landing.

"Floor two and floor seven *cámaras están muerto*, I know," Che said. "No *cámara* repair come for one, two week *más*."

Bret stopped, holding the stairwell railing. "Che, you've been very helpful," he said. "But, how can you know about the, the security setup, non-working cameras and the repair schedule?" The hollow sound of his words echoed throughout the 100-foot vertical shaft.

"*No comprendo . . .*"

"You understand," Bret snapped. "Where'd you get your information?"

"How do you know about the building security?" Abby asked. Although less insistent than Bret, she realized Che *was* aware of many inside details.

Che sat on a step, his assault rifle clacking against the stairs. "Johnson tells me to meet jou at smuggling field."

"Sure," Bret said. "But, he couldn't have learned the security arrangements. He'd just learned our schedule."

He stared up at Bret, then said, "Ees true. Johnson geeve me four hours time before I meet jou. I spend eet to learn facts of thees building."

"A security guard lets you in and says, 'look everywhere you want, *señor*'?"

Che lowered his eyes and studied a ventilation duct on the wall directly across from him. "I, I get help to learn secrets een *edificio*."

"Who did you get to help?" Abby asked.

"I promise not . . ."

"Hold it, you little shit," Bret yelled, and grabbed hold of his right shoulder. "This is a life and death operation. We aren't playing kids' games."

"Che," Abby said, "this man"—she pointed to Bret—"who you know as a colonel in the National Police, speaks truthfully. We are on a very risky assignment. Major General Serrano Cadeña would not have given him such an important station if it weren't absolutely necessary."

Che nodded. "*Dije a mi padre*, agent Duchamps."

"Your father?" Bret asked. "How could he help?"

He answered, "My father ees, ees *comandante* of PJR een Boyacá Department. His *jefe* ees same as jours, *señor* colonel . . . he ees on orders of General Serrano."

"Damn, Che," Bret snapped his fingers. "I forgot to report to him after all the shit we went through."

"My father—he ees named Colonel Augustin Cordoba—understands. He has been, um, advisored . . ."

"'Advised' Che?" Abby provided the correct verb.

"*Si*, others een *policía* and military ad—vise him of jour Magdalena travels."

Bret was puzzled. "What 'advisor' could know of my trip, and where I was?"

"Jou meet *capitán* een Plato, colonel Parra. Capitán Camargo ees a brave and honest police officer of Colombia."

Bret nodded. "Can't forget Captain Camargo. Did he tell your father that Russell and I were heading toward the emerald digs?"

Che stood and brushed dust from his trousers. "*Si*, he, and *mi padre*, fight for the day when Colombia ees free of *narco mágicos, guerrilleros y terroristas*."

"With men like your father and that captain," Abby said, "your nation has a good chance to break free of corruption."

"Okay," Bret spoke. "It's time we got this road show back on schedule. We could still have problems getting into the Muzo offices."

Bret blindfolded the ninth-floor hallway camera. Duct tape from Abby's "magic backpack," as Che called it, was slipped over the lens from below. Although the security officer on duty covered for *comandante* Cordoba, the camera was blacked out to protect him from possible retaliation.

A scan of the offices from outside the entrance revealed infrared, motion and sound detectors. Abby jammed the defenses. Based on the principle of radar jammers, the Morensse "Negator 2100" reverses the direction of their microwaves. It monitors the detectors before they "see" or "hear" intruders, thereby beaming *neutral* signals to the central alarm station. Once inside, they checked the area for radio-transmitted sound and video equipment. The Muzo Properties offices were debugged.

Observing the cubicles and desks, Bret said, "Not one computer. Any business in the States couldn't run without databases and word processors."

"One door locked, Colonel," Che said from behind a cubicle.

Bret walked into it and read the sign on the closed door: *Provisiones de la oficina. Autorizó personal sólo.* "That sign says 'Office supplies. Authorized personnel only', doesn't it, Che?"

"*Si*. Why ees only locked door on a room that hold pencils and paper?"

"Good question."

Abby said, "*Oui*, especially since there is a large Steelcase cabinet across the room filled with office supplies."

Bret pulled a small penknife from a pocket and snapped open a thin blade. He carefully slipped the blade between the door and its frame, running the blade around all four edges. "No trip wires or alarm tape," he said.

Abby walked to the door and pushed the working end of her automatic lock pick into the keyhole. "Tough sucker, double dead bolts." Despite the second heavy bolt, the lock clicked open in twenty seconds. She pushed the latch down and opened the door.

Inside it was dark, but the flick of a wall light switch illuminated a small, sparsely furnished room. A long table held an AST 80786/

999 personal computer. A 20-inch monitor and H-P color laser printer were connected to it, plus external speakers, microphone, TV camera, DVD-ROM and a one gigabyte Iomega backup drive. Plastic cases held floppy disks and CD's of varying sizes. Five or six boxes of popular software programs lay at one edge of the table. A wooden chair faced the keyboard and monitor.

"Didn't spend much for an interior designer," she noted. The walls were unpainted plasterboard, and nail heads presented a classic carpenter's pattern against unseen wooden studs. A cheap frosted-glass ceiling fixture held a low wattage bulb.

"Che," Bret said, "check around for possible 'bugs' . . . you know, small transmitting gadgets."

"I," Abby said, dropping to her knees, "having been once bit, am twice shy." She scuttled under the table, beneath the central processing unit. She examined each cable and wire, still enraged that Claude had rigged a 'burglar alarm' that nearly killed her.

"Housekeeping's for shit," Abby muttered as she slid back out from under the computer table. She whisked away a swirl of dust from kneecaps, skirt and blouse. "No dirty tricks, though."

"No boogs, Colonel," Che called from atop the chair where he'd checked inside the light fixture. "Thees ees las' place I look."

"Clean room, clean computer," Bret said. "Time to tackle cyberspace."

Having dusted herself off, Abby sat on the stark chair. Che dragged the chair he'd used as a ladder next to her and sat in it. Bret stood next to her facing the computer. "No lock," Abby said, as she studied the CPU. She flicked all 'power' switches on.

Muzo Properties's main menu enveloped the screen, yellow type superimposed against the image of an enormous green emerald. This computer was part of a small network. A short list of other sites included 'Bogotá international office' and 'Muzo field office.' Abby clicked the mouse on the button for the Muzo mine site.

Another screen appeared, with yellow background and a

rectangle in the center bordered in green. Above the rectangle were the Spanish words *PALABRA ENTRAR*.

"Password," Che said, pointing at the Spanish words.

"The field office has to be ... something like ..." Abby typed MUZO MINES in the rectangular opening. Tapping the Enter key only emptied the rectangle.

"Maybe as one word," Bret suggested.

She typed MUZOMINES, then hit Enter. No response. "Not it."

"What's 'field office' in Spanish, Che?" Bret asked.

"Um, *'oficina del campos'*."

Abby typed MUZO OFICINA DEL CAMPOS. Nothing. "Shit!" She deleted 'MUZO', leaving OFICINA DEL CAMPOS, but again nothing changed.

"Dammit," Bret said. "It's a mine office ... *oficina del minas.*"

Abby typed OFICINA DEL MINAS and hit 'Enter.' No change. "*Merde*, maybe simply Muzo *minas.*" She typed MUZO MINAS, giving the Enter key another whack. The screen dissolved into the familiar Windows menu page with its 'fanfare' welcome.

Bret stared at the monitor. There were at least two dozen icons spotting the menu screen. "All right, I see icons with software names, hardware and, um, five or six names of people. Where do we go from here?"

"We want to get into the files of the guy Claude owned at Muzo. Name was ... I think it started with 'V' or 'W'."

"There's a Valenzuela, lower left on the screen." He pointed at an icon with the name of Jaime Valenzuela written beneath it.

"Sounds close, J. Val ... ," Abby said. "Why do I question that name?"

Che searched the icons, then said, "Maybe ees Javier Velasco?" He pointed near the top of the screen, beneath the list of items on the text bar.

"J. Velasco," Abby cried, "that's it. He signed his e-mail to Claude as *Señor* J. Velasco. You're wonderful, Che," she beamed.

Suddenly, the digital phone/two-way radio on Bret's belt vibrated. He pulled it from the cloth holder, pressed the key strip and answered, "Orphan One here. Go."

"Orphan, this is Pulsar. Had trouble with three armed guerillas. My 'fifties' made sure they won't be goin' home to momma. Others could show up any minute. What's your ETA? Over." His voice was calm, but it had an edge to it.

Abby began typing furiously at the keyboard. "Tell him I've almost hacked into Muzo field office. I'd say no more than a half-hour."

"Orphan, did you copy? Over." The Stealth copter pilot sounded more concerned this transmission.

"Copied you perfectly. Entered the offices. Hacking into a network computer." He stared at Abby at the computer. "Hang on for another half-hour. Copy?"

"Radar shows more bad guys. Do my damndest, but half-hour's gonna seem like a week. Pulsar out."

"Okay, CalColo001, let's see your own screen at the mining camp," she mumbled, fingers racing across the keys. "Hah, gotcha!"

"Ees good hackinck," Che said. He sat in the clunky, wooden chair he'd climbed on to search for hidden transmitters. "Jou have Muzo screen on line."

"*Oui*, with his own ColomSat Internet site." Abby double-clicked the icon for ColomSat Online version 6.1, then did the same with the primary linking icon. Within fifteen seconds the phone connection was made with the closest telephone tie-in. A screen popped up that read: *Ninguna conexión hizo. Por favor trata de otra vez.*

"He say telephones een use, try him again," Che translated.

"Come on, little connection," Abby murmured to the PC, clicking the mouse button repeatedly. The same message continued to appear. "Forgot how few phone lines there are in this part of Colombia."

Bret could imagine the Stealth pilot's frustration. He probably wanted to say 'The hell with those spooks, I'm savin' my ass'. It would be an easy solution . . . crank up the two powerful T800 turboshaft engines. Rise out of harm's way. At that moment he noticed Abby had gotten on line.

"Into his mail box," Abby breathed, smacking the keys so fast it seemed they'd split. "He delete his e-mail?" she asked herself aloud. She clicked the mouse on the small 'file folder' icon, then clicked it open. "Nope, never deleted his mail."

"Jou look at one to make for sure he ees what jou want," Che said. He nearly lay on the keyboard, studying the screen.

Abby double-clicked a file Velasco had called 'Easy as Pie'. "All right," she said, "Claude and Velasco have a little interest in food." The text read:

> Subj: Easy As Pie
> Date: Feb 21 (present year) 18:20:45 EST
> From: CalColo001
> To: ClaudeTLux
>
> Mr. Tomasso: SalMex e-mail to order 1000 tbs sugar. Also she want 500 cup flour for Acapulco pie and 500 tbs baking soda for Tijuana pie. Both pie to be serve at dinner March 14. No gummy bear for decirate. To bad.
>
> Sr. J. Velasco

"Eet ees code message for sure," Che declared.

"Yeah, and a lot like the one Abby saw in Claude's own files."

"All we need now is a 'Rosetta stone' file, a list that will prove our code-breaking theories," she said.

"Maybe Velasco download messages to hard drive or floppy," Che suggested.

"Right, let's check the hard drive. If they're there, we can copy them to floppies or a writable CD."

Quickly minimizing the Internet provider, then Windows, Abby clicked onto Dos Shell. Choosing the "word search" option, she typed 'CalColo001' to pull up any file on C-drive with that particular word in it. A few moments passed, and there it was, a directory named *Recetas*.

"Ees word for 'recipes'," Che said.

"Shows 'CalColo001' mentioned in 87 different files." "Think we've got it." Fingers rapidly typing, she pulled up the first file in the *Recetas* directory.

"Hot damn," Bret cried. "The first file is our Rosetta stone. Look,"—he pointed at the screen—"there's the list of code words!" Listed vertically on the page were about a dozen words in English, mostly condiments. Opposite each word was its decoded equivalent, in English and Spanish. "You're incredible, Abby," Bret said, grasping the young woman's head and kissing her on the cheek.

"*Mon dieu*," she sputtered, "how impetuous. I believe I deserve a raincheck for more peaceful times."

As Bret started to reply, he felt the radio/phone pummel his right side. He answered it, saying, "Orphan One. Go Pulsar."

"Dammit, Orphan, ain't gonna leave y'all, but I'm between big rock an' hard place." His plight was punctuated by the sound of his .50 caliber machine guns. "Got more guerillas on my landin' patch."

Bret began to reply, but Che grabbed the phone. "Hang in, *amigo*," he shouted. "We get jou *policía* help *rapido*, hombre. Orphan Dos over." Before the helicopter pilot's reply was heard, Che toggled to basic digital phone mode.

"Che, what the . . . ?" Bret began. He noticed Abby shove a CD-R disk into the CD-R/RW backup drive. She began punching keys.

As Che tapped a telephone number, he said, "We mus' send *policía* to stop *terroristas*." In Spanish, he began to speak to someone who answered the phone. "This is an emergency. I must speak to Colonel Cordoba, immediately." He hesitated as the person on the other end of the line spoke to him.

Bret could make out most of the conversation.

"Si," Che said, "this is his son. I am phoning at the directive of Major General Serrano, *comprendes?*" He grinned at Bret and Abby, nodding his head.

"Looks like the heir to the Cordoba millions made his point," Bret said. "Never hurts to drop names."

" . . . Especially when it's a matter of life or death," she added, thinking of the army pilot taking on a hit squad of vindictive guerillas.

Abruptly, Che spoke into the phone. "*Padre*, it is Benito. I am with the American who Captain Camargo told you about." He stopped as his father questioned him about an "emergency."

"It is true, *papá*. General Serrano's American and a woman agent of the French national police arrived in a helicopter at the north valley smuggling grounds. I drove them here, but now, the pilot is under attack by terrorists. He needs help." Che became quiet, listening to his father.

Cupping a hand over the phone speaker, Che said, "My father tells his men about jour pilot. *Papá* will save him."

"I wish I were as confident as Che about our pilot," Bret whispered to Abby.

Che began speaking to someone on the phone, again. "He is alone. I believe the raid is by a large group of terrorists." Another pause, then Che said, "That is wonderful news. Many thanks, *papá*. I must leave now. *Si. Hasta la vista*." He switched off the phone and returned it to two-way transmission. "Pulsar, this is Orphan Two," Che spoke. There was no answer. He tried two more times without reaching the Stealth pilot.

Bret said, "let me check the battery." He pressed two buttons on its dial pad. Several LEDs shone. "Shows plenty of charge. Maybe the satellite's at a bad angle." Bret thought, *It never gets out of range . . . something's wrong at the drop zone.* "I'll try again in a few minutes." *Can't blow this mission now that we're down to the wire.* "Making headway on downloading the files, Abby?"

"Just burned the last disk. It's time to pack up and move out."

"That's our clever spy," Bret told Che. "Superior I.Q., great beauty and a computer whiz to boot." He began to gather tools, papers and other belongings.

Che held Abby's knapsack while she wrapped two 700-megabyte CD-R's in some clothing. She put the disks that held Velasco's file copies inside the cloth bag.

They raced from the hot, damp room, turning out the light as they walked into the main office. Abby closed the door, making certain it was locked. From beneath the security camera, the duct tape was ripped from the lens. They descended nine flights of stairs, and the pivotal Muzo mission seemed to be nearing completion.

Reaching the lobby, Bret stood back from the large picture window. Behind him, Abby stared out at the surging crowd.

"More people now than when we came in," she said.

"A little rowdier, a little more inebriated," Bret said. "Helluva lot more masks and costumes than I want to see."

"We mus' go to jour 'copter pilot," Che interjected.

"I'll try him again." Bret keyed the two-way radio and said, "Pulsar, this is Orphan team. How do you read me?" There was no reply. Frowning, he tried to reach the army pilot again: "Pulsar, Orphan. Come in, over." Silence.

"Probably too busy to talk," Abby suggested, hoping she was right.

Suddenly the green LED light beneath the phone switch began blinking, and the entire device vibrated. Staring at the compact radio/telephone, Bret asked, "Che, did you give our number to the *com* . . . , your father?"

"I do not know thees number." No numbers were displayed anywhere on the government issue device.

Nodding, Bret toggled over to the digital phone function. "*Bueno, quién habla?*"

"*Bueno*. Here ees Colonel Cordoba. Do I speak with Colonel Parra?"

"You do, sir. I'm sorry for not contacting you when we got to Chiquinquira. We had some problems."

"I understand, Colonel Parra.

"Colonel, were you able to send your men to the landing zone? The helicopter pilot's last message sounded like he was in trouble."

"Eet ees why I *telefono* to jou, *mi amigo*. My *capitán* chust report they engage *terroristas* and they haf been terminate."

"Fantastic, colonel. Please tell me, is the pilot safe?"

"Ees hokay. Little hurtings, but not so bad for taking to *clínica*, um, hospital."

"That's great news, Colonel. We appreciate your help." Bret hesitated, then asked, "Er, Colonel, how were you able to find our phone number?"

Chuckling, the Colombian police officer said, "Eet ees not beeg secret, Colonel Parra. I chust press "star, six-nine"—and get automatic callback of last number to this phone."

Chapter Thirty-Three

The distance from the front lobby to the '82 Chevy was about a hundred yards, Bret figured. "Time to move out. Stay together. It's a portable cemetery out there."

Skulls, ghostly white zombies and death masks leaped and shouted, lunged and shrieked. These obstacles blocked the progress of the trio. Bret led, Abby squeezed in the middle, and Che took up the rear.

Music, Bret thought, *Latin rhythms, definitely not religious.* It seemed the band must be on the other side of the plaza. Noise invaded their space—spinning clackers, harsh whistles, firecrackers. "Stayin' with me?" he shouted, turning his head.

"Keeping up," Abby yelled. Her voice was barely audible in the midst of the crowd.

"Okay, thirty, forty yards to go."

Inexplicably, the crowd began to thin ahead of them. Bret saw a grim reaper twenty feet in front of him. The reveler carried a realistic-looking scythe, sweeping it dangerously close to a death's head and a festering zombie. Then, without warning, the grim reaper lurched toward Bret. It raised the scythe, and prepared to swing it at him. "This isn't happening," he shouted.

An automatic weapon brandished by a ghoul sliced down the grim reaper five feet from Bret. The scythe clanged to the pavement, sliding against Bret's shoes. A ghostly form lunged toward them from the right side. Pistol shots dropped the machete-wielding ghoul close enough for Abby to see blood spurt around its masque.

A Satanic form rushed at Bret, and he raised his MAC-10. The weapon was suddenly jerked from his hand by someone wearing a death's head. He felt his .22 caliber pistol pulled from his waistband. In a twinkling, three demonic forms dragged him along the scene of carnage and unearthly screams.

"Let me go, you bastards." Bret bellowed, swinging his arms as best he could. An open car door took form, seeming to be straight from Hell. He was shoved inside and grabbed by a man in civilian clothes who'd been sitting on the rear seat. "What do you assholes want with us?"

"*Vamos*," a uniformed man in the passenger's seat ordered. He yelled to Bret who still struggled in the back. "Colonel Parra, I am Comandante Cordoba. Do not fight my officers. They save jou from *terroristas* at the fiesta."

The police officers in the back seat pulled Bret up between them. The man costumed as 'death' tore off his mask and threw it to the floor. Sweat covered his face and neck. He saw that his weapons lay on the floor.

"We take jou from thees crowd, colonel. My officers shoot two *terroristas, pero* for certain others are in the plaza."

He shook his head. "Abby, your son. Are they okay, colonel?"

"Look at *carro* who follow us, Colonel Parra. They are een same good feelings as jou." The husky Colombian police commander smiled. "Jour *dama amiga* from French *Sûreté* almos' shoot my officer."

Inwardly, Bret smiled. He thought of her raising her skirt to grab the pistol from her holster. "Your officer is lucky he is still breathing." He looked out the rear window. She smiled at him through the windshield of a closely-following Ford sedan. Bret waved. *Yeah*, he thought, *I'd never try to sneak up on that spunky lady.*

Chief Warrant Officer Walter Romanski showed them several cuts and scratches he'd gotten while fighting the guerillas. He described spinning the Comanche helicopter a foot off the ground to aim machine guns at the enemy. Sometime during the attack his radio/phone had been knocked out of service. He hadn't known until after the Colonel's troops had arrived that Bret had received his Mayday.

"The Stealth is damaged," Abby noted, inspecting the RAH-66 Comanche. "Do you think it's airworthy?"

"Little lady," he answered, "this bird's also an attack 'copter. Like its Apache brother, it's a goddam flyin' Abrams tank. Shit, nasty 7.62mm ammo like those AK-47 assault rifles the guerillas fired won't dent this baby. Even .50's can't pierce its thick hide."

"Eet ees a beautiful *máquina*," Che spoke, admiring the deadly aircraft.

"Now here's a lad appreciates the finer things in life," the CWO said, placing a paternal arm over Che's shoulder.

Smiling at the pilot's banter, Bret asked, "How'd you get those injuries if the Stealth's so invulnerable?"

"Guess you'd hafta say 'sheer stupidity'," he muttered. "Saw the radio antenna get shot off, so I went out to fix it. Bastards started layin' down a real barrage when they saw me leave the bird."

"They didn't shoot you, though," Abby said.

"Naw, that's the stupid part. I ran to get back in the cockpit an' slipped off a foot well. Fell onto the freakin' landing gear. Shitload of scratches."

"Mean you won't get a Purple Heart, Walter?" Bret asked.

The pilot scowled at him. Turning to Abby, he said, "Mebbe you woulda been better off leavin' Indiana Jones back in town, little lady." He limped to the helicopter, using a flashlight to begin his pre-flight check, then supervised the refueling from a large Colombian military tank truck.

"I believe you hurt Walter's feelings," Abby said.

Before he could reply, Colonel Cordoba strode up to them. Che was following the army pilot around his aircraft. "We haf cleared the field of dead *terroristas*, Colonel Parra *y agente* Duchamps."

"You did a thorough job," Bret said. "Outstanding marksmanship by your troops. I don't believe there was a single prisoner taken, colonel."

His sarcasm was not lost on the commander. "Colonel, or may I call jou Mr. Lamplighter, America ees ver' beeg. America ees not 70 percent control by *terroristas*, jou call *guerrilleros*. We want freedom. We want safe *ciudads* and peace een the, um, countryside. We mus' stop smuggling *drogas, armas, oro, plata, y esmeraldas.*"

"We know most people of all nations want Colombia to be free and law-abiding."

"I understand," Cordoba replied, "but thees mean peoples of Colombia mus' not fear *terroristas*. Not *paisa, policía, politicos,* army *antinarcotraficantes. Terroristas* mus' be wiped out to las' person." He looked at his son, who held CWO Romanski's flashlight. "Do jou understand M-19 *terrorista* words *'plata o plomo'*?"

"'Silver or lead'" Abby answered. "Take a bribe or take 'lead poisoning'. Also, it is a threat I have heard used in Marseille."

Just then, a police lieutenant approached and saluted the Colonel. He whispered to him and handed him an envelope.

"Thees ees for jou, *señor*," the colonel said, handing the note to Bret. "*Hasta la vista* Colonel, *agente* Duchamps." Cordoba walked toward his staff car, then stopped, turned and said, "May jour mission be one of great success." He saluted his two allies in this meadow splattered with blood.

* * *

The Stealth helicopter sliced through the darkness on a due west heading. Ahead, the sky was a brilliant orange near earth, where the sun had set almost an hour before. Rapidly, the sky turned deep blue, then black several degrees above the horizon. Before Bret had ripped open the envelope, they had looked forward to returning to St. Martin.

Now they flew toward Cali and an uncertain visit with one of

Colombia's most feared *narco mágicos*. The short note from Johnson, typically obscure, had been typed by a machine far beyond its planned obsolescence. It read:

> Mister Lamplighter and Miss Duchamps:
>
> When leave Chiquinquira one must therefore fly by helicopter to the city called Cali. This flight official by order of Colombia national defense minister. U.S. Army South Command give official notice from General Markley [and more high]. Arrive to city of Cali, telephone by radiophone numbers as following: [57] 1-224-2224. This presents *señor* Enrique Vargas Mantilla for talk. Land helicopter to Vargas casa. Deal with Vargas [this order from U.S. Justice department attorney general]. Enjoy rest.
>
> Your friend, señor Johnson, Esq.

"Certain we translated this right?" Bret was becoming used to checking Johnson's messages several times, searching for flaws in his and Abby's deciphering.

"It won't change. We have to meet Vargas tonight in Cali."

"Y'all gonna hafta use your own phone when we get near Cali," the pilot yelled. "Damn broke antenna don't give me radio transmission capabilities."

"Glad that's all that doesn't work on the Stealth," Abby said over the roar of the twin turboshaft engines.

"Radio compass an' altimeter outta whack, too," Romanski exclaimed.

"Walter," Bret yelled, "you've been flyin' over these mountains, in pitch darkness, without knowing where we're going or how close we are to crashing?"

There was a long pause from the pilot's niche. "Got all m'bases covered, Colonel." Turning around, they saw he wore infrared goggles. He held up a 59-cent plastic Wal-Mart compass, the kind you put on the dash of a '76 Dodge. "Always keep this little shitter for 'mergencies."

Bret shook his head. "Odds are real good you've been flying with infrared landing lights on."

"Yeah, Colonel," he hollered back, "ever since we lifted off." His westerly course meant they'd bypass Medellín one hundred miles south of the city. He'd continue flying west until he reached the Cauca River. Then he intended to follow the Cauca river valley southerly to the outskirts of Cali.

"Got our ETA for Cali, Chief?"

"'Bout forty more minutes. We're south of Medellín now. Gonna pick up the Cauca River any moment, then it's 130 miles to 'Sugar Town'."

"Is 'sugar' slang for their cocaine production?" Abby asked.

"You'd think so," he shouted. "It's a paradox. Cali *is* the sugar capital of Colombia. Surrounded by huge sugar cane plantations."

The Comanche helicopter turned ninety degrees to the left. Abby and Bret looked down to see a silvery ribbon of water snaking its way beneath them. At a higher altitude, the Cauca River would have been invisible to pilot and passengers.

He can't be more than 300 or 400 feet above the river, Bret thought. "Any reason to stay this low, Chief?"

"DEA and Colombian *anti-narcoticos* have their own planes and 'copters. Don't get military radio transmissions."

"So they don't . . ." Abby said.

" . . . don't know us," Romanski finished her sentence. "To them, we're most likely 'caine or hemp smugglers."

"Thought we were 'invisible'," Bret said.

"Stealth's invisible to radar, not to the naked eye. If we get forced down, we'll be a lot more likely to land safely from this altitude."

The reconnaissance/attack helicopter rushed southerly at 190 miles an hour. Twisting Cauca River blurred below. Hills raced alongside and above. Brilliant night sky over Cali loomed ahead. Three voyagers were intent in thought.

A silvery half-moon rising in the east frosted the tops of ridges above the valley. Ten, then twenty, then thirty minutes passed.

"Gettin' close to Cali, folks. Better get on the horn."

"Yep," he answered. "Phone's here somewhere." He felt around the floor until he found the telephone lying near his feet.

"Over the 'burbs, colonel," the pilot yelled. "Time to give your contact a ring."

Contact? Bret thought. *Damn drug smuggler's hardly a contact.* He dug through his pockets and got Vargas' phone number. "Hope these are good directions. That's a big city down there."

"Metro area's about two and-a-half million people," Abby said. "Number three city in Colombia."

Bret nodded at her, then tapped keys on the phone pad. The sound of the phone ringing pulsed in his ear.

"*Buenó. ¿Quién está?*"

"Colonel Parra. Johnson arranged for me to meet with *Señor* Vargas."

"Are you traveling from the north?" the man asked.

"Yes, we followed the Cauca river into the northern suburbs."

"I understand. You are in a helicopter?"

"Yes." Bret held a hand over his left ear to hear the man better.

"Have the pilot hover where you are. You are probably close to our location."

"Hold on." He lowered the phone and yelled, "Chief, our associate says to stop where we are. Thinks we're probably damn near over him."

"We're stoppin', colonel." The Stealth bucked like a spirited colt, then hung in the sky. The panorama of the large city stilled. Houses, cars, people, vast suburban haciendas stood out beneath the bright moon.

An LED on the phone displayed green, and a voice said, "*Coronel* Parra, we are going to turn on a bright light to show our location. Understand?"

"Understood. We'll look for it." He spoke loud enough for

Abby and the pilot to hear, "They're gonna turn on a light for us to see where the landing area is."

The city and suburbs were brightly lit at this time of night. No one in the Stealth asked how they'd find the beacon from among millions of lights.

"Kee-rist!" Romanski exclaimed. The sky suddenly blazed as if Cali had exploded in a cataclysm.

"Shit! It's a huge searchlight beam, and we're damn close to the middle of it."

They had aimed the searchlight vertically from its couplings on the ground. A giant beam spewing millions of candlepower of intense light shone less than a mile from the RAH-66 Comanche.

"At least it's serving its purpose," Abby said. "Move a bit closer, Walter, so we can see where to set down."

The pilot slowly moved the Stealth toward the blinding beam of light, losing altitude simultaneously. The searchlight was on the rear compound of a palatial mansion.

"Tell 'im to kill the light, colonel. Too bright for me to move any closer."

Bret said, "We're above your beacon. Turn off the light."

"We see you. It will be turned out." In a second, the searchlight began to dim. Nearly a minute passed before the carbon arc elements faded to a level suitable for landing the Stealth.

"What's a Jolly Green Giant doing at your friend's house?" Romanski asked. He stared beneath the Comanche at a heliport built for a potentate.

"Huge helicopter," Bret said, while a dozen men pushed the big HH-53C to the edge of the landing pad. "Military gray but no insignia, no markings."

"Someone's traveling incognito, and doesn't want to be recognized."

The Comanche slowly descended. "Watch for hostiles," the pilot shouted to them. "Could be a trap, knowing these drug lords."

As the U.S. Army RAH-66 touched down, the warrant officer

cut its engines and popped the canopy. As the Plexiglas top rose, the scent of tropical flowers mixed with high octane fuel fumes. The mixture of uniformed soldiers and business suited civilians all held assault rifles at the ready.

"We wait until someone tells us to get out," Bret briefed.

In two or three minutes, a man and woman approached the aircraft, both dressed in expensive suits of the latest fashion. They stopped at the side of the helicopter, oblivious to the still-spinning rotor blades.

"My first look at a Stealth helicopter," the man shouted from the eerie artificially-lighted heliport pad. "Very impressive, very sinister."

No one in the aircraft spoke. They stared at the well-spoken, handsome Colombian, and waited for instructions.

"Welcome to Garden City, Colombia" the woman said. She was in her early thirties and attractive. The suit fit as if it had been tailored for her in Paris or Milan. "I know nothing of helicopters." She paused, then said, "My associate"—she nodded at the man by her side—"and I assist *Señor* Vargas."

"I trust you had a pleasant journey," the man said. He was in his late thirties and wore an immaculate lightweight Armani suit. Like his 'associate', the suit was tailor-made. He barely moved an index finger, and two men in coveralls rolled a portable steel staircase against the Stealth. "Leave any weapons in the aircraft," the spokesman declared. "The pilot will now deplane, after locking down all weapons controls."

Romanski thought of protesting. *Nah, they might take it out on m'passengers*, he thought. Walter flipped switches and turned knobs, then hauled himself up in the cockpit. "Stay healthy, little lady—colonel." He stepped to the platform, swayed down the stairs and was escorted by two 'uniforms' toward a small bungalow.

"Colonel Parra and agent Duchamps," the woman announced, "it is now time to deplane." As with her companion, she spoke flawless English. "We will have the lady first," she said, smiling.

Abby rose unsteadily. It had been a long flight in cramped

quarters, and she needed full feeling to return to her legs. She picked up her backpack and stepped over the edge of the cockpit. Holding the handrail, she descended the eight steps. "I have important documents in this bag." She held the backpack out to the woman.

"Ramón," she said. She beckoned to one of the personnel surrounding the helicopter, who jogged over beside her.

He slung his Russian Draganov assault rifle over one shoulder and ran a hand-held metal detector over the backpack. A piercing screech sounded from the small device, startling several onlookers.

"*Abre la bolsa*," the woman said, pointing to the bag.

The guard opened the backpack and picked it up, holding it for the woman to inspect. As her partner shone a flashlight inside, she dug within. She shook her head as she inspected various items. She pulled a small knife from the pack and handed it to the guard. She nodded to him, and he set the bag down and zipped it shut. "You walk around with enough electronic spy gear to equip the NSA."

"It's barely enough to help DST officers survive terrorists and drug lords."

"Check the woman next," Armani told the guard with the metal detector, in Spanish. His features, as those of his female companion, had stiffened. "Hands behind your head," he instructed Abby.

The guard slowly moved the wand of the detector over the front and back of Abby's blouse. As the detector passed over Abby's midriff, it chirped. When it neared her abdomen, it whined. Lowered close to her right thigh, all hell broke loose. The guard pulled the screeching gadget away and switched it off. The silence was menacing.

The Colombian woman sneered at Abby. "If you wore hose, I might believe the metal was a clasp on your garter belt." She moved within inches of Abby, grabbed the hem of her skirt and snatched it up.

"How dare you," Abby yelled. Nonetheless, she didn't retreat.

"We told you to leave weapons on the helicopter," the woman

said, as matter-of-factly as if scolding a child for some minor misdeed. "Beautiful tan. Very small bikini line," she added.

"What are you . . . ?" Abby began to ask.

Still holding up her skirt, the woman jerked the pistol from its breakaway holster. Clutching the weapon, she let the skirt drop. "A vintage but lethal pistol, the MAS 1950," she said. "But, then, French intelligence savors tradition."

She handed Abby's pistol and knife to the guard, saying something to him. He nodded, climbed four stairs by the aircraft, and handed the weapons to Bret.

"You are our guests, *señorita*," 'Armani' reminded Abby in way of explanation. "Any other time, I'm afraid those deadly objects would be confiscated."

And their holders neutralized, Abby reminded herself.

"*Coronel* Parra," the woman said, gazing up at the cockpit. "Please join us. I'm so sorry you had to wait."

He descended the stairs. At the bottom, he put hands behind his head and allowed the guard to scan him with the metal detector. No sounds came from the portable device.

"*Bueno, coronel*," the man in the blue Armani suit said. "Now, if you and your unexpected guest will follow us . . ." He never finished the sentence, his intent having conveyed volumes. The two assistants to Cali cartel's *narco mágico* Vargas turned and walked toward a huge doorway of the palatial *hacienda*. Two armed bodyguards strode behind Bret and Abby.

The house was enormous, the furniture and fixtures elaborate, the security cameras and armed domestics too many to count. The six people in the petite parade entered an elevator large enough to haul freight. It was so lavish, it boasted oil paintings and leather padded chairs. No one sat.

In a large conference room/study, Vargas' assistants sat across from their guests at a broad table. The two bodyguards leaned against walls inset with immense bookcases and antique bric-a-brac.

"You must be hungry after your long flight from Chiquinquira," the woman said. "Would you like a snack or something to drink?"

Does everyone know where we flew from? Bret wondered. *Guess Johnson told Vargas where I'd been.* "Black coffee sounds great."

"Coffee, please," Abby answered.

The coffee came, and another half-hour went by. Finally, their host appeared. Enrique Vargas Mantilla was tall and pleasant looking. His suit, shoes and personal bearing spoke major money, accumulated through decades of smuggling, financial 'laundering' and carnage. Two other men were with him. Bret and Abby recognized Claude Tomasso, whose face was flushed and sweaty. He'd lost any semblance of the vain, overconfident thug he'd portrayed on St. Martin. The third man was impossible to identify, since Energy and Mines Minister Rodrigo Gomez was again dressed in his yellow military jumpsuit and wore a yellow head mask. Both visitors sat in chairs set against opposing walls of the room.

"Welcome to my humble *casa*, Colonel Parra, and officer Duchamps." Speaking to her, Vargas said, "Your visit to our country is a surprise, *mademoiselle*. However, we are always delighted to have a French intelligence officer as a guest."

How many French DST agents have been guests here? Abby wondered. "I'm surprised to be here myself, *Señor* Vargas."

He nodded, but he didn't pursue the subject. He walked close to Bret. "Our mutual acquaintance, Mister Johnson, suggested this meeting, colonel."

"That's what his message said. I don't know why he wanted me to see you."

Claude's complexion went from pink to red, and new beads of sweat quickly replaced those dripping in his lap.

"Mr. Lamplighter," Vargas said, "you and a man called Russell boated down the Magdalena River. It wasn't a pleasure cruise. With the approval of the national police commander, you were on a covert mission."

"It was *hardly* covert. Seems much of Colombia knew about our journey."

Vargas strode to a chair across from Bret and Abby. Sitting, he said, "I am surprised you admit to your intended raid on the legitimate trade in coca and poppies."

Bret and Abby exchanged knowing glances, nearly smiling. "Legitimate or not," Bret said, "Russell, Mademoiselle Duchamps and I have no concern with narcotics."

"You work with the *yanqui* DEA," Vargas snapped.

"I was discharged by the DEA quite awhile ago," he said, "and was never reinstated by the organization."

Vargas looked away from him and asked Abby, "You are with a French police organization, *señorita?*"

"You are aware of that."

"Why work with him?" Vargas gestured toward Bret.

Abby took a breath. "Initially, my organization was suspicious of Mr. Lamplighter when he arrived in St. Martin—a French territory."

Vargas nodded. The room was silent except the hiss of air conditioning.

"I soon learned he was an insurance investigator for an American company. They'd sent him there to recover a valuable theft, if possible. It was a sizable loss."

"What was he sent to recover?"

Staring at Claude, Abby said, "Colombian emeralds. Eleven million dollars' worth at wholesale."

Leaping from his chair, Claude screamed, "I object. It's a lie."

The two bodyguards rushed to him and pushed him back in the chair. As they held him down by his shoulders, Claude became silent.

Vargas stood and gazed at Claude. "First, this is hardly a court of law. Secondly, why would you object to Miss Duchamps' description of an emerald theft?"

"I am very—yes, very—upset, that anyone . . ."

"Quiet, Claude," Vargas directed. He turned to Bret, saying, "I recall hearing of a large emerald, er, heist on the British island of Anguilla. About a month ago, wasn't it?"

"That's the one, *señor* Vargas. A buyer for a large gemstone consortium was murdered for eighteen exquisite emeralds"

"*Esmeraldas de Colombia?*" the Energy and Mines Minister asked.

"*Patrón, por favor,*" Vargas spoke to the yellow mask. He

turned back to Bret. "You are certain the stolen emeralds came from this country?"

Patrón? Bret thought. *Coming from the Capo of Cali?* Bret nodded. "All emeralds have internal particles that show their source. The Philipsburg emerald merchant identified all eighteen that were stolen as being from Muzo mines."

"I see," Vargas said. He turned to his male assistant. "Guillermo, what was the name of the candy we heard spoken on the tape recording?"

"'Gummy bear', *señor* Vargas."

Despite the two guards' hold on his shoulders, Claude jumped to his feet. "You're crazy! I object! He lies! So does the Frenchwoman," he screeched.

The bodyguards jammed Claude back to the chair, one of them pressing a handkerchief to his mouth. His arms were wrested behind the chair and a guard handcuffed him tightly.

The yellow-clothed figure gawked at Tomasso in loathing. "Betrayer," he said in highly-accented English.

"Gummy bear is his code word for 'emeralds'," Abby said. "I have the proof in my knapsack." She picked up the bulky bag.

As Vargas watched her pull articles from the pack, he asked Bret, "What made you suspect my trusted marketer of emeralds, Lamplighter?"

"Do you want a dozen reasons, two dozen?"

Vargas' American college education became apparent as he said, "Just the first time you 'knew' he'd ripped off your insurance company."

"Lots of things pointed to him. The guy who stole the emeralds and murdered their buyer ended up dead, and he was a part-time lackey of Claude's."

Vargas nodded.

"The manager of the hotel where I took a room, who was blown up trying to kill me, owed favors to Claude."

"Those are circumstantial . . ."

"That man your men are holding down works closely with two others."

Vargas didn't like being interrupted, but he asked, "Doing what?"

"Smuggling, murdering, threatening and stealing from you."

"If they stole emeralds, they were from a client your insurance company represents." Vargas replied.

"Agent Duchamps," Bret said, turning toward Abby, "why don't you show our host the proof you spoke about a few minutes ago."

Abby stood. "Do you have a personal computer with a CD-ROM?" She held several compact disks.

"Of course," Vargas asserted. "Guillermo," he ordered, "bring a computer here with, um, the ROM *señorita* asks for."

Guillermo rose and hustled toward the door. His expression suggested that he wasn't quite sure that a CD-ROM drive was installed on any of their PC's.

"Lamplighter, Duchamps," Vargas said as he again sat in a chair near the conference table, "you are here because Johnson said I should see you. He is often helpful to Colombian businessmen."

Abby said, "You spoke of 'gummy bears', *señor* Vargas. In what context were they mentioned?"

Vargas nodded slightly and turned to his female assistant. "Cecilia, read me the portion the French *Sûreté* agent asks about."

Cecilia snapped open her briefcase. She removed a manila folder from the valise and opened it. "*Aquí está, patrón. ¿Empezaré?*" She requested Vargas' permission before she read the quote.

Vargas nodded.

"Mr. Tomasso asks, 'This talk. How specific did it get?' The man Wilson answers, 'Very specific, even to mentioning many different gummy bear sizes. It also included possibly turning states's evidence . . .'"

Even with the hefty bodyguards holding Claude, he rose several inches from his chair. A squawk managed to escape his tightly-clamped lips. The guards nearly lay on the man to curb his jerking motions.

"Go on," Vargas said.

Cecilia continued, " . . . 'particularly the names of sugar and spice traders in exchange for the fed's WPP'." She'd emphasized 'sugar' and 'spice'.

Vargas asked Bret, "The WPP is your nation's witness protection program?"

"Yes, Claude and Wilson were afraid their partner, Hough, would give names and dates in return for a more desirable prison sentence."

Vargas nodded again. He left his chair and walked to the man dressed from head to toe in yellow. The room was deathly quiet, but the drug lord's conversation with Minister Gomez was conducted in hushed whispers.

The silence was interrupted by the return of Guillermo, who'd shoved the door open. Walking behind him was Jaime, head of security for the drug lord. Vargas' assistant pushed a tall metal stand on wheels that held a personal computer and an array of peripherals. An internal CD-ROM drive was visible in the CPU. Atop the stand rested a large 35-inch monitor. Cecilia hurried over to her partner to help set up the equipment. The computer and monitor were powered up.

Enrique Vargas concluded his discussion with the man in yellow. He walked to his chair and said, "It is time we view your presentation."

Chapter Thirty-Four

Abby began issuing instructions to the computer through its keyboard. "First, I'll show you several downloaded files sent between Tomasso and an accomplice in Muzo." She inserted a disk into the CD-ROM drive, typed its location and tapped 'Enter'.

"The messages were sent over the Internet," Bret explained. "The files were found on Claude's personal computer at his automobile dealership. There are hundreds of them, but we'll show you a small sample."

As the files appeared on the screen, Abby said, "These were taken from a backup cache on his computer. I didn't have time to check, but if he'd deleted any files from the PC, they would have stayed in the cache."

Claude struggled in his chair, but it was futile. There were now three security men to make sure he stayed where he'd been put.

"*Señor* Vargas, would you select a random file for us to show the group." The cursor blinked at the top file on the screen.

"I choose the thirtieth file from the top."

Abby hit the down arrow thirty times. It stopped on a file named '*bistec con frió papas*', steak with fried potatoes. She tapped the 'enter' key. The message was examined by everyone in the room . . .

Subj: Bistec con Frió Papas
Date: Dec. 11 (two years ago) 21:45:55 EST
From: CalColo001
To: ClaudeTLux

Mr. Tomasso: Friend CubaJoe5 make grate e-mail to me. Want six gummy bear for Habana sweet shop. Bes ask next: 500 tbs sugar and also 1000 cans flour. For desert, want 500 cups spice gos to 69SemperFi at Guantanamo. Mos happy with last time holiday pak. Prepays here.

Sr. J. Velasco

Abby printed a half-dozen copies of the file. Bret passed them to the disguised Minister of Mines and Energy, Vargas, his two assistants and the security chief. He set a copy on the CPU for Abby. Bret would look at Cecilia's copy, if necessary.

Vargas motioned to his security chief, indicating he wished to speak with Claude. The bodyguard removed the handkerchief and his hand from Claude's mouth. Vargas asked, "How do you explain this message?"

Claude sputtered, trying to get some sympathy. "It, it, it's exactly what you, er, see," he said, pointing at the monitor. "Condiments for a, um, little pastry shop in . . ."

" . . . in Havana, Cuba, Claude?" Bret asked. "Illegal for U.S. citizens, isn't it?"

"No, no, Lamplighter. Only . . ."

" . . . enough, Claude," Vargas bellowed. "Why would a car dealer, my marketer of emeralds, send little notes about condiments?"

"That's a h-hard one t-to answer . . ."

" . . . who is *señor* J. Velasco? Where does he communicate *from*?"

"*P-patrón*, why all these q-questions? I only . . ."

". . . Officer Duchamps," Vargas interrupted the whimpering Tomasso. "Do you have more of your show-and-tell?"

"Yes. As you are aware, Lamplighter and I just arrived from Chiquinquira. We went to the local headquarters of Muzo mines, located nearby."

"I know this," Vargas said, glancing over at his chief of security.

"We found evidence of Claude's man Velasco, and probably others, skimming off the rarest emeralds mined at Muzo."

The gasp from Minister Rodrigo Gomez was nearly as loud as Claude's screech. The security chief swatted his hand against Claude's mouth.

"Do you have this evidence on CD's, *mademoiselle*?" Enrique Vargas Mantilla seethed with fury, but was courteous with her.

Abby said, "Yes." She removed the first disk and replaced it with another. "This group of files was copied from a downlink with Velasco's personal file at Muzo. I cannot change data on such a link, just read and record it."

"Officer Duchamps," Bret stated, "entered Velasco's personal computer system from a file server in Chiquinquira, *señor*."

"Show me the Muzo files." Vargas was in a hurry. He kept glancing at the man who was powerful enough to commandeer a military HH-53C helicopter to check on a thief and a smuggler.

"These files came from Velasco's 'mail sent' directory. I assume he never felt they could be compromised. Do you have another random number, *señor* Vargas?"

"*Si*," Vargas answered. "*número dieciocho*, my daughter's age."

"Eighteen it is," Abby said, and she tapped the down-arrow key eighteen times. She highlighted the file called, unbelievably, 'Bulgarian Pork with Sauerkraut'. A tap on the Enter key pulled up the file . . .

> Subj: Bulgarian Pork with Sauerkraut
> Date: May 7 (last year) 03:31:55 EST
> From: CalColo001
> To: ClaudeTLux
>
> Mr. Tomasso: Friend Jacques424Fr gives us with magnifisent order of 2,000 tbs spice and 2,000 tbs sugar. All go to Sofia30Tali after flies from Marsaile. Bes suprise . . . 5 can hi-quality coffee and 50 can grapes. We do swell bizness, my amigo. Bes to Fredrik.
>
> Sr. J. Velasco

"Remarkable, *mademoiselle*," Vargas exclaimed. "My emerald chief even has ties to France and Sofia, Bulgaria." In a somber tone, he said, "Claude never mentioned those European alliances to me."

"I am as surprised as you, *señor*," Abby said, "as I am headquartered in Marseille. Perhaps 'shocked' is the all-important word."

Across the room, Gomez stood, back against a large bookcase. Jaime, Vargas' security chief, stood near him, but not so close as to make him feel uncomfortable.

Bret rose from his chair, walked to the PC console, and picked up the pages Abby ran off the printer. As he walked around the room, handing out copies of the second Internet message, he spoke. "We have hundreds more communications between Tomasso and Velasco. All look like the strange memos you have copies of," holding up Cecilia's copies. He then set them back in front of the woman.

Vargas asked, "But, how do we know what 'gummy bear' means?, and what 'spice' means ?"

"We knew we *had* to see a code key if we were to understand exactly what they were stealing, smuggling and selling. We have all seen that these 'faithful employees' had buyers worldwide."

"Where is the 'code key' you speak about?" Vargas said.

"Abby," Bret said, "would you answer the question?"

"Our 'Rosetta Stone' is the first file in the directory I have on the screen." She began to type on the keyboard. A file appeared on the screen, all in English except for the title:

RECETAS

CODE WORD	PRODUCT	CODE WORD	PRODUCT
Apples	= Silver	Baking Soda	= Raw Coca
Coffee	= Diamond	Flour	= Marijuana
Grape	= Gold	Gummy Bear	= Emerald

CODE WORD	AMOUNT	CODE WORD	AMOUNT
Can	= Ounce	Cup	= Pound (U.S.)
Tablespoon (Tbs.)	= Kilo	Teaspoon (T)	= ½-kilo Bag

"As you see, it's not complicated at all," Bret said, "but worth millions, maybe *billions?*, to Claude Tomasso and his associates."

Abby collected the hard copy from the printer, and handed out the RECIPE to all concerned. "This," she held up her copy, "is the key to all of Claude's dealings, and those of his accomplices: Wilson, Hough and Velasco."

The Minister of Mines and Energy was quivering with rage. He walked in front of Tomasso, who was bent over nearly double—eyes shut, face white. Sweat dribbled from his face. Urine covered the floor beneath his chair. The repulsive odor of human feces caused the bodyguards to turn their heads and gasp. The man in yellow strode to Enrique Vargas Mantilla.

They walked to the far end of the room, behind the computer stand and conference table. They hovered near a mahogany-paneled wall, lined with more book shelves. They compared the various computer printouts. The man in yellow spoke louder and grew more animated with each passing second.

"Miss Duchamps," Vargas spoke in the hushed room, "my

good friend, and I, wish to know if it is possible to alter the data on the CD's you have shown us."

"No, *señores*," Abby answered without hesitation. She pushed a button below the CD tray, and it slid out with its compact disk. Lifting the disk, she displayed it to everyone in the room. She said, "As you see, this disk says CD-R, meaning it can be recorded upon only *one time*. If it were designated CD-RW, it could be written over or edited anytime, in other words, ReWritable." She said, "In fact, most people deliberately select a CD-R to assure *no alterations*. It's a safety device." She handed the disk to Cecilia, who carried it to Vargas and Rodrigo Gomez.

They conversed quietly, with the woman pointing to and even tapping at the compact disk. In a few minutes they nodded their heads. Cecilia turned and brought the CD-R back to Abby, who reinserted it into the disk drive.

Suddenly, the government minister shouted something unintelligible at Vargas. He spun around and smashed a fist into the shelving filled with books. No one turned to see what happened. Claude's whimpers were the only sounds in the stench-filled library.

Gomez stalked from the library. Bret heard him say the words 'Lamplighter' and 'Tomasso', but the context was lost with his departure. As he passed Claude, Rodrigo Gomez smashed his fist into the side of his head. Claude continued to sob.

Enrique Vargas walked over to his security chief, who was breathing in shallow spurts next to Claude. He spoke quietly despite his obvious disgust with his 'emerald marketer'. Jaime nodded several times to the Cali cartel chief, then they hauled Claude to his feet and dragged him from the room.

As Abby returned to her chair, she asked Bret, "Refresh my memory. What's the Spanish word for 'disappear'?"

He turned and stared at her, realizing why she asked the question. "*Desaparece*."

Abby nodded. In a whisper she said, "Our host told his security man that Claude was to 'disappear'."

Vargas took his seat at the table. He drummed his fingers on the fine mahogany. "Our friend Mr. Tomasso caused a bad odor in here," he said. "My men removed him so we could continue our discussion."

"I'd say the talking is finished," Bret said. "We proved our assertion."

"Commendable detective work. But, has it helped return the gems to your insurance company?"

"No more than you have recovered your emeralds, and any other stolen merchandise," Bret said.

"After an exhaustive search through all the disks," Abby added, "I believe we'll be able to find Ultragem's missing emeralds."

"Cecilia," Vargas said to his female assistant, "fetch the blue satchel, *por favor*."

As she arose to get a satchel, a sudden roar like that of an erupting volcano startled everyone. It was only after a few moments that it was apparent the clamor came from the engines of the huge Sikorsky helicopter.

"Damn," Bret said, "two fully-revved 3,500 horsepower engines would bring down a less-sturdy house." The din lasted for twenty or thirty seconds, far longer than usual for such an aircraft to become airborne. Books fell from their shelves, the monitor abruptly toppled from the multimedia stand and hundreds of loose objects vibrated. No one verbalized that the Jolly Green Giant was intentionally being used to vent the spleen of one yellow-clothed visitor.

"Your friend certainly leaves with a bang," Abby said.

Must be very high up in the government, Bret thought. *Still, in Colombia, it's not healthy for even the most-powerful people to piss-off a drug lord.*

Enrique Vargas sat back in his easy chair, fingers intertwined across his trim midriff. They saw a look in Vargas's eyes that said a multitude: No one humiliates Cali's *droga mágico* and lives long to boast of it.

Cecilia entered the room and handed a beautiful, soft blue leather tote to Vargas. He set it in front of him.

No larger than a man's size 10-D shoe box, Bret thought.

Such an elegant portmanteau, Abby considered.

"Claude Tomasso is a terrorist," Vargas asserted. "You two gave me the proof I needed to realize that fact."

"We're glad to have helped *señor* Vargas," Bret replied. "The CD's we found should help us find Multistate Insurance's missing 'green'."

"What is it, Guillermo?" Vargas asked, looking toward his assistant who held a hand over the mouthpiece of a cellular phone.

"Jaime gives me a report of an aircraft accident, *patrón*."

They couldn't have gotten him that fast, Bret thought.

"Pardon me," Vargas excused himself. He walked to the far side of the room with Guillermo.

"Could it be our honored visitor?" Abby wondered.

Before Bret answered, Cecilia leaned over and whispered, "I believe we would have heard the helicopter crash, as it would still be very close."

They glanced at Cecilia and nodded.

On the far side of the room, Guillermo listened intently to Vargas. He incessantly nodded or shook his head. After five minutes of the one-sided conversation, Vargas approached the conference table. His face was stern, but less agitated than when his visitor had buffeted the hacienda with sound waves.

Vargas surveyed Bret and Abby. "Before you go, my assistants will show you bath facilities. I'm certain we can probably find you clean changes of clothing, as well."

"That would be most welcome, *señor*," Bret said, smiling.

"Nothing sounds more wonderful," Abby agreed. "My deodorant perished somewhere in Chiquinquira."

"It's the least I can do for you. You've tracked down traitors in my employ and saved me millions."

Billions, Bret thought. Emeralds were small change to the man who controlled more than half the illicit drugs trafficked throughout the world. Claude's slide back into drug dealing was the ultimate deceit. He'd pay the ultimate price.

"I'm afraid your army lost another pilot, Lamplighter."

"Is this about the aircraft crash?" Bret asked.

"Claude's partner, the army captain, died in his ancient C-47," Vargas continued. "This teaches us a lesson. Governments should ground aircraft after a half-century of use."

"Where," Bret began, "did the plane . . . ?"

" . . . the old plane disintegrated. It was making its final approach to George Town airport in the Caymans."

Any plane will disintegrate when a pound of C-4 is detonated by a barometric ignition, Bret knew.

"Wilson was going to Grand Cayman?" Abby asked. "Must be where he banked his share of money from drugs and gems he smuggled from Colombia."

A British colony, the Cayman Islands are famous for their secret bank accounts. Some sources believe the Cayman international banking center rivals that of Switzerland. True or not, George Town brings in untold billions of dollars in confidential banking transactions every day.

"Was our mutual friend, Wilson, the only crash fatality?"

Vargas raised his eyebrows and turned toward Guillermo.

Vargas' assistant said, "According to *our* representative in George Town only the pilot died. Two tourists on a sport fishing boat were slightly injured by falling debris."

"Little bag," Vargas said out of the blue. The drug czar seemed to have his own set of rules for conversation. He said, "I have a going away present for you, Mr. Lamplighter." Turning his head, Vargas said: "Guillermo . . ."

Guillermo rose and said, "Thank you, *patrón*. Yesterday morning, after our chief of security spoke with Tomasso for eleven hours, I accompanied Jaime to Sint Maarten, Netherlands Antilles."

Abby asked, "What information . . . ?"

Vargas turned to her and, finger to mouth, made a 'hush' sound.

"Using Mr. Tomasso's house keys, Jaime and I entered his *casa*. The house was empty, Mrs. Tomasso having left no word where she could be found. The furniture was covered to keep off dust.

"Following Claude's directions, the security chief and I went to the basement and a large Mosler walk-in safe. Claude assured us nobody could have entered since he was last there, since only he knew the combination."

"How did you know he hadn't rigged a booby-trap?" Bret asked.

Guillermo said, "We entered the numeric combination that he had given us, then *opened* it from a distance of four hundred meters with an electronic remote control servo."

"Good thinking."

Vargas' assistant continued. "When we entered the safe, we found much cash in many currencies. We also found gemstones and bullion—platinum, gold and silver."

"Why hadn't Claude put it in a Swiss, Cayman or Bahamian safety deposit box?" Abby asked.

"Claude had always told me he didn't trust those 'secret' accounts," Vargas said. "He was afraid once he put valuables in he could never get them out."

"So Guillermo and Jaime emptied Tomasso's safe?" Bret said.

"Not at all," Vargas answered. "However, now we can identify what is rightfully mine, from your computer disks." He studied the blue bag. "Guillermo did bring back a few items we knew belonged here in Cali." Vargas pushed the blue packet in front of Bret. "This is yours, Lamplighter—for services rendered."

Bret's heart leapt as the bag came to rest only a few inches from his folded hands.

"I don't know what to say," Bret remarked.

"Say nothing. Simply open the satchel."

Bret pulled the tote bag nearer. It was heavier than he'd suspected. Looking for a clasp, he realized the 'satchel' was actually a clever breakaway device held together on all sides with Velcro. The bag stretched out as a single blue leather 'flat,' about twenty-four inches wide and thirty inches long. It contained twenty-four 'pockets', four in width by six in length.

The top eight pockets were expanded, as were the bottom eight. Two additional pockets protruded.

"Looks like we have eighteen individual items in most pockets," Bret said.

"Isn't that the number of emerald's stolen from Ultragem?" Abby asked.

Bret began to open a pocket on the bottom, the closest to him. It was held shut with Velcro, and he pulled the two clinging pieces apart. He reached inside and withdrew an item the size of a Pink Pearl pencil eraser, wrapped in blue satin. His hands wavered slightly as he unwrapped the cloth covering.

"*Mon dieu!*" Abby exclaimed. She stared at an immaculate emerald that radiated its blue-green hue to all parts of the room. "It's almost alive. A living, breathing gem."

All eighteen stolen emeralds were encased in soft blue leather pockets, each more perfect than its neighbor. Even Vargas Mantilla gazed in wonder at the array of remarkable gemstones.

* * *

Bret let the phone ring. It was ten o'clock in Cali, which meant it was nine in Chicago. He had no doubt that George Princeton would welcome his call as no other phone call he'd ever received. Five rings, six.

"Hello," Princeton answered breathlessly.

"Hey, George. You smoking so much ya can't catch your breath?"

"Who the . . . ? Oh, for shit's sake, it's Sam Spade. Nah, jist walked through m'front door. How th'hell are you, ole buddy?"

"Never better, George. Never better. Y'know, maybe Sam Spade's *not* dead."

"Now, there's a change of tune. Where y'at, Bret, O'Hare?"

"No, farther away than that—Cali, Colombia."

"Still in Colombia?" George replied. "DEA told us you were pokin' around there. Thought you'd be chasin' emerald banditos in the Caribbean." Another pause. "Uh, speakin' of those green stones, I jist got home from a meetin' with Gruener, The Colonel and Mrs. D. They're concerned about the Ultragem emerald heist."

Bret foresaw a distant red flag. "Some coincidence. What was their conclusion?"

"First, your two-week deadline for finding the emeralds has elapsed."

"Only two days past. No company would hold anyone to a mere two days." The imagined red flag began waving.

"Ultragem lowered their finder's reward. They don't think it's worth a quarter-mil to get them back."

"They're worth eleven and a half mil, George, wholesale. So they'll bring twenty-five to thirty on the world market."

"We're aware of their potential value, good buddy. Jist find 'em and bring 'em back alive," George chuckled. "You'd still get a great piece o'change."

"What would the initial two-hundred, fifty thousand dollars diminish to, George?" The red flag flapped as if it pulsated in a hurricane.

"Look, it's not only the money, it's the prestige that really counts, as Henry explained to me. You'd have so many clients you'd have to get an unlisted phone number." George knew Bret was still on the line, waiting for an answer. "All expenses, Bret—plus twenty thousand cash."

Epilogue

July in Buenos Aires, Johnson explained to Bret, is similar to July in Natchez, Mississippi. He believed that the weather 32 degrees south of the equator would be similar to weather 32 degrees *north* of the equator. So be it. Bret didn't argue.

Sitting on the rear patio of Bret's villa, they sipped fresh guava juice and gazed toward the estuary of the Rio de la Plata. The wide bay, separating Argentina from Uruguay, teemed with ships from many nations. On a clear day such as today, Colonia was visible twenty-five miles north on the Uruguayan side of the *bahía*.

"Many thanks for being a messenger for me."

Johnson smiled. "I make good *dinero* to be messenger *para* many people." This was a sizable understatement. Johnson was a millionaire many times over.

The smallest emerald of the Ultragem collection fetched one and one-half million dollars U.S. in Philipsburg one week before. Johnson's commission, one hundred, fifty thousand dollars, had been earned after two hours of haggling, shouting and ultimate shrewd bargaining. Bret's share had been placed into a Swiss account, a Grand Cayman account and a split of cash into five Buenos Aires bank money market investments.

The seventeen remaining emeralds rested in a safe deposit box of a large Chicago bank, across the street from Multistate Insurance. Abby had conceived of the idea. She felt that the emeralds' proximity to Gruener, The Colonel and Mrs. D. was just retribution for the broken business arrangement.

Once more, Bret read the e-mail printout he'd received four hours before. It was short and to the point: *Mon cher Bret: I shall begin my summer holiday in Buenos Aires two weeks from today. Please meet me at Ezeiza Airport. Je t'aime, Abby.*

It was a magnificent July day in Buenos Aires.